The Mental Health Act Commission

Risk, Rights, Recovery

Twelfth Biennial Report 2005-2007

Laid before Parliament by the Secretary of
State for Health pursuant to Section 121(10)
of the Mental Health Act 1983

London: **The Stationery Office**

information & publishing solutions

Published by TSO (The Stationery Office) and available from:

Online
www.tsoshop.co.uk

Mail, Telephone, Fax & E-mail
TSO
PO Box 29, Norwich, NR3 1GN
Telephone orders/General enquiries: 0870 600 5522
Fax orders: 0870 600 5533
E-mail: customer.services@tso.co.uk
Textphone 0870 240 3701

TSO Shops
16 Arthur Street, Belfast BT1 4GD
028 9023 8451 Fax 028 9023 5401
71 Lothian Road, Edinburgh EH3 9AZ
0870 606 5566 Fax 0870 606 5588

TSO@Blackwell and other Accredited Agents
(see Yellow Pages)

First published 2008

ISBN 978 0 11 322807 2

Mental Health Act Commission,
Maid Marian House,
56 Hounds Gate,
Nottingham,
NG1 6BG

Tel: 0115 943 7100

Printed in the United Kingdom for The Stationery Office

Acknowledgements

The principal author of this report was Mat Kinton of the MHAC Policy Unit. Other Policy Unit staff played significant roles. In particular, Rose Sibley liaised with and provided an account of the Service User Reference Panel (SURP). Ron Rushbrook provided research and oversaw the production of the report for the MHAC.

We are grateful to all SURP members past and present who have worked with the MHAC, and particularly to the following for their contributions to this report: Danuta Allan, Dawn Cutler-Nichol, Monica Endersby, D P Gilbert, Mark Gray, Deborah Hickman, Richard Holmes, Margaret Jessop, Michael Lang, Emma Laughton, Kay Reed, Anthony Stephens, L Summers, Stuart A Wooding, and one other member who preferred to remain anonymous. We are also grateful to Sarah Dewey for her account of a hospital admission, printed between chapters one and two.

Statistical advice and services were provided by Jo Simpson (now Senior Project Manager for Mental Health and Community Care at the Information Centre), and her successor as Count Me In Census Project Manager, Christine Marriott. MHAC data has been retrieved by Stephen Klein, Regional Director for London and the South-east.

A number of MHAC members and staff provided comments or information. Thanks to Faizan Ahmed, Simon Armson, Leanne Bacon, Barbara Brooks, Dr Patrick Callaghan, Karen Carder, Patricia Chadderton, Stephanie Chandler, Luke Clapham, Jeff Cohen, Ann Curno, Barbara Davis, Barry Delaney, Suki Desai, Martin Donohoe, Kate Doohan, Andrew Evans, Petrina Douglas-Hall, Jay Harman, Prof Christopher Heginbotham, Phil Howes, Katherine Herzberg, Elizabeth Holland, Deborah Jenkins, Craig Jennings, John Knox, Jane MacKenzie, Stephen Maloyd, Sue McMillan, Steve Nelson, Gemma Pearce, Kay Sheldon, Sue Turner, Philip Wales, Denise Walker, Anthony Williams. We are also grateful to Drs Peter Jefferies and Simon Halstead, members of the SOAD panel. Full lists of both MHAC members and second opinion panel appointees are in the appendices: we are grateful to all for their contributions, which provide the data behind this report.

We also owe various debts to Malcolm Alexander of Medical Justice, Prof Peter Bartlett, Christopher Curran, Rowena Daw, Dr David Hewitt, Chris Gale, Chris Higgins (Ontario Ministry of Health), John Horne, Dr Mark Morris, Andrew Parsons, Fiona Ritchie, Lucy Scott-Moncrieff and Dr George Szmukler. We do, of course, take full responsibility for the contents of this report, none of which may be taken to reflect the views of those who are kind enough to discuss with us our thoughts and concerns. We thank the patients and staff of hospitals that we visit for their co-operation with our work.

The cover image, "Psychotopia", was created as a part of an Active Arts patient workshop held at Kneesworth House Hospital, part of the Partnerships in Care (PiC) group of hospitals. We are grateful to the hospital for allowing us to permission to use the image.

This report is dedicated to the memory of Gordon Lakes CB MC (1928–2006), member of the MHAC between 1991 and 2001, leader of the visiting team to Ashworth Hospital for three of those years, and Acting Chairman from August 1998 to November 1999. He remained a good friend of the MHAC after the end of his period of appointment and his counsel will be missed.

Contents

4. The Mental Health Act in Practice: Hospital admission and detention under the Act

5. The Mental Health Act in Wales

6. Medical treatment under the Mental Health Act

Chairman's Foreword

Risk, Rights, Recovery

The Mental Health Act Commission's Twelfth Biennial Report

As this report goes to publication, the MHAC has a projected lifespan that would make it our penultimate biennial report. Government has announced its intention that the MHAC will merge to become a part of the generic health and social care inspectorate to be known as the *Care Quality Commission* in April 2009. I find myself once again succumbing to the temptation to write a valedictory foreword, given the possibility that this is now the last report that will be published whilst the MHAC is still a going concern. Of course, we have waved goodbye at least twice before, and I may once again be premature in doing so here.

I will assume, however, that the MHAC may not survive to celebrate the bicentenary of the *Parliamentary Inquiry into Madhouses* of 1815/6, which was perhaps the earliest significant report on psychiatric care in England and Wales; a forerunner of both the Lunacy Commission and Board of Control reports to Parliament, and of our own biennial reports to the Secretary of State. It might reasonably be asked what possible comparisons there could be between the care of mentally disordered people in the early nineteenth and twenty-first centuries, given the enormous differences in medical knowledge, forms of treatment and indeed social structure between the two periods. It is true that when the 1815 Inquiry condemned the overuse of 'restraint', for example, the term referred to something very different, and much more horrific, to what is implied by that term today. It is also true that some of the problems of today's services – in particular I have in mind the startling overrepresentation of some Black and minority ethnic groups amongst the detained population – are matters without direct historic parallel. I nevertheless find some striking parallels with our concerns today in *some* of "the following basic evils of the system" listed by the 1815 Inquiry:

1st.   Keepers of the houses receiving a much greater number of persons... than they are calculated for... which greatly retards recovery;

2ndly. The insufficiency of the number of Keepers, in proportion to the number of persons entrusted to their care, which unavoidably leads to a greater degree of restraint than the patients would otherwise be under;

---

[1]   Although a case might be made for parallels between present-day overrepresentation of BME patients in coercion and the routes taken by the poor, or by women, into the asylum system.

3^{rdly}. The mixing of patients who are outrageous, with those who are quiet and inoffensive;

4^{thly}. The want of medical assistance, as applied to the malady for which persons are confined… as the practice very generally is to confine medical aid to corporeal ailments;

5^{thly}. Restraint of persons much beyond what is necessary…;

6^{thly}. The situation of the parish paupers in houses for insane persons… [and] in parochial workhouses;

7^{thly}. Detention of persons the state of whose minds did not require confinement;

8^{thly}. Insufficiency of certificates on which patients are received into the madhouses;

9^{thly}. The defective visitation of private madhouses.[2]

The first three items on the above list, were it not for the archaic terminology, might serve as chapter headings in this report. Overcrowding (which we now call 'over-occupancy') is, amazingly, once again a key concern of staff and patients that we encounter on visits, as is the shortage of staff in many hospitals. Inadequate numbers of qualified and experienced nursing staff in many wards no doubt continue to limit the potential for relational security to be preferred over more physical barriers to patients' freedom. As acute inpatient beds become more of a last resort with the development of community services, patients admitted to such beds are increasingly highly disturbed, and acute wards can be frightening places to reside (all the more so for women who feel vulnerable in being locked up with disturbed male patients).

In some ways the fourth 'evil' identified by the 1815 inquiry – that 'treatment' in hospital was limited to that for physical ailments rather than mental disorder – is quite the opposite of concerns today. Detained patients will usually now receive treatments from the modern pharmacopoeia of psychiatry, but will often have physical health care needs overlooked or poorly managed. We discuss this at chapter 2.79. In recent years we have seen the wider prescription of newer (and more expensive) antipsychotic drugs, which may be more effective and less debilitating than older drugs, and so the medical treatment of mental disorder in some ways continues to improve. But in other ways the 1815 concerns are still valid. Many detained patients (and the professionals caring for them) today bemoan the lack of access to psychological therapies, such as Cognitive Behavioural Therapy (CBT). It is encouraging that access to such therapies generally is a part of the government's agenda[3], but better access to psychological therapy for detained patients should be a priority in terms of ethics (given that the provision of the most effective treatment should be reciprocal

---

2   First report, Minutes of evidence taken before the select committee appointed to consider of provision made for the better regulation of madhouses, in England. Ordered by the House of Commons to be printed 25 May 1815. In Hunter R & McAlpine I (1963) *Three hundred years of psychiatry 1535-1860*. Oxford University Press, p.697

3   Speech by the Rt Hon Patricia Hewitt MP, Secretary of State for Health, 10 May 2007: *Improving Access to Psychological Therapies National Stakeholder Conference*

benefit of their loss of liberty) and possibly also on grounds of health economics (given that this might reduce the frequency and/or duration of hospitalisation).

Regarding the physical care of patients, an uncomfortable parallel with 'asylum dysentery' of the nineteenth and early twentieth centuries is suggested by the extremely concerning outbreaks of hospital 'superbugs', such as the *Clostridium difficile colitis* deaths over the winter of 2005/06 in physical healthcare wards at Maidstone and Tunbridge Wells NHS Trust[4], and with the current widespread public fear of hospital-acquired infection. Asylum dysentery was probably the result of contaminated water supplies or poor hygiene practices, possibly coupled with a lack of resistance to the infection on the part of patients for various social or clinical reasons[5]. It was

> caused by a close relative of *E.coli, shigella*. It occurred in every mental hospital. In a bad year it ranked as the third most common cause of death in them, after syphilis of the brain and tuberculosis. Patrick Manson … called it 'the very fatal type of dysentery, euphemistically called "colitis", which is the scourge and disgrace of lunatic asylums'.[6]

Professor Hugh Pennington has argued that, whilst hospital infection control had little regulation (at least in 2005 when he was writing)

> there is one very important historical exception to this generalisation: Victorian lunatic asylums. From 1845 they were inspected by the Lunacy Commissioners. This was a powerful incentive for cleanliness. Cleaning was done by inmates with military thoroughness and routine regularity because it was superintended by matrons ruling with rods of iron. My grandfather was chief attendant in one, my grandmother worked for years in an asylum's dysentery wards, and my own employment in two left an abiding memory of their smell: strong soap and floor polish, with only a fleeting hint of faeces. For all this they were the seat of the longest ever recorded epidemic of hospital-acquired infection[7].

There may be an important lesson from history here. Not, certainly, that Lunacy Commission visits (or their MHAC equivalent today) are in some ways a protection against hospital infections, although our Commissioners do and will continue to raise concerns about dirty living environments for patients. Rather, the point is that even in the carbolic-soaped environment of an old-style psychiatric ward, infections still occurred. It is important that mental health patients are protected from hospital-acquired infection, but there is a real danger, as we discuss at chapter 2.15 of this report, that we concentrate on making sterile the places that our patients must call their home for the duration of their detention, without allowing them to be comfortably habitable.

---

[4]   Healthcare Commission (2007) *Investigation into outbreaks of Clostridium difficile at Maidstone and Tunbridge Wells NHS Trust* October 2007

[5]   Firth R H (1908) *The Theory and Practice of Hygiene,* quoted by Andrew Roberts on his extraordinary Mental Health History Timeline (http://www.mdx.ac.uk/WWW/STUDY/mhhtim.htm). Although not mentioned in these sources, it may be that the more aggressive psychiatric 'treatments' of the nineteenth century (such as purgatives) were similarly deleterious to the body's natural resistance to e-coli type bacteria as antibiotics are proving to be today.

[6]   'Don't pick your nose – Hugh Pennington on MRSA'. *London Review of Books* 15 December 2005. See also Pennington H (2007) 'Wash your hands' *LRB* 15 November 2007.

[7]   ibid.*(LRB 15 December 2005)*

As I have mentioned, what the nineteenth and twenty-first centuries referred to as restraint (the fifth evil of the 1815 Inquiry) are quite different matters: we rarely see physical restraints (such as body-belts that restrict the movement of the limbs) today, and only as very last resorts[8]. But we still have unregulated restraint by the human hand, and we still have patient injuries and deaths. We deal with this at chapter 2.125. The MHAC is also still concerned at some seclusion practices, which we feel have a potential to traumatise patients and therefore may still retard recovery.

The MHAC's longstanding concerns over the lack of legal protection for patients who are deprived of their liberty without recourse to the formal powers of the 1983 Act (and particularly those who are incapacitated by their illness or disability) perhaps provides a parallel with the 1815 Inquiry's sixth evil: the situation of pauper patients, especially those in workhouses. The parallel is simply one of unregulated exercise of detention on grounds of mental disorder, and the amendments to the Mental Capacity Act 2005 by the Mental Health Act 2007 are designed to address these. In the meantime the MHAC is legally blind to these patients, although our Commissioners may walk past them on their way to interview the formally detained. This was and is deplorable, and is discussed further below.

When the 1815 Inquiry listed its seventh and eighth evils – unwarranted detention and inadequate detention documentation – the law was in its infancy. Such 'unwarranted' detention as now exists is most likely the result of delayed discharges for want of appropriate post-discharge support (see chapter 1.10 and 1.51). The oversight by hospital managers and the MHAC on its visits is a good check on detention documentation, although the MHAC still often has cause to criticise hospitals' documentation of other legal aspects of treatment, especially as regards consent to treatment (see chapter 6.22) or leave of absence (see chapter 4.41). In reviewing Lunacy Commission reports, Hunter and McAlpine noted how 'asylums may fall behind with the passage of time'[9], an observation that is supported by the experience of the MHAC.

The final 'evil' noted by the 1815 report – the want of adequate visiting – touches the very heart of the MHAC's purpose. Critics of the MHAC have questioned whether the MHAC has been as effective as it might be in its monitoring of the Act, either through want of adequate powers of sanction; or because it is insufficiently independent of its main funding body, the Department of Health; or because of the limitations of its remit (which excludes the *de facto* detained, for example); or because it may not always have confined its observations to matters encompassed directly within that remit[10]. The coming period of transition will be an opportunity for these criticisms to be debated more widely, and as such I finish with a few observations of my own.

---

[8] At least in the population of patients detained under Mental Health Act powers. The Healthcare Commission inquiries into the treatment of learning disability patients in Cornwall and Surrey published in this reporting period (see chapter 3.32 below) support our 2003 observation that groups who are less likely to have formal detained status (such as the frail elderly and learning disability patients) are the most likely to be subjected to forms of mechanical restraint (MHAC (2003) *Tenth Biennial Report 2001-2003: Placed Amongst Strangers,* para 11.39).

[9] Hunter R & McAlpine I (1963) *Three hundred years of psychiatry 1535-1860.* Oxford University Press, p.992. The authors note that St Luke's Hospital, having been singled out in 1815 as the standard for other asylums to attain to, was criticised in the Lunacy Commission's 1850 visit report.

There are a number of tensions at the heart of the MHAC's operations. Throughout its existence, the MHAC in practice has pushed at the constraints of its remit, whether this is in relation to aspects of patient care which Richard Jones has argued to be outside of its concern (including, for example, the environmental standards of wards where patients are detained[11]), or groups of patients that fall outside of our remit[12]. In the latter case, we have instructed Commissioners that they must not misuse the authority of the MHAC in raising concerns about the treatment of patients who are not formally detained under the Act, although we recognise that this can place them in the invidious position of being seemingly required to ignore the plight of some very disadvantaged patients that they cannot but become aware of in the course of their official duties. As such the MHAC accepts that its Commissioners may raise matters about such patients in a personal capacity, or indeed pass on concerns to the Healthcare Commission through the MHAC offices. In the meantime, we await government action to provide formal oversight for these patients.

As to the question of whether the MHAC has the right to raise broad issues around the care and treatment of detained patients on visits or, especially, in its Biennial Reports, I believe that we do so in a long and honourable tradition established by the Seventh Earl of Shaftesbury in his first report for the Metropolitan Commissioners in Lunacy (1844):

> Throughout the course of the visitations we have endeavoured to carry into full effect the spirit as well as the letter of the Acts… and … have extended our enquiries to many subjects beyond those which are specifically mentioned[13].

Another tension underlying the MHAC's role is its operation as an arm of the Secretary of State, but entrusted to monitor the operation of legal powers with a degree of independence that may involve doubt about or criticism of government policy. This was certainly the case over the passage of the Mental Health Bill 2007. This tension is healthy neither for the monitoring body itself, nor for its prospective function as a part of the mechanism of safeguards required by this country's status as a signatory to the Operational Protocol for the Convention Against Torture (OPCAT), which is discussed at chapter 8. Here is one potential advantage of the MHAC's functions being taken by the Care Quality Commission, which should be granted a greater constitutional independence, rather than being directly accountable to the serving Minister and his or her officials. Whether in fact the Care Quality Commission will enjoy proper independence is uncertain as I write. As presented to Parliament, the Health and Social Care Bill 2006 contains several clauses requiring the new

---

[10] For the latter, see in particular Jones R (2005) *Mental Health Act Manual,* tenth edition, preface.

[11] The MHAC does not accept the validity of Jones' analyses of the constraints of its legal remit in respect of 'powers and duties', and there is no evidence that it ever has interpreted its remit in the way he suggests (including during the period of his membership). See, for example, MHAC (1985) *First Biennial Report,* pages 16 – 33, and specifically: "particular care is paid [on MHAC visits] to the conditions of the wards where detained patients are placed, and to the facilities available for the preservation of individual dignity and personal choice, when living is necessarily restricted within a close community such as a hospital ward. Many suggestions for improvement made by Commissioners have quickly been taken up by units, and a more homely and creative atmosphere created for the patients" (para 8.6(b)).

[12] See, for example, MHAC (1985) *First Biennial Report,* which devotes space to discussions of guardianship, *de facto* detention and the treatment of incapable but compliant patients, which are all matters outwith the MHAC remit .

[13] Quoted in Hunter R & McAlpine I (1963) *op cit.* n.9, p.925

Commission to seek the Secretary of State's approval for its methodology in assessing quality and safety, including approval over the frequency of inspection. I do not believe that this constraint will best serve the public interest in having a robust and independent regulator unafraid to point out the failings in health and social care to the government of the day.

The great potential disadvantage of the subsuming of the MHAC into a general health and social inspectorate such as the Care Quality Commission would be, of course, if this reduced or ended the practice of visiting hospitals and meeting directly with detained patients. Over the years of debate regarding the future of the MHAC, it is this aspect of its function, rather than the organisation itself, that we have consistently argued to preserve. We are encouraged that, notwithstanding my concerns over the drafting of the Health and Social Care Bill 2006, our argument that there is no substitute for the direct visiting of closed institutions where persons are deprived of their liberty has been sympathetically received by government, no doubt in part because of OPCAT requirements. The difficulty that will remain is how to retain the MHAC's primary visiting methodology whilst merging it with the much larger health and social care inspectorates who are committed to the quite different approaches of sampling and self-assessment for services.

Professor Lord Patel of Bradford OBE

Introduction – Rights, risk, recovery

> I initially thought when I went into hospital that I would lose all my rights and freedom, but it hasn't proved to be the case.
>
> *Dawn Cutler-Nichol, s.37/41, Derbyshire*

(i) The above statement, made by a member of the MHAC's service user reference panel[14], highlights several interrelated matters that we wish to acknowledge at the outset of our report. Patients who are detained under Mental Health Act powers, unless they are too ill to consider such matters at all, are very likely to view their new status with fear and perhaps anger, not least because of the cultural baggage that, from the gothic novels of the nineteenth century to today's tabloid brutalities, has accumulated around the process of being 'sectioned'[15]. However, these fears are not always borne out; patients may be relieved to find that the law which takes away their liberty also contains some checks and balances that a patient can use to regain control throughout their recovery process, and which stand against any overenthusiastic exercise of powers granted to those who detain that patient. The Mental Health Review Tribunal (MHRT) is one such check and balance; the Mental Health Act Commission (MHAC) another. Our MHRT colleagues have the job of hearing appeals against detention itself: the MHAC role is to monitor the way in which the powers and duties of detention are exercised. In doing so, we are bound to pay close attention to those duties upon detaining authorities which are themselves designed to check the unjustified exercise of power, such as the duties to provide information about rights, to assess capacity and work within the consent to treatment framework of the Act, and so on.

(ii) Much of what we say in this report is critical of services provided to detained patients. We are unapologetic about this: our criticism is more useful than our praise, and we do not wish to lose a focus on what needs to be changed by highlighting that which is changing. The Department of Health has established its own agencies in England to promote good

---

14 See page 23 below on the MHAC service user reference panel

15 In pre-Mental Health Act days, the term would be 'certified'. We do not use the term 'sectioned' in our work, preferring the descriptive term 'detained'. Throughout this report generally we refer to those detained or otherwise resident in hospital as 'patients' and people who receive outpatient mental health services as 'service users' (one notable exception to this general rule is the MHAC's own 'service user reference panel', which is comprised of both hospital patients and other service users).

practice[16], which we welcome and support, and whose work we do not wish to duplicate. However, we are aware that our critical tone may obscure the immense amount of compassion and care that is to be found in mental health services. We have highlighted examples of good practice in the care and treatment of detained patients in this report. Indeed, given the extraordinary power over other people that is given to mental health practitioners by the Act, seeing the way in which such power is exercised can be a heartening experience. But there are dark exceptions, and in a service that is running under extreme pressures, there is an ever-present danger of the cursory or careless exercise of power, which might barely register in the mind of the mental health professional but deeply scar the patient concerned.

(iii)   One thread that runs through much of this report is established in the first chapter: we are concerned at the pressure on admission wards, which we believe makes it very difficult to provide good care to patients, and which has a negative effect on care throughout the inpatient mental health service.

(iv)   The busy acute wards that we visit appear to be tougher and scarier places than we saw a decade ago. Something needs to be done about this. It is scandalous that we are forcing vulnerable people onto mental health wards that are frightening and dangerous places. This should not happen at all, but it should be a matter of extreme priority that children are not placed in such situations, and that women's safety from sexual harassment, abuse and assault is addressed within the mental health service. We note that the government has recognised these problems, and indeed that funding has been pledged to address the safety of both women and children in psychiatric hospitals[17]. We discuss this funding further at chapters 2.29 and 3.60 below. We hope that, whether or not they are in receipt of the new funding, all services will give real priority in the next reporting period to the provision of suitable accommodation and care to women and children.

(v)   The next year will be a busy one for mental health services, as they prepare for the implementation of the Mental Health Act 2007. Providers of NHS mental health services will have received a self-assessment tool from NIMHE/CSIP to gauge their preparedness for the changes to mental health legislation. We have seen some very positive responses to this from some services. Barnet, Enfield and Haringey Mental Health NHS Trust, for example, have established a Board-level *Mental Health Act Scrutiny Committee,* with user, carer and clinician representation. The committee not only oversees preparations for the changes in the law, but also receives monitoring and audit reports on the Trust's exercise of its statutory duties and reports on these quarterly to the Board itself.

(vi)   Such arrangements are an excellent example of mental health services' internal control mechanisms. They are vitally important to instigate local action to ensure that the services provided to detained patients are appropriately resourced and safe for patients. They should

---

[16]   Including the National Institute for Mental Health in England (NIMHE), Care Services Improvement Partnership (CSIP),and National Patient Safety Agency (NPSA).

[17]   "Government invests £31m in children and young peoples' psychiatric wards". Department of Health Press Release, 14 November 2007; Department of Health (2006) 'Capital allocation process: £30 million for improvements in safety on adult inpatient mental health wards' letter to all chief executives of NHS mental health Trusts & SHA chief executives, 2 November 2006.

also help to ensure that the service for which they are responsible meets its statutory obligations and discharges its legal duties in operating the Act.

(vii)   We discuss the proposed dissolution of the MHAC and creation of a new, generic Care Quality Commission (CQC) at chapter 8 of this report, and have reproduced our open letter to the Secretary of State at appendix 1. Our primary concern over the merger is that the visiting role of the MHAC must not disappear when our organisation is dissolved, even though our visiting methodology (focussing on visiting all services to meet with patients in private) may run counter to assessment methodologies likely to be adopted by the new body in carrying out its main work. The government's obligations to people that are deprived of their liberty would not be met by reactive visits alone. We do not believe that the internal monitoring mechanisms of detaining authorities should be relied on to determine whether to visit their detained patients, or even as uncorroborated evidence to determine the frequency of such visits. In this report we show examples where our visits to hospitals have shown considerable and dangerous gaps between self-assessment and reality (see chapter 2.14).

(viii)   We have completed this report in the wake of a successful MHAC conference (November 2007), at which Commissioners and service users shared experiences and enthusiasm for the potential for change in mental health services. On the following pages we set out some of the comments received when MHA Commissioners were asked to record the worst thing that they had seen in the previous six months, and the change or improvement that they had been able to make that had given them the greatest satisfaction. Following this, we explain the role of the Service User Reference Panel (SURP) in the MHAC's work. The first of these documents shows why a body such as the MHAC is necessary. In our view the second and third demonstrate the achievements of the MHAC, and as such represent a legacy that we are proud of.

The most disturbing incidents seen by individual Mental Health Act Commissioners in the six months prior to November 2007

Older people consulting a list of when they were able to have a bath in the week, (according to staff available).

Six patients sharing a poorly decorated room; and one of them refusing to go out on leave for fear of losing this bed – because when she came back she could be in an even worse room with a high risk of violence.

A patient being nursed by four nurses in a bare room, with a mask on her face to stop her spitting; three nurses holding her.

Three members of staff restraining a patient in a way that involved holding a towel across his mouth and holding it from behind so that the patient had difficulty breathing.

A dying man nursed in a dining room of an elderly unit whilst other patients having their lunch (lack of staff to nurse him appropriately).

Vulnerable women housed with predatory men – alleging physical / sexual abuse – unwilling to take complaint forward due to fear of what would happen and lack of control over the process. Had told male member of staff who had laughed it off.

Observation blinds to patients' rooms kept permanently in the open position for staff convenience. (Most of patients' rooms were off main corridor i.e. no gender designation)

A male patient who is secluded 90% of the time – no quality of life – no other service willing to take him.

Seclusion room with no privacy to use the toilet – only disposable bedpans.

Visit to rehab/assess unit. Female patient from black minority ethnic group, frequently verbally abused by male patient of a racist nature and during the past month physically abused. Commissioner highlighted the same issue on previous visit-no adequate response.

A detained patient who clearly lacked capacity being treated with a Form 38. This patient …was also being treated for physical problems that were probably side effects of his psychiatric treatment.

Three new acute wards with 135% bed occupancy – patients sleeping in day rooms – no curtains – mattresses stowed away by day – no space for belongings – staff run off feet.

Finding detained patients sleeping on mattresses on floors on wards, doctor's office, quiet room, etc., due to bed over occupancy levels.

A ward where the plaster on the walls had been removed bit by bit by a patient. Some rooms looked like they were in the process of being demolished – staff seemed resigned to the conditions – patients very upset & angry about the living conditions.

An unsustainable workload on acute unit: i.e. 100% occupancy; high numbers on s.17 leave; 17 out of 24 patients detained; informal patients admitted to a psychiatric intensive care unit (PICU) as no other beds available; 6 on close observation; 2 ward rounds taking place; nurses working flat out. Patients saying nurses have no time to speak to them.

A hospital where due to staff shortages, patients had to collect their belongings in a bin bag each morning, take them to another ward where they would spend the day then only return to their ward each night. This happened for several weeks.

The effect on a detained patient (X) being kept in seclusion for about two weeks due to financial closure of PICU, and the knock-on effect on the rest of the patients who had to be 'secluded' every time staff needed to move X to bathroom, smoke-room etc. One female patient was terrorised, being convinced "he will kill me".

CCTV in patient bedrooms supposedly switched off following complaints by male and female patients, but reported to come back on randomly.

Of six women SURP members responding to project on women in detention, four described personal experience of serious abuse or serious sexual harassment.

An overcrowded PICU with very active group of men with not enough access to fresh air or space for vigorous activities leading to some prone restraint (more than for the three minutes) because of daily incidence of violence.

An all male PICU located in an extremely cramped upstairs ward with no secure access to outside. Patients without s.17 leave NEVER have access to fresh air or outdoor exercise. Many patients detained were on s.37/41. Little daylight reaches communal areas, central heating on even when outside temperature is more than 18 degrees.

The mix of patients on an acute ward, i.e. older patients, learning difficulties. Patient on one to one observation, able to hang himself in his room with door open and nurse sat outside.

Removal of education facilities for 16-18 years at an adolescent unit leaving no proper link between the unit and local colleges.

A woman in seclusion who was deprived of sanitary protection whilst menstruating.

A male member of staff using his mobile phone to photograph a female patient naked in a bathroom (she was in the bathroom being supervised by other staff members)

A Hindu woman offered Halal meat.

A patient ready to move on from secure services but with nowhere to go, so detained longer than needed.

A detained patient who contracted TB whilst an inpatient.

A deaf man who has been in special hospital for 60 years.

Mice and cockroaches on the wards.

A detained young man with learning disability with a double facture of his arm as a result of 'restraint'.

One detained patient told me he was very worried about his life and future as he had raped another detained patient and nobody had discussed these issues with him. When we brought it up with the manager, they said that it had been 'dealt with'.

A patient discharged into the community without a care plan, support from social services or a place to stay. The patient subsequently left the ward, and was found dead at bottom of a viaduct in a nature reserve.

A bedroom on a PICU with no door and the inhabitant frightened.

Changes or improvements with which individual Commissioners had been involved in the six months prior to November 2007

The introduction of a protocol for ensuring that consent to treatment (s.58) process is properly applied rather than simply having lip-service paid to it.

Much improved and well recorded re-presentation of rights information to patients – patients clearly better informed and more aware of their rights.

A joint visit with Healthcare Commission to a womens' secure unit at 7 p.m. one night found appalling conditions, practices and care. Joint letter to managers, notice served by HCC, followed by changes and improvements.

A man in a medium secure unit for more than a year had been told that he was to move to a rehabilitation unit the next day. He was upset about this because he wanted to say goodbye to friends (other patients) by cooking a meal for them. Negotiated with ward for move to be delayed for a few days for him to be able to do this.

Persuading a hospital to introduce independent advocacy services for the first time.

Better s.58 [consent to treatment] compliance – corrections of s.132 [information for patients] deficits.

Improved partnership working between agencies on a ward where substance misuse was having a negative and dangerous impact on patient care and experience, and staff safety and morale.

Seeing improvement in level and quality of activities on one particular ward, following sustained feedback.

The introduction of a new policy for the application of s.132 [information for patients] and the application of an audit on the implementation of this section, based entirely on issues that we had raised in the annual report.

A learning disability patient living in a 'cell' with a commode chained to a radiator being properly assessed and provided with more appropriate and humane living facilities.

Cutting the over-occupancy rates in one trust from 12 wards at 115% to one ward in one year.

An independent unit where I questioned whether they were able to provide patient care – no nurse call; no attack alarms; ligature points throughout; staff not Care Programme Approach trained; provision inadequate for disabled patient etc. Next visit, the unit had been renovated, addressing all environmental issues. A new manager and clinical lead had been appointed, and staff training had dramatically improved. All contributed to better patient care.

Persuading a multi-disciplinary team to change their minds about transferring a patient back to prison four months before the end of his sentence, after four years in hospital. In prison he would have received no resettlement plan. In hospital plans were put in place for a structured discharge with family support and involvement.

Access to fresh air for patients at Rampton. Vast improvement in completion of s.132 so that virtually all wards now have evidence.

RMOs recording capacity and consent (sometimes).

The Trust Executive claimed 85% bed occupancy to their Board but visiting Commissioners found between 90 – 125% occupancy. By persisting in keeping this on the agenda in all my discussions, the senior management have now acknowledged that they are running over-full and have recommended to their Board that there should be no more bed closures.

Having had several visits over 2 to 3 years to a ward with dormitory of 8 to 10 patients, and saying this ward was no longer fit for purpose and it was not acceptable for the Trust to say that this would be resolved in 5 to 10 years time with a new build, to visit last week and find the dormitories have been closed and are being changes into single bedrooms, and a new lounge, dining room, kitchens etc.

On a visit to a PICU, having suggested advance directives to manage seriously disturbed patients, as I'd heard that some patients preferred rapid tranquilisation, and others seclusion etc. Then to visit the same unit 9 to 12 months later and listen to a nurse describe an initiative 'they' started which considered patient's wishes as to their management when they were behaving in a disturbed way.

A patient who had been on a low secure 'rehab' ward for over ten years who had not had a CPA meeting for several years & the staff had given up on. Following my visit and recommendations, a CPA meeting was held, a placement found and funding agreed. When I next visited the patient had started the gradual process of moving. He told me that he would like to train as a screen-printer and a placement at a return to work project was found to provide this.

Early closure of high risk learning disability service which would probably still be open without MHAC intervention – and individual needs assessments used to relocate patients, rather than all moving to one new unit.

Instant removal of two identified ligature points on one busy acute ward.

Persuading a Trust not to place single women on an eight-bedded PICU with acutely unwell males. They were continuing this practice despite an allegation of rape by a previous female patient.

Constant criticism about an inpatient unit contributing towards the Trust reconfiguring the wards to include en-suite facilities and a wholly better patient environment.

The possibility of a future for an extremely abused and vulnerable young woman who had been on s.3 for over a year with no movement (also had been abused / raped on unit): the making of a care plan; the input of psychological services and activities; the reconstruction of the acute ward to provide separate vulnerable adults area (long planned but not activated before).

Improved compliance with annual physical examinations at a high secure hospital.

Getting a Trust to take concerns about female patients seriously.

Uncovering poor MHA admissions and practice – returning 10 months later to find good systemic change and all recommendations addressed.

Visiting hospitals out of my local area where there was a history of poor compliance of section 132. Examining the process in detail and making suggestions for change which have now been implemented.

Improvements in practice in relation to seclusion

Compliance-medication charts with Form 38/9 in regional secure unit. Not yet complete but some wards are now auditing regularly.

The Service User Reference Panel: service user involvement in the MHAC

The Mental Health Act Commission seeks to involve users of mental services in all aspects of our work. We believe this helps us to respond more effectively to the needs of patients who are detained under the Mental Health Act and so bring about improvements in services to detained patients. To this end, we work closely with a Service User Reference Panel (SURP) made up of 20 to 30 people who are currently detained, or have recently experienced detention.

For the MHAC, service user involvement is part of a wider strategy that puts equality and human rights at the centre of our work, to help us to be inclusive of the rights of all detained patients and respond well to the complexity of individual service users' needs. We recognise that it is important to include the perspective of service users with a range of experience in this work, because of the different issues they may face in relation to detention under the Act. We have targeted recruitment to encourage the involvement of a diverse range of service users, ensuring the panel's diversity in terms of ethnicity, age, gender, sexuality, geography, disabilities and experience of mental health services.

The SURP was set up in 2005 as part of our service user involvement strategy to provide the MHAC with a service user perspective on all aspects of its current and projected activity, to influence all aspects of the Commission's work programme, including advising and commenting on priorities for visiting, development work, research and publications, and to contribute to particular projects through participation in steering groups or in other ways. Over the two years since introducing this strategy, service user involvement has helped change the culture of the organisation, and has become a regular and integral feature of our work.

The SURP has demonstrated that service users want to be involved, to be listened to, and to influence mental health services and the work of the MHAC. Its members have been enthusiastic about developing the way we involve people in our work. They have helped with responses to formal consultations, taken part in training our workforce, influenced our programmatic development work, and been involved in specific projects, such as the *Count me In* census and our human rights case study *Making it real*[18]. SURP members have helped develop our equality schemes for race, disability and gender, and contributed to improvements in our communications materials for patients and the public. They have also contributed directly to publications, and examples of their views and experiences appear throughout this biennial report.

A most significant area of development is how service users influence the day to day practice of visiting Commissioners. In 2006 the SURP argued that service users should be more directly involved in visiting activity. Service users worked alongside Commissioners to pilot methods for doing this in a project called *Acting Together*. Evaluation of the project showed that direct service user input into visiting activity has clear benefits: patients at the sites visited were more willing to engage in discussion, and the visiting service users were able to provide an independent but user-focused view of the service. Commissioners involved in

---

[18] http://www.mhac.org.uk/files/48529%20Bklt%201st%20proof%20of%20flyer.pdf

the project reported that the experience from the joint visits would continue to influence the way they visit in future. The outcome of the pilots will be further joint visits between Local Commissioners and SURP members, and will form part of training and development for the Commissioners. A report of the *Acting Together* pilot project is available on the Service User Involvement page of our website, or by contacting the MHAC office.

The MHAC has learnt much from the SURP about the need to be flexible in our approach and how to adapt ways of working to facilitate involvement. We use a range of methods to encourage people to get involved in a variety of different ways. Workable solutions are needed to overcome barriers to engagement, such as communication difficulties, bouts of ill-health, detention in secure settings, or deeply negative experiences of public authorities. We aim to meet practical needs for communication and support: for example, where service users have no email access, or prefer to give views face-to-face or by telephone rather than in writing. Whilst we realise that we have more to learn, and will continue to develop our user involvement strategy, we believe that many of the lessons from our service user involvement have wider applicability for public services wishing to involve service users, particularly those concerned with mental health. With support from the Department of Health, we are producing a report, *From Strength to Strength*, outlining the development of our service user involvement strategy, to be published this year.

The context of detention under the 1983 Act

Hospital beds

We no longer rely on beds to help people with serious difficulties.

Professor Louis Appleby, National Director for Mental Health[19]

[The coroner] described the current trend for treating mentally ill patients at home as "imperfect". He said: "there are concerns here that a woman who was seriously ill went back to a home that left a great deal to be desired. Time was when that a person like this would have been cared for in a safe, warm environment. But there has been a change where people are not kept in institutions but are cared for in the community"

'Schizophrenic woman died in freezing room', *Wandsworth Guardian*, 7 June 2007. The patient in question was discharged (having been detained under section 2) to the care of a relative who also had mental health problems. She died of hypothermia after sleeping in a freezing room without adequate clothing or covers.

1.1   In 2005/06 the NHS spent about £575 million, or more than two-thirds of its budget for clinical mental health services, on acute psychiatric in-patient hospital care[20]. Nevertheless, as we have noted in previous reports, there are fewer mental health beds now than at any time during the lifetime of the Act. Figure 1 below shows that NHS mental illness beds in England have reduced by almost two-thirds since 1983[21].

---

[19]   'Mental Health Tsar pledges further reforms' Press Association, 11 May 2007.

[20]   Mental Health Foundation (2007) *The fundamental facts; the latest facts and figures on mental health.* London, Mental Health Foundation, p. 47.

[21]   See MHAC (2006) *Eleventh Biennial Report 2003-2005: In Place of Fear?* London, Stationery Office, figure 6 (p.115) for previous data between 1983 and 2003/04. The Eleventh Report's discussion of that data (para 2.15, p.114) incorrectly gives the reduction to 2003/04 as 40% (it should read 60%).

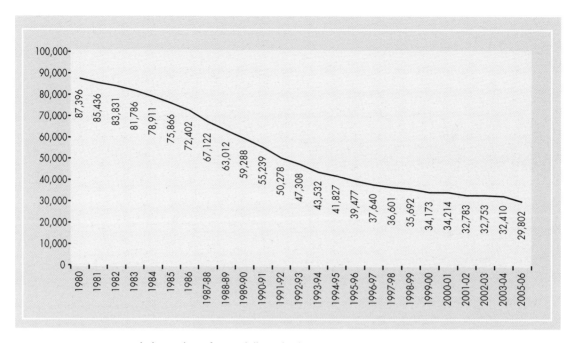

Fig 1: Average daily number of mental illness beds in NHS Trusts, England, 1980 – 2005/06

Data source: Department of Health[22]

1.2   In contrast to the downward trend in bed numbers shown at figure 1 above, a trend-line describing detentions of patients over the lifetime of the Act shows something of an inverse curve (see figure 15, chapter 3.1 below). Whilst the annual incidence of detentions under the Act appears to have levelled off around the 45,000 mark, this represents a one-third increase from 1990/01, the earliest year for which comparable data is available (see figure 2 below).

1.3   The number of detentions under the Act is sometimes used as a crude measure of the success of 'community care' alternatives to hospital admission for severe mental health problems. In the Department of Health's report on progress with implementing its National Service Framework for mental health, it is stated that "perhaps most importantly, the use of the Mental Health Act has remained constant in recent years"[23]. Whilst this is one way of approaching the statistic, data in the Department of Health's report itself shows that, whilst the number of detentions may have remained relatively stable, it has done so in a period of a 10% decline in *all* mental health admissions (formal and informal), and as such the *proportion* of mental health in-patients who are detained has grown slightly[24]. At ward level, many acute services now report to us that they care for an increasing proportion of detained patients.

---

[22] DH returns SK3/KH03, Hansard HC 15 July 2003: col 228W; (2003/4 - 2005/06 data from www.performance.dh.gov.uk/hospital activity/).

[23] Department of Health (2004) *The national service framework for mental health - five years on*, p.26.

[24] *ibid.* In 1998/9 there were 135,460 admissions, of which 46,298 involved detention under the Act at some point. In 2002/3, there were 122,260 admissions overall, of which 45,484 involved detention at some point.

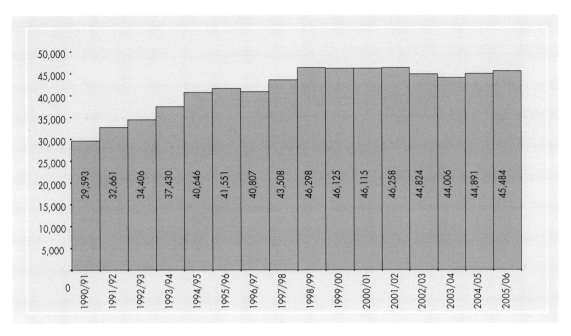

Fig 2: Detentions under the Mental Health Act (admissions and inpatient detention), mental health and learning disability, England, 1984 – 2005/06

Data source: Department of Health / Information Centre statistical bulletins
"Inpatients detained under the Mental Health Act 1983 and other legislation" 1986 - 2007[25]

1.4 The data behind figure 2 suggests roughly one-third more incidences of detention under the Act in NHS facilities annually than there are beds in the whole NHS mental illness sector[26]. This is, perhaps, a surprising figure, especially given that it excludes informal patients, who are the most populous patient group using these beds[27], but it is not sufficient by itself to indicate any crisis in bed provision. Indeed, a sense of the throughput in many mental health wards can be gauged by the Department of Health statistic that the median length of stay for all adult mental health inpatients has been 'stable' at between 18 and 19 days in recent years[28]. We discuss lengths of stay for detained patients at chapter 3.8 below.

1.5 Nevertheless, there is some evidence to suggest that there may be insufficient numbers of beds for the adequate care of patients in some areas of the service. We report on the severe

---

[25] See figure 15, chapter 3.1 below for more detailed data.

[26] Discounting all admissions under the Act to independent hospitals (an average of 1,523 patients over each of the last five years recorded at figure 2) and also learning disability patients admitted to NHS facilities (based upon the average of 132 patients with mental impairment classification admitted to NHS wards in each of the five years). We cannot, from available data, quantify and therefore discount the number of existing inpatients who were detained either in independent hospitals or with a legal classification equating to learning disability, although these are not likely to be very large numbers of patients. Data source: *"Inpatients detained under the Mental Health Act 1983 and other legislation"* 2002 – 2007, tables 9 and 6 respectively.

[27] In 2002/03 there were 122,260 NHS adult mental health admissions in total: see Mental Health Foundation (2007) *The fundamental facts; the latest facts and figures on mental health.* London, Mental Health Foundation, p. 47. Data at fig 2 above suggests that 44,824 of these were detained on or after admission. This suggests a 2:1 ratio of informal and detained patients in that year. On admission (i.e. discounting informal patients who become detained after admission), the ratio is closer to 7:2 (see fig 15, chapter 3.1 for data).

[28] Department of Health (2004) *The national service framework for mental health - five years on.* p.26.

difficulties in finding beds for urgent admissions of patients under the Act at chapter 4.1. More generally, we continue to note widespread over-occupancy on wards that we visit. Over this reporting period, 37% of all wards visited by Mental Health Act Commissioners were running at over 100% occupancy, where some patients will have been given leave to free up beds for others (figure 3), and a further 27% were running at 100% occupancy when we visited.

| Occupancy Band | 2005/06 | | | 2006/07 | | |
	Number of Wards	Percentage band		Number of Wards	Percentage band	
<= 90%	128	< 100%	35.9%	139	< 100%	37.0%
90%+ to <100	61			61		
Exactly 100%	135	= 100%	25.7%	148	= 100%	27.4%
100%+ to 105%	11			30		
105%+ to 110%	55			37		
110%+ to 115%	28	> 100%	38.4%	38	> 100%	35.6%
115%+ to 120%	28			28		
120%+ to 125%	17			17		
> 125%	63			42		
Total	526		100%	540		100%

Fig 3: Bed-occupancy levels in 1,066 wards visited by the MHAC over 2005/6 and 2006/7

Data source: MHAC data

1.6   Problems with high rates of bed occupancy in acute wards are most prevalent in urban areas, with London showing a particularly high percentage of wards running over 100% occupancy, with considerable numbers of wards visited having very high levels of over-occupancy (figure 4).

Occupancy Band	Number of Wards	Percentage band	
<= 90%	50	< 100%	26.0%
90%+ to <100	26		
Exactly 100%	71	= 100%	24.3%
100%+ to 105%	8		
105%+ to 110%	18		
110%+ to 115%	21	> 100%	49.7%
115%+ to 120%	23		
120%+ to 125%	16		
> 125%	59		
Total	292		100%

Fig 4: Bed-occupancy levels in 292 London acute wards visited by the MHAC over 2005/6 and 2006/7

Data source: MHAC data

1.7   MHAC bed occupancy data counts patients 'on the books' of a ward, whether or not they are physically present at the time of our visit. A number of such patients will in fact be on leave.

> K was detained for four months on an over-occupied ward. Although she did not have to move or go on leave, she shared a locker and en-suite bathroom and toilet with a woman who did "sleep out" on another ward. As the dispensing of medication was done late at night (sometimes as late as midnight), the other patient could not go to her own bed until after that time, and consequently was still sharing K's space until then.
>
> Service user experience, *from Who's been sleeping in my bed?*

1.8   In December 2006 the MHAC published *Who's been sleeping in my bed?*[29], a short report on the findings of its bed occupancy. The survey reinforced our concern that bed pressures and over-occupancy of acute services have a deleterious effect on the care of detained patients at their most vulnerable time. The measures taken to manage such bed pressures contribute to and exacerbate wider problems experienced in acute services, including difficulties in maintaining the safety, dignity and privacy of patients. The clinical treatment and care of patients may also be compromised: patients and staff reported concerns over a lack of continuity in care caused by the movement of patients within wards or hospitals, or the sending of patients on leave, to ease bed pressures. In some units ward staff perceived that the day-to-day demands of bed-management diverted them from their primary nursing role. A number of staff members acknowledged that the frustration and stress of bed-management in an over-occupied ward was harmful to staff morale, and that this had an indirect effect on the quality of patients' experience on the ward.

1.9   The survey also established that, in some services, there is a serious lack of service user involvement in finding solutions to bed over occupancy problems. In some hospitals, patients appear to be given very little or no choice about where they are to sleep, resulting in poor relationships with staff and a heightened sense of coercion in acute care services. Where patients did feel involved and respected by nursing staff, they reported bed-management arrangements (such as being asked to take leave) much more positively, and were likely to acknowledge the potential for therapeutic benefit in leave or short-term 'sleeping-out' arrangements.

> **Recommendation 1:** Hospitals should review their bed-management practice and seek to ensure that it does not unnecessarily compromise patients' treatment or well-being. Particular attention should be paid to fostering a culture of patient involvement in decisions over bed-management that affect their care and treatment.

[29]   MHAC (2006) *Who's been sleeping in my bed? The incidence and impact of bed overoccupancy in the mental health acute sector.* Findings of the Mental Health Act Commission's Bed Occupancy Survey. Suki Desai & Mat Kinton. MHAC, Nottingham, December 2006. Available from www.mhac.org.uk

1.10 One cause of pressure on beds in the acute sector is delay in discharging patients or transferring patients to other services. Data collected by NHS Trusts for the Department of Health (figure 5) suggests that around 9% of acute beds are occupied by patients, detained or informal, who should no longer be there but cannot move for want of an agreed follow-on destination. Details on the causes of such delayed discharges are set out at figure 9, paragraph 1.51 below.

	Delayed Transfers of Care (DTOC)	Average MH & LD beds occupied	% of MH & LD beds occupied by DTOC
November 2006	2,375	24,862	9.6%
December 2006	2,210	24,368	9.1%
January 2007	2,229	24,479	9.1%
February 2007	2,246	24,290	9.2%
March 2007	2,198	24,229	9.1%
April 2007	2,174	24,783	8.8%
average over six months	2,239	24,502	9.2%

Fig 5: Percentage of beds occupied by delayed transfers of care (DTOC), mental health and learning disability patients (detained or informal), Nov 2006 – April 2007, England

Data source: Department of Health SitReps[30]

1.11 Trusts have identified a range of methods for managing bed pressures, some of which were reported in a positive light by staff members. Innovative and beneficial practice should be shared more widely between and within Trusts. There is some evidence to suggest that as crisis resolution and home treatment services become more established this has resulted in some easing of pressure on beds. Some Trusts use such teams to facilitate an earlier discharge for patients from acute psychiatric wards. The impact of this on service users has yet to be explored.

1.12 The Care Services Improvement Partnership and National Institute for Mental Health in England have produced a good practice toolkit aimed at providing best practice guidance on reducing the current levels of delayed discharge experienced by adults and older people in mental health services[31]. This document, which should be studied by all ward managers and service commissioners, covers admissions planning between community and inpatient care teams.

---

[30] Department of Health SitReps (Situation Reports) collected by NHS Trusts: see www.dh.gov.uk/en/Publicationsandstatistics/Publications/PublicationsPolicyAndGuidance/DH_4070304

[31] CSIP/NIMHE (2007) *A Positive Outlook: A good practice toolkit to improve discharge from inpatient mental health care.* Accessible from www.virtualward.org.uk

> **Recommendation 2:**
>
> i) Services should adopt the CSIP/NIMHE discharges toolkit.
>
> ii) Discussions with patients (and, where appropriate, carers and relatives) over bed-management arrangements, especially as this relates to leave of absence from hospital, should be recorded by staff in patients' notes.

Reinstitutionalisation of mental health services?

1.13   The continuing development of community services appears to be changing the profile of patients admitted to acute wards with serious mental illnesses, principally by keeping the least unwell out of hospital. It may also be having wider effects on the profile of inpatient services themselves. The Department of Health reports a net loss of 680 NHS acute beds between 1998/99 and 2002/03 (or a fall of 4.7% of the total), but a net gain of 310 NHS medium secure beds (a rise of 18%) over the same period[32]. We are unable to quantify the growth of secure beds in the independent sector during this period, but we believe that were these taken into account the overall pattern in available beds would appear to be shifting towards secure services. In 2005 independent hospitals provided 1,827 medium secure beds, or 39% of the total provision of 4,713 such beds[33].

1.14   The Sainsbury Centre for Mental Health has reported that the total number of people detained in forensic services has been increasing year on year for more than a decade. There were 3,658 people detained in forensic services at the end of 2006, up seven per cent on 2005. By July 2007 the number had reached 3,723, a record high[34].

1.15   There are a number of plausible reasons for this growth in the medium and intermediate secure sector, not least a starting point of wholly inadequate service provision[35]; the increased demand for 'step-down' beds with the retraction of the High Secure Hospitals; and a massive prison population with high levels of psychiatric morbidity (of which see chapter 7.2 below).

1.16   The pressure to create more secure beds is not only a demand for 'step-down' places: it is also a pressure from below, from the acute sector and the community. There is no statistical evidence of any significant rise in the number of patients detained under part III rather than civil powers[36]: indeed, the proportionate use of part III powers to detain patients has

---

[32]   Department of Health (2004) *The national service framework for mental health - five years on*, p.26. The number of NHS short-stay (acute) beds for adult mental health fell from 14,420 in 1998–99 to 13,740 in 2002–03, while the number of NHS medium secure beds increased in the same period from 1,750 to 2,060.

[33]   Rutherford M & Duggan S (2007) *Forensic Mental Health Services: Facts and figures on current provision.* Sainsbury Centre for Mental Health 'Forensic Factfile 2007', September 2007. Appendix (based on Laing & Buisson (2006) *Mental Health and Specialist Care Services UK Market Report 2006).*

[34]   *ibid,* page 8.

[35]   Coid J, Kathan N, Gault S, Cook A Jarman B (2001) 'Medium secure forensic psychiatry services: Comparison of seven English health regions' *Br J Psychiatry* 178: 55-61.

[36]   That is, detained through the criminal justice system (by court order or prison transfer) rather than under the 'civil' powers of ss.2 and 3.

decreased over the lifetime of the Act (figure 6 below). As such, it would seem that at least some of the new secure-sector beds are being occupied by patients detained under civil sections of the Act.

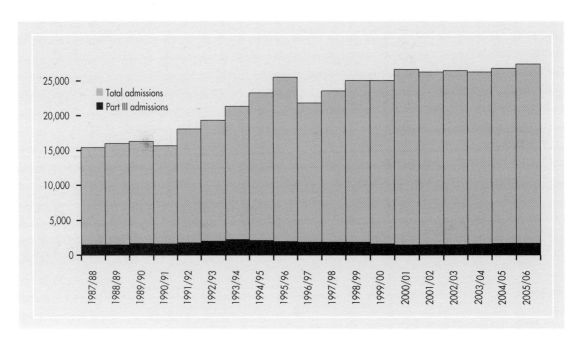

Fig 6: Admissions from court or prison (part III admissions) as a proportion of total admissions under the MHA 1983, England, 1987/88 – 2005/06.

Data source: Department of Health / Information Centre statistical bulletins
"Inpatients detained under the Mental Health Act 1983 and other legislation" 1986 - 2007

1.17   The policy of 'zero-tolerance' of violence towards NHS staff, discussed in our previous reports[37], may also lead to action being taken against inpatients detained under civil sections of the Act that lead to their 'progression' up hospital security levels, perhaps even (when prosecution takes place) as patients subject to hospital orders under part III of the Act. In some cases this may be entirely appropriate, but we have seen some worrying examples of 'zero-tolerance' that could have perverse consequences in terms of healthcare outcome. There is also a terrible irony that patients who act out when detained in unsuitable, frustrating or frightening hospital environments (see chapter 2.8 below) could become more deeply enmeshed within the hospital system and within the coercive powers of the Act as a result.

1.18   The following example describes an apparently questionable prosecution. It is easy to see how this sort of case could lead to adverse health events for the patient, precipitating civil readmission, or to readmission as a forensic patient.

> A Wigan mum is calling for changes to the law after her daughter was charged with assaulting a mental health nurse... during a struggle with a team of professionals attempting to restrain her from walking out of Leigh PICU. She was sectioned under the Mental Health Act for six months

---

[37]   See, for example, MHAC (2006) *Eleventh Biennial Report 2003- 2005: In Place of Fear?*, paras 4.141-6, 4.202-6.

after suffering from manic depression ... [but] returned home a month ago after the order was revoked. [She] was shocked to be summoned to Wigan police station for questioning and later bailed on an allegation of assault. Now her devastated mother ..., fears the trauma of spending virtually a full day in the cells at Wigan police station – and the prospect of a possible assault hearing – could push her daughter back into the abyss of mental illness. ...She said "Helen was very ill indeed at the time of this incident. Are we now saying that people should be punished for falling ill? ... this has had a terrible effect on Helen again, coming so long after the incident, and pushing her back towards the tipping point"

'Mum's fight for her daughter' *Wigan Evening Post*, 29 June 2007.

1.19   The increased use of secure beds for civil detainees may also be a simple reflection of the practice of hospitalising patients only at the point at which they become very unwell with quite complex needs, but even such a practice could be seen as a manifestation of a process discussed as "reinstitutionalisation" in our last report[38], and similar to that described in a Canadian study as "forensicisation"[39]. This unhappy coinage describes a process whereby "the only way many seriously mentally ill people can access increasingly scarce inpatient services is to become a forensic patient"[40], and was observed in relation to Ontario services in the ten years to 1998, during which time psychiatric bed numbers reduced generally but the numbers of forensic beds doubled[41]. The Ontario studies, which compared hospital populations from 1990 with 1997, interestingly concluded that the increase in forensic beds had not been accompanied by a lowering of the average risk level posed by the forensic population: rather clinicians used the resources as an opportunity to "more accurately assess risk" leading to increased levels of "retaining patients (and providing interventions) in accordance with risk"[42]. In other words, forensic psychiatrists were finding new levels of risk in the patients presented to them and in the patients that they already had. There is even a possibility that this discovery of previously unnoted risks raises the bar still further for psychiatric inpatient care: the Ontario study suggested that the retention of the new burgeoning forensic population relied upon the release of "lower risk" patients[43].

---

[38]   MHAC (2006) *Eleventh Biennial Report 2003- 2005: In Place of Fear?*, para 2.53 *et seq*. See also Lamb H R & Weinberger L E (2005) 'The Shift in Psychiatric Inpatient Care From Hospitals to Jails and Prisons' *J Am Acad Psychiatry Law* 33:529-34; Lamb H R & Bachrach L L (2001) 'Some perspectives on deinstitutionalization' *Psychiatric Services* Vol.52, No.8; Lamb H R (1981) 'What did we really expect from deinstitutionalisation?' *Hosp Community Psychiatry* 32:105-109.

[39]   Rice M, Harris G et al (1999) *Planning Services for Forensic Psychiatric patients in Ontario: Results of the 1998 Forensic Survey*, October 1999. Quoted in Champlain District Mental Health Implementation Task Force (2002) *Final Report: Foundations for Reform. Section 9.5, Building Community Based Services and Supports in Forensics*. Ontario, July 2002. For published version, see Rice, M.E., Harris, G.T., Cormier, C.A., Lang, C., Coleman, G., & Smith Krans, T. (2004) An evidence-based approach to planning services for forensic psychiatric patients. *Issues in Forensic Psychology* **5**, 13-49 British Psychological Society.

[40]   Champlain District Mental Health Implementation Task Force (2002) *op cit* n.39, p.4.

[41]   Rice M, Harris G *et al* (1999) *op cit* n.39.

[42]   *ibid.*, p.34.

[43]   *ibid.*

Risk

1.20 The Ontario experience discussed above suggests that 'forensicisation' can be a result of a particular type of focus on risk described by Jonathan Green as a "spiral of precaution" which

> privileges an often indeterminate future risk over possibly less apparent current benefits; and, furthermore, disregards the possibility that future advances may neutralise current or future risks. Since it is impossible to prove the complete absence of risk we may in this way end up increasing it.[44]

1.21 In recent years there has been considerable development of standardised and structured risk assessment tools, but also questions over the objectivity in the way such tools are applied, and the choices of risk to which they are applied[45]. The Royal College of Psychiatrists has called for services to move beyond "the politics of risk assessment of violence", the dominance of which it suggests has the potential to distort clinical priorities and may lead to "defensive psychiatry"[46]. Szmukler has suggested that a focus on predicting violence in psychiatric practice has a risk of creating false positives (i.e. wrongly classifying patients as dangerous), and may also:

- emphasise control and containment at the expense of treatment;
- divert resources towards those assumed risky and away from the majority of people with mental disorder;
- reinforce sterotypes of mentally ill people as dangerous; and
- deter people (including 'risky persons') from engaging with services. [47]

1.22 In May and June 2007 the Department of Health published two guides to best practice in risk-assessment (the first covering all NHS services, the second specifically for mental health services)[48]. We hope that mental health services will utilise both documents as the basis for practice, as cumulatively they emphasise a version of risk assessment that is, indeed, much wider than the 'homicide and suicide' focus that some may have adopted. Both documents emphasise the role of "positive risk management", developed in collaboration with users and carers, which seeks to build on users' strengths and plans for recovery[49]. Patients who are detained under Mental Health Act powers must not be excluded from such approaches.

---

[44] Green J (2006) 'Avoiding a spiral of precaution in mental healthcare' *Advances in Psychiatric Treatment* **12**, 1-4. See also MHAC (2006) *Eleventh Biennial Report 2003-2005: In Place of Fear?* para 2.57 *et seq.*

[45] See Maden T (2003) 'Standardised risk assessment: why all the fuss?' and Szmukler G (2007) 'Risk assessment: 'numbers' and 'values" *Psychiatric Bulletin* **27** 201-207

[46] Morgan J F (2007) Giving up the culture of blame: *Risk assessment and risk management in psychiatric practice* Briefing document for the Royal College of Psychiatrists, Feb 2007.

[47] Szmukler G (2007) *op cit.* n.45

[48] Department of Health (2007) *Independence, choice and risk: a guide to best practice in supported decision-making*, May 2007; (2007) *Best practice in managing risk: principles and evidence for best practice in the assessment and management of risk to self and others in mental health services.* Document prepared for the National Mental Health Risk Management Programme, June 2007.

[49] See also Morgan S (2007) 'Visions of risk' *Openmind* 146, 7-8; Raven C (2007) 'Breaking the cycle of risk behaviour' Openmind 146, 9-10, for discussion of risk management as a therapeutic tool.

Recommendation 3: Services should ensure that risk assessment of detained patients takes account of 'positive risk management' and is undertaken in collaboration with patients and, where appropriate, carers and relatives.

The litigious hospital environment

1.23   In November 2006 the Court of Appeal held Nottinghamshire Healthcare NHS Trust liable for injuries inflicted by a patient on six staff members at Rampton Hospital, when that patient attacked one member of staff, and injured five others who went to restrain her, on a night-shift in March 2001[50]. At that time, the hospital had yet to implement the 'Tilt' Safety and Security Directions, which had come into force in November 2000[51], and the court found that this was relevant insofar as, had the directions been implemented, a risk-assessment would have resulted in the patient being locked into her room at night and thus not at liberty to assault the staff member.

1.24   The Trust's argument was that any breach in its duty of care towards its staff should be tested according to *Bolam* principles, which is to say on a test of whether it could be shown that no responsible body of clinicians would have failed to confine the patient[52]. The judge accepted that the duty of care towards staff must take into account the sometimes competing duty of care owed to the patient, but if the Trust could take precautions so as not to expose its employees to needless risks and still not be in breach of its duty to a patient, then it might well be in breach of duty if it failed to take those precautions[53]. There is some danger that such rulings may be interpreted by already risk-averse service managers as additional liability for staff safety that further tips the balance towards defensive practices involving greater confinement and control of patients, at the expense of opportunities for patients to exercise limited freedoms and regain their autonomy.

Staffing levels

Nursing staff

1.25   In August 2007 the Royal College of Nursing released results of a survey of RCN nurses in mental health[54], in which 66% of respondents considered that staffing numbers were insufficient, with 42% reporting that low staffing levels compromised patient care at least once in every week. Seventy per cent of respondents reported recruitment freezes, and the survey claimed that training days had reduced by two days per year since 2005.

---

[50]   *Buck & Others v Nottinghamshire Healthcare NHS Trust* [2006] EWCA Civ 1576

[51]   On the HSH Safety & Security Directions, see MHAC (2001) *Ninth Biennial Report 1999-2001*, Chap. 5.

[52]   *Bolam v Friern Hospital Management Committee* [1957] 1 WLR 582

[53]   *Buck & Others v Nottinghamshire Healthcare NHS Trust*, per Waller LJ at para 10.

[54]   Royal College of Nursing (2007) *Untapped potential: a survey of RCN nurses in mental health 2007*. RCN, London, August 2007.

1.26 There is, as yet, no formula to calculate 'adequate' staffing levels in use in the UK, although other jurisdictions have introduced mandatory staffing ratios[55] and the NIMHE Acute Care programme and National Workforce Programme are undertaking a joint project to identify and support the development of different approaches to staffing levels and skill mix in acute inpatient areas that should result in published guidance[56]. In this reporting period we have observed staffing levels that we feel to be unsafe, and that have been identified as such to us by the nursing staff themselves. Patients and staff that we have met with on visits in this reporting period have frequently expressed concern at the effect of staffing shortages on patient care. We noted that many wards experienced high rates of staff-sickness, including long-term, stress-related sickness. Coupled with a number of recruitment bans as a result of budgetary constraints, and staff moving to work in community-based provision, there have been serious constraints on staffing over this period. In some cases staffing provision did not appear to take account of the consequences of these constraints:

> The ward has experienced a reduction in staffing levels, as part of the financial recovery plan... [and] also a loss of experienced staff to the new community teams. The current staff team is therefore predominately newly qualified, inexperienced staff who require extensive training on the job, support and supervision. The staffing levels should take into account this additional requirement.
>
> October 2006, Cumbria and Lancashire Commission visiting area

1.27 In the above example, the inexperience of staff was not necessarily a result of their employment status, although both patients and staff on some visits complain that the use of agency or bank staff creates particular difficulties. Figure 7 below shows the percentage of agency staff on the wards that we visited in this reporting period. The majority of wards (86.8% overall) had 10% or less agency staff, and the proportion of agency staff is less in the second year. Nevertheless, in 2006/7, there were around 75 wards that we visited where every third nurse was agency employed.

---

[55] e.g. Belgium, Victoria Australia and some American states. See RCN (2003) *Setting safe nurse staffing issues: an exploration of the issues.* Cherill Scott. RCN, London, page 15 .

[56] Department of Health (2006) *From Values to Action: the Chief Nursing Officer's review of mental health nursing.* April 2006, para 5.4.9.

% of agency staff	no of wards (cumulative total)		% of wards (cumulative %)	
	2005/6	2006/7	2005/6	2006/7
90+ to 100	3 (3)	2 (2)	0.15 (0.15)	0.10 (0.10)
80+ to 90	0 (3)	0 (2)	0 (0.15)	0 (0.10)
70+ to 80	0 (3)	1 (3)	0 (0.15)	0.05 (0.15)
60+ to 70	2 (5)	6 (9)	0.10 (0.25)	0.30 (0.45)
50+ to 60	5 (10)	10 (19)	0.25 (0.50)	0.50 (0.95)
40+ to 50	31 (41)	14 (33)	1.55 (2.05)	0.70 (1.64)
30+ to 40	64 (105)	43 (76)	3.20 (5.24)	2.14 (3.78)
20+ to 30	70 (175)	52 (128)	3.50 (8.74)	2.59 (6.37)
10+ to 20	125 (300)	102 (230)	6.24 (14.99)	5.08 (11.45)
<10	1,702 (2002)	1,779 (2009)	85.01 (100)	88.55 (100)

Fig 7: Percentage of agency staff on wards visited by MHAC, 2005/06 and 2006/07.

Data source: MHAC data

1.28 Even where there is not a high proportion of agency staff, there may be a wide use of 'bank' staff[57]. We frequently find that many nurses on wards that we visit are doing bank shifts from other parts of the Trust, and that consequently nurses are unfamiliar with the ward and the patients:

> The ward seems to have a serious staff shortage. There was only one nurse on duty who was entirely familiar with the ward. Two of the nurses, including the nurse in charge, were doing bank shift from other wards. The fourth nurse was very new to the ward.
>
> High Security Hospital, February 2006

> …significant difficulties with staff numbers at the moment … some night shifts are all bank.
>
> North West London Commission visiting area, February 2006.

1.29 Patients informed us that it is very difficult to develop a rapport with a constantly changing nursing staff, partly due to the use of bank and agency staff. In many wards we noted staff observing but not interacting with patients, alongside a general lack of meaningful activities for patients (see chapter 2.43 below). Some patients complained that nurses 'relied upon'

---

[57] Staff 'bank' systems operate similarly to agencies, usually filling temporary or part-time positions. The key difference is that the bank system is organised and managed by the Trust or on behalf of NHS Trust consortiums. Staff are able to work flexibly to suit their circumstances but are paid nationally agreed rates and can receive the same general benefits as full time staff. Many are current employees using the bank system to receive additional payments for extra shifts worked.

restraint, medication and confinement in order to manage them. It is possible that staffing levels are an influence on the numbers of locked wards (see chapter 2.103 below), although, perhaps because the Code of Practice condemns the locking of wards because of staffing restriction[58], we have not encountered staff acknowledgement that this may be the case.

1.30   Nursing staff frequently complain of being too busy to develop 'therapeutic rapport' with patients. In some wards, 'patient protected time' initiatives are used effectively to ensure that nursing staff have the opportunity to interact with patients for at least some set periods without distractions of administration, meetings, or other tasks. Such initiatives were supported in the Chief Nursing Officer's 2006 review of mental health nursing[59] and are recommended by the RCN "wherever possible"[60]. Oxfordshire Mental Healthcare NHS Trust[61] and Pembrokeshire and Derwen NHS Trust[62] have won awards for their protected time schemes in this period. In Oxfordshire, nurses and other clinical staff spend therapeutic time directly with service users from 11.00 a.m. to 12.30 p.m. each day, including during lunch. No non-clinical visitors are allowed on the ward during this time, no meetings take place, and any messages must be left with the ward clerk. A pilot project in the Highgate Mental Heath Centre in north London ran such protected time from 9 a.m. to 12.30 p.m. every day. The protected time scheme in Bryngofal ward in Llanelli (Pembrokeshire and Derwen NHS Trust) differed in that each patient was allocated specific time to have contact with nursing staff on a one-to-one basis.

1.31   Protected patient time schemes have been reported not only to enhance therapeutic interactions, but also to have wider benefits. The Highgate study found reduced incidents of aggression on the ward, not just in protected time but over the whole day. There were no reported incidents involving substance misuse, although this had been a problem prior to the study. Patients were also more engaged with occupational activites[63]. The protected time periods can help bring structure into patients' days; encourage attentiveness to personal care; help with social interactions and building relationships; and ultimately promote self-esteem and confidence, leading towards earlier discharge[64].

1.32   The following example of a MHA Commissioner's report from a busy north London hospital ward provides a fairly positive example of a ward environment in the acute sector,

---

[58]   *MHA 1983 Code of Practice*, para 19.24.

[59]   Department of Health (2006) *From Values to Action: the Chief Nursing Officer's review of mental health nursing.* April 2006, p.44.

[60]   'New survey shows mental health low staffing levels are impacting on patient care' Royal College of Nursing Press release, 1 Aug 2007.

[61]   Department of Health (2006) *From Values to Action, p.44: Oxfordshire MH Trust won an award "in the Thames Valley 'Patients first' category".*

[62]   'Mental health initiative up for second top award', Welsh Assembly Government press release, 26 Sept 2006. The initiative was given an award by the Welsh Assembly Government and short-listed for a *Nursing Times* award.

[63]   Soong S and Soobratty I (2007) 'Patient Protected Time: is it a waste of time?' *Mental Health Practice* 10:8, 31-33.

[64]   *ibid.*

although even here patients, advocates and the staff themselves expressed concern over staffing pressures leading to limitations on patient care:

> There was a ward round in the morning, the atmosphere was calm and orderly. Despite the size of the ward, it was pleasing to see that the ward was not locked. ... some patients did praise staff and said they were well looked after: "staff are OK", "nurses are very kind". Some patients said they were doing groups and classes, and I saw patients being encouraged to go to a movement and dance class. One patient said he was able to go swimming. Community meetings take place on Fridays and there is a communal cooked breakfast on Wednesdays. Although I saw a significant number of patients in bed throughout the morning, the situation improved in the afternoon. Patient Protected Time is going well, and some patients said they welcomed having more time with nursing staff.

1.33 Protected time initiatives cannot resolve all the problems faced by under-staffing of wards. In some hospitals staffing levels have limited the effectiveness of such initiatives, and we frequently hear of protected time being under pressure on wards. In the summer of 2006, a MHA Commissioner wrote after visiting one west London-based unit that

> I was concerned to find many patients still in bed late in the morning, and some apparently still in bed in the afternoon. I heard that some patients are not always getting their 1-1 with nurses, and that authorised leave is not always given. I saw little evidence of nurses spending time with patients. One patient said: "it would be nice if a nurse came and sat down to talk with me for ten minutes". Another said: "staff are always busy". I heard nevertheless that there were new initiatives for New Working and Protected Time, which should ensure more engagement of staff with patients.

A year later, the Commissioner was still reporting to the Trust that

> I saw little staff engagement, and many patients were alone on their beds for much of the day. I understand that it had been a busy day, and that Protected Time was beginning in the afternoon. Because of the ward round [on the day of the visit], and the consequent pressure on staff time, moving the Protected Time is being discussed. Staff said that most days, s.17 leave had to be negotiated with patients. I also heard strong representations about the complement for night shifts. The frequent occurrence of 1-1 observations, out of hours admissions, taking breaks and perhaps supporting other wards all led to levels of staffing that put significant pressure on nurses and put staff and patients at risk. The Commission understands the financial constraints, but I heard of the toll on nurses. One commented: "I know it's about budgets, but we're human beings".

Recommendation 4:

- *All hospital wards caring for detained patients should instigate "patient protected time" schemes, where patients are guaranteed time with nursing staff apart from all other distractions.*

- *Ward managers should audit the performance of protected time schemes, keeping records of problems in observing protected time and taking account of patient experience.*

1.34   Many hospitals who employ ward clerks find that they play a valuable role in safeguarding staff time for patient interaction. We believe that such clerks can therefore make a significant contribution to patient care, even though they are vulnerable to cost-trimming cuts as non-clinical post-holders. It is also noticeable that wards without administrative support appear to be more likely to make legal errors in the operation of the Act, whether this is in relation to its consent to treatment provisions (i.e. failing to request Second Opinions when one is legally required, or to submit reports on treatment to the MHAC) or in relation to the renewal of detention, authorisation of leave, or other matters.

1.35   Patients often complain that staffing shortages reduce opportunities for escorted leave from the ward, whether this was just for the purpose of getting fresh air in the hospital grounds or as a part of planned leave arrangements. In some hospitals we suggested that investing money to make an outdoor area of the hospital estate safe and secure so that it could be used by patients with less staff supervision could provide a cost-effective solution. As we note at chapter 2.60 *et seq* below, the impending smoking ban within hospital buildings provides another reason to ensure that the design of hospital estates does not confine patients indoors unnecessarily.

1.36   We noted many cancellations of planned and authorised leave for want of available escorting staff, and many services where staffing levels clearly restricted patients' leave arrangements. This in itself may hold back patients' recovery and discharge from detention in hospital:

> General pressures and staffing difficulties on [the] ward … are having an effect on leave arrangements. It was reported that escorted leave beyond the hospital grounds may not routinely be requested by nursing staff due to difficulties facilitating this. Patients may therefore need to wait until they are ready for unescorted leave prior to significant leave being given.
>
> Cheshire and Merseyside Commission visiting area, July 2006

1.37   In some cases, staff acknowledged that they did not routinely request that patients undertake escorted leave outside the hospital grounds because of staffing limitations. In others, patients were frustrated to be unable to take advantage of escorted leave authorised by their RMOs. We discuss this further at chapter 4.45 below.

1.38   Staffing levels can impact upon staff training, and the availability and competence of staff to deal with medical emergencies:

> Staff continue not to receive appropriate and mandatory training (e.g. control and restraint refresher training, basic life support skills and Mental Health Act updates) … certain members of staff are expected to carry out certain responsibilities (e.g. restraint) but they have not had recent update training to carry out these responsibilities. The ward manager is aware of the situation and agrees that it is unacceptable. Whilst training was available it was not always possible to release people from the ward due to staffing levels.
>
> Cheshire and Merseyside Commission visiting area, Nov 2005

The combination of the following makes it difficult to have confidence that [the unit] could respond to a medical/psychiatric emergency to a level expected of somewhere catering for patients detained under the Act, many of whom often have concurrent physical health complications:

a)   patient rooms are not equipped with a nurse call button;

b)   staff do not carry personal attack alarms;

c)   staff are not trained in and do not use Control and Restraint;

d)   no member of staff with whom I talked had undertaken either breakaway training or even de-escalation techniques within the last 18 months;

e)   no member of staff with whom I talked had completed even the most basic first aid or life support training within the last year;

f)   no 'ligature cutters' are available to staff; and

g)   staffing levels of 1 qualified member and 2 support workers per shift.

It was further noted that the project is not equipped for dealing with 'advanced life support', in as much as staff are not adequately trained and equipment (oxygen etc) is not available.

Greater Manchester Commission visiting area, Oct 2006

1.39   In 1998 the Royal College of Psychiatrists suggested that it was "unlikely that a ward of 15 acute patients could be safely managed with less than three registered nurses per shift during the day and two at night, irrespective of other staff available"[65].

1.40   The RCN survey (see paragraph 1.25 above) found the mean ratio of registered nurses and unqualified care assistants on mental health ward day shifts to be 50:50 (41:59 in elderly mental health wards)[66]. Our own findings of the percentages of trained staff on the wards that we visited in this reporting period are set out at figure 8 below. Untrained staff made up at least half of the nursing complement of two-thirds (66.7%) of the wards that we visited.

[65]   Royal College of Psychiatrists (1998) *Not just bricks and mortar: report of the working party on the size, staffing structure, siting and security of new adult psychiatric in-patient units.*

[66]   Royal College of Nursing (2007) *Untapped potential: a survey of RCN nurses in mental health 2007.* RCN, London, August 2007.

% of trained staff	no of wards (cumulative total)		% of wards (cumulative %)	
	2005/6	2006/7	2005/6	2006/7
<10	19 (19)	18 (18)	0.95 (0.95)	0.90 (0.90)
10+ to 20	124 (143)	124 (142)	6.19 (7.14)	6.17 (7.06)
20+ to 30	202 (345)	159 (301)	10.09 (17.23)	7.91 (14.98)
30+ to 40	509 (854)	468 (769)	25.42 (42.66)	23.30 (38.28)
40+ to 50	508 (1,362)	546 (1,315)	25.37 (68.03)	27.18 (65.46)
50+ to 60	222 (1,584)	248 (1,563)	11.09 (79.12)	12.34 (77.80)
60+ to 70	172 (1,756)	188 (1,751)	8.59 (87.71)	9.36 (87.16)
70+ to 80	167 (1,923)	170 (1,921)	8.34 (96.05)	8.46 (95.62)
80+ to 90	13 (1,936)	25 (1,946)	0.65 (96.70)	1.24 (96.87)
90+ to 100	66 (2002)	63 (2009)	3.30 (100)	3.14 (100)

Fig 8: Percentage of trained staff on wards visited by MHAC, 2005/06 and 2006/07.

Data source: MHAC data

1.41 The benefits of having trained staff on the ward can only be realised where they are given an opportunity to use their nursing skills. The RCN survey found that a significant proportion of trained nursing staff (43% across both community and inpatient services) felt that their skills were underused because of insufficient time with patients. Fifty-nine per cent of the inpatient staff surveyed felt that too much time was spent on paperwork[67]. We do not imagine that nursing staff can be relieved of all the burdens of paperwork, and indeed many criticisms levied by the MHAC on hospital visits relate to poor record-keeping and management of patients' medical notes and legal documentation. Nevertheless, we do recognise that having trained nursing staff diverted to managerial or domestic tasks can be a waste of a very precious resource, and we endorse Baroness Murphy's call, in the debates over the 2007 Act, for new ways of organising nursing priorities:

> Staff … need to feel pride in specific therapeutic skills which enable them to treat people, and wards must be properly managed. Training for ward leadership is cursory; qualified nurses can suddenly find themselves managing 50 staff and a budget of £1.5 million without any training whatever. What nurses should do with their patients is often a mystery. They have control and restraint training but no education and specific training for therapeutic skills or behavioural training, interpersonal support skills, family interventions and so on.

> … wards are still run on traditional hospital ward lines, and I cannot for the life of me see why they have to be run by nurses at all. We need nursing skills but wards could be run by bright

---

[67] *ibid.*

people with all kinds of skills—social work and management are two examples. This has been done in learning disability services, for example, during the late 1980s, with great success. We are still too stuck in the traditional model of nursing care, which has been abandoned outside the hospital but not inside.[68]

1.42 The RCN recommend that services need to undertake reviews of their staffing levels and skills mix, not just once but at least biennially, with such reviews undertaken by executive nurse sponsors and nurse leaders with the active involvement of ward managers and ward-based staff. Such reviews should inform executive and Board-level decisions about risk and quality of care. We urge Boards to consider radical approaches to resolve staffing or skills shortages that are identified in such reviews.

> **Recommendation 5:** Psychiatric nursing skill mix and staffing levels should be reviewed using the principles outlined in the Royal College of Nursing's 2007 report *Untapped Potential.*[69]

Medical staff

1.43 In our last report[70] we highlighted the difficulty for many services in implementing (were they minded to do so) the recommendations of the David Bennett inquiry that a doctor be present wherever mentally ill patients are restrained, or at least available within twenty minutes of being called[71]. The government responded to the Bennett inquiry by saying that it would "repeat that message" to services but did not direct that services should comply with it. The situation described in our last report has not changed: we discuss this further at chapter 2.127.

1.44 At chapter 2.98 *et seq* we discuss patient's contact with their responsible medical officers. In many hospitals this is not ideal, often simply because consultant psychiatrists have too many patients or too many other calls on their time. Some problems raised by this in relation to ascertaining patient's consent status as required by the Act and Code of Practice are discussed at chapter 6.66 below.

1.45 The Department of Health's 'new ways of working' initiative[72] aims to decentre power and responsibility from the consultant psychiatrist and share it amongst the clinical team. This aim could be distorted towards saving money or other resources to the detriment of patient care or patient safeguards, but it has the potential to provide a better, more patient-orientated and responsive services.

---

[68] Hansard (HL) 12 Jun 2006: Col 92-3 (Baroness Murphy)

[69] For a summary of the report and a complete list of the twelve principles for nurse staffing reviews, see RCN Policy Unit Briefing 10/2007 *Untapped potential: a survey of RCN members working in mental health* (July 2007). www.rcn.org.uk

[70] MHAC (2006) *Eleventh Biennial Report 2003-2005: In Place of Fear?* para 2.33 -2.39.

[71] Norfolk, Suffolk and Cambridgeshire Health Authority (2003) *Independent Inquiry into the Death of David Bennett.* December 2003, p.53

[72] Department of Health (2004) *Guidance on new ways of working for psychiatrists in a multi-disciplinary and multi-agency context: National Steering Group interim report,* August 2004; (2005) *New ways of working for psychiatrists: Enhancing effective, person-centred services through new ways of working in multidisciplinary and multi-agency contexts. Final report,* October 2005.

1.46   One of the complaints about current practice made by the *new ways of working* review was that

> history and ambiguous guidance has led to the widespread expectation that consultant psychiatrists carry 'medical responsibility' for all people who are referred to secondary care services. The Responsible Medical Officer role is a legal requirement under the Mental Health Act - it does not apply to informal patients; yet this has been extrapolated to other service users. In turn, consultants have developed unmanageable workloads, whilst Trusts, and indeed the general public, have developed unrealistic expectations of consultants.[73]

1.47   The passing of the Mental Health Act 2007 has changed this position, and brought services for detained patients much more readily within the scope of *new ways of working*. The extent of these changes will only become clear when the Act is implemented and services develop within its framework. The revisions of the 2007 Act do, however, widen the parameters of who may be the equivalent of the 'responsible medical officer' under current law, so that any suitably trained mental health professional may be eligible[74]. As the new name suggests, the 'responsible clinician' under the revised Act nevertheless retains a centralised authority in many ways, including the authorisation of leave of absence; discharge from hospital (whether absolute or onto a CTO); renewal of detention (albeit with the agreement of another colleague); the recall of CTO patients; and (at least where the responsible clinician *is* a doctor) providing authority for treatment under the Acts. We discuss the new lines of responsibility created by the 2007 Act in relation to consent to treatment at chapter 6.66 below.

1.48   There is clearly a balance to be struck between maintaining adequate patient safeguards for patients subject to psychiatric compulsion, and not excluding them from any service developments fostered through *new ways of working*. Thus, whilst we remain concerned at the possibility that non-medical practitioners will have authority under the revised Act to renew psychiatric detention (see chapter 4.51), and see potential for confusion over responsibilities regarding part IV of the Act, we also recognise that being the nominal responsibility of a consultant who is overburdened with patients and other duties provides no genuine protection to detained patients. As such, we cautiously welcome the devolution of powers to the clinical team, but urge vigilance amongst detaining authorities that this does not allow for the poor administration of legal requirements under the Act.

Community services & inpatient wards

1.49   It is vital that service reconfigurations do not create a gulf between community and inpatient services. Good care planning, especially in acute and rehabilitation wards, requires a seamless service between the hospital and the community. We continue to see patients whose discharges are unnecessarily delayed for want of arrangements having been made for their support in the community:

> several patients were recognised as delayed discharge and no longer requiring acute care - with some requiring high dependency/longer term care and those that are ready for discharge but

---

[73]   Department of Health (2004) *ibid.*, para 5.7.

[74]   Mental Health Act 2007, ss.9 – 17.

issues relating to home circumstances preventing them from returning. For example, two patients could not be discharged due to housing and/or benefits issues not being fully addressed. Several patients also appear to have had adjourned Tribunals with specific action required on the authorities to progress transfer/discharge. It is recommended that for those relevant patients, robust aftercare planning should take place.

Cheshire and Merseyside Commission visiting area, August 2006

1.50 As discussed at paragraph 1.10 above, around 9% of acute inpatients beds are occupied by patients awaiting delayed discharge or transfer. The reasons for such delays are set out at figure 9 below.

reason for transfer delay	NHS		social services		both		total	
	no.	%	no.	%	no.	%	no.	%
awaiting completion of assessment	116	5.3	92	4.2	35	1.6	243	11.1
awaiting public funding	104	4.7	154	7.0	44	2.0	302	13.8
awaiting further non-acute mental health care	225	10.2	-	-	-	-	225	10.2
awaiting home placement – residential home	149	6.8	359	16.3	-	-	508	23.1
awaiting home placement – nursing home	100	4.5	208	9.5	57	2.6	365	16.6
awaiting care package for own home	33	1.5	63	2.9	10	0.5	106	4.8
awaiting community equipment/ adaptions	8	0.5	8	0.5	6	0.5	22	1.0
patient or family choice	125	5.7	59	2.7	-	-	184	8.4
disputes	45	2.0	27	1.2	-	-	72	3.3
housing if not covered by NHS & C. Care Act	172	7.8	-	-	-	-	172	7.8
total	1,076	49.0	970	44.1	151	6.9	2,197	100

Fig 9: Average number of mental health and learning disability patients (detained or informal) subject to delayed transfer of care (DTOC), March 2007, England

Data source: Department of Health SitReps[75]

1.51 The most common cause of transfer delays – accounting for nearly 40% overall – is a want of residential or nursing home accommodation to receive discharged patients. Nearly two-thirds of such delays in the above table were the result of problems in social services provision. For elderly patients who are not treated in the mental health or learning disability sectors, social service delays are subject to 'cross-charging' whereby social services are held financially accountable for beds blocked in the NHS due to inadequate social care provision. We were a party to the debates over why the mental health and learning disability sectors were excluded from the Community Care (Delayed Discharges) Act 2003[76], and accept that there are good reasons to be cautious over the extension of this legislation to such services. Nevertheless, the continuing disparity whereby social services authorities are subject to financial penalties for failing to provide for patients other than those in the mental health or learning disability sectors may be a disincentive for investment in appropriate aftercare facilities for mental health or learning disability patients.

---

[75] Department of Health SitReps (Situation Reports) collected by NHS Trusts: see n. 30 above.

[76] MHAC (2003) *Tenth Biennial Report 2001-2003: Placed Amongst Strangers* para 9.68-7.

1.52 Just as the divide between the NHS and social services authorities with regard to mental health and learning disability services continues to be largely entrenched, in many NHS Trusts there continues to be a divide between inpatient and community services. We have written before of our concern that inpatient services may suffer neglect in comparison to newer, developing community services[77]. Inpatient services must be seen as a vital part of an integrated mental health service.[78] Commissioning and provider bodies need to develop ways of overcoming the divide between community and inpatient services. Baroness Murphy has spoken of the need

> …to create an integrated service in which community team and ward staff all rotate as one team and are managed under the same budget. That seriously encourages alternatives to acute ward care. The Norfolk and Waveney Mental Health Partnership NHS Trust has done much of this circulating of staff to ensure that people keep up to date and understand each other's work. Other units have tried joint management, but few stick with it. At present in-patient staff never get to know a patient or service user except in crisis and do not get to establish a relationship as the community team worker does. For the community team at the moment there are negative incentives to admit when an alternative residential care or day care place might be better. Budgets are institution bound and do not facilitate movement. Joint management prevents in-patient units being allowed to deteriorate physically while new community health teams get all the capital spend. You see all the time new teams being set up yet the physical environments being reduced.[79]

Commissioning and funding mental health services

1.53 In our last report we questioned whether present arrangements for the commissioning of mental health services might not militate against the government's concerns for service improvement and best use of resources[80].

Retraction of services due to financial pressure on PCTs

1.54 On many of their visits in this reporting period, Mental Health Act Commissioners have heard concerns of clinical staff and indeed managers of mental health inpatient facilities over financial and other pressures on the services that they provide. Government has denied that mental health services have been disproportionately hit by spending cuts designed to balance NHS budgets in this reporting period, although the National Director for Mental Health acknowledged in 2004 that "many, though certainly not all, PCTs, faced with their own financial pressures, have not given sufficient priority to mental health care in comparison with other priorities"[81]. The mental health charity *Rethink* and the Royal College of Psychiatrists both submitted evidence to the Health Select Committee in 2006 claiming "a substantial disinvestment in mental health services" in London and "cuts ... not

---

[77] MHAC (2006) *Eleventh Biennial Report 2003-2005: In Place of Fear?*, para 2.27

[78] Burns T & Kent A (1994) 'Failure in community care - inpatient care is a part of the integrated approach' (letter) *BMJ* 1994;308: 1235-37.

[79] Hansard (HL) 12 Jun 2006 : Column 92 (Baroness Murphy)

[80] MHAC (2006) *Eleventh Biennial Report 2003-2005: In Place of Fear?*, para 2.21.

[81] Department of Health (2004) *The National Service Framework for Mental Health- Five Years On*, p.69. A longer quotation is given in MHAC (2006) *Eleventh Biennial Report, 2003-2005: In Place of Fear?*, para 2.23.

to do with inefficiency or non-effectiveness of the mental health services, but …to subsidise other parts of the health service going into overspend"[82]. The Health Select Committee report of December 2006 stated that "mental health services appear to have been particularly targeted" and that the cuts "mean a significant step back in the provision of mental health services" involving (as it was informed by the Chief Executive of Central and North West London Mental Health NHS Trust) "a reduction in the number of acute mental health beds and the cessation or reduction of some of the new teams that have been set up under the … National Service Framework for Mental Health"[83].

1.55   A number of Mental Health Act Commissioners have suggested to us that there have been deep cuts in the areas that they visit, involving ward closures and other retractions of services provided to patients. In many ways mental health services are an easy target for cuts, as they evince less public sympathy than many other clinical areas and may have seemingly 'peripheral' non-clinical expenses, such as advocacy services (see chapter 4.38).

1.56   Commissioners of publicly-funded beds in independent hospitals retain a power to transfer patients that they place there, whether or not the clinical team caring for the patient consider this appropriate[84]. This leaves such patients vulnerable to decisions based upon cost or organisational need that may be detrimental to their care and progress in recovery. We outline an example of the use of such power in chapter 5.14 below.

Establishing the responsible service commissioner

1.57   Establishing the responsible commissioner of services for detained patients has led to a number of disputes between PCTs and local authorities. Department of Health guidance is now available on the rules for determining the responsible commissioner[85]. The rules are rather complicated in the case of detained patients' admission and discharge from hospital, especially in relation to s.117 aftercare.

1.58   The responsibility for funding the hospital placement of a detained patient falls to the PCT that holds the contract for the GP practice where that patient was registered, or to the PCT where the patient was "ordinarily resident"[86] prior to hospitalisation if s/he was not registered with a GP.[87] If the patient has no fixed abode or is unable to give an address, the responsible commissioner is usually the PCT where the receiving hospital is located. Where

---

[82]   See Royal College of Psychiatrists (2006) *Response from the Royal College of Psychiatrists into the Health Committee Inquiry into NHS Deficits.* 1 May 2006; Rethink (2006) "Select Committee back's Rethink's warning on mental health cuts" press release, 13 December 2006; House of Commons Health Select Committee (2006) "Failure in NHS Financial Management", press release, 13 December 2006.

[83]   House of Commons Health Select Committee (2006) *NHS Deficits First Report of Session 2006–07,* HC 73-1, paras 152-4.

[84]   See paragraph 7(4) of the Mental Health Regulations 1983.

[85]   Department of Health (2007) *Who Pays? Establishing the Responsible Commissioner.* September 2007.

[86]   *ibid.,* see Annex A for a definition of 'ordinary residence'.

[87]   Or, in the case of s.47 or 49 prison transferees of no fixed or determinable abode, the place in which the offence was committed with which the detainee is either charged or convicted.

the patient was "ordinarily resident" in a certain area prior to admission[88], the PCT for that area will remain responsible for aftercare provided under s.117 of the Act upon discharge, even if the patient is discharged to a different geographical area. However, if the patient is not entitled to s.117 aftercare (or is entitled to s.117 aftercare but had no known fixed abode prior to admission), responsibility for aftercare provision will fall to the PCT in the area to which the patient is discharged.

1.59   As this report was being completed, we heard that some practitioners have been instructed that they are required to identify the commissioning authority, and get approval for the funding of a hospital pace, prior to using the powers of the Act to admit a patient to hospital. Thus the implication is that this should be done as a part of the Mental Health Act assessment, where it would technically fall to the doctor (according to the Code of Practice paragraph 2.22d), although we understand that in practice the identification of a bed often falls to the ASW. In our view, it is improper that any hospital admission under the Act (which by its very nature is a matter of necessity and is usually urgent) should be delayed, not only by the unavoidable need to search for an available bed, but also by an entirely avoidable requirement to ascertain its funding prior to admitting the patient. We have proposed to the Department of Health that the revised Mental Health Act Code of Practice should seek to ensure that this distortion of the aims of the Act is not allowed to become accepted practice.

1.60   In 2007 the *Count Me In census* team made great efforts to ensure that information on the commissioning organisation for each patient was completed and validated. Although 99% of NHS patients' data was validated, data problems with 75 independent sector hospital returns prevented the validation of 29% of all independent hospital patients' data. As such, the breakdown of independent hospital commissioning into percentages (and thus the breakdown of overall commissioning) set out at figure 10 below is liable to some distortion. It is clear, however, that PCTs commission the vast majority of care from NHS hospitals, and a large proportion of independent hospital care. Local authorities are the second largest funders of learning disability services from both NHS and independent sector.

---

[88]   Irrespective of GP registration: responsibility for s.117 aftercare is determined by ordinary residence, but not by registration with a GP practice.

Commissioner	Mental health services						Learning disability services					
	NHS		PVH[89]		Total		NHS		PVH[90]		Total	
PCT	23,204	86.3%	1,553	50.8%	24,757	82.7%	2,612	81.2%	280	42.1%	2,892	74.5%
Care Trust	370	1.4%	18	0.6%	388	1.3%	39	1.2%	1	0.2%	40	1.0%
other Trust	849	3.2%	343	11.2%	1,192	4.0%	62	1.9%	61	9.2%	123	3.2%
Scottish LHB	1	0.0%	13	0.4%	14	0.0%	3	0.1%	3	0.5%	6	0.2%
Welsh LHB	1,695	6.3%	119	3.9%	1,814	6.1%	163	5.1%	10	1.5%	173	4.5%
local authority	306	1.1%	118	3.9%	424	1.4%	265	8.2%	156	23.5%	421	10.8%
other agency	216	0.8%	260	8.5%	476	1.6%	18	0.6%	91	13.7%	109	2.8%
SHA	4	-	-	-	4	0.0%	-	-	6	0.9%	6	0.2%
privately funded	-	-	235	7.7%	235	0.8%	-	-	-	-	-	-
invalid	123	0.5%	280	9.2%	403	1.3%	6	0.2%	46	6.9%	52	1.3%
recorded not known	127	0.5%	120	3.9%	247	0.1%	49	1.5%	11	1.7%	60	1.5%
Total	26,895	100%	3,059	100%	29,954	100%	3,217	100%	665	100%	3,882	100%

Fig 10: Mental health and learning disability service commissioners by provider type (detained and informal patients)

Data Source: *Count Me In* census 2006

---

[89] Less returns from 75 independent providers (1,233 patients) invalidly completed.

[90] As n.89 above.

Reflections on an admission

After two weeks in hospital I needed a long, hot soak in my own bath. The two bathrooms I found on the ward had no locks and the patients discussed various ways of making them secure. For me this lack of personal safety on a mixed ward was made worse as my single room had no curtain at the door to give privacy. I found it easier to avoid washing than take any risks!

I had recently moved to London and was struggling to settle to a new environment, job and home. As I became increasingly unwell I grew acutely aware of the loss of support from the mental health service previously familiar to me. Having only met my new psychiatrist once for an initial assessment, I was unsure how I would cope with an inpatient unit and unfamiliar staff for whom I would be an unknown patient with a long history and numerous admissions.

Unfortunately, when I was admitted, the unit five minutes walk away from my home was full and I was placed informally in a private hospital across London. I felt like a criminal as my possessions were searched and my i-pod and mobile taken off me. Taking away my means of communication and music which help me to relax added to my sense of bewilderment and increased my agitation. I couldn't understand why they were doing this to me. This sense of confusion was compounded the following day when I was transferred to an NHS unit on the edge of London and even further from my home and husband. The decision seemed to be entirely based on cost and the move certainly had a negative impact on my mental state.

As I became more unsettled, I became suicidal and made frequent attempts to leave the ward although most of the time the doors were locked. It felt inevitable that I would be sectioned and indeed I was put on a section 2. In a depressing physical environment, the two weeks felt incredibly long as boredom set in with only meal times and visitors to break the tedium. What some might see as small frustrations became magnified.

Although it got easier as time passed and I became more settled, it was difficult to feel any sense of trust in a whole new staff team. I found some of the psychiatrist's questions in ward round intrusive, all the more so as I had never set eyes on him before. They were questions I wouldn't ask a close friend! Their total lack of communication with the team from my previous mental health service meant that much we had learnt together was not passed on. I feel the lack of background information resulted in the ward team being unduly cautious, keeping me on a section longer than need be.

I left and was transferred effectively to the local CRT and my own consultant. I was determined to avoid readmission if at all possible. Sadly, despite the efforts of a friendly nursing team, the uninspiring physical surroundings and unrelenting boredom remain the more powerful memories.

Sarah Dewey, October 2007

2

The experience of coercion

The care of the self in hospital environments

Many of our hospital wards are now frankly scandalous. We can only guess at the horror of patients and carers as they walk (or are dragged) into a ward that is filthy, offers no sexual privacy and has an atmosphere of predatory violence. Partly, this is a matter of resources…but it is a matter of attitudes too.

Mike Shooter, former president of the Royal College of Psychiatrists, 2007[91]

2.1 The MHAC's most recent biennial reports have all highlighted our concern over ward environments, both in the sense of the physical state of wards within which patients are detained, and in relation to the atmosphere on such wards. There are some examples of excellent new facilities for acute inpatient care, but all too often patients' experience of inpatient care at times of mental health crisis involves dirty or shabby wards where they are inactive, confined, bored and anxious over their safety or for the security of their possessions. Women patients often report feeling unsafe on mixed wards, or on wards which are nominally gender-segregated but where male patients are still perceived as and experienced to be a threatening presence. Patients continue to complain that they do not receive sufficient nursing staff attention, and that consultation with doctors can be rare and perfunctory, often confined to the semi-public ritual of the ward round.

2.2 Patients who are detained under Mental Health Act powers are placed in a quite different situation from many other NHS funded inpatients. They have not agreed to come into hospital and in some cases do not accept that need for admission, yet they may not discharge themselves from a ward that they find insupportable. They may experience no physical disability through their illness, and yet be confined, even by force, with a building with little access to exercise or fresh air. If they are smokers, they may be denied access to a place where they can smoke for hours or days at a time. Thus, although acute psychiatric inpatient wards may not be unique in their sometimes chaotic atmosphere, or in their potential to compromise the privacy, dignity, or even physical safety of the patients who find themselves

---

[91] Commentary from Chapter 10 of *Experiences of mental health in-patient care: narratives from service users, carers and professionals,* edited by Mark Hardcastle, David Kennard, Sheila Grandison and Leonard Fagin. London, Routledge, 2007.

admitted, the context of such admission can make a very real difference. Ideally an acute inpatient ward should perform the positive function of *asylum:* a safe and supportive place that facilitates recovery.

2.3   This biennial report is being published shortly before the release of the Healthcare Commission's 2006/07 acute inpatient service review. We expect that many of the concerns expressed here will find an echo in that review. The National Director of Mental Health has stated that too much good work goes unreported and unrecognised in mental health wards, and characterised mental health publications as being too often "another list of what is wrong"[92]. There is much truth in this, although we take the view that pointing out what is wrong is intrinsic to our role, and even the publication introduced by the National Director's remarks puts its suggestions into the context that "the state of acute wards is so far from what users, carers and staff want" and that "inpatient stays tend to be characterised by an absence of therapeutic or even recreational engagement"[93].

2.4   We welcome initiatives such as *Star Wards,* which promulgate solutions to the problems of patient care that we have highlighted in our reports. *Star Wards* has been developed by Marion Janner, a service user with experience of detention under the Act that she describes in her report as "unusual" in its positive aspects, largely due to the care of two nurses who were "approachable, concerned and good company", "patient and non-judgmental"[94]. We commend the ongoing work of the *Star Wards* initiative to all acute services.

> **Recommendation 6:** All acute inpatient mental health service managers should be familiar with the *Star Wards* initiative and the Sainsbury Centre report *The Search for Acute Solutions*[95], and should consider their proposals for improving patients' experience in hospital.

2.5   A number of other initiatives aim towards service improvement and peer-group support for those managing acute inpatient wards. The Royal College of Psychiatrists has established *Accreditation for Acute Inpatient Mental Health Services* (AIMS)[96], to which services can sign up for accreditation and peer-review on the model of the now established ECT Accreditation Service (ECTAS). The National Institute for a Mental Health (NIMHE) and Care Services Improvement Partnership (CSIP) have produced a handbook of best practice guidance to "make the best of" the Healthcare Commission's 2006/07 acute inpatient service review[97] and have produced a *virtual ward* as a source of information and positive practice in acute mental health care[98]. There is also a *National Association of Psychiatric Intensive*

---

[92]   Louis Appleby, introduction to Marion Janner (ed) (2006) Star Wards: Practical ideas for improving the daily experiences and treatment outcomes of acute mental health in-patients. www.starwards.org.uk

[93]   Marion Janner (ed) (2007) *op. cit* n.92 pages 8 & 5.

[94]   *ibid.*, p.5

[95]   Sainsbury Centre for Mental Health (2006) *The Search for Acute Solutions*

[96]   See www.rcpsych.ac.uk/AIMS

[97]   CSIP Acute Mental Health Programme (2007) Onwards and Upwards: sustaining service improvement in acute care. June 2007. Available from www.virtualward.org.uk

[98]   See www.virtualward.org.uk

Care Units (NAPICU)[99] which played a leading role in the development of the National Minimum Standards for PICUs[100].

Ward environments

2.6   Many patients describe the physical environment in which they are confined as "grim"; "depressing"; "institutional" or "tired" and "dirty".

> The décor was pretty grim, made one feel quite depressed it was so awful, but this was an old building and we were told that nothing could be done without spending money… This was a private hospital taking NHS patients onto a PICU and long-stay medium secure / low secure units. When I finally convinced the MHRT that I should not be held on a PICU, and I was moved downstairs to the private open ward … wow … what an eye opener… it was a totally different world, and I had only come down to the ground floor in a lift.
>
> Monica Endersby, detained under s.2 then s.3

2.7   Compulsory admission under the Act is likely to be a frightening experience for most patients, but it is one that should be mitigated through being received into a comfortable, welcoming and safe environment:

> I felt very scared when I first went into hospital. It is very scary. Sometimes people hit out and it can be very unsettled on the ward.
>
> Danuta Allan, detained under s.3 in Northampton

2.8   Sarah Dewey's account of her admission leading to detention (see page 50 above) shows how, despite some kindness from nursing staff, the "depressing physical environment", "uninspiring physical surroundings" and "unrelenting boredom" magnifies small frustrations. As the Healthcare Commission's National Audit of Violence[101] demonstrated, these can be a causative factor of disturbed behaviour:

> In the first few days I felt like a caged animal and reacted violently. I was held down and placed in a padded room.
>
> Kay Reed, detained under s.3

2.9   Some "small frustrations" that are pointed out by MHA Commissioners draw criticism of commentators, who argue that it is not our role to comment on environmental issues such as "a broken toilet seat"[102]. We have not been informed by the Department of Health that we may not make such observations, and as we consider that such matters can have a great effect on detained patients' experience of care and treatment under the Act, we shall

---

[99] See www.napicu.org.uk

[100] Department of Health (2002) *National Minimum Standards for Adult Services in Psychiatric Intensive Care Units and Low Secure Services.*

[101] Healthcare Commission (2005) *National Audit of Violence 2003 – 2005.*

[102] Jones R (2006) *Mental Health Act Manual*, tenth edition, preface, page v.

continue to do so. We do not consider these trivial matters, but even apparently trivial matters can be of importance to patients. For example, one recently redecorated ward upon which much effort had been made to improve patients' environment, window cleaning had been overlooked to the extent that it was difficult to see through the glass. This easily rectifiable detail unnecessarily increased patients' sense of confinement within the unit.

2.10 The Department of Health *Essence* of Care provides assistance for Trusts to establish 'benchmarks' for the patient care environment, and sets benchmarks for best practice in (amongst other areas) allowing patients to:
- feel comfortable, safe, reassured and welcome;
- experience care in a tidy and well maintained area;
- experience care in a consistently clean environment;
- have their personal environment managed to meet their needs, including:
    - appropriate lighting, temperature, noise, ventilation and security;
    - appropriate furniture , décor and flooring;
    - appropriate recreational space available and an opportunity to engage in communal activities and experiences;
    - access to fresh air and outside spaces;
    - staff recognition of the need for quiet and rest periods, especially at night;
    - clear and accessible visiting guidelines; and
    - safe storage of belongings; and
- have their care supported by appropriate linen and furnishings, with systems in place to monitor, condemn and replace furnishings[103].

2.11 All of these areas have been the source of concern on MHAC visits during this reporting period. We have found wards that are unventilated and hot in summer but cold in winter; wards where there is little natural light; noisy and smoky wards; and broken, worn and stained furniture, sticky floors and bad smells; peeling paint and graffiti; and non-existent or broken lockable storage for patient's belongings. We have had cause to comment on broken and dirty toilet facilities, and even on inadequate numbers of toilet and bathroom facilities provided for certain wards:

> The seclusion room floor was dirty, one of the patient toilets off the corridor had liquid around it that appeared to be urine, and the bath was still dirty from a patient who had used it after soiling herself.
>
> Norfolk, Suffolk and Cambridgeshire visiting area, November 2006

2.12 Many wards about which we have raised environmental concerns are those built in dormitory style, many of which are quite rightly due for closure or reprovision as wards with single rooms. In our experience, patients greatly appreciate single-room sleeping accommodation, both for the sense of privacy and security and also as a place to spend quiet time during the day, where daytime access to such rooms is allowed. Where closure is intended, the environments of some old wards are allowed to deteriorate beyond a point that should be acceptable.

---

[103] Department of Health (2007) *Essence of Care: Benchmarks for the Care Environment.* 31 Oct 2007.

2.13   In one hospital in southern England, a patient told us that he had been complaining about a smell in his room for two weeks, with no result. The smell was also apparent in a clinic room next to the patient, and had been blamed on the air-conditioning, which had been serviced. The MHA Commissioner asked senior managers why the patient had not been moved, and why no further action had been taken to investigate and remove the smell. She was told that senior managers were not aware that the problem was affecting a patient, and moved him within two hours. The next day the smell was identified as a dead rat in the cavity wall.

> Having my own room helped enormously.
>
> *Female patient, s.3, Yorkshire*

2.14   Another London hospital, based in a Victorian asylum building, was infested with mice and cockroaches in this reporting period. A patient had also contracted legionnaires' disease in the hospital's aging facilities, which suggests poor maintenance. An interview room made available for us to meet with patients in the hospital was unusable due to its dreadful smell, which staff attributed to the mice. A patient on one of the wards told us that "there are mice everywhere on the ward; in the bedroom, dining room, day room. They sometimes crawl up on the table when we have our meals". Although we had raised the issue of cleanliness and vermin infestation with the Trust, the hospital concerned had self-assessed itself as compliant with Healthcare Commission hygiene standards throughout this reporting period. Were it not for our visits to the hospital concerned this disparity would not have been evident.

Infection control

> The environment has unclean toilet facilities. The Commissioner was warned by one patient on the ward to "make sure your hands are clean [because] it's so dirty in there you could catch MRSA".
>
> North West London visiting area, December 2007.

2.15   Many people, and perhaps the elderly in particular, are anxious that admission to hospital may expose them to 'super-bug' hospital-acquired infection and so pose a serious risk to health (see Chairman's foreword, page 12 above). Although the most notorious outbreaks of such infections have not occurred in mental health facilities, it is quite proper that reasonable action is taken to limit the likelihood of hospital-acquired infection by attending to basic cleaning and hygiene. The Healthcare Commission's Annual State of Healthcare 2006 report noted "very poor standards of cleanliness" in many mental health wards, with wards for older patients found to be particularly poor[104].

---

[104] Healthcare Commission (2006) *Annual State of Healthcare 2006*. October 2006. www.healthcarecommission.org.uk/nationalfindings/stateofhealthcare.cfm

2.16 The *Essence of Care* benchmarks[105] provide a basic outline of sensible infection control practice, which we hope will be adopted across all inpatient units where patients are detained, and we note that mental health Trusts in England are covered by the *Health Act 2006 Code of Practice for the Prevention and Control of Health Care Associated Infections*[106]. There is something of an irony that the government has instructed mental health Trusts that compliance with *this* Code of Practice is mandatory (in that failure to comply may result in the issue of an improvement notice or a Trust being placed on 'special measures'[107]), but has allowed (and indeed supported) that compliance with the *Mental Health Act Code of Practice* is not such a requirement[108]. Nevertheless, compliance with the Health Act Code should provide some significant improvements to patient environments, for example by ensuring that hospital cleaning contracts are flexible enough to enable nursing staff to obtain additional cleaning services for spills or to correct previously unprofessional routine work[109]; and in providing a duty to keep wards clean and in good physical repair and condition. In a number of hospitals we have been told that cleaning contracts preclude or hinder remedial cleaning work. The government has also announced that all NHS hospitals in England will be deep cleaned before year end[110], which for some units that we have visited will be a long-overdue event.

> Patient in single room, blood on floor, patient has open wound (MRSA patient). Not noted by staff until I went into room to interview patient. I recommend that room be checked at least hourly.
>
> Due to shared washing areas, patients' toothbrushes all together on side of sink – danger of cross-infection. Please review arrangements for storage.
>
> West Yorkshire visiting area, February 2007.

2.17 It must be remembered, however, that some mental health units are patients' place of residence for extended periods of time, and should be homely as well as clean. As this report was being finalised we heard that the ward manager in one London inpatient unit had been informed by an infection control manager that staff could no longer assist with patients' cookery activity in occupational therapy sessions (thus effectively ending such sessions) because of the risk of cross-contamination. As this report goes to press we are hoping for an outbreak of common-sense to stop such restrictions on already limited patient activities.

---

[105] Department of Health (2007) *Essence of Care : Benchmarks for the Care Environment* , Factor 5 – Infection control precautions.

[106] Department of Health (2006) *Health Act 2006 Code of Practice for the Prevention and Control of Health Care Associated Infections.*

[107] *ibid.*, page 1.

[108] The Department of Health's submission to the Court of Appeal stage of the *Munjaz* case, which argued against mandatory status for the MHA Code of Practice, is discussed in MHAC (2003) *Tenth Biennial Report 2001-2003: Placed Amongst Strangers,* para 3.4. This argument succeeded only in the House of Lords: see MHAC (2006) *Eleventh Biennial Report 2003-2005: In Place of Fear?* pages 35-7.

[109] See also Department of Health PL letter "Improving cleanliness and infection control" 1 November 2007 (PL/CNO/2007/6)

[110] *ibid.*

Refurbishment of wards

2.18 We have noted considerable refurbishment work being undertaken in some of the older hospital sites. In the best of these refurbishment projects, service users and staff are involved in the planning and decision-making processes: although in one south west London unit staff felt excluded from the consultation process as a project progressed and pressures to make quick decisions mounted. As a result, the staff felt that some poor decisions had been made that would affect the quality of care for patients. In a number of units, both refurbished or otherwise, we have noted inappropriate or dangerous fittings, such as poorly secured glass mirrors in secure areas, including in one high secure hospital facility, and ligature points.

> **Recommendation 7:** Hospitals should consult with staff and service users over the redesign or reprovision of mental health services to accommodate detained patients.

Patients' contact with their families

I was detained about 50 miles from where I live and only got to see my children once a week for an hour.

Deborah Hickman, s.3, Bolton

2.19 In 2006 we collaborated with Barnardo's and the Family Welfare Association in a project commissioned by the Care Service Improvement Partnership designed to look at how mental health services can promote family contact when a parent is in hospital. Mental Health Act Commissioners were funded by the project to visit 60 services in July and August 2006, where they looked at policies and family visiting facilities, and interviewed 56 inpatients (33 of whom were women, and 28 of whom were detained) who were the parents of at least one child under 18 years of age.

2.20 The reports from this project, published in July 2007, are available on the MHAC website[111]. Services should obtain a copy of at least the summary report and implement its recommendations. It is of relevance to note here that:

- overall, visiting policies were good and conformed with (indeed quoted from) the Code of Practice and Department of Health Guidance on the visiting of patients by children[112]; but evidence provided by Commissioners' observations for some units was disappointing in the light of good policies in their Trust. For example, one Trust had

---

[111] Robinson, B, Scott S & Day C (2007) *Parents in Hospital: How mental health services can best promote family contact when a parent is in hospital. Final Report.* CSIP, MHAC, FWA & Barnardo's, July 2007. A summary report is also available.

[112] *MHA 1983 Code of Practice* 26.3 -26.4; DH Circular HSC 1999/222. For High Security Hospitals, see HSC 1999/160.

easy-to-read and comprehensive policies, but there were no dedicated rooms in two of its units that we visited.

- Despite the intentions of service providers, hospital provisions were not always ideal for visiting children. The quality of facilities provided varied within Trusts, and in one case within the same hospital, where one visiting area was identified as 'good' and another as 'poor'. Only 5 of the 39 visiting facilities described in the checklists were deemed to be 'good', in that they had flexible booking arrangements; a dedicated family room in an appropriate location; pleasant décor and furniture; and a range of toys and activities for children. Twenty-one settings were rated as 'adequate', providing visiting rooms that were clean, accessible and generally child-friendly. What these generally lacked was a dedicated room; a truly pleasant environment; or sufficient activities and information for parents and children. Thirteen settings were identified as being 'poor', meaning that family visiting areas were in a poor location, cleanliness and décor were often inadequate and little effort had been made to create a space where children would feel welcome and comfortable.

- The evidence of this review is that the identification of patients as parents is not automatic, that patients and their carers take most responsibility for maintaining family contact and would welcome more support, and that families often feel that children are not entirely welcome visitors.

> **Recommendation 8:** Mental health services should obtain a copy of the *Parents in Hospital* report and implement its recommendations.

2.21   Patients can also find it difficult to maintain contact with adult relatives and even partners:

> John came to visit me on Saturdays … we requested a couple of hours visiting time as he was coming a long way and this was granted. I challenged my Trust … that they should be responsible for John's travelling expenses to get to me. It took a lot of arguing and a lot of time, but finally the Trust agreed to fund John's fares after visits. So he had to use his credit card and then wait for ages to receive his travel money back again.
>
> Monica Endersby, detained under ss.2 then 3. John is Monica's husband.

2.22   Given the importance of maintaining contact with relatives and carers throughout the inpatient stay, detaining authorities should be prepared to provide guidance on help available with visitor's travelling expenses, if not help with the funding of such travel. Hospitals should also ensure that visiting facilities are suitable for the purpose.

2.23   We continue to find cases where family members or carers are designated as 'escorting' patients out of the hospital during their visits[113]. It is not always clear that the term 'escort' in such circumstances has the meaning given under s.17(3) of the Act (which would confer upon the relative or carer the powers of a constable should the patient go AWOL whilst outside the hospital) or, if this is meant, whether it is appropriate that the relative or carer

---

[113] We raised this matter in our *Ninth Biennial Report 1999-2001*, para 4.25.

should be expected to fulfill this role. If a patient requires an escort under the terms of s.17(3), we advise particular caution over conferring this role on relatives or carers, rather than making staff available to ensure the safety of the patient or others. The designation of a relative or carer as an escort under s.17(3) must be in writing to take legal effect. Where there is no intention to designate a relative or carer as an 'escort' under s.17(3), another term should be used to describe their presence if this is a condition of the patient's leave to avoid confusion, such as that a patient may take leave within certain parameters 'accompanied' by their relative or carer.

> **Recommendation 9:** Mental health services should only authorise relatives or carers to 'escort' patients on leave under the terms of s.17(3) after careful consideration that this is an appropriate legal responsibility to devolve from nursing staff.

Women's safety

2.24   A 1987 article in *Openmind magazine*[114] reported that women patients were at risk on mixed wards that had separate, dormitory style provision at night, and highlighted the case of a patient who had been raped in a dayroom out of sight of nursing staff on such a ward. The rape victim was "disbelieved" by the hospital managers when she reported the incident to them.

> The wards that I have been on are all mixed. The atmosphere was strained and uncomfortable, I didn't feel safe and spent most of the time in my room... I have sat in my room for four or five hours at a time without anyone checking if I was OK.
>
> *Deborah Hickman, s.3, Bolton*

2.25   Twenty years ago, some hospitals had no single-sex accommodation, partly as a legacy of 'normalising' ward life, but also as a means of simplifying bed management so that any bed was available for male or female patients. It is now an expectation that all mental health wards will provide segregated accommodation facilities, although this has not been achieved meaningfully for many patients. The disputes over numbers outlined below can overshadow what is a truly scandalous and tragic situation: as a society, we are forcing some of the most vulnerable women to reside in places where they are frightened, and may have reason to be frightened, for their safety.

2.26   Half way through our reporting period, the Department of Health and its National Patient Safety Agency (NPSA) had been passing back and forth a draft publication prepared by the latter body which stated that 122 'sexual safety' incidents had been reported to it between November 2003 and September 2005.[115] Of these incidents, there were 19 alleged rapes

---

[114] Catherine Grimshaw (1987) *All Mixed Up*. Openmind No 27, June / July 1987, p.6.

[115] National Patient Safety Agency (2006) *With Safety in Mind. Patient Observatory Report 2*. www.npsa.nhs.uki

(11 allegedly perpetrated by staff members); 13 cases of exposure; 18 cases of unwanted sexual advances; and 26 cases of 'invasive touching'. We understand that the Department of Health made many suggestions as to the drafting of the report, but it was also on record as wishing to verify the most serious incidents before making the report public. The report was released in July 2006 after it had been leaked to a national newspaper[116], alongside a statement from the National Director of Mental Health that he had not been able to substantiate the rape allegations.

2.27 There was stark evidence of the difficulties that patients have in reporting sexual abuse in the 2005 report of the Kerr / Haslam inquiry[117]. During this reporting period, a legal case gave further indication of just how alleged incidents might leave no substantiating evidence. In September 2006, a mental health Trust settled out of court in two compensation claims made on behalf of patients who made separate allegations of rape and sexual assault against the same member of staff at an older adult mental health assessment unit[118]. In one case, the police had been involved after a delay but, although criminal proceedings took place, the nurse was acquitted. In part the damages claimed related to alleged failings to investigate the reported incidents: the Trust settled with the estates of the patients (who were by then deceased) for £30,000 and £17,500 respectively.

2.28 In the face of the controversy over the NPSA's figures, *Community Care* magazine sought information on sexual safety incidents directly from mental health Trusts, using the Freedom of Information Act. Forty-four Trusts (out of 70 approached) reported over 300 incidents over the three years between 2003 and 2006, 224 of which involved assaults by patients on other patients[119]. The *Count Me In* census survey of service users for 2005 found that 20% of respondents reported having experienced unwanted sexual advances (16% from other patients, and 4% from staff). We have found that not all senior managers are sufficiently aware of the provisions of the Sexual Offences Act 2003, which prohibits any sexual activity between *any* care worker (the definition of which extends to clinical staff; receptionists; cleaning staff; advocates; and voluntary helpers) and *any* person with a mental disorder placed in a relationship of care with that care worker[120].

2.29 Following release of the NPSA report, the Department of Health wrote to mental health Trusts emphasising, *inter alia*, the need to comply with its guidance on single-sex accommodation, encouraging the development of single-sex inpatient facilities; and stating that "any sexual safety incident should be thoroughly investigated and local vulnerable

---

[116] "100 women raped or assaulted in hospital - health ministers sit on damaging report for months" *The Times,* July 10, 2006: see also leader column: "publish and reform"; and 'Out of Sight', Catherine Jackson, *Mental Health Today* September 2006, p.8

[117] Department of Health (2005) *The Kerr/ Haslam Inquiry.* Cm 6640-1

[118] *E and B v Birmingham & Solihull Mental Health NHS Trust* [2006]. Health Care Risk Report, September 2006; RadcliffesLeBrasseur Mental Health Law Briefing Number 107 *Harrassment and sexual assault by staff,* November 2006.

[119] *Community Care,* 20 July, p.6. See also *Community Care,* 27 July, editorial and *Mental Health Today* September 2006, p.8.

[120] See MHAC (2003) *Tenth Biennial Report 2001-2003: Placed Amongst Strangers,* para 11.56 *et seq.* For information on the Sexual Offences Act, see Home Office (2004) *Working within the Sexual Offences Act.* May 2004 (leaflet) SOA/4s.

adults' procedures and/or the police involved where necessary"[121]. In November 2006 the National Director for Mental Health wrote again to mental health Trust chief executives inviting bids for funding to develop women-only facilities, including whole wards and crisis houses, but also women-only areas of wards; single rooms; *ensuite* facilities etc[122]. To qualify for some of the £30m funding made available, Trusts would have to show compliance with the higher-priority area of having hospital-based s.136 facilities and with critical requirements for existing or planned PICUs[123].

2.30 In May 2007 the Department of Health released *Privacy and Dignity*, a report by the Chief Nursing Officer into mixed-sex accommodation in hospitals[124]. The report claimed 99% compliance with the objective of "providing safe facilities for patients in hospital who are mentally ill, which safeguard their privacy and dignity"[125], although it otherwise did not cover mental health Trusts. Other studies, including the Healthcare Commission's 2006 survey of the views of hospital inpatients in England[126], had shown a very different picture. It is clear that hospitals have reported themselves as compliant with the Department of Health guidelines over single-sex accommodation where they had in fact provided inadequate segregation (such as curtains between beds) or none at all[127]. This is all the more disappointing given that the Department of Health's definition of single-sex accommodation only requires segregated sleeping areas (which might be bays on a dormitory-style ward); a women-only day room; and designated toilets and bathrooms that are accessible without walking through an area occupied by members of the opposite sex[128].

2.31 Just after 6 p.m. on the 13 August 2007, a female inpatient was strangled by a male inpatient on a mixed-sex ward at Birch Hill Hospital in Greater Manchester. The victim, aged 58, was an informal patient. Her attacker was aged 36.

2.32 The *Count Me In* census collected information on whether inpatients were in single-sex accommodation as defined by the Department of Health. The results of the 2006 census collection in relation to women patients are shown below at figure 11 below. Overall, 58% of women patients were not considered to be in single-sex accommodation by the staff completing the census returns. The data shows significant numbers of patients from Black and minority ethnic communities (including, for example, over 200 Asian or Asian British patients) in mixed-sex accommodation. For some of these patients, requiring women to reside in mixed-sex accommodation may be culturally insensitive.

---

[121] Department of Health (2006) 'Patient safety in mental health services' letter to all chief executives of NHS mental health Trusts, 19 July 2006

[122] Department of Health (2006) 'Capital allocation process: £30 million for improvements in safety on adult inpatient mental health wards' letter to all chief executives of NHS mental health Trusts & SHA chief executives, 2 November 2006.

[123] *ibid.*

[124] Department of Health (2007) *Privacy and Dignity - a report by the Chief Nursing Officer into mixed-sex accommodation in hospitals.* May 2007.

[125] *ibid.*, p.18. This is 'most recent information, measuring compliance at December 2004'.

[126] Healthcare Commission (2007) *Inpatients - The views of hospital inpatients in England. Key findings from the 2006 survey.* http://www.healthcarecommission.org.uk/_db/_documents/Inpatient_survey_-_briefing_note.pdf

[127] 'Hewitt admits failure on mixed-sex wards pledge', *Guardian* 10 May 2007; .

[128] Department of Health (2000) *Safety, privacy and dignity in mental health units - Guidance on mixed sex accommodation for mental health services*

| Ethnicity | Is patient in single-sex accommodation? | | | | | | |
| | yes | | no | | not known | total | |
	number	%	number	%	number	number	%
British (White)	4,512	38.1%	7,167	60.5%	171	11,850	100%
Irish (White)	100	38.3%	156	59.8%	5	261	100%
any other White background (White)	200	35.9%	346	62.1%	11	557	100%
White and Black Caribbean (Mixed)	36	42.9%	46	54.7%	2	84	100%
White and Black African (Mixed)	14	35.9%	23	59.0%	2	39	100%
White and Asian (Mixed)	14	51.9%	13	48.1%	-	27	100%
any other Mixed background (Mixed)	26	50.0%	26	50.0%	-	52	100%
Caribbean (Black or Black British)	150	44.4%	225	58.0%	13	388	100%
African (Black or Black British)	89	44.3%	109	54.2%	3	201	100%
any other Black background (Black or Black British)	62	44.9%	73	52.9%	3	138	100%
Bangladeshi (Asian or Asian British)	20	42.6%	26	55.3%	1	47	100%
Indian (Asian or Asian British)	67	44.7%	82	54.7%	1	150	100%
Pakistani (Asian or Asian British)	49	47.1%	47	45.2%	8	104	100%
any other Asian Background (Asian or Asian British)	35	38.5%	52	57.1%	4	91	100%
Chinese (other ethnic groups)	21	52.5%	18	45.0%	1	40	100%
any other ethnic group	46	43.8%	57	54.3%	2	105	100%
not stated	48	32.9%	93	63.7%	5	146	100%
total	**5,490**	**37.0%**	**8,559**	**57.7%**	**232**	**14,821**	**100%**

Fig 11: Female psychiatric inpatients (informal and detained) in single-sex and mixed-sex accommodation, all hospitals, England, 31 March 2006.

Data source: *Count Me In* census 2006

2.33 Over the last decade, male and female patients have been admitted under the Act in roughly equal numbers, although there are fewer women patients resident at any particular time, with women patients accounting for about one third of the total resident detained population (see chapter 3.4 *et seq*). However, the proportions of women to men in any particular unit can vary greatly. In many mixed units, women will be in a minority. It remains the case that bed management can frustrate attempts to segregate sleeping areas in mixed units. The following example is from a May 2007 visit letter from the Bedfordshire and Hertfordshire visiting area:

> The ward is split into two: male at one end and female at the other. However, due to recent demand, more males have been admitted, resulting in males being cared for at the female end. Additionally, the MHA Commissioner noted a male patient in the 'female lounge' and this was acknowledged by staff as an increasing occurrence. The Trust are requested to inform the MHAC how it intends to address the privacy, dignity and safety of women patients in a unit that clearly isn't able to provide a single-sex environment.

2.34 In the following example, taken from a visit in north west London in May 2006, the pressures on accommodation were from female admission:

> Despite the gender separation of the ward, because of the numbers of female patients, it has been necessary to accommodate females in the male area, with all the concomitant difficulties of staffing such an imbalance.

2.35 The provision of secure and forensic services for women patients has historically been poor, although a number of units have opened in this reporting period as the policies set out by the Department of Health's 2002 document *Into the Mainstream* have been implemented[129]. Some of these units are reportedly funded from costs recouped through bringing patients back from out-of-area placements[130].

2.36 Women in the forensic sector are still at risk of being housed in mixed wards (albeit with some degree of separation between the sexes). On a visit to Buckinghamshire NHS Trust in the spring of 2006 we met with one female restricted patient who had been recalled from conditional discharge, and who should have been admitted to the acute ward of the Trust's medium secure unit, which at that time was entirely populated by male patients, many of whom had committed sexual offences. The multi-disciplinary team responsible for her care at the Trust recognised her vulnerability were she to be admitted to this ward, and made special arrangements to admit her to a rehabilitation ward in another unit where there was another female patient; less risk of predatory behaviour from male patients; and where she would be nearer her family from whom she received regular supportive visits. Additional agency staff cover was provided to ease the pressures on the rehabilitation unit staff posed by this arrangement. In our view this was a commendable and sensitive response to the patient's needs, although it does also illustrate the dilemma of placing women in secure accommodation, and also show how some nominally 'mixed' units are in fact becoming single-sex male wards by default. As such, there may be a danger that the *de facto* closing of

---

[129] Department of Health (2002) *Into the Mainstream*; (2003) *Mainstreaming Gender and Women's Mental Health*

[130] 'The Safer Sex' *Health Service Journal*, 22 June 2006, p.24-5

beds available to women in the mixed-sex forensic hospitals could offset the developments of specialist units. We are concerned that women who are shut out of forensic psychiatry beds will all too often end up, by various routes, swelling the ranks of seriously mentally disordered prisoners (see chapter 7.2 below).

2.37   From April 2007 all public authorities have been required to have due regard when carrying out their functions to the need to eliminate unlawful discrimination and harassment; and to promote equality of opportunity between men and women[131]. In practice, this requires NHS Trusts and independent hospitals who detain patients under the Act to have in place a gender equality scheme, along the lines of the requirements for a race equality scheme under the Disability Discrimination Act 2005. We hope that this legal duty will provide a lever for change that appears to be badly needed in many parts of the service.

> **Recommendation 10:** Detaining authorities' compliance with gender equality duties should be monitored by their own Boards and by commissioning agencies funding the detention of patients. Particular attention should be paid to the avoidance of mixed-sex accommodation and the safety and security of women patients.

2.38   The MHAC is preparing a separate report, *Women in Detention*, for publication in 2008.

The safety and security of older patients

2.39   We have some concerns over the placement on acute mental health wards of older patients[132] suffering from mental illnesses, including dementia. This has been reported to us as largely a result of ward closures elsewhere in mental health services. Some such patients have complained of feeling vulnerable and unsafe. They felt anxious witnessing the volatile behaviour by some of the more acutely ill younger patients and by the constant loud noise. At one hospital in the Wirral and Cheshire visiting area, an older patient complained of having been slapped by a younger patient. It may also be the case that staff on acute wards do not have experience of dealing with this particular age group and consequently do not understand their needs.

> **Recommendation 11:** The admission of elderly patients with functional mental disorder to acute units should be avoided wherever possible, and such admissions should trigger particular vigilance over the safety and security of the patient involved, and the training and engagement levels of staff involved in their care.

---

[131] Sex Discrimination Act 1975 (Public Authorities) (Statutory Duties) Order 2006. For the statutory Code of Practice see Equal Opportunities Commission (2007) *A Gender Equality Duty Code of Practice*. http://www.equalityhumanrights.com/en/forbusinessesandorganisation/publicauthorities/Gender_equality_duty/Pages/Genderequlaitydutydocuments.aspx

[132] i.e. patients over 65 years of age.

Physical health on psychiatric wards

My need of wholesome exercise and occupation was denied. My idleness of mind and body left me at the mercy of my delusions … my want of exercise produced a deadly torpor in the moral functions of my mind, combined with the ruin of my spirits by their diet and medicines.

John Perceval (1840) *A Narrative of the Treatment Experienced by a Gentleman During the State of Mental Derangement*[133].

2.40   People with a severe mental health problem (schizophrenia or bipolar disorder) are twice as likely as the rest of the population to die prematurely[134]. They are more likely to smoke, to be obese, and have significantly greater risk of heart disease, respiratory disease and stroke[135]. They are more than twice as likely as the general population to have diabetes[136]. There are significantly higher rates of bowel and breast cancer amongst people with schizophrenia than in the general population[137].

2.41   People with learning disability are also more likely to die prematurely and have high rates of obesity and unmet health needs[138].

2.42   Despite this, hospital wards where patients are detained under the Act can be difficult places to maintain or promote healthier lifestyles. The following sections of this report look at aspects of this in more detail.

Patient activity and education

For a rehab ward there was a distinct lack of rehab activities and a number of patients were complaining of boredom. No occupational therapy activity… low staffing levels, no pool table or games facilities on the ward. Other than leave, patients complained there was little to do.

Cumbria and Lancashire Commission visiting area, April 2006

2.43   There is a great disparity in opportunity for detained patients to engage in meaningful or educational activities across various sectors of mental health services, unrelated to the capacity of the patients themselves to engage in activities. In July 2007 an anonymous

---

[133]   Bateson G (ed) (1961) *Perceval's narrative; a patient's account of his psychosis 1830-1832*. California, Stanford University Press, p.39.

[134]   Harris SC, Barraclough B (1998) 'Excess mortality in mental disorder' *British Journal of Psychiatry* 173; 11-53, referenced in Nocon A, and Owen J (2006) 'Unequal treatment' *Mental Health Today*, February 2006, 27-30.

[135]   Disability Rights Commission (2006) *Equal Treatment: Closing the Gap*. London, DRC, chapter 3. For research paper see Hippisley-Cox J and Pringle M (2005) *Health inequalities experienced by people with schizophrenia and manic depression: analysis of general practice data in England and Wales* at http://www.drc.gov.uk/library/health_investigation/research_and_evidence.aspx

[136]   *ibid*. In its response to the DRC recommendations, the Department of Health recognises that the antipsychotic drugs Olanzapine and Risperidone have been associated with increased risk of diabetes. See Department of Health (2007) *Promoting Equality*, p.7.

[137]   *op. cit.* n. 135

[138]   Disability Rights Commission (2006) *op. cit.* n. 135. Researchers for the DRC were unable to identify learning disabled people accurately from primary care records to provide reliable data on specific health conditions such as diabetes, etc (see p.40 of the DRC report).

employee of a medium secure unit in the north west of England wrote to the Guardian newspaper[139] contrasting the generally good provision of basic skills education in the high secure hospitals (as evidenced by an earlier newspaper article on the DSPD unit at Rampton Hospital[140]) the with the paucity of such opportunity in the MSU. Regarding education, the correspondent stated that it was "a shame that, when the Rampton offenders are released into medium secure units, believing they are moving on, they will be greeted with virtually no resources".

> There were lots of activities at first but had problems getting to them due to staff shortages.
>
> *Richard, detained under s.3 in Hull*

2.44   It is true that High Secure Hospitals have generally good education and activity programmes, partly because of their considerable estates, although in this reporting period we have encountered waiting lists for education at Broadmoor Hospital, where opportunities for patients to take leave or even attend off ward activities in the hospital's education centre also appear to have been curtailed due to the unavailability of staff to escort patients. In one disappointing example, a Broadmoor patient who had won a Koestler award for creative work complained that she had not been able to attend the 2006 awards ceremony because "the money was not available"[141]. We have also encountered familiar problems with patient motivation in the high secure hospitals, as is shown by the example at chapter 7.60 below. Nevertheless, we have seen some evidence to support the contention that the step-down from high security can involve a drastic reduction in patients' opportunities for education and activity. In one visit to a London-based NHS medium secure unit in December 2005, for example, we were told by the head of occupational therapy that there was insufficient funding to support a reasonable education programme there. Some, but not all, of the patients on that unit had access to no more than thirty minutes of maths, English and computer tuition each week, with no activity programme at all during weekends. This continuous confinement of patients in a building where there was little to do was profoundly counter-therapeutic for the patients. We suggested that additional funds might be made available to increase the programme in the next financial year.

> Lack of activities in some hospitals has led to a decline in my mental health
>
> *Dawn Cutler-Nichol, s.37/41, Derbyshire*

2.45   Mental Health Act Commissioners have even had cause to raise concerns about activities in rehabilitation units. The following is an extract from a letter to the managers of one such unit after a visit in 2006:

---

[139] *The Guardian*, 31 July 2007 'Educating Rampton' (Education Guardian Letters, anonymous letter).

[140] *The Guardian*, 24 July 2007 'Good days and bad days' (Education Guardian Article)

[141] The hospital did what it could to mitigate this patient's disappointment by subsequently arranging an award ceremony.

Patients raised a number of issues around their daily activities. It was clear that the unit has an impressive ideology of community integration. Trips to the local shops, leisure centre, etc, are to be commended. However, for those without leave, the unit appears less successful at meeting their needs. There is no facility for any form of physical exercise and higher risk patients may not even get good access to the garden area. While a number of activities are in place for patients, a high percentage of these are essentially leisure focused. Whether it be the successful dance competition which took place on the day of the visit or the craft activities, the on-site activities seem only to a limited extent linked to the assessed needs of the patients, who reported some of them as somewhat childish. Of particular note was that there appears not to be an energetic adult education program which would benefit a number of the patients of the unit.

2.46 On our next visit we wrote that:

It is of concern to the MHAC that the situation has not improved for those patients who are not able to access community facilities. The patient group requires an energetic rehabilitation regime which might include, social skills training, anger management, relapse prevention, basic education, computer skills, budgeting etc. It is unacceptable that, on a rehabilitation unit, a patient may get to cook once a month, while bingo is the most regularly reported event.

2.47 When we asked the unit management to inform us of the steps they planned to take to develop a rehabilitation ethos on the ward discussed above, they initially provided a wholly unacceptable justification of the level of service provided to patients:

The purpose of the on-site activities is that they be available to all service users, and not to discriminate against those whose mental state does not allow for long periods of concentration and focus. This ensures that for the small number of service users who are not granted leave due to their mental state, there is still a full programme available to them.

2.48 We see a great danger here. It is simply unacceptable that ward-based activities or educational opportunities should be limited to that in which the most incapacitated patient can participate - this will necessarily leave the majority of patients under-employed and dissatisfied. Furthermore, particularly in forensic or secure services, it is important that activities and educational opportunities are not unnecessarily limited by an exclusive focus on the positive symptoms of patients' illnesses, such as anti-social or violent acts; sexual misconduct; drug and alcohol abuse; etc. This was certainly the case with the above unit, where, with the exception of compliance with medication and personal hygiene, there was little focus in care plans on the negative symptoms of patients' presentations, such as lack of motivation; poor communication skills; lack of concentration; poor practical household skills; and lack of education. It is vital that such matters are properly addressed in the CPA process and in the daily life of wards.

> I was greatly concerned about lack of motivation and activity on the ward. A large proportion of patients were encouraged to get up for breakfast but then went back to bed until lunch time. Patients complained that they were bored and that planned activities did not take place as no-one was interested in them.
>
> *Visit report to an acute ward in south London,* November 2006

2.49 In the debates over the Mental Health Bill, Baroness Murphy (who is both a psychiatrist and Chair of a Mental Health Trust) suggested that ward staff other than nurses should be organising activities on the wards:

> ...at the moment we employ hardly anybody with the right skills to do that. This is not an OT function and, given the youth and educational disadvantage of many patients, we really need teachers and sports or gym supervisors on our wards....[142]

2.50 Lady Murphy went on to suggest that specific focus should be given to creating links with employment specialists who can help patients find or retain employment:

> We know that education and training for work and finding and keeping work are at the heart of patients' priorities. We must see the inpatient stay as a time when everything possible is done to keep a job or to get linked to the opportunities to give the person the chance of a job. At present, no one in the service thinks that it is their role to do that. We need mental health employment specialists whose task is just that. Of course, much of that work will go on outside hospital, but we need to keep people linked to those precious jobs and ensure that they do not lose them.[143]

Recommendation 12: Hospital managers should audit and review educational and other activities available to the patients detained in their care, seeking to improve opportunity of access for such patients

Food

2.51 As one MHA Commissioner noted in a post-visit letter to a womens' service in the independent sector: "food is of particular importance to patients who stay on the ward for a very long time". Indeed, Commissioners frequently report that detained patients from all kinds of wards raise concerns about the quality, and often also quantity, of food that is made available to them.

2.52 The most common concern raised about food are that it is unappetising, no longer hot, and of poor quality: variously "tasteless, dry and cold"; "mushy"; "greasy"; "unwholesome"; "fatty"; "monotonous"; etc. Many patients asked for more healthy options, and complained that fresh fruit, salads and vegetables were insufficiently available.

---

[142] Hansard (HL) 12 Jun 2006 : Column 93

[143] *ibid.*

2.53 In many cases patients complained that portion sizes were too small, leaving them hungry. Patients often supplemented hospital food provision through the purchase, not only of snacks, but of take-away meals. This was a particular problem in those services which served the last cooked meal of the day as early as 4.30 p.m., as patients were often hungry later in the evening. Some patients were buying in significant amounts of take-away food, either to supplement hospital food or to substitute for it. This could leave patients with little money to purchase other necessities such as toiletries, and also constituted a very unhealthy diet.

2.54 Some patients reported "undignified" processes at mealtimes. Patients disliked queuing to be served food from a trolley, and many found the lack of effective choice (or indeed simply the quality of food made available to them) demeaning. Some patients were required to state menu choices up to a week in advance; although others were given no choice over food at all.

> *"Staff told me that they wouldn't eat the food"*
> From a MHAC visit report, north west London visiting area, July 2006

2.55 In one London forensic unit, patients were provided only with poor-quality plastic cutlery, which was not only difficult to eat with but snapped easily into dangerous, sharp edges, thus presumably undermining the purpose of its provision. In other secure units, patients complained at blanket restrictions on cutlery provision, irrespective of risk assessments; or that, in one unit where patients had better cutlery, the procedure for its retrieval took too long, so that patients were made to remain seated at table long after finishing their meal.

2.56 In one hospital, the dining area doubled as a smoke-room outside of mealtimes; in other hospitals food and drink vending machines were situated in smoke-rooms.

2.57 Religious or ethnic food requirements are not always met: even in hospitals in large cities such as London we have found halal or kosher food to be unavailable to patients who request them; in a Surrey hospital one Jewish patient complained that food served to him often contained pork-products (i.e. ham in quiche, etc); and a patient who was a practising Rastafarian was not provided with appropriate food in a north London hospital. Patients raised with us their wish for culturally appropriate food in a number of hospitals serving significant Black and minority ethnic populations. In most cases this related to Afro-Caribbean menu options, although not exclusively: a patient in a Manchester hospital, for example, complained that he was not provided with any Chinese food. In many cases a lack of such provision indicates a wider insensitivity towards culturally appropriate services.

2.58 Patients who were vegan, vegetarian or who had special dietary requirements were also often poorly provided for (see paragraph 2.74 below). A number of vegetarian patients complained of monotony and lack of adequate nutrition in the food provided to them.

2.59 Some patients are given food allowances from which to buy and prepare their own meals, or supplement hospital meals. The amount of such allowances varies from hospital to hospital, and on several occasions patients have complained to visiting Commissioners that their food allowances are inadequate for healthy eating. In some cases it may be that such patients need additional help with budgeting or menu-planning as a part of rehabilitative work, although in some cases the allowance was probably inadequate (see example at chapter 7.61 below).

Smoking and detained patients

It seems to me that the atmosphere of psychiatric wards is all too often a deep and unhealthy fug of compulsion and deprivation.

A Mental Health Act Commissioner's comment on the smoking ban, 2007.

2.60 In the public consultation on the implementation of the Health Act 2006 regarding smoking bans in enclosed public spaces, the MHAC supported the aim of smokefree hospital environments for patients and staff, but took the view that patients who are detained in hospitals (and who may therefore be denied any opportunity to smoke offsite) should not, as a consequence of their detained status, be *forced* to give up smoking whilst they are required to reside in hospital[144]. We stated then that we do not believe that patients who are deprived of their liberty through use of the Mental Health Act to detain them in hospital for psychiatric treatment should, as a consequence, be forced to abstain from smoking. Having suggested in our last report that enforcing a smoking ban on patients whose detention in hospital is justified for the purposes of psychiatric treatment could be found to be an unjustifiable interference in their human rights if this were subject to legal challenge[145] (see paragraph 2.67 below), we therefore suggested that hospitals where detained patients are resident should have the same exemption from the smoking ban as was being considered for prisons.

2.61 The subsequent regulations require all mental health units to be smoke-free from 1 July 2008[146]. From that date, it will be against the law to smoke in any enclosed or substantially enclosed part of any mental health establishment in England. Wales has established different regulations that allow exemptions for psychiatric units where patients are resident, which we discuss at chapter 5.19.

2.62 The MHAC has and will continue to take a great interest in the facilities and arrangements hospitals have for their patients' access to outdoor space and fresh air, regardless of whether they are smokers or non-smokers. Having had sixteen months' notice of the legal requirement that all patients must now smoke outside, it is our view that hospitals should at the very least have prepared for the change by ensuring that patients are not confined indoors for lengthy periods of time. Such confinement is a frequent complaint of patients on our visits.

---

[144] MHAC response to Smoke-free Regulations Consultation, 10 August 2006.

[145] MHAC (2006) *Eleventh Biennial Report 2003 – 2005, In Place of Fear?* para 4. 88

[146] Regulation content announced by the National Director of Mental Health, 1 February 2007 (letter to Chief Executives of Mental Health Trusts & Strategic Health Authorities, Gateway No: 7783, Department of Health). Made by Parliament on the 7 March 2007 as *The Smoke-free (Exemptions and Vehicles) Regulations 2007*, (SI 2007/765).

2.63 The National Director for Mental Health has stated that "an extra year is being allowed for wards to prepare outdoor smoking areas" in a letter to a national newspaper defending the smokefree policy[147]. Many, but not all, hospitals are making preparations for the legal requirements in July, and some hospitals have already implemented the smoking ban and dispensed with smoking rooms. In most such hospitals patients are theoretically able to smoke outside the hospital buildings, but we have encountered many patients who complain that they are unable in practice to access the open air, as in the following extract from a report of a summer 2007 visit to a locked PICU in the West Midlands:

> Patients without leave have no access to fresh air or outdoor exercise. This was the main complaint made with great feeling by every patient seen … in June 2005 [and] July 2006. This problem is exacerbated by such patients being denied the freedom to smoke, a choice which all other patients are free to exercise… as a consequence considerable tensions arise on the ward which have placed patients and staff at risk and have sometimes necessitated increased use of medication.

2.64 The above unit had plans to build a secure outdoor area at the time of our visit. In our view it was premature to implement a smoke-free policy within the unit before arrangements for patients to smoke outside had been put in place, especially given the fact that we had been raising the problem of outdoor access for such a long time.

2.65 As an impetus to the creation of accessible outdoor spaces in hospital grounds, the smokefree regulations may in fact have a positive effect on the life of even those patients who wish to continue to smoke. It is important, however, that spaces provided for patients to access outdoors are safe and, if necessary, secure. The MHAC has already heard of worrying instances, such as patients at a rehabilitation unit within a residential housing estate being pelted with stones by local youths as they stand outside the front entrance to smoke; and a patient who sought to use a discarded hosepipe in a hospital garden area as a ligature.

> **Recommendation 13:** NHS and independent hospital managers should consider as a matter of priority patients' access to outdoor space with appropriate safety and security levels.

---

[147] "No smoke without ire", *Guardian* society section, letters, 14 Feb 2007.

Smoke-free policies across hospital estates

2.66 A number of NHS Trusts who have anticipated the impact of smokefree legislation have extended their smoking bans across the whole hospital estate, encompassing hospital grounds as well as hospital buildings. One of these, Nottinghamshire Healthcare NHS Trust, is the manager of Rampton High Security Hospital, where patients may not leave the hospital grounds without leave (in most cases requiring the consent of the Secretary of State). For all detained patients in such Trusts (but especially for those held in secure conditions), such a policy effectively strips patients of any choice as to whether they should give up smoking. We deplore this, and have received many complaints from patients who are affected.

2.67 In March 2007 an application for judicial review was launched by one patient at Rampton, arguing that "an immediate and unconditional ban on smoking at Rampton Hospital … constitutes a disproportionate interference with the Article 8 right of respect for the home and private life of the patients detained there who wish to continue smoking". The Trust disputed the claim, arguing that allowing smoking in the hospital's outside areas would still subject escorting staff to passive smoking (especially as the nature of many patients requires such escorts to keep a close physical proximity to patients under escort), and that the ban on smoking was not a disproportionate interference with Article 8 rights in the context of high security care: "it is submitted that a smoking ban is no greater invasion of Article 8 rights than, for example, the prohibition of alcohol"[148]. The Trust further maintained that its policy allows for exemptions to be made on an individual basis, but it is not clear how this would be facilitated; patients are not aware of what criteria would be applied; and to our knowledge no such exemption has been made to date.

2.68 At the time of writing this report (December 2007) the outcome of the application for judicial review was not known.

Smoking cessation services

2.69 In hospitals where patients have been prevented from smoking cigarettes at any time, nicotine replacement therapy (NRT) is offered as a substitute. In a letter to one complainant, Nottinghamshire Healthcare NHS Trust stated that

> it is true that if patients cannot leave the hospital site and if they do not fall into an exemption category then they cannot smoke. But the provision of nicotine replacement therapy will help patients who are prevented from smoking… Lighting a cigarette merely addresses the craving to reduce the withdrawal symptoms from the last cigarette. Nicotine replacement therapy can reduce these cravings by replacing the nicotine which

---

[148] R (on the application of x) and Nottinghamshire Healthcare NHS Trust, summary grounds for defence, May 2007. We have removed the patient's name from this as yet unheard case reference.

is in cigarettes in a way that does not harm health. A range of other types of support will also be available.[149]

2.70   In such circumstances, patients are not using NRT as an aid to giving up smoking voluntarily, but as simply as a means of staving off cravings for the cigarettes that have been denied them. We believe that this is neither a use for which smoking cessation services promote NRT, nor the context in which smoking cessation services are likely to achieve their aim.

2.71   It is vital that smoking cessation services are offered to all detained patients as a matter of choice, and the MHAC will take a special interest in the provision of such services to detained patients in the period leading up to the closure of all hospital smoking-rooms. Effective smoking cessation support for patients will require staff training and specialist input. It has been reported that some psychiatrists have shown a reluctance to prescribe sufficient NRT to their patients, and that the targets set for the PCT commissioners of smoking cessation services (which measure numbers of people who have stayed smoke-free for four weeks) may hinder the targeting of psychiatric patients and other 'difficult' cases[150]. Detained patients should not be disadvantaged by any target-based priorities created for smoking cessation services, and we hope that any evidence that this is happening will be addressed with specific funding.

> **Recommendation 14:** The Department of Health should consider specific funding of smoking cessation services within psychiatric services to counter any unintended consequences of public health targets. Smoking cessation services must remain voluntary for detained patients.

2.72   It is also extremely important that smoking cessation, although clearly a priority in the coming years, does not become *the* priority at the expense of wider health promotion and physical health care for the detained population. Making anti-smoking measures the key 'physical health' intervention will reinforce the service user perspective that issues of patient behaviour and lifestyle in mental health units are addressed more energetically by interventions of deprivation and restriction than of provision and action. Voluntary smoking cessation should therefore be one aspect of a wide range of interventions discussed below.

The physical health care of patients

2.73   In this reporting period, the Disability Rights Commission (DRC) called for more support from specialist mental health and learning disability providers to enable people with learning disabilities and/or mental health problems to access primary care and take care of

---

[149] Nottinghamshire Healthcare NHS Trust response to a patient's complaint over the smokefree policy at Rampton Hospital, April 2007.

[150] 'Quitting Time' *Mental Health Today*, July / August 2007, p.10-11.

their physical health. There is a surprising lack of such support for many detained inpatients. We concur with the DRC recommendation that this be an area of patient care addressed in the ongoing review of the Care Programme Approach, although we have some concerns that the CPA review may in fact be taking a different course (see paragraph 2.95 below). We suggest that priority should be given to the areas discussed below.

> Physical healthcare is often left unattended or delayed until the last minute regardless of certain staff being qualified in general nursing.
>
> *male patient, section 37/41, West Midlands*

Patients' dietary needs

2.74 As discussed at paragraph 2.51 *et seq above*, the food available to inpatients is often of poor quality, or insufficient quantity, or is served at odd times of the day, so that in many units we find patients supplementing their diet with unhealthy takeaway foods. Department of Health guidelines require dieticians to check hospital menus to ensure that nutritional requirements are met[151], and hospital menus should enable a diet which is lower in fat, based on complex carbohydrates and includes plenty of fruit and vegetables[152]. Dieticians should also have regular and more general input to psychiatric inpatients' care[153], given the widespread incidence of nutrition-related ill-health (whether relating to malnutrition or obesity, with the latter sometimes exacerbated by side-effects of psychiatric medication). In particular, dieticians and specialist clinicians should be involved in the care of patients with complex dietary requirements, such as coeliac disease, newly diagnosed and unstable diabetes, obesity, hyperlipidaemia, malnutrition or food refusal[154].

> Patient 1 has diabetes. She has not seen a podiatrist and needs to see a dietician. She is not getting food that is suitable for a diabetic and to help control her weight.
>
> *Visit report to a psychiatric acute ward in a general hospital, NE England, 2007*

2.75 The NSF for Diabetes recognised that people with mental health problems or learning disabilities may receive poor quality care for diabetes. People of South Asian, African, African-Caribbean and Middle Eastern descent have a higher than average risk of Type 2 diabetes, as do less affluent people. Therefore, risks may accumulate if an individual belongs to more than one of these groups[155].

Recommendation 15: hospital menus should be reviewed to ensure that healthier options are made available, with the involvement of dietitians in both overall reviews of food quality and choice and in the care of individual patient's needs.

---

[151] See http://195.92.246.148/nhsestates/better_hospital_food/bhf_content/introduction/home.asp

[152] Department of Health (2002) *National Service Framework for Diabetes: Implementation details and draft service models.* London, DH, p.2. See http://www.dh.gov.uk/en/Publicationsandstatistics/Publications/PublicationsPolicyAndGuidance/DH_4002951

[153] Department of Health (2002) *Policy Implementation Guide on Acute Care Provision.* London, DH.

[154] See Sainsbury Centre for Mental Health (2007) *Delivering the Government's Mental Health Policies; Services, Staffing and Costs.* Jed Boardman and Michael Parsonage. London, Sainsbury Centre for Mental Health, p.41.

[155] Department of Health (2001) *National Service Framework for Diabetes: Standards,* p.9. http://www.dh.gov.uk/en/Publicationsandstatistics/Publications/PublicationsPolicyAndGuidance/DH_4002951

Regular access to exercise

2.76 Patients should also have opportunity to exercise wherever possible. For adults, the current guideline is to undertake at least 30 minutes of moderate intensity activity (such as brisk walking or sport) on at least five days of the week[156]. Many detained patients do not have sufficient opportunity to achieve this. Many patients do not have access to exercise equipment and a gymnasium, and some hospitals with such facilities lack sufficient trained staff to make them regularly available for patient use. We have noted at paragraph 2.63 above widespread problems in accessing outdoor areas for detained patients.

2.77 The Department of Health has accepted the Disability Rights Commission's recommendation that contracts with service providers should require that patients have opportunity for healthy eating and exercise, although it has also stated that it is for PCTs "to set local standards for quality improvement to reflect local priorities"[157]. Given that there are likely to be challenging problems with providing many psychiatric inpatients with the facility to exercise (even in terms of access to an open space and fresh air within existing hospital estates), we doubt that this will be sufficient to provide the 'robust' quality standards called for by the DRC. However, we note that the Department of Health has indicated that it will keep this matter under review and consider whether to set national standards for quality improvement in the next financial year[158].

Health promotion groups

2.78 A number of services now run health promotion groups, including (but not limited to) weight-watchers style programmes. Such groups are, however, often presented to visiting Commissioners as an innovative project rather than a standard part of the ward environment.

Physical health care checks and monitoring

2.79 A number of hospitals have good relations with general practitioners who provide primary care physical healthcare for their patients. However, regular medical examinations for long-stay patients are far from universal, and patients whose mental health treatment involves high doses of antipsychotic medication or polypharmacy do not always receive the physical health monitoring recommended by the Royal College of Psychiatrists (see chapter 6.32).

---

[156] Department of Health (2002) *National Service Framework for Diabetes: Implementation details and draft service models*, p.2.

[157] Department of Health (2007) *Promoting Equality*, p.18.

[158] *ibid.*

2.80   As this report was being finalised, we learned of some problems occurring in relation to contracts between general practitioners and detaining authorities. A GP practice in Cheshire withdrew its services to a rehabilitation unit that had been recently registered as a hospital with the Healthcare Commission (the establishment had previously been registered as a nursing home with the Commission for Social Care Inspection). The GP practice had, until it withdrew its services at 24 hours' notice, been responsible for prescribing all psychiatric medication, including monitoring associated with the prescription of clozapine, and providing physical healthcare to patients in the unit. Four patients on the unit were undergoing physical treatment at the time of the withdrawal of service, including one terminally ill patient prescribed pain relief. The GPs' services were withdrawn because the practice determined that it could take no responsibility for the provision of medical care or the renewal of prescriptions in secondary care settings (which the rehabilitation unit had become, by definition, through being registered as a 'hospital'), and that it had no indemnity insurance to enable its GPs to provide such services. The unit was without a service for just over a week (during which time the terminally ill patient died[159]) until agency services could be arranged. At the time of going to press, the GP contract was being renegotiated to allow the restoration of a service to this unit. A similar problem arose between a GP practice and a learning disability unit in Wales. We fear that these problems could occur across the health service and have sought to have this matter considered at a national policy level.

2.81   We support the DRC's call for the Department of Health to ensure that service commissioners can require that consultants in psychiatry cease to have overall sole responsibility for the physical healthcare of inpatients, and that this responsibility should instead be held by the primary health care professionals providing regular in-reach, so that psychiatrists and psychiatric nurses provide psychiatric treatment and have a complementary role in monitoring and providing treatment for physical health problems as specified by the primary health care team[160]. The expansion of responsibility for the physical healthcare of patients beyond the hospital ward would ensure that patients whose coercive treatment takes place outside of hospital (whether on leave arrangements or under the CTOs established by the 2007 Act) are not disadvantaged. One London-based consultant told us that

> the problem with some GPs and A&E staff is that 'mental patients' are sometimes treated less well than non-mentally disordered patients. They are not examined in as much detail, and have fewer investigations. Assumptions are sometimes made that complaints of physical symptoms are somehow related to the mental disorder and do not need normal levels of attention. A&E staff are keen to get the patients out as quickly

---

[159] There is no suggestion that the death of this patient was hastened by the lack of GP service, although the rehabilitation unit reported problems in obtaining pain relief medication and an ambulance to take the patient to a hospice because the GPs would not sign relevant forms.

[160] See Disability Rights Commission (2007) *Initial DRC response to Promoting Equality: Response from Department of Health to the Disability Rights Commission Report 'Equal Treatment: Closing the Gap'*. April 2007. http://www.drc.gov.uk/library/health_investigation/research_and_evidence.aspx

as possible. For patients in supported community supported accommodation, arranging for a GP visit can be very difficult, although this varies from practice to practice. Given that physical illness is so common in our patients, especially now with the metabolic complications of the new antipsychotic drugs, poor quality services can have very serious outcomes.

I accept that some patients may be difficult to treat because of their mental illness - histories may be harder to obtain, they may be less co-operative with investigations, they may appear less grateful etc., but the problem goes far beyond this. I think there is, as in so many areas of our patients' lives, old-fashioned discrimination.

Dental services

2.82 A study of patients in one long-term medium secure unit published in this reporting period found that more than half had significant dental problems[161]. Although this sample was small, there is undoubtedly a need amongst longer-stay detained patients for dental care, which is not always met. As this report went to press we were aware of one medium secure unit that had lost access to dental health care due to the local practice withdrawing its services. The primary care NHS Trust responsible for the service was having great difficulty in finding a replacement service.

Facilities for the physically disabled

2.83 We continue to hear of instances of poor facilities for and management of physical disability in mental health services[162]. In this reporting period Commissioners have noted poor services provided to patients with a range of disabilities, including deaf and blind patients, and patients requiring walking aids or special equipment for safe and comfortable living. From December 2006 NHS Trusts have been under a legal duty to promote equality of opportunity for disabled people and should address facilities for disabled patients in their Equality Action Plans[163].

> It took weeks for the ward to find a chair with a high back for me to sit in, there were no facilities for bathing for disabled patients, no suitable furniture anywhere on the ward, in the day room, television room, or anywhere to support my needs. I spent nearly seven months sitting in my room, all alone, on the chair they finally found for me… patients who came to my room to talk to me were removed at once as there was a no accessing other rooms policy…I got patients to move my chair into the doorway … but nurses then said I was creating a fire hazard.
>
> *Monica Endersby, detained under ss.2 and 3*

[161] Power N, Harwood D, Akinkunmi A (2006) 'Tilting the balance: the first long-term medium secure unit in the NHS in England and Wales'. *Psychiatric Bulletin* 30, 25-28. Of 18 patients audited between November 2003 and January 2004, only one had no physical health problem. Three patients had diabetes, 5 were obese, 9 had cardio-vascular problems, 8 dermatological problems, and 6 gastro-intestinal problems, two of whom had hepatitis C.

[162] MHAC (2006) *Eleventh Biennial Report 2003-2005: In Place of Fear?* Chapter 4.105 *et seq.*

[163] See http://www.dotheduty.org/files/Code_of_practice_england_and_wales.doc

2.84 At one NHS Trust we have ensured that a blind patient was allowed regular visits from her guide dog which had previously not been allowed, and that legal correspondence regarding her ongoing divorce was read aloud to her promptly on delivery, as she had requested, to ensure that she could take timely action. The Trust also provided rights information in an audio format for this patient after some prompting.

The Care Programme Approach

2.85 The Care Programme Approach (CPA) is designed as a framework for effective mental

> I felt as though I were a spy watching in when we had the weekly meeting with psychiatrists – they just talked as though I was not there.
>
> *Deborah Hickman, s.3 Bolton.*

> The biggest thing that made a difference was meeting my care co-ordinator – knowing that my voice was being heard.
>
> *Michael Lang, South Yorkshire*

> Quite often care plans have been written for me without me knowing what they entail.
>
> *Dawn Cutler-Nichol, s.37/41, Derbyshire*

health care for people with severe mental health problems, which should ensure that health and social care needs are assessed and addressed through a regularly reviewed care plan, overseen by a key-worker but designed in consultation with the service user and, where appropriate, any carer[164]. The current policy on CPA is set out in the Department of Health booklet *Effective Care Co-ordination: Modernising the Care Programme Approach*[165], although this is under review.

2.86 The patchy implementation of the CPA has been a recurring theme of our past Biennial Reports[166], and was the subject of our 2005 report *Back on Track*[167], produced in collaboration with the Sainsbury Centre for Mental Health. The implementation of CPA has

---

[164] Department of Health (2006) *Reviewing the Care Programme Approach 2006. A consultation document.* November 2006, para 1.

[165] Department of Health (1999) *Effective care co-ordination in mental health services: modernizing the care programme approach – A policy booklet.*

[166] See, for example, MHAC (1999) *Ninth Biennial Report 1999-01*, chapter 3.1-2; (2001) *Tenth Biennial Report 2001-2003: Placed Amongst Strangers*, Chapter 8.27; (2006) *Eleventh Biennial Report: In Place of Fear?* chapter 2.75 *et seq.*

[167] Sainsbury Centre for Mental Health (2005) *Back on Track? CPA care planning for service users who are repeatedly detained under the Mental Health Act.* Published in association with the Mental Health Act Commission. www.scmh.org.uk.

drawn criticism for its bureaucracy and arguable over-emphasis on risk-assessment rather than recovery[168], but there is also general support for its principles amongst professionals (including professional bodies[169]) and service users. Kingdon and Amanullah reported in 2005 that "pressure from the Department of Health Inspectorates and Mental Health Act Commission on one hand and from users and carers who want care plans and clear points of contact on the other has had some effects" in terms of CPA implementation[170].

2.87   In this reporting period, a number of inquiries into homicide and suicide have underlined deficiencies in the implementation of the CPA[171], and the Department of Health has

> Towards the latter part of my hospitalisation the ward's Practice and Development nurse introduced me to a new psychological and social model developed by my Trust aimed at the planning, management and execution of aftercare. I was initially very enthusiastic…three meetings were held with the nurse and I thought that she was incorporating into the model all of the psychological and social factors relevant to me. There then ensued a meeting with my aftercare care co-ordinator. I was totally disillusioned and my care co-ordinator (an occupational therapist) was bewildered as the practice development nurse had eliminated anything psychological and/or social in favour of a strictly medical model approach. Even now, six weeks after discharge, I remain without any planned and co-ordinated aftercare.
>
> *Stuart A Wooding, detained under s.3 in London.*

acknowledged "increasing concern that a number of key groups which should meet the characteristics for enhanced CPA are not being identified consistently"[172].

Patient involvement in CPA

2.88   We have noted some good practice over patients' involvement in care planning under the CPA. In Oxleas NHS Foundation Trust, nursing staff complete the care plan during the CPA meeting with the patient and clinical team, projecting the document onto the wall so that all can see what is being typed. The Dene Hospital in Sussex provides its patients with a "have your say form" designed to aid their input into CPA meetings. The form explains the purpose of CPA and gives a space for a patient to summarise their wishes and views about

---

168 Department of Health (2006) *op cit.* n.159, introduction.

169 See, for example, Royal College of Psychiatrists (2004) *Good Psychiatric Practice* (2nd ed) (Council Report CR125). London: RCPsych.

170 Kingdon D, Amanullah S (2005) *Care Programme Approach: relapsing or recovering?* Advances in Psychiatric Treatment 2005 vol 11, 325-329.

171 See, for example, the *MN Inquiry* Report (see n.182 below]); *Barrett Inquiry Report* (NHS London, 2006); Francis R, Higgins J & Cassam E (2000) *Report of the independent inquiry into the care and treatment of Michael Stone.* South East Coast Strategic Health Authority; Maden T (2006) *Review of Homicides by Patients with Severe Mental Illness* (report commissioned by the Department of Health); National Confidential Inquiry into Suicide and Homicide by People with Mental Illness (2006) *Avoidable Deaths: five year report of the National Confidential Inquiry into Suicide and Homicide by People with Mental Illness*, December 2006.

172 Department of Health (2006) *op cit.*,n.159, para 3.4.

their care, as well as repeating a structured question under a number of headings, including "housing", "money", "physical health", "daily living skills", "family/carer issues", etc. The structured question has three parts, relating to past events, current situation, and wishes for the future. In terms of past events and current situation, patients are prompted to think about what did or did not go well, and how they coped. The form suggests that patients write down "what else... I need" in terms of their current situation, and think about both their strengths and needs for the future. It is made clear that not all of the questions have to be answered[173].

Financing leave and rehabilitation activities

2.89   As patients progress towards discharge or to a move down the security system, it is likely that they will have increased leave and rehabilitative activities that incur expenses from their own funds. This is often appropriate and, indeed, managing their own funds may well be a part of a patient's rehabilitative programme. We welcome the end of hospital downrating of benefits, which should have made a substantial difference to many long-stay patients' incomes (see paragraph 2.14, but also chapter 7.56 *et seq*). However, we have noted some patients who are expected to contribute towards rehabilitation trips to a questionably appropriate degree. One independent hospital told us that the ward had a budget of £20 per week to reimburse staff spending on escorted trips, and each patient was therefore only allowed one escorted trip which incurs expense to staff through the use of public transport, etc. If the patient required or wished to have further trips incurring staff expense, that expense was reported to come from the patient's own money. At another independent hospital we met with a patient who contributed partially towards some of the activities within her weekly programme. The unit manager told us that this was because the commissioning authority did not contribute adequately to the patient's recreational needs. In cases such as these we suggest that the CPA process should provide a platform upon which costs can be negotiated over and built into individual commissioning arrangements covering patients' clinical, rehabilitation and therapeutic needs.

Census data on CPA status of detained patients

2.90   Figure 12 below shows the CPA status of 13,856 patients who were detained under the 1983 Act at the time of the 2006 census. A majority (11,745 patients, or 85% of the whole detained group) were subject to enhanced CPA. Nearly twelve-hundred patients (1,198, or 9% of the whole group) were subject to standard CPA, and CPA was not being applied at all to 836 patients, or 6% of the whole group, 482 of whom (4% of the whole group) were adults of working age.

---

173   A full copy of the "have your say form" can be seen as the appendix to the MHAC's response to the Care Programme Approach consultation, available on our website. For further information or permission to reproduce the form contact Mr Sam Ishmail, Mental Health Act Office, The Dene, Gatehouse Lane, Goddards Green, West Sussex BN6 9LE.

		CPA status by diagnostic category								Totals	
		Neither CPA nor SAP		Standard CPA		Enhanced CPA		Single Assessment Process			
		MI/PD	LD	MI/PD	LD	MI/PD	LD	MI/PD	LD	MI/PD	LD
Age Band: 17 and under	Count	19	-	12	-	81	23	2	-	114	23
	% of age band in diagnostic category	16.7%	-	10.5%	-	71.1%	1.7%	1.8%	-	100%	100%
18-24	Count	78	21	141	12	1,067	264	8	2	1,294	299
	% of age band in diagnostic category	6.0%	12.3%	10.9%	18.2%	82.5%	19.3%	0.6%	50.0%	100%	100%
25-34	Count	123	36	176	20	2,496	357	5	1	2,800	414
	% of age band in diagnostic category	4.4%	21.1%	6.3%	30.3%	89.1%	26.1%	0.2%	25.0%	100%	100%
35-44	Count	134	50	202	21	2,937	398	4	-	3,277	469
	% of age band in diagnostic category	4.1%	29.2%	6.2%	31.8%	89.6%	29.1%	0.1%	-	100%	100%
45-54	Count	76	36	148	6	1,746	233	7	-	1,977	277
	% of age band in diagnostic category	3.8%	21.1%	7.5%	9.1%	88.3%	17.1%	0.4%	-	100%	100%
55-64	Count	71	16	128	7	1,114	72	8	-	1,321	95
	% of age band in diagnostic category	5.4%	9.4%	9.7%	10.6%	84.3%	5.3%	0.6%	-	100%	100%
65-74	Count	52	9	130	-	531	18	15	1	728	28
	% of age band in diagnostic category	7.1%	5.3%	17.9%	-	72.9%	1.3%	2.1%	25.0%	100%	100%
75 and above	Count	112	1	195	-	407	1	24	-	738	2
	% of age band in diagnostic category	15.2%	0.6%	26.4%	-	55.1%	0.1%	3.2%	-	100%	100%
Totals	Count	665	171	1,132	66	10,379	1,366	73	4	12,249	1,607
	% of age band in diagnostic category	5.4%	10.6%	9.2%	4.1%	84.7%	85.0%	0.6%	0.2%	100%	100%
	CPA status as % of all detained patients	6.0%		8.6%		84.8%		0.6%		100.0%	

Fig 12: CPA status of patients detained under the MHA, 31 March 2006

Source: *Count Me In* census 2006

CPA and patients aged under 17 years

2.91 Upon its introduction in 1991, CPA was focused solely on adults of working age, and there is still no explicit policy requirement that children and younger people have their needs assessed through formal CPA mechanisms, although in 1999 it was stated that "the principles of the CPA are relevant to the care and treatment of younger…people with mental health problems"[174]. Thus it is expected that younger people will still be subject to

[174] Department of Health (1999) *Effective care co-ordination in mental health services: modernizing the care programme approach – a policy booklet*, para 17. See also Care Programme Approach Association (2004) *The CPA Handbook 2004*. CPAA, Chesterfield, p.4-5.

assessment of need, and the development and review of a care plan, but without this taking place within the formal CPA framework. Our data shows that a majority of detained patients below the age of 17 are, in fact, recognised as having a formal CPA status, and that this is usually at enhanced level. It is, nevertheless, unsurprising to note that, of all patients in hospital for primary treatment of mental health rather than learning disability, this age group has the highest percentage of detained patients without a formal CPA status.

CPA and older patients

2.92   There are two alternative frameworks of care planning for older people with severe mental illness[175]. Where a patient's diagnosis relates to a psychotic disorder, the government requires the use of "the full CPA"[176], but where the diagnosis relates to functional or organic mental health problems, such as depression or dementia, services are expected to assess needs through the "Single Assessment Process" (SAP) for older people, introduced by the National Service Framework for Older People of 2002. The SAP, like CPA, is a process of determining need through assessment and the drawing up of a care plan, which may be led by a co-ordinator where there are complex needs. Where older patients have functional or organic mental health problems that would have merited CPA status in any adult of working age, extant guidance suggests that "aspects of CPA" should be "integrated into SAP"[177].

2.93   The Department of Health's current guidance around CPA and older patients thus weights a diagnosis of psychotic illness over any other[178], although it has been argued that diagnosis (which addresses the *nature* but not the *degree* of a disorder) has a marginal contribution to defining severe mental disorder[179]. Given that conditions other than psychotic illness may lead to equally severe disability and need, making psychotic illness alone an indicator of the need for "the full CPA" may lead to some equally seriously disordered patients being denied the benefits of the CPA process.

2.94   The single assessment process (SAP) is not limited to older patients, but may also be applied to other service users with health and/or social care needs. Our data shows, however, that it is very rarely used as the care-planning framework for detained patients, and hardly at all for patients of adult working age or for minors.

Who should be subject to CPA?

2.95   We are concerned at the government's suggestion that 'standard CPA' could be abolished as a means of simplifying CPA requirements and focusing on those with "complex

---

[175] See Department of Health (2001) *Guidance on the Single Assessment Process for Older People; (2002) Care Management for Older People with serious Mental Health Problems* (HSC 2002/001; LAC (2002)1).

[176] Department of Health (2002) *ibid.* n.175, annex A.

[177] *ibid.*, para 4 and annex A.

[178] *ibid.*, see annex A.

[179] Kingdon D, Amanullah S (2005) Care Programme Approach: relapsing or recovering? *Advances in Psychiatric Treatment* 2005 vol 11, 325-329.

needs"[180]. We are concerned that the assessment of "complex needs" will be subjective (and subject to distortion by resource availability), so that patients could slip through the care-planning net. The *National Confidential Inquiry into Suicide and Homicide by People with Mental Illness* found that 71% of preventable homicides and 45% of preventable suicides were by patients who were not subject to appropriate CPA plans, despite clear evidence of severe mental illness, previous violence, self-harm or admission under the Mental Health Act[181].

2.96 The report of the independent inquiry into the care and treatment of *MN*, published in this reporting period[182], pointed out that a significant contributing factor to the patchy implementation of CPA is that the criteria for instigating the CPA in relation to a particular patient's care is nowhere unequivocally set out. The inquiry team recommended that the criteria for CPA should be capable of objective determination wherever possible. It suggested the following non-exhaustive list of criteria, any one of which should be considered sufficient to indicate a need for CPA at some level:

- a risk of violence and/or self harm as assessed according to a standardised, structured risk assessment;

- treatment with medication for a severe mental illness coupled with a history of non-compliance;

- more than one professional providing care and treatment to the service user and carer;

- when a request for CPA review is made by a service user or carer;

- following a first episode of assessment or treatment; or

- when subject to MHA s.3; on s.17 leave; or whilst subject to s.117 aftercare[183].

2.97 In particular, the inquiry urged the Department of Health to consider patients detained for treatment, on s.17 leave, subject to s.117 aftercare or subject to a Community Treatment Order as a key group which should receive *enhanced* CPA, on the grounds that such patients

---

[180] See MHAC (2007) *Mental Health Act Commission response to the Care Services Improvement Partnership and Department of Health consultation document Reviewing the Care Programme Approach 2006*. February 2007 www.mhac.org.uk

[181] National Confidential Inquiry into Suicide and Homicide by People with Mental Illness (2006) *Avoidable Deaths: five year report of the National Confidential Inquiry into Suicide and Homicide by People with Mental Illness*. http://www.medicine.manchester.ac.uk/suicideprevention/nci/Useful/avoidable_deaths_full_report.pdf

[182] *Independent Inquiry into the Care and Treatment of MN. A report commissioned by Avon, Gloucestershire & Wiltshire Strategic Health Authority*. Gillian Downham, Richard Lingham, John McKenna & Anthony Deery. June 2006. Henceforth "MN inquiry report (2006)". Available from: http://www.agwsha.nhs.uk/board/june06/Item_2.1_REPORT_7_JUNE_2006_Final.pdf.

[183] *Independent Inquiry Report into Care and Treatment of MN. Report by the Inquiry Team on the Six Month Review of Progress in the Implementation of Recommendations*. 26 February 2007. Henceforth "MN report six-month review (2007)". Available from http://www.southwest.nhs.uk/boardpapers/2007Mar15/Independent_Inquiry_Report_into_the_Care_and_Treatment_of_MN.pdf

have presented, by legal definition, a risk to themselves or to others of some nature. We would go further: in our view any patient who has been detained for assessment or treatment under the Act, or under any of the powers in part III of the Act should be subject to CPA at some level.

> **Recommendation 16:** Any patient who has been detained for assessment or treatment under the Act, or under any of the powers in part III of the Act should be subject to CPA at some level.

Patients' contact with their responsible medical officers

2.98   In the 1983 Act as it is currently in force, a detained patient's "responsible medical officer" is defined simply as a registered medical practitioner who is "in charge of the treatment of the patient"[184]. The amendments made by the 2007 Act will change the title to "responsible clinician", defined (for detained or community patients) as "the approved clinician with overall responsibility for the patient's case"[185].

2.99   The identification of an RMO of a detained patient is thus "a question of fact"[186], in contrast to the identification of an RMO for a patient subject to guardianship, who may be nominated by a social services authority[187]. As we discuss below, it is not always clear, as a matter of "fact", just who is "in charge" of the patient's treatment, and in practice there can seem to be an aspect of nomination in the identification of the RMO. Under the changes made by the 2007 Act, whereby the responsible clinician (who need not be a doctor at all) is defined as an approved clinician "with overall responsibility for the patient's case"[188], it is possible that this element of nomination will be increased.

2.100   In January 2007, we were contacted by a legal member of the MHRT, who had presided over a Tribunal hearing where a patient's RMO had neither written nor countersigned the medical report. The RMO appeared to have last seen the patient three months before the Tribunal hearing. We visited the unit unannounced and examined evidence of the RMO's involvement with patients. We found that an associate specialist had regular contact with patients, but we had serious concerns that the engagement of the nominal RMO with the unit (one session per week) was compromising the lawful management of responsibilities under the Act, particularly in relation to certifying consent to treatment and authorising patients' leave of absence. The Trust concerned submitted an action-plan to us in respect of

---

[184]   MHA 1983 s.34(1), definition at (a) under 'responsible medical officer' prior to amendment under the MHA 2007.

[185]   MHA 1983 s.34(1), definition at (a) under 'responsible clinician', as amended by MHA 2007, s.9(10)

[186]   Jones R (2006) *Mental Health Act Manual*, tenth edition. Sweet & Maxwell, para 1-468

[187]   MHA 1983, s.34(1), definition at (b) under 'responsible medical officer' prior to amendment under the MHA 2007.

[188]   MHA 1983, s.34(1), definition at (a) under 'responsible medical officer' as amended by MHA 2007, s.9(10).

all of the concerns raised on our visit, which generally satisfied us that matters were being addressed. One aspect of that plan was the formal transfer of RMO responsibilities to the associate specialist, so that the associate specialist was from that time recognised as the RMO.

2.101 Whilst there is no legal requirement that a patient's RMO should have consultant status, the Memorandum on the Act establishes an expectation that detained patients will be under a consultant's care. The Memorandum suggests that the RMO's functions should normally be exercised by "a consultant who is in charge in the sense that he [*sic*] is not responsible or answerable for the patient's treatment to any other doctor"[189]. It allows that another doctor "who is for the time being in charge" can be recognised as the RMO when the usual RMO is unavailable through sickness or annual leave, although even here it suggests that the stand-in doctor should normally be another consultant or a specialist registrar approved under section 12(2)[190].

2.102 In the case discussed above, the hospital managers chose to address the legal questions raised by the infrequent attendance of a consultant-grade psychiatrist to a mental health unit by formally passing the RMO role to an associate specialist (who is by definition responsible to a named consultant[191]). As such, they presumably removed the need for the consultant-grade psychiatrist to visit the unit at all, which is something of a perverse result in terms both of patient welfare, and of the 1983 Act's clear intention to provide clear authority and accountability in identifying the person in charge of a patient's treatment.

The hospital as a disciplinary environment

Locked doors

"[I] felt embarrassed, claustrophobic, locked in, an inmate ... fourteen again"

Unnamed service user view from Humber M H Trust research on user experience of locked wards

2.103 The majority of acute wards that we visit operate a locked door policy. Figure 13 below shows the number and percentage of locked and open wards visited between the October 2004 and April 2007. A patient admitted to an acute ward, whether detained or informal, is more likely to be held in a locked environment than not. A Swedish study published in 2006 identified, through semi-structured interviews, that staff reported more disadvantages than advantages associated with locked wards[192]. The advantages included having control over patients; creating a secure and structured environment; protecting patients from theft, drugs or harassment from outside; reassuring relatives, carers or the patients themselves; and that having the door locked as a matter of policy reduces anxiety and discussion that

---

[189] Department of Health & Welsh Office (1998) *Mental Health Act Memorandum on Parts I to VI, VIII and X*, Stationery Office, para 60.

[190] *ibid.*

[191] See Royal College of Physicians, *Guidance on job descriptions/job plans and setting up an AAC for an Associate Specialist.* http://www.rcplondon.ac.uk/professional/aac/aac_associate.htm

[192] Haglund K, von Knorring L & von Essen L (2006) 'Psychiatric wards with locked doors – advantages and disadvantages according to nurses and mental health nurse assistants'. *Journal of Clinical Nursing* 15, 387-394

would be caused on the occasions where it might otherwise have to be locked. The disadvantages included patients feeling confined, frustrated, aggressive, depressed or anxious; increasing patients' sense of helplessness, dependence and ill-health; adapting the ward for the sake of those who are most unwell to the detriment of others; reinforcing the power relationships between nurses and patients; and creating the impression of a non-caring environment with an emphasis on keys and physical barriers. Further research on locked wards has been commissioned by the Department of Health from Professor Len Bowers, whose 2006 study on observation and outcomes in acute wards suggested positive associations between locked wards and patient self-harm, although without being able to determine the direction of causality[193].

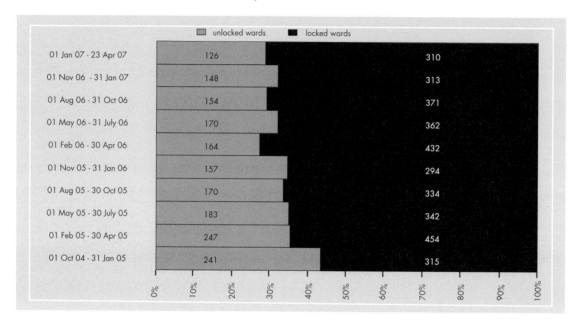

Fig 13: Locked or open door status of acute wards visited by the MHAC, Oct 2004 to Jan 2007

Data source: MHAC data

2.104 For patients who are not detained under the Act who wish to leave a locked ward, the door should be opened at their request, although we know that this is not always done and as such informal patients may be subject to the unlawful deprivation of liberty referred to in previous MHAC reports as *de facto* detention[194]. In December 2006 we wrote an open letter to the National Director for Mental Health (in his capacity as the director of the National Confidential Inquiry) questioning statements in the *Avoidable Deaths* report[195] that remarked upon informal patients leaving wards "without permission" or referred to them as

---

[193] Bowers L, Whittington R, Nolan P, Parkin D, Curtis S, Bhui K, Hackney D, Allan T, Simpson A & Flood C (2006) *The City 128 Study of Observation and Outcomes on Acute Psychiatric Wards.* Report to the NHS SDO Programme, December 2006, p.8.

[194] See MHAC (2006) *Eleventh Biennial Report 2003-2005: In Place of Fear?* para 3.18 – 3.26 for an extensive discussion of locked wards and *de facto* detention.

[195] National Confidential Inquiry into Suicide and Homicide by People with Mental Illness (2006) *Avoidable Deaths: five year report of the National Confidential Inquiry into Suicide and Homicide by People with Mental Illness*.

"absconders". The National Director suggested that we were misunderstanding the way in which "permission" is used in his report; that "when staff say that a patient may leave the ward, they are saying whether it is safe or consistent with the care plan, not explaining the patient's legal entitlement"; and that people in clinical practice would understand that it was not meant "in a legal sense". We doubt that such a distinction between the exercise of 'clinical' or 'legal' authority is clear, either to clinicians or, especially, to the patients whose liberty is in question. The correspondence between the MHAC and the National Director on this issue is available on the MHAC website.

2.105 Notwithstanding our concerns over *de facto* detention, we recognise that it would be a mistake to make a fetish of open wards, or fail to recognise that even on an open ward some patients' movements may be restricted and patients' movements supervised. The issue is not whether there should be controls, but what sort of controls are appropriate. Having an open-door policy does not preclude having arrangements whereby patients are asked to 'sign out' when leaving the ward (and it is surprising how in many units the nursing office is neither alongside nor within sight of exits that might facilitate this). Nurses on open wards may be required to keep a close watch on particular patients and may have to prevent individual patients from leaving the hospital as necessary using appropriate legal powers[196]. Developing ideas about observation practice suggest that it can play a part in building therapeutic relationships as well as controlling patient behaviour or movement[197].

2.106 A number of wards have sophisticated electronic swipe-card operated systems, where each patient is issued with a programmable swipe card that can be used to access individual bedrooms and lockers, gender-appropriate washing and toilet facilities, and (if the patient's card is so programmed) to come and go through the locked ward door. Such systems that we have observed appear to work well, with patients taking great care of their cards.

Closed-Circuit Television (CCTV)

2.107 Commissioners increasingly find CCTV installed in mental health units, particularly in newly built establishments. In some cases staff have inadequate understanding of the constraints around its proper use. The MHAC has published guidance on the legal and ethical framework for the use of CCTV, derived in part from the requirements of the Data Protection Act 1998 and the Information Commissioner's CCTV Code of Practice[198]. Managers should consult this guidance where CCTV is used on their premises, and ensure that staff are familiar with its basic points. Commissioners frequently visit wards where the notices stating that CCTV is in use are absent and where patients are unaware of their rights to view recorded material.

---

[196] Kinton M (2006) 'Is it time to close the doors?' *The Mental Health Review*, Volume 11, Issue 3, Sept 2006. See Rae M (2006) in the same issue for a defence of locked wards.

[197] Buchanan-Barker P & Barker P (2005) 'Observation: the original sin of mental health nursing?' *Journal of Psychiatric and Mental Health Nursing* 12, 541-549; Vråle G B & Steen E (2005) 'The dynamics between structure and flexibility in constant observation of psychiatric inpatients with suicidal ideation' *Journal of Psychiatric and Mental Health Nursing* 12, 513-518

[198] MHAC (2005) *The Use of CCTV in NHS and Independent Mental Health Units: a framework for assessment.* Nottingham, October 2005. http://www.mhac.org.uk/files/Microsoft%20Word%20-%20CCTV%20GUIDANCE%20-%20FINAL.pdf

2.108 Hospital managers should also have a clear rationale for the use of CCTV in patients' living areas. The use of CCTV in communal or especially private areas of hospital wards should be justifiable as a proportionate interference with patients' rights to privacy under ECHR Article 8. We consider that there is a considerable burden on service providers to justify the placing of cameras in bedrooms, seclusion rooms and toilets, particularly if these were linked to recording devices rather than real-time monitors, and that such justification must be applicable to each individual patient subject to CCTV monitoring[199].

2.109 In June 2004, CCTV with 24-hour monitoring by non-clinical security staff was introduced at the John Meyer ward, a PICU then split over two floors at Springfield Hospital, southwest London. This was one a number of measures taken in response to an incident in 2003 where a healthcare assistant who had been left unaided on one floor of the ward was fatally attacked by a patient. In a review of this use of CCTV undertaken a year after installation[200], it was reported that the system did not effectively fulfil its original function of providing a real-time system for the prevention of potentially violent incidents on the ward, but that it was largely used as a retrospective tool to review incidents. The review noted that:

- viewing CCTV footage had become the first resort in such incident reviews, supplanting colleague accounts;
- some staff were less likely to use 'therapeutic touch' as a clinical tool for fear that it might be misconstrued from CCTV footage; and
- some staff were more likely to use physical restraint because they felt confidence that the CCTV footage would evidence their proper conduct.

2.110 The use of security staff rather than ward staff to monitor real-time CCTV footage may have been a factor in its limited effectiveness in preventing incidents: the review noted that ward staff observed incidents that were not picked up by security staff (so that no alert had been given), whilst security staff created some 'false alarms' by reacting to behaviour that clinical staff would have tolerated.

2.111 Whilst patients were reported generally to feel safer on the unit in the presence of CCTV, there was an increase in non-compliance with staff from some patients, with patients suffering from paranoia being a particular management issue. The experience of the John Meyer ward would appear to suggest that monitored CCTV is a poor-value but high-cost intervention to improve safety in psychiatric units, and will not necessarily resolve problems caused by blind-spots and other dangerous aspects of ward design. More effective measures include providing staff with radios; training; and the reprovision of units where there are structural obstacles to patient and staff safety.

---

[199] For further discussion on the use of CCTV, see MHAC (2005) *ibid*.

[200] South West London & St George's Mental Health NHS Trust (2005) *Review of CCTV use on John Meyer Ward*. Trust board meeting paper, 28 July 2005.

Restrictions on communication

Telephones

2.112 Throughout March, April and May 2006, the MHAC asked patients that it met with a series of questions relating to access to, and privacy in using telephones. We collected responses from 425 patients, the results of which are set out at figure 14 below.

2.113 Of the 425 patients that we met with, 73 (17%) claimed that they had no access to a free-of-charge telephone to call either their solicitor or the MHAC. Of those who had such access, 119 (28%) claimed that they could not use the telephone in private. In many cases, this is because the telephone made available for patient use is the ward telephone in the nurses' office, so that patients might have to use it with staff working in the room, even if they wished to speak with their solicitor or the MHAC. In some cases, staff would insist on remaining in the office to ensure the privacy of patient records held there, even though this prevented patients from having privacy to make their call. Of the 145 patients (34%) who reported restricted access to a telephone, many explained that this was because it was in the nurses' office. Such restrictions might be because patients had to wait until staff were not using the phone, or the office was not busy, or handover times had ended. A number of patients explained that their ward rules time-limited any call made on the office telephone (in one case, for example, all calls to solicitors on the office telephone were restricted to five minutes' duration). Some patients reported better arrangements, with cordless handsets available from the nurses' office so that calls could be taken elsewhere in the ward, although even in such cases patients expressed concerns over privacy.

2.114 Most patients (84%) were aware of a payphone either on the ward (77%) or nearby (7%). For some patients, this was their only means of speaking to their solicitor, although in most of these cases patients reported that staff would telephone the solicitor and arrange for him or her to ring in on the payphone to speak with the patient. Such systems were clearly felt to be cumbersome by the patients interviewed, who expressed concerns that the payphone did not always audibly ring (and that calls had been missed as a result) or that staff might 'forget' to call solicitors. Some of these impressions may result from solicitors being unavailable to call back at the time that staff members make contact, leaving staff with no option but to leave a message.

2.115 Several patients reported that they used their own mobile telephones to contact both family and solicitors, given the inconvenience and lack of privacy in using ward-based telephones. The cost of this was remarked upon by some of the patients reporting the use of their own mobile telephones. By contrast, Broadmoor Hospital's telephone system has the MHAC's telephone number programmed to be available with neither restriction nor cost to patients.

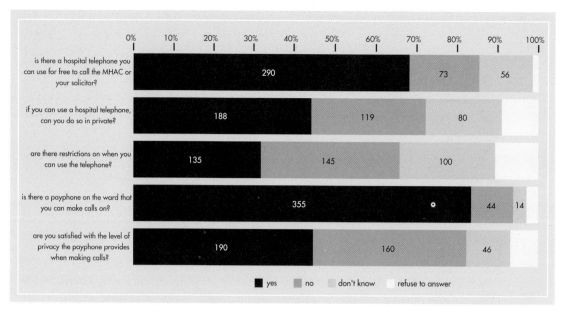

Fig 14: Responses of 425 patients met with on MHAC visits to a structured questionnaire on access to and privacy in using telephones

Data source: MHAC data

Mobile telephones

2.116 In our Tenth Biennial Report[201] we noted the results of our 2001 survey of a third of all detaining hospitals regarding patient's access to their mobile telephones. Although 84% of the services that we surveyed reported having no policy on the matter, over half (54%) reported operating restrictions on patients' access to mobile telephones. We suggested then that hospitals should have policies on the use of mobile telephones, based upon an assumption of unfettered access (at least in units not within the secure sector), modified in accordance with clinical risk assessments. In that report we reflected the common assumption that wards within general hospitals may have widespread restrictions on the use of mobile telephones to protect sensitive hospital equipment on the site. It has since been clarified that such restrictions need only apply within the immediate proximity (i.e. 2 metres) of such equipment[202].

2.117 Some acute wards have more recently imposed bans on all mobile telephones, on the basis that their digital camera facilities could be misused to record and transmit inappropriate images of patients. Indeed, we have witnessed the taking of such images of a female patient when she was washing, albeit by a (male) member of staff, whom we reported to hospital managers. The Department of Health has recognised the risk to patient confidentiality of such digital technology, and suggested that hospitals have a duty to take action to protect

---

[201] MHAC (2003) *Tenth Biennial Report 2001-2003: Placed Amongst Strangers,* para 11.67 *et seq.*

[202] Department of Health (2007) *Using mobile phones in NHS hospitals.* Best practice guidance, May 2007, page 4.

patients' ECHR Article 8 rights to privacy, but it does not advocate a hospital-wide ban[203]. Unless there are reasons for restricting the use of mobile telephones on more general security grounds (as there might be in secure facilities), mental health services should seek to comply with the Department of Health's best practice guidance and provide areas within the hospital where mobile telephone use is permitted, and clearly signpost areas where it is not. In this way hospitals can protect patients from unwarranted intrusion through the use of camera facilities, and also try to contain the disruption of mobile telephone use (including noisy ring-tones and inbuilt music players) away from the immediate ward environment.

Access to the internet

2.118 Many detained patients express a wish to access the internet whilst in hospital, although this is often unavailable. Internet access can provide leisure and education opportunities for patients (on more than one occasion in this period we have met with long-stay patients who wish to undertake Open University courses), and can play such a significant part in patients' lives outside hospital that its unavailability may appear to be a privation[204]. Many people now use e-mail to keep in contact with friends and family. Only in the High Security Hospitals is there an outright ban on internet access. We encourage all other hospitals to consider ways in which patients might be provided with internet access, and recommend that all long-stay units should have an IT facility with more than one terminal for general computing and internet access, available to any patient for whom such access is not a security problem.

2.119 Whilst supervised access to the internet can be a useful and purposeful activity in the often barren environment of psychiatric hospitals, unrestricted access in certain contexts has certain risks. We have heard of one training group in a medium secure unit being shown the workings of internet search engines, which one patient then used to look up the index offence of another who had, until that time, kept this a secret from other patients.

Drug misuse on psychiatric wards

2.120 Some services that we visit struggle with a major problem of illegal drug use amongst patients. In one ward in London in the summer of 2007, all six patients interviewed by a visiting Commissioner stated that they had continuing access to illegal drugs. It was clear from the interviews that drug misuse had been a major element in the problems leading to many of these patient's readmissions to inpatient care, and yet one patient stated that it was difficult to stay away from drugs on the ward. Staff recognised the serious drugs problems on the ward, but were not confident about their rights to search patients and visitors, and uncertain of what they might expect from the police.

---

[203] ibid., page 10.

[204] Mark Ellerby (2006) contribution to Viewpoint page, *Mental Health Today*, November 2006.

2.121 In our Tenth Biennial Report we noted that some psychiatric services were using drug dogs to try to address the use of illicit drugs on wards[205]. From January to June 2006 Camden and Islington Mental Health and Social Care NHS Trust conducted an evaluated pilot study on the use of drug dogs in mental health units at St Pancras Hospital and Highgate unit[206]. Although the study reported hostility to the pilot from some patients at the start of the study, and some ambivalence during the pilot itself, overall the perception of patients and others around the issue of drug use on the wards showed a marked improvement, and during the course of the project service users spoke of wishing to have "drug-free wards" where their treatment would be in an environment free of illicit drug use.

2.122 In the course of the pilot, sixteen searches were undertaken, resulting in seizures of just two cannabis cigarettes and two crack pipes, but the effects of such searches (combined with the use of drug testing kits towards the end of the study) appear to be significant in terms of patient experience. The percentage of patients who felt that they had been affected by the use of illicit drugs reduced by from 48% before the pilot to 21% after it had finished. There were falls in the numbers of patients who reported witnessing drug use; being offered or using illicit drugs; being victims of aggression; and feeling that such aggression was due to the influence of drugs. There was, however, an increase in *recorded* incidents involving drug misuse (quite possibly as a result of heightened staff vigilance). At the end of the pilot 58% of people reported feeling safe in the units, whereas 48% felt safe prior to the study. The Trust acknowledged that this is still not good enough, but it does indicate progress and we recognise that illicit drug use is only one of many causes of patient insecurity in mental health units.

2.123 As a result of the pilot study, the Trust will continue to seek to bring drug dogs on to wards in response to intelligence that problems with illicit drugs exist[207]. We are pleased that the Trust will target searches in this way, rather than using them a general preventative measure: this both targets resources and avoids making discriminatory assumptions about people in psychiatric care, which was one concern raised by a patient representative in the pilot study. We are also pleased to see that the Trust undertook a race equality impact assessment on its pilot, and will specifically address race equality issues in its training. Although no formal complaints were made during the pilot, two Muslim patients remarked that the dogs were unclean according to their beliefs. Staff ensured that all bedding was replaced after the search had passed through these patients' rooms

---

[205] MHAC (2003) *Tenth Biennial Report 2001-2003: Placed Amongst Strangers*, para 11.51

[206] Contact Mr Kuruvilla Punnamkuzhy, Highgate Mental Health Centre, London N19 5NX, tel: 020 7561 4070. kuruvilla.punnamkuzhy@candi.nhs.uk

[207] In the immediate aftermath of the pilot study (and in the wake of the July 2006 London tube bombings), the Metropolitan Police Service dog section had been unable to assist with further searches due to the increased demands of anti-terrorist activity on the service. However, we understand that the MPS dogs are now once again working at the Trust. The Trust had looked into contracting a private company to undertake searches with dogs, although the costs of this (which could be around £500 per visit) would be likely to limit the extendibility of the pilot within the Trust and to other parts of the mental health service.

2.124 Although the pilot study in Camden and Islington some positive results, there remain some ethical and practical concerns over the use of sniffer dogs. If a dog is allowed to roam freely through a populated ward, it would be practically difficult to comply with the Code of Practice requirement that patient's permission is at least sought before any search takes place[208]. There is some danger of false positives in identifying patients who have been using drugs, as a dog may detect the smell of cannabis on a patient who has been where others have been smoking the drug[209] (and this may well have been in the inpatient unit itself). A positive identification, whether correct or not, may well take place in view of other patients, leading to unfair stigmatisation or distress. Perhaps most importantly, the use of drug dog searches should not supplant good nursing practice in observing patients and developing appropriate therapeutic relationships that should enable patients to discuss drug-use issues openly, and staff to establish drug control methods based upon a hierarchical model starting with patient self-reporting and patient contracts, but also involving urine screening and therapeutic interventions such as brief therapy and joint working with dual-diagnosis services[210]. It is also important that nursing staff remain vigilant to the potential for misuse of prescribed or non-prescribed medication that would not be detected by sniffer dogs, whether through trafficking, or swapping medications, or self-medicating with non-prescribed medications, or hoarding medication for possible suicide attempts[211].

Seclusion and restraint

2.125 We accept that psychiatric services will in many instances have no option but to resort to the physical restraint and/or seclusion of patients to prevent harm to self or to other people. Research by Professor Len Bowers has shown that patients on acute wards found restraint, seclusion and coerced intra-muscular medication to be the least acceptable methods of dealing with self-harming behaviour[212]. The study found that three measures could lead to lower rates of such behaviour: increase the use of special observation; ensure that there is a good programme of patient activities; and increase the numbers of qualified nursing

---

[208] *MHA Code of Practice*, para 25.4. See also Nash M J (2005) 'Who let the dogs in? The use of drug sniffer dogs in mental health settings'. *Journal of Psychiatric and Mental Health Nursing* **12**, 745-749, from which we have drawn many of the concerns expressed in this paragraph.

[209] Nash M J (2005) *ibid.*, p.746.

[210] *ibid.*, p.748.

[211] *ibid.*

[212] Bowers L, Whittington R, Nolan P, Parkin D, Curtis S, Bhui K, Hackney D, Allan T, Simpson A & Flood C (2006) The City 128 Study of Observation and Outcomes on Acute Psychiatric Wards. Report to the NHS SDO Programme, December 2006.

staff[213]. Services with high incidences of restraint and/or seclusion should look carefully at their clinical practice, staffing levels, patient mix and ward environment for improvements that could reduce patient frustration and distress.

Restraint

2.126   The following example shows clearly how one ward's physical environment, patient mix and staffing establishment appeared to create serious management problems that were being addressed by restraint, but which exacerbated the negative effects of restraint on the general ward population:

> There appears to be a diverse mix of patients on the ward at the moment. Patients expressed concerns around bullying and intimidation and staff talked about the challenges of keeping patients safe. This is made more difficult by ... patients likely to engage in grooming behaviour and patients vulnerable to that behaviour on the ward. Staff report high levels of overt grooming behaviour taking place; one man with challenging behaviour is having to be regularly restrained owing to the difficulties of trying to manage him within the wider patient group; layout of the building means that when restraint is taking place that part of the ward is closed off. Patients can then find themselves stranded in a room until the incident is over; both staff and patients commented that staffing levels do not seem to be adequate to manage the ward.

Cumbria and Lancashire Commission visiting area, December 2006

2.127   The practice of restraint is now subject to National Institute of Clinical Excellence (NICE) guidance[214], which should be available to and used by all services. The guidance stipulates that resuscitation training (and a defibrillator) must be in place where rapid tranquilisation is used, that a crash bag must be available within three minutes of a restraint situation, and that a doctor should be on scene within 30 minutes of being called[215]. In our Eleventh report we noted that many services are unable to meet either the Bennett inquiry's recommendation of having a doctor available within 20 minutes of being called, or the NICE requirement for a doctor's attendance within 30 minutes[216].

2.128   The very real dangers of physical restraint were highlighted again during this reporting period, first by the findings of the coroner's court into the death in 2003 of Andrew Jordan[217], and also by the report of the inquiry into the 2004 death of Geoffrey Hodgkins[218]:

---

[213] ibid., p.6. See also 'Warning over self-harm by mental health patients' *The Guardian*, 14 May 2007.

[214] NICE (2005) *Violence: the short-term management of disturbed / violent behaviour in inpatient psychiatric settings and emergency departments.* Clinical Guidelines, 25 February 2005.

[215] On NICE and NIMHE guidance, see MHAC (2006) *Eleventh Biennial Report 2003-2005: In Place of Fear?* para 4.211, 4.217-8 and fig 85, p.303.

[216] MHAC (2006) *Eleventh Biennial Report 2003-2005: In Place of Fear?* para 2.33 -2.39.

- Andrew Jordan was 28 years old, 6ft tall, originally from Guyana, and had a history of schizophrenic illness. He was restrained face-down for more than 10 minutes in his own house during a Mental Health Act assessment, with his knees on the floor but his upper body pressed down onto a sofa, then carried (again face-down) strapped to a trolley-bed to an ambulance. He died (seemingly still in a face-down position) in the ambulance, having received little or no medical intervention that the jury considered might have saved his life. The ambulance crew appeared to have no meaningful knowledge of the dangers of positional asphyxia. The jury returned a lengthy narrative verdict which suggested that, had he been raised from the kneeling position in his house, or given oxygen in the ambulance, the death might have been avoided.

- Geoffrey Hodgkins was a 37 year old white male with a history of paranoid schizophrenia who had been in hospital for 18 years, excepting limited time spent in the community with his family. On the day of the restraint incident that led to his death he had been detained under s.3, partly in response to a restraint episode lasting 2½ hours in the previous week. The ward where he was detained experienced four separate episodes of restraint during the afternoon shift (none involving Mr Hodgkins) requiring assistance from security guards and staff from other wards. It had, as the inquiry report put it, been a "really busy" afternoon shift. At around 8 p.m. Mr Hodgkins threw a glass cup at another patient, and went into the (otherwise empty) 'family room' holding a glass and a fork. Staff locked him in the room and called for help. A discussion on how to restrain Mr Hodgkins took place outside of the room, and then eight nurses and security guards entered the room, carrying a quilt to throw over him and towels to place under him and around themselves, as he was known to spit and bite whilst being restrained. No attempt to talk to or reason with Mr Hogkinson appears to have been made at any point. He was held face down for about 25 to 30 minutes and given an injection of haloperidol and lorazepam. He stopped breathing whilst under this restraint. Attempts were made at resuscitation and he was transferred to the local A&E department by ambulance, arriving just before 9.30 that evening. His family arrived at the hospital in the early hours of the next morning, and at 8.30 a.m. he was declared dead and his life-support machine turned off.

---

[217] 'Prone to fatal error' *The Guardian*, 8 February 2006

[218] Hampshire and Isle of Wight Strategic Health Authority (2006) *Independent Mental Health Inquiry into the Care and Treatment received by the late Geoffrey Hodgkins*, September 2006

2.129 Geoffrey Hodgkins' death occurred after the David Bennett inquiry had recommended that "under no circumstances should any patient be restrained in a prone position for any longer than three minutes"[219], and indeed his care plan (which the inquiry recognised as a generic document based upon a template and unmodified to meet his needs[220]) seems to have stipulated that after three minutes of prone restraint he must be raised to a kneeling position[221]. It is clear, however, that this plan had not previously been followed and was not followed on the night of his death, although the departure from the care plan was neither noted nor was any record made of discussions of an alternative care plan made. The inquiry noted with concern that the existence of this care-plan that stipulated actions not reflected in practice created a false sense of compliance with best practice[222]. This underlines that it is not enough to check that a service has the correct policies in place: both service managers and external regulatory or monitoring bodies must try to ascertain whether the policies are followed in practice. We believe that a key component of such checking should be private interviews with patients: neither hospital managers nor, especially, external monitoring bodies should be satisfied with self-assessment by those implementing policies or by 'paper' checks.

2.130 Although we are disappointed that the Department of Health has refused to endorse a time limit for face-down restraint, as we believe that this would send a clear signal to services over the dangers of positional asphyxiation, we do recognise that such a time limit would be little more than a guideline and is not therefore the most important aspect of safe restraint. It *is* vital, however, that services fully implement the existing NICE guidelines when using physical restraint, particularly in having a member of staff at the patient's head who co-ordinates the restraint throughout its duration; monitors breathing and vital signs; and ensures that the patient is moved from any prone position as soon as it is possible to do so.

2.131 There have been some positive developments in restraint practice. The NHS Security Management Service has orchestrated a national "Promoting Safer and Therapeutic Services" training initiative, which aims to equip ward staff to act as trainers themselves within their workplace over the identification, de-escalation and safe management of violent incidents[223]. It was stated in December 2006 that, by March 2008, all frontline mental health and learning disability staff will have received training through the trickle-down effect of this scheme, and such training is a mandatory requirement in terms of health and safety commitments[224]. This, however, is mandatory training in non-physical interventions: what is needed next is mandatory training on physical restraint itself.

---

[219] Norfolk, Suffolk and Cambridgeshire Health Authority (2003) *Independent Inquiry into the Death of David Bennett.* December 2003, p.53

[220] Hampshire and Isle of Wight Strategic Health Authority (2006) *op cit.*, para 4.7.5

[221] *ibid.*, para 4.6.1

[222] *ibid.*, para 4.7.6

[223] NHS Security Management Service (2005) *Promoting Safer and Therapeutic Services: implementing the national syllabus in mental health and learning disability services.* October 2005. http://www.cfsms.nhs.uk/doc/psts/psts.implementing.syllabus.pdf

[224] Adam James (2006) 'Proportionate Response' *Mental Health Today,* December 2006, p.10-11

Recommendation 17: Mandatory training should be developed for all mental health and learning disability staff expected to engage in physical restraint interventions to complement the current mandatory training in non-physical interventions.

Seclusion

2.132 We continue to see euphemisms used for seclusion practice, so that patients are in effect secluded but without any of the appropriate safeguards. In the Thames Valley visiting area, for example, we found in May 2006 that one patient was locked in his bedroom at night and also occasionally during the day, without the safeguards of the seclusion procedure in the Code of Practice. Areas of the bedroom presented significant risks to the safety of both the patient and staff caring for him. We wrote to the Trust chief executive about this requesting a review of the patient's care.

2.133 In previous reports we have suggested that confining a patient in a room without adequate sanitary facilities is a potential breach of the ECHR Article 3 prohibition of degrading treatment[225]. In this reporting period we have continued to see disturbing treatment of patients in seclusion in this respect. In a high security hospital, for example, we saw a patient being held in a seclusion room, the en-suite facility of which had been locked off for security reasons. The patient was suffering from diarrhoea, and had not had his used chamber-pot removed and changed. In another hospital, a recently secluded patient, who was also reported to be hepatitis positive, had carried out a 'dirty protest'. The room had not been cleaned thoroughly afterwards, which clearly constituted a general health hazard and could have serious consequences were it used subsequently for the seclusion of any patient. We have seen seclusion rooms similarly left unclean when patients had urinated in them.

2.134 The Code of Practice requires all hospital managers to have written guidelines on seclusion and to monitor and regularly review seclusion practice[226]. We commend the explicit statement of values in the seclusion policy of West London Mental Health Trust, which we feel could be emulated by other services:

> Adherence to this policy will
>
> - Limit the use of seclusion to exceptional circumstances and promote alternative approaches to the care and treatment of disturbed behaviour;
>
> - Ensure that patients' rights are respected and adhered to if seclusion is initiated;
>
> - Set out the proper management and monitoring of the patient whilst in seclusion in order to ensure that his or her safety is paramount, and that accountable decisions are recorded regarding the commencement, supervision and termination of the seclusion process;

---

[225] See MHAC (2006) *Eleventh Biennial Report 2003-2005: In Place of Fear?* para 1.200 on *Napier, re petition for judicial review* [2004] ScotCS 100. On the environment of seclusion rooms, see Curran C *et al* (2005) 'Seclusion: factors to consider when designing and using a seclusion suite in a mental health hospital' *Hospital Development* Jan 05, 19-26. www.hdmagazine.co.uk

[226] *Mental Health Act 1983 Code of Practice*, paras 19.17, 19.23.

- Ensure that when seclusion is used it is terminated at the earliest and safest opportunity;
- Detail the formal responsibilities of all employees from ward level to the Board for the maintenance of appropriate records of the use of seclusion.

2.135 We have seen some excellent examples of such monitoring in practice, including within the high security and independent sector. The National Forensic Audit Group (NFAG), which is a network of professionals from various disciplines within the forensic sector with an interest in service audit who meet to share and discuss findings, has piloted a national audit of collaborating services' seclusion facilities and practice. We look forward to the further development of this project and hope that it may provide lessons or models for application across all services.

Stigma and detention under the 1983 Act

2.136 According to the Department of Health's 2007 survey, public attitudes towards mental illness have generally worsened in recent years. In 2007, more than half of respondents defined a person who is mentally ill as someone who "has to be kept in a psychiatric or mental hospital"; and there was less agreement that there should be more tolerance towards people with mental health problems than there had been in 1994[227]. Younger people were more likely overall to be frightened of the mentally ill, and to not want to live next door to someone who is mentally ill[228]. The Minister has stated that "the attitudes of a significant minority reflect prejudices that should be as unacceptable as racism in a civilised society"[229]. It has been suggested by Mind and the Mental Health Foundation[230] that the better results in surveys in Scotland[231] may reflect Scotland's better funding of anti-stigma campaigns, as well as the very different emphasis placed upon the process of legislative reform in Scotland.

2.137 Within this general trend there are some positive results. For example, fewer people now believe that people with a history of mental health problems should be excluded from public office, or given other responsibilities, with younger people appearing to be especially tolerant in this area[232]. Whilst we believe that government should lead rather than follow public opinion about mental illness, this shows that government would not be pushing against public opinion in combating discrimination relating to public appointments. People occupying positions of responsibility are increasingly open about their use of mental health services, and service users are visible in many other ways. The chief executive of Nottinghamshire Healthcare NHS Trust, for example, is a service user who is open about his experience of being a patient.

[227] National Statistics (2007) *Attitudes to mental illness 2007 report*. June 2007, p.23 & 7 respectively.

[228] *ibid.*, p.15-17

[229] 'Prejudice against people with mental illness rises', *Community Care* 12 July 2007, p.8. The Rt Hon. Ivan Lewis MP quoted.

[230] *ibid.*

[231] Scottish Government Social Research (2007) *Well? What Do You Think? (2006): The Third National Scottish Survey of Public Attitudes to Mental Health, Mental Wellbeing and Mental Health Problems*. Simon Braunholtz, Sara Davidson, Katherine Myant and Dr Rory O'Connor.
http://www.scotland.gov.uk/Resource/Doc/197512/0052833.pdf

[232] National Statistics (2007) *ibid.*, p.11-12

2.138 Failing to respect the human rights of patients who come into contact with the powers of the Mental Health Act may amount to unlawful discrimination, but also creates a cultural lack of respect for the humanity of patients. Behind every diagnosis, and every statistic in this report, is an individual who has a right to be included in the government's drive to give NHS provision a 'personal' focus, and for whom the process of recovery from severe mental illness is likely to involve reconstituting or rediscovering his or her personhood and place in the community. Insofar as public services and structures discriminate against people with severe mental disorder they therefore impede recovery and management of the conditions concerned.

Voting and patients detained under civil powers of the MHA 1983

Traditionally... consumers of psychiatric services have been denied the right to the franchise and other rights associated with the exercise of political choice and influence.

Larry Gostin, 1983[233]

2.139 Disenfranchisement is part of the historical stigmatisation of and discrimination against people with mental disorder. In our last report we discussed and welcomed the changes made in 2000, allowing detained patients to use their hospital address to register to vote[234]. We were, however, critical of the requirement that such votes may only be cast by postal voting or proxy, arguing that there was no reason why the law should prohibit patients from voting in person where they were practicably able to do so (i.e. under leave arrangements). We recommended that this bar to voting in person be lifted.

2.140 We are pleased that the MHAC recommendations were taken up by the Disability Rights Commission and, through the DRC, by Liberal-Democrat peers Lords Rennard and Goodhart. The latter tabled amendments at committee stage reading of the Electoral Administration Act in March 2006, which was received sympathetically by the then Minister Baroness Ashton of Upholland. A government amendment was adopted at report stage.

2.141 The law now allows that detained patients (with the exception of "mental patients who are detained offenders": see chapter 7.64 *et seq* below) may vote by post or proxy or, "in person (where he is granted permission to be absent from the hospital and voting in person does not breach any condition attached to that permission)"[235]. In our view, the qualification of the right to vote in person is designed solely to ensure that leave status alone does not provide a right to attend a polling station when leave has been given for a purpose that precludes this, such as leave for treatment in another hospital, or to appear in court etc; or that the right to vote is not interpreted to override any condition of leave that a patient does not go to a specified geographic area. Clinicians should be able to justify as necessary any such conditions that may restrict a patient's ability to attend a polling station.

---

[233] Larry Gostin (1983) 'the ideology of entitlement: the application of contemporary legal approaches to psychiatry' in Bean P (ed) *Mental Illness; Changes and Trends*, p.23.

[234] MHAC (2006) *Eleventh Biennial Report 2003-2005, In Place of Fear?* paragraph 2.105

[235] Representation of the People Act 2000, schedule 4 para 2(5A), as amended by the Electoral Administration Bill 2006.

Jury service

2.142 Under the Juries Act, a mentally disordered person is excluded from jury service if resident in hospital or a similar institution, or if he or she "regularly attends for treatment by a medical practitioner"[236]. The definition of 'mental disorder' follows that of the Mental Health Act, and has been amended by the Mental Health Act 2007, so that it must now be interpreted as "any disorder or disability of mind". Technically, this change in the law has widened the scope for excluding people from jury service on grounds of mental disorder[237], although government has already accepted that the previous criteria "could be applied very widely, such as covering people with minor depression prescribed medication by their GP"[238].

2.143 It is an uncomfortable irony that the criteria for jury exclusion should be widened as a result of the Mental Health Act amendments, given that many of the other historic exclusions for eligibility for jury service were removed with the passing of the Criminal Justice Act 2003[239], and, more importantly, that government promised in its social exclusion unit report of June 2004 that there would be public consultation on how "to remove removal of unnecessary barriers to community roles such as jury service"[240] by changing the mental health criteria for jury duty[241]. In May 2007, government informed Parliament that it could not give a timetable for such a consultation, and had experienced difficulty in devising criteria "that would allow those mentally disordered persons who are capable of undertaking jury service to serve, while excluding those who are incapable of serving, and yet be clear, easily understood and readily operable in practice".[242] We urge government to give further consideration to this matter and redress the increased discriminatory effect of the 2007 Act.

> **Recommendation 18:** Government should bring forward its consultation on the mental health criteria for jury service to ensure that exclusions are for functional rather than discriminatory reasons.

---

[236] Juries Act 1974, Schedule 1 part 1. A person under guardianship or deemed incapable of managing his or her property and affairs by a judge is also excluded.

[237] Prior to the 2007 Act, the phrase was defined to mean either mental illness, psychopathic disorder, mental impairment or severe mental impairment, rather than simply 'mental disorder' as used in the 1983 Act pre-amendment.

[238] Office of the Deputy Prime Minister (2004) *Mental Health and Social Exclusion. Social Exclusion Unit Report*, June 2004, p.78.

[239] Criminal Justice Act 2003, Schedule 33, s.321.

[240] Office of the Deputy Prime Minister (2004), *ibid.*, p.9.

[241] *ibid.*, p.109.

[242] Hansard HC 21 May 2007, Col 1144W (Mr Sutcliffe).

School governorship, other public appointments and civic duties.

2.144 In our previous reports we have discussed the rules concerning membership of public bodies, particularly with regard to appointment as a school governor[243]. Following our criticism of the rules whereby a person 'liable to be detained' under the Mental Health Act was excluded from such appointment, the school governor regulations were revised (without consultation with us) to specify that it was detention, rather than liability to detention, that triggered the exclusion. Our argument that this does not address the discriminatory aspect of such rules has gone unheeded by government, and no further action has been taken. It seems to us to be profoundly discriminatory that the law requires a person to forfeit his or her appointment as a school governor upon being detained under the Act, even if that detention is of a short duration and that the person returns to the community fully able to resume his or her previous roles and responsibilities. A member of the MHAC's own Service User Reference Panel[244] was forced to resign from her position as a school governor as a result of the revised rules.

2.145 During the passage of the 2007 Act we suggested that the rules regarding Members of Parliament and detention under the Act could be updated to serve as an exemplar of anti-discriminatory practice. We regret that an amendment tabled to have this effect was not accepted by government, and was not pushed to a debate in the house, so that the opportunity was lost. Nevertheless, even without the amendments that we suggested, the rules regarding Members of Parliament and detention under the Act are less discriminatory in effect than those applicable to school governors. Members of Parliament are not required to forfeit their seats immediately upon being detained under the Act, but only if they have been detained (or on leave) for a period of six months. We can see no reason why public appointees such as school governors should be subject to more stringent rules and therefore recommend that the school governor regulations are revised, with civil detention under the Mental Health Act treated no differently to any other hospital admission, and fitness to continue as a school governor decided on whether a person's mental disability prevents them from undertaking the duties of the role.

> **Recommendation 19:** Government should revise the school governor regulations as suggested above, to ensure that exclusions are for functional rather than discriminatory reasons.

---

[243] MHAC (2003) *Tenth Biennial Report 2001-2003: Placed Amongst Strangers,* para 6.34 *et seq*; MHAC (2006) *Eleventh Biennial Report 2003-2005: In Place of Fear?,* para 2.101 *et seq.*

[244] See p.23 for a description of the MHAC service user reference panel.

Patients' benefits

2.146 In our last report we discussed the problems faced by patients subject to 'hospital-downrating' of their state benefits after a certain period in hospital, and looked forward to the implementation of a government announcement that it would change the benefits rules and end the curtailment of benefits in these circumstances[245]. We were pleased to see the abolition of hospital downrating from the 10 April 2006 for most patients, but extremely disappointed to learn of the government's decision not to extend this to those detained under s.45A and some patients detained under s.47. This decision introduced a degree of arbitrary discrimination amongst forensic patients that was understandably experienced as unfair by those who lost all benefit-related income at a time when many patients saw their income rise significantly. It also created some managerial difficulties for forensic hospital services and has passed an admittedly small economic burden from the Department of Social Security to the Department of Health. We discuss this further at chapter 7.56 *et seq* below.

Section 136 and criminal records

2.147 We understand that the use of s.136 of the Act (see chapter 4.58) may be disclosed through enhanced Criminal Records Bureau checks. In one reported case[246], such disclosure took place when a young student, whose symptoms of schizophrenia were in complete remission three years after a breakdown, applied for a holiday job as a gardener at a local rest home. He was understandably concerned that, having returned to his studies, such disclosure would lead to discrimination against him both in student placements and eventual employment prospects. Although the local chief constable had the discretion to remove the information from the disclosure form, he declined to do so on the grounds that "the details were factual at the time".

2.148 Persons may be detained by a policeman under s.136 on the grounds that they are in a public place and "in immediate need of care or control". It is not a requirement that the person should be engaged in any activity that is potentially unlawful, or even dangerous, even though the detention is technically an 'arrest' under the Police and Criminal Evidence Act. In previous reports we have noted the (quite legitimate) use of this section to take into protective custody persons who are wandering and seemingly confused.

2.149 The correspondent who raised the above case in the pages of the *Psychiatric Bulletin*, Dr Lars Hansen, viewed the recording of s.136 incidents for the purpose of Criminal Records Bureau checks as unnecessary and discriminating[247]. We agree. If the decision whether to remove such incidents from records *must* be left to the discretion of Chief Constables (and we would prefer a ruling that s.136 should never count as a criminal record in any

---

[245] See MHAC (2006) *Eleventh Biennial Report 2003-2005, In Place of Fear?* para 2.98.

[246] Hansen L (2007) 'Legislative discrimination against people with mental health problems' (correspondence) *Psychiatric Bulletin* **31**: 33.

[247] *ibid.*

circumstances), we would like to see national guidance provided that would suggest a presumption of removal, only to be overturned in exceptional circumstances. If the police, having brought a person in under s.136, believe (after the assessment of that person under the Act has been completed) that something of that person's behaviour was of a criminal nature deserving sanction, then they should charge or caution that person under criminal justice powers.

> **Recommendation 20:** National guidance should instil a presumption that s.136 incidents are not to be recorded as a police 'criminal' record.

Section 139 and access to the courts

2.150   Section 139 of the 1983 Act prevents any criminal or civil proceedings (other than those covered by s.127) from being brought against any person (with the exceptions discussed below) in relation to their exercise of powers and duties under the Act without the permission of the High Court or Director of Public Prosecutions, and that no such action can succeed unless the court is satisfied of bad faith or lack of reasonable care in the actions of the person proceeded against[248].

2.151   In July 2007 the House of Lords gave its judgment[249] in the case of Mr Seal, a litigant in person who wished to claim for damages against false imprisonment after having been detained under s.136 by South Wales police (see chapter 4.63 below). The claim was made close to the applicable six-year limitation period[250], but without the leave of the High Court. It is unlikely that Mr Seal knew of the requirement for such leave, but without it his case had been determined to be invalid. The House of Lords was asked whether s.139 should be interpreted in this way, to nullify any claim made without permission, or whether the proceedings could be given legitimacy by a successful application for permission after they have commenced, where the requirement for such permission was not known at the time of the commencement. Their Lordships decided by a majority of three to two that the section should be interpreted so as to nullify any case brought without permission, so depriving Mr Seal of his access to the courts in this case.

2.152   Although the Department of Health proposed the abolition of s.139 in its draft Mental Health Bill of 2004[251], the 'modernising' amendments of the Mental Health Bill 2007 did not address its powers in any respect. We regret this, especially as the 2007 Act was passed in the wake of this division amongst the Law Lords as to the proper interpretation of the section, and a call from one Law Lord that it be repealed[252].

---

[248]   For a detailed and critical discussion of access to the law for detained patients, see Bartlett P & Sandland R (2007) *Mental Health Law Policy and Practice,* 3rd edition, Oxford University Press, chapter 12.

[249]   *Seal v Chief Constable of South Wales Police* [2007] UKHL 31.

[250]   See s.2, Limitation Act 1980.

[251]   Department of Health (2004) *Draft Mental Health Bill* Cm 6305-1, clause 298.

[252]   *Seal v Chief Constable of South Wales Police,* para 60 (Baroness Hale of Richmond).

2.153 The blanket restriction on access to the courts set by s.139 does not apply to potential litigation against the Secretary of State or NHS authorities (including Special Health Authorities such as the MHAC). These exemptions from the scope of s.139 were introduced in government amendments at a late stage of Parliament's reading of the bill that led to the Mental Health Act 1983: a process that has been described critically by David Hewitt[253]. The amendments anticipated – incorrectly, as it happened – the success of a human rights-based legal challenge against the requirement upon a Broadmoor patient to obtain leave to litigate against his health authority and the Secretary of State in respect of his transfer delay[254]. In the event, the European Commission of Human Rights and the ECtHR ruled that there was no breach of the ECHR in the 1959 Act's provisions[255], but by this time the legislative patch that had been applied to address the purported incompatibility had been enacted. Hewitt suggests that the scope of the exclusions was therefore a contingent response to a legal challenge of the day, rather than a more considered policy determination, and points to the anomaly that s.139 protects social services authorities but not NHS Trusts in relation to the exercise of powers of detention under the Act[256].

2.154 The rationale behind such restrictions on access to the courts was expressed by Lord Simon in *Pountney v Griffiths*:

> Patients under the Mental Health Act may generally be inherently likely to harass those concerned with them by groundless charges and litigation[257]

This has been criticised as little more than prejudice[258], and it remains true today that there is no evidence that litigants who are aggrieved over the use of Mental Health Act powers are any more likely to be vexatious than any other litigants. Indeed, a recent study of the Court of Appeal suggested that the litigant in person[259] (whatever his or her cause) characteristically "finds it difficult to apply objectivity to legal and factual reality"[260], although Lord Justice Sedley has argued that this "undifferentiated and hostile" assertion cannot be backed up with evidence[261].

---

[253] See Hewitt D (2000) 'Something less than ready access to the courts: section 139 & local authorities.' *Journal of Mental Health Law*, 73-82.

[254] Under s.141 of the Mental Health Act 1959, the immediate forerunner of s.139 in the 1983 Act. The challenge claimed a breach of Articles 5(4) and 6(1) of the ECHR.

[255] *Ashingdane v United Kingdom* (1985) 7 EHRR 528

[256] Hewitt D (2000) *ibid.*, p. 79-80

[257] *Pountney v Griffiths* [1975] 3 W.L.R. 140, p.141. Bartlett P & Sandland R (op cit., n.248, p.579) provide a "shocking" quotation from Lord Denning's 1957 judgment in *Richardson v London County Council* to argue the paternalistic basis of the law at s.139, where Denning LJ compares the mentally disordered to children or dumb animals who resent being given medicine for their own good, and states that as such they "are apt to turn round and claw and scratch the hand that gives it".

[258] See, for example, Gostin (1975) *A Human Condition: The Mental Health Act from 1959 to 1975*. Vol 1. Mind publications, London.

[259] i.e. a litigant who has no qualified legal representation.

[260] Drewry G, Blom-Cooper L, Blake C (2007) *The Court of Appeal*. London: Hart, p.134.

[261] Sedley S (2007) 'Second Time Around', *London Review of Books*, 6 September 2007, 14-15.

2.155 Staff at the MHAC regularly field persistent and even aggressive approaches from a limited number of persons who believe, sometimes on what appears to be clearly delusional bases, that they have been mistreated or denied human rights, and who demand that the MHAC undertakes an investigation or other action. More than one ex-detainee in this reporting period has demanded that the MHAC arranges their medical examination (in one case in an open court) to disprove their continuing diagnoses, and in a number of examples a refusal to concede to such wishes has been interpreted as incompetence or collusion with persecution. Some contacts extend over a number of years, and take up considerable staff time. However, despite the fact that the MHAC is excluded from the protections of s.139, only once in the last decade at least has a detainee or ex-detainee filed a claim with a court that has required any defensive action on our part (see below)[262]. Whilst the MHAC is not, perhaps, the most likely body to attract litigious action from persons who are aggrieved at their treatment under Mental Health Act powers, this fact (and our experience of dealing with the claim itself) may be helpful to future discussion of the appropriateness of the law in this area.

2.156 At the end of this reporting period the MHAC was served with a county court claim for an unspecified amount of damages, on grounds that it had failed in a legal duty to protect the claimant from allegations that he was suffering from a mental disorder and from perceived harassment from the psychiatric profession subsequent to discharge from detention under the Act. This was one of eleven claims lodged by a litigant in person, all seeking damages for alleged abuses of human rights from public authorities. Some of these bodies (such as the police and Royal College of Psychiatrists) had the protection of s.139, whilst others (such as NHS authorities and the MHAC) did not. After two months (and after staff time had been taken up in contacting the court for advice and filing a defence), the claim was struck out as disclosing no reasonable cause of action. We understand from the claimant that all eleven claims were struck out, and doubt that the 'protection' of s.139 made significant material difference to bodies to whom it applied.

---

[262] We refer only to criminal or civil litigation as covered under s.139 of the Act: particularly in its role of indemnifier of Second Opinion Doctors appointed by the MHAC for the purposes of the Act, the MHAC has been involved in a number of judicial review cases over its existence: see MHAC (2003) *Tenth Biennial Report 2001-2003: Placed Amongst Strangers*, para 3.32 *et seq.*

3

The Mental Health Act in practice: admission and population data

Admissions under the 1983 Act

3.1   After six years of stability, the number of patients admitted from the community to hospital under civil powers of the 1983 Act in England rose slightly in 2004/05 and 2005/06 to a total of 25,054 and 25,618 respectively (figure 15). The number of informal patients detained under the Act's powers was 18,173 in 2004/05 and 18,202 in 2005/06. The total number of times that the Act was invoked in England, according to this data, stood at 44,891 in 2004/05 and 45,484 in 2005/6.

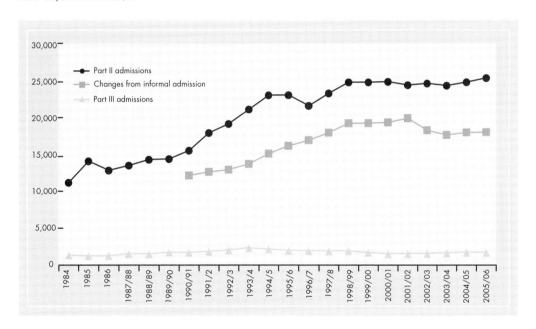

Fig 15: MHA admission trends, England, 1984 – 2005/06

Data source: Department of Health / Information Centre statistical bulletins
"Inpatients detained under the Mental Health Act 1983 and other legislation" 1986 - 2007

3.2   Although this means that more patients than ever before were admitted to hospital under civil powers in 2005/06, the cumulative use of the Act remains slightly below the peak years of 1998/9 (46,298) and 2001/02 (46,258).

3.3 The growth in admissions for civil patients (i.e. under part II of the Act) has not been matched by a similar rise in the use of part III powers. This may indicate that at least some of the apparent growth in the use of civil powers can be accounted for by re-admissions of civil patients, given the trend towards short but repeated admissions of civil patients (a trend that obviously does not extend to patients sent to hospital under criminal justice powers). Nevertheless, the fact that part III admissions peaked between the years 1991/92 and 1998/99 should be of concern given the massive rise in the prison population over the last two decades (see chapter 7.2 below).

The gender mix of the detained population

3.4 In both England and Wales, women patients account for roughly half of all informal inpatients, but only around one third of the resident detained population. Just under 5,000 women were detained in hospital in 2006. The gender split of detained patients resident in English hospitals is shown at figure 16 below (for data on Wales, see figure 59, chapter 5.5 below).

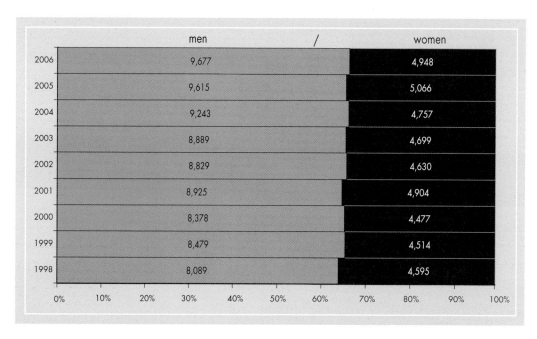

Fig 16: Male and female resident patients detained under the MHA, all hospitals, England 1998 to 2006

Data source: as for fig 15

3.5 Admission rates over the last decade in both England and Wales show a roughly even split between male and female patients, although at the end of the 1980s there were slightly more women than men admitted under the Act (figure 17 below).

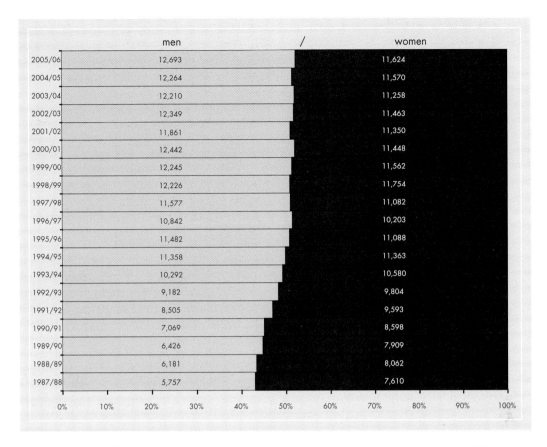

	men		women
2005/06	12,693		11,624
2004/05	12,264		11,570
2003/04	12,210		11,258
2002/03	12,349		11,463
2001/02	11,861		11,350
2000/01	12,442		11,448
1999/00	12,245		11,562
1998/99	12,226		11,754
1997/98	11,577		11,082
1996/97	10,842		10,203
1995/96	11,482		11,088
1994/95	11,358		11,363
1993/94	10,292		10,580
1992/93	9,182		9,804
1991/92	8,505		9,593
1990/91	7,069		8,598
1989/90	6,426		7,909
1988/89	6,181		8,062
1987/88	5,757		7,610

Fig 17: Male and female admissions under Part II of the MHA, all hospitals, England, 1987/88 to 2005/06

Data source: as for fig 15

Age of patients

3.6 Patients who are detained under the Mental Health Act show a distinct age profile to those who are resident informally. At figure 18 below, we show the age on admission to hospital of patients reported to the 2006 *Count Me In* Census, and at figure 19 the age of such patients on the census day itself. Both graphs show that detained patients are younger on average than informal patients. There are two distinct 'peaks' in the age ranges of informal patients in both graphs, indicating highest rates of admission and hospitalisation in patients aged between 30 and 45 years of age, and in those aged over 65 years. For detained patients, there is no second 'peak' in admissions of elderly patients.

3.7 At figures 25 (paragraph 3.18), 32 (paragraph 3.41) and 39 (paragraph 3.55) respectively we show data on the age ranges of patients with mental illness, learning disability and personality disorder.

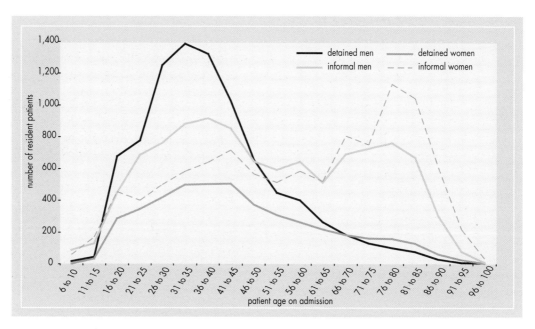

Fig 18: Distribution of detained and informal patients by age on admission to hospital and gender, all hospitals, England and Wales, 31 March 2006

Source: *Count Me In* census 2006

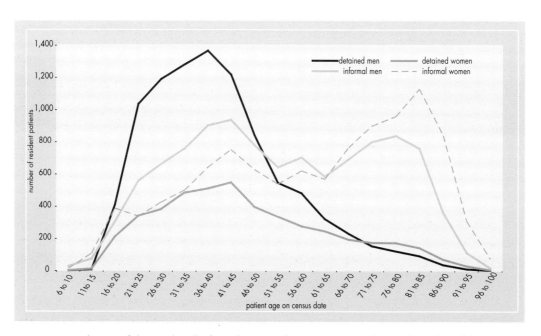

Fig 19: Distribution of detained and informal patients by age at census date and gender, all hospitals, England and Wales, 31 March 2006

Source: *Count Me In* census 2006

Length of hospital stays

3.8   The length of hospital stay for patients who were detained under the main civil and criminal justice sections of the Act at the time of the 2006 census is shown at figures 20 and 21 below.

			Length of hospital stay in 5 year bands									Total
			0-5 years	6-10 years	11-15 years	16-20 years	21-25 years	26-30 years	31-35 years	36-40 years	41 + years	
Legal status (at census date)	section 2	Count	1,123	4	4	2	1	0	1	1	4	1,140
		% within legal status	98.5%	0.4%	0.4%	0.2%	0.1%	-	0.1%	0.1%	0.4%	100%
	section 3	Count	8,213	289	84	39	17	11	8	1	7	8,669
		% within legal status	94.7%	3.3%	1.0%	0.4%	0.2%	0.1%	0.1%	0.0%	0.1%	100%
	section 37	Count	898	72	18	9	5	2	0	0	0	1,004
		% within legal status	89.4%	7.2%	1.8%	0.9%	0.5%	0.2%	-	-	-	100%
	section 37/41	Count	2,004	235	76	36	21	10	5	0	0	2,387
		% within legal status	84.0%	9.8%	3.2%	1.5%	0.9%	0.4%	0.2%	-	-	100%
	section 47	Count	59	0	0	0	2	0	1	0	0	62
		% within legal status	95.2%	-	-	-	3.2%	-	1.6%	-	-	100%
	section 47/49	Count	491	36	15	7	4	0	0	0	0	553
		% within legal status	88.8%	6.5%	2.7%	1.3%	.7%	-	-	-	-	100%
	Total	Count	12,788	636	197	93	50	23	15	2	11	13,815
		% within all legal status	92.6%	4.6%	1.4%	0.7%	0.4%	0.2%	0.1%	0.0%	0.1%	100%

Fig 20: Length of hospital stay for categories of detained patients on the 31 March 2006

Source: *Count Me In* census 2006

3.9   'Length of hospital stay' does not necessarily equate with length of detention under the section of the Act shown, but includes any period spent as an informal inpatient, or subject to another section of the Act, if such a period was a part of a continuous inpatient stay[263] . It is notable, for example, that the mean length of stay for section 2 patients[264] is nearly six months (figure 22), because of a small number of long-stay patients who were subject to that legal power on the census day. In an attempt to avoid any distorting effects of the extreme outlying cases, we also show at figure 22 the "5% trimmed mean" (an average taken from data shorn of the highest and lowest 5% of returns), and the median length of stay. The 5% trimmed mean length of stay for s.2 patients is two weeks; for s.3 patients[265] it is one year. The median length of stay for s.2 patients is three weeks; it is five months for s.3 patients.

---

[263] For example, 'admission' for a s.3 patient does not necessarily mean admission to hospital under s.3, but could also include patients admitted informally, or under s.2 or a holding power of the 1983 Act.

[264] Section 2 allows for detention for assessment and treatment of mental disorder for up to 28 days.

[265] Section 3 allows for the detention for treatment of mental disorder for up to six months, renewable for another six months and then renewable annually.

3.10 Of course, many s.3 patients have much shorter hospital stays. At figure 21 we show the distribution of s.3 patients who had been in hospital for less than a year according to the number of weeks since their admission. One-third of these s.3 patients had been in hospital for six weeks or less, and half for twelve weeks or less.

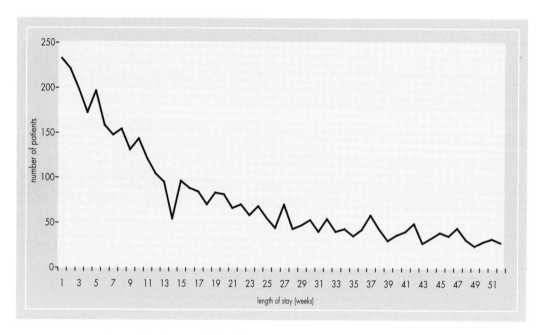

Fig 21: Patients detained under s.3 who had been in hospital for less than one year on the 31 March 2006, by number of weeks from hospital admission. All hospitals, England and Wales

Source: *Count Me In* census 2006

		Legal status (at census date)					
		section 2	section 3	section 37	section 37/41	section 47	section 47/49
Length of stay	mean (weeks)	23.64	75.38	134.91	192.22	137.39	150.51
	5% trimmed mean (weeks)	3.03	48.40	107.54	158.94	77.88	121.34
	median (weeks)	2.00	21.00	71.00	119.00	65.00	89.00
	maximum (weeks) (to nearest ½ year)	2,413.00 (46½ yrs)	3,661.00 (70½ yrs)	1,400.00 (27 yrs)	1,858.00 (35½ yrs)	1,647.00 (31½ yrs)	1,291.00 (25 yrs)

Fig 22: Mean and median lengths of hospital stay for patients detained under sections 2, 3, 37 or 47 on the 31 March 2006

Source: *Count Me In* census 2006

3.11 It is notable that the longest hospital stay – of more than 70 years - was recorded for a patient detained under the civil power of s.3. This is more than twice the longest time spent in hospital by any patients detained after conviction of an offence, whether by court order (ss.37, 37/41) or after having been transferred from prison (ss.47, 47/49).

3.12   Patients who had been sent to hospital by the courts after conviction had been there, on average, for between 2 and 2½ years if they were unrestricted, and between 3 and 3½ years if restricted. Patients who had been serving a prison sentence but had been transferred to hospital had been in hospital for an average of between 1½ and 2½ years if unrestricted, and 2½ to 3 years if restricted.

Patients with mental illness

3.13   The 2006 census data suggests that, of all patients (both detained and informal) who are in hospital in England or Wales for the treatment of mental illness, approximately 40% (12,157) are detained under the Mental Health Act 1983 (figure 23). This group of detained patients is very heterogeneous, in that it includes a wide range of diagnoses. The census collation allowed patients to be classified as being in hospital for the treatment of more than one category of mental disorder (just as the 1983 Act allows this with its own classification system), and so the 'mental illness' category discussed below will also include patients who have concomitant learning disability or personality disorder. Patients classified with more than one type of mental disorder made up approximately 5% of the detained sample from the 2006 census.

3.14   Figure 23 below shows the distribution of patients being treated in hospital for mental illness by ward type. The category of 'assessment and treatment wards' (which includes acute admission wards) is by far the most-populated single census category of ward for both detained and informal patients. Such wards housed 44% of all patients detained primarily for treatment of mental illness on the 2006 census date, and 41% in 2007. These national statistics show that there are more informal patients than detained patients on such wards, in that detained patients average at approximately 38% of the general ward population. The MHAC does, however, encounter significant variation in the proportion of detained patients found in general mental health wards. Especially in acute admission wards, it is not uncommon to find that more patients are detained than not. There are also significant numbers of detained patients on both long and short stay wards not counted in the 'assessment and treatment' category, and here we also found a similar proportion of detained to informal patients when taken as a national average. As might be expected, detained patients form the majority of the population on high dependency and intensive care wards, where they account for an average of 85% of the ward population.

3.15   It is rather more surprising to find that about half of the population of rehabilitation wards were detained under Mental Health Act powers (i.e. an average of 49% across the two years). It may be that such a group of patients – and there were over 2,000 of them in census counts from 2006 and 2007 – form the most likely pool of patients to whom the new powers of Supervised Community Treatment (Community Treatment Orders) will be applied.

Ward type		Detained patients			Informal patients			Total
		Count	% of all detained patients	% within ward type	Count	% of all detained patients	% within ward type	
Assessment & treatment	2007	**5,389**	44.3%	36.9%	**9,196**	48.9%	63.1%	**14,585**
	2007	**5,571**	41.2%	39.6%	**8,499**	48.1%	60.4%	**14,070**
High dependency, extra or intensive care, PICU	2006	**1,420**	11.7%	84.3%	**264**	1.4%	15.7%	**1,684**
	2007	**1,688**	12.5%	85.5%	**286**	1.6%	14.5%	**1,974**
NHS campus bed / old long stay	2006	**35**	0.3%	5.8%	**571**	3.0%	94.2%	**606**
	2007	**122**	0.9%	22.7%	**415**	2.3%	77.3%	**537**
Long stay (>1 yr)	2006	**1,366**	11.2%	37.1%	**2,315**	12.3%	62.9%	**3,681**
	2007	**1,643**	12.2%	40.4%	**2,425**	13.7%	59.6%	**4,068**
Short stay (<1 yr)	2006	**1,587**	13.1%	34.4%	**3,020**	16.1%	65.6%	**4,607**
	2007	**1,614**	11.9%	35.8%	**2,891**	16.4%	64.2%	**4,505**
Rehabilitation	2006	**2,013**	16.6%	45.5%	**2,409**	12.8%	54.5%	**4,422**
	2007	**2,389**	17.7%	52.5%	**2,163**	12.2%	47.5%	**4,552**
Other	2006	**345**	2.8%	25.3%	**1,017**	5.4%	74.7%	**1,362**
	2007	**491**	3.6%	33.2%	**990**	5.6%	66.8%	**1,481**
Total	2006	**12,156**	100%	39.3%	**18,792**	100%	60.7%	**30,948**
	2007	**13,518**	100%	43.3%	**17,669**	100%	56.7%	**31,187**

Fig 23: Ward type for detained and informal 'mental health' patients from 2006 and 2007 census collections

Source: *Count Me In* census 2006, 2007

3.16 Census returns on residents in 'old' long-stay and NHS 'campus' beds are combined in figure 23, although they formed separate categories in the census return. It is difficult to interpret these returns due to a number of data quality issues with these categories. Firstly, there appears to be a significant underreporting of NHS 'campus' beds[267]. Department of Health figures suggest that there were at least 1,600 patients resident in NHS 'campus' beds in June 2007[268], although the census only counted 700 occupied 'campus' beds in total. It may be that the beds missing from the census data are placed in establishments that are not classed as hospitals, but registered as care homes under the Care Standards Act 2000 and regulated by the Commission

---

[266] Category of 'other' includes brain injury units (49 detained and 146 informal patients in 2006; 41 detained and 61 informal patients in 2007); and respite beds (16 detained and 122 informal patients in 2006, 1 detained and 64 informal patients in 2007).

[267] The Department of Health defines NHS campus beds as "a service that is NHS provided long-term care in conjunction with NHS ownership/management of housing; commissioned by the NHS; and Includes people who have been in assessment and treatment beds for more than 18 months, who are not compulsorily detained or undergoing a recognised and validated treatment programme" *Capital funding for the NHS campus closure programme*, 9 August 2007.

[268] "Opening the door to a new life for people with learning disabilities' Department of Heath press release, 9 August 2007. See also "Data black hole undermines NHS campus closure target", *Community Care* 14 June 2007 p.7 on the possible underestimate in DH figures.

for Social Care Inspection, in which case they would fall outside of the census scope[269]. Secondly, the 2007 return identified 88 *detained* patients amongst campus residents, although only one such patient had been identified in the previous year's census return. It is possible, but perhaps not likely, that the 87 'new' patients were existing inpatients who were newly detained under the Act, perhaps after having been assessed as being subject to unlawful deprivation of liberty[270]. Thirdly, although the census returns for the category 'old long stay' ward were consistent between 2006 and 2007 (with, in respective years, 35 and 34 detained mental health patients, and 568 and 406 informal mental health patients reported), it is not clear *how* this category was interpreted by those completing the returns.

Security levels

3.17   At figure 24 we show the distribution of patients in the 2006 census across the various security levels of psychiatric inpatient services. More than half (55%) of detained patients are in general wards; 20% are in low secure wards; another 20% in medium secure wards, and about 5% in the high security hospitals. As we discuss in relation to learning disabled patients below at chapter 3.45, the significant numbers of informal patients in units with designated levels of security raises the question of *de facto* detention and lawful deprivation of liberty. We do not, of course, presume that all informal patients within secure units are necessarily being unlawfully deprived of their liberty, and we are not suggesting that detention under the formal powers of the 1983 Act is necessarily a criterion for a patient to be lawfully nursed in conditions of medium security. Nevertheless we are concerned to note that in both years over 200 patients were in medium secure units without any of the safeguards of the 1983 Act being applicable to their treatment and care.

		Ward type									
		General		Low security		Medium security		High security		Total	
		2006	2007	2006	2007	2006	2007	2006	2007	2006	2007
Informal	count	6,701	7,352	2,438	2,638	2,373	2,711	645	817	12,157	13,518
	% of all detained patients	55.1%	54.4%	20.1%	19.5%	19.5%	20.1%	5.3%	6.0%	100%	100%
	% within security type	28.3%	31.0%	60.6%	71.8%	91.7%	0.9%	100%	100%	39.3%	43.3%
Detained	count	16,970	16,402	1,582	1,035	216	225	-	-	18,791[271]	17,669[272]
	% of all informal patients	90.3%	·92.8%	8.4%	5.9%	1.1%	1.3%	-	-	100%	100%
	% within security type	71.7%	69.0%	39.4%	28.2%	8.3%	99.1%	-	-	60.7%	56.7%

Fig 24: Security type for mental illness patients from 2006 census – detained and informal patients

Source: *Count Me In* census 2006

---

[269] See FAQ question 10, "Should learning disability respite units and tenanted houses run by the NHS be included in the census?" http://www.mhac.org.uk/census/2007FAQs.php

[270] i.e. subsequent to the government's interim guidance on the European Court of Human Rights decision in *HL v UK*: see MHAC (2006) *Eleventh Biennial Report 2003-2005: In Place of Fear?*, Chapters 1 and 3, and also Department of Health (2004) *Advice on the decision of the European Court of Human Rights in the case of HL v UK (The "Bournewood" Case)* 10 December 2004

http://www.dh.gov.uk/en/Policyandguidance/Healthandsocialcaretopics/Mentalhealth/DH_4077674

3.18   The detained 'mental illness' group identified by the census showed some particular characteristics. Male inpatients in this group were more likely to be detained under the Act: detained patients counted for 47% of all male patients with mental illness and 30% of all female inpatients with mental illness. Detained patients with mental illness were also significantly younger than their informal counterparts: detained patients had a mean age of 43, whereas informal patients had a mean age of 59. That these averages are the result of quite different age profiles is shown by the data at figure 25.

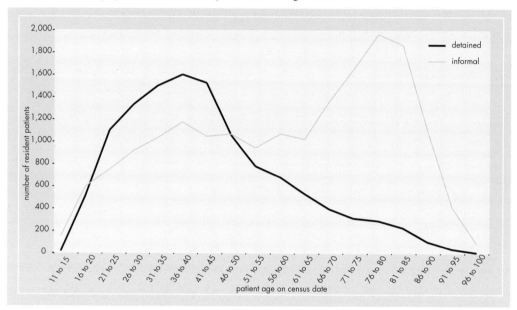

Fig 25: Distribution of detained and informal patients in hospital for reason of mental illness, by age at census date, all hospitals, England and Wales, 31 March 2006

Source: *Count Me In* census 2006

Private funding of detained patients' treatment and care

3.19   The 2007 census attempted to ascertain who was commissioning (i.e. paying for) the care and treatment of patients that it counted. There were data problems in the returns of 75 independent providers, so that 4.9% of all data collected about commissioning from independent hospitals was invalid, compared to only 1% of invalid data from NHS providers. Discounting this invalid data, it is notable that 235 beds (or nearly 8% of all mental health beds in the independent sector) were privately funded. Of these beds, 39 were reported to be occupied by detained patients.

3.20   The Commission was contacted by the parent of one privately-funded detained patient during this reporting period. His adult daughter, who suffers from bipolar affective disorder, was admitted under s.2 to a private hospital in London following a Mental Health Act assessment at the family home. The father of the patient was the nearest relative

---

[271]   Twenty-three patients out of the total 18,791 informal patients noted by the 2006 census (0.1%) could not be accurately ascribed a security status.

[272]   Seven patients out of the total 17,669 informal patients noted by the 2007 census (0.03%) could not be accurately ascribed a security status.

applicant for admission and financed the contract with the hospital. From soon after her admission, the parents expressed their concern over the co-ordination between members of staff and a lack of supervision over the patient, who was, for example, allowed to use her mobile telephone all through the night, and make unsupervised visits to shops, banks, off-licenses and public houses. The s.2 was allowed to run its full course (indeed it appears that the parents of the patient were concerned that the patient would not co-operate with informal care), and shortly after the detention lapsed the patient was further detained under sections 5(2) and 3. At the time of this further detention, the hospital had told the parents that the patient could stay with them no longer, as she had broken the no-alcohol house rules. The parents arranged a transfer to another hospital in the Midlands, where the patient remained for over five weeks as a private patient and received, in the parent's view "excellent care and attention". The bill from the first hospital (where the patient had resided for 30 days) came to over £23,000: the parents of the patient sought unsuccessfully to recover some of this amount on account of their dissatisfaction with their daughter's care and treatment in that hospital.

3.21   It would appear that there were conflicting expectations about the care and treatment of this patient under the Act, which illuminate some of the curious aspects of privately funded psychiatric detention. The parents agreed to admission under detention with the understandable expectation that this would empower the hospital to take the necessary actions to confine and protect their daughter in the manic phase of her illness. They were subsequently disappointed with the degree to which their daughter was allowed to use her mobile telephone at unsocial hours, both to telephone them and to arrange apparently unrestricted visits to the hospital by her friends (especially as they had agreed to limit their own visits whilst their daughter's mania was at its height); consume alcohol (whether by smuggling bottles of vodka into the hospital, or by visiting public houses and friends when on leave or absent without leave); access and spend money (including buying an expensive second mobile telephone from another patient); and "come and go" at will from the hospital after an initial period of intensive nursing. The hospital countered that it was "not run as a prison"; that the management of bipolar disorder is a matter of negotiated co-operation with the patient. As such the hospital argued that it would have been a disproportionate exercise of power to restrict visitors (the hospital particularly relied upon the Code of Practice statement that such restriction should only be undertaken in "exceptional circumstances"[273]); or prevent any opportunity to obtain alcohol (although it did random checks to try to prevent alcohol being brought onto the ward); or lock otherwise open wards to prevent the patient from going AWOL.

3.22   Whilst, in many ways, the hospital's approach to the care of its patients is understandable and humane, its response to the parents' concerns highlights a culture that is built around the voluntary status of most of its clientele. For example, the hospital argued that refraining from the consumption of alcohol was "one of the conditions of admission"; that the patient was given a copy of these conditions; and that discharge from hospital was a response to failure to comply with those conditions, albeit a response "not thought to be appropriate here". It is notable that in this case, the "terms of admission and financial agreement" form

---

[273]   MHA Code of Practice, para 26.1.

used by the hospital, which is usually signed by both patient and the person acting as surety for payment, was completed only by the patient's father as surety. It is understandable why the father, as the actual contracting party, felt aggrieved, when the hospital (in many ways also understandably) treated his daughter as though she had contracted care from the hospital, whereas she had not done so.

3.23   We highlight this case only as an example of an otherwise obscure area in the application of Mental Health Act powers. Whilst other examples of privately-funded detention may be different in their particulars (we believe that a more common situation may be where existing inpatients who are privately funded are detained under MHA powers), there is always likely to be something of a paradox at the root of their situation, in that the person paying for the detention (whether or not that person is the patient him or herself) is to some extent unable to determine how such powers are exercised.

Acquired brain injury and detention under the MHA

3.24   It is generally accepted that the categories of mental disorder defined at section 1 of the Mental Health Act exclude patients with brain injuries, in that an acquired brain injury is neither a mental illness nor, for the purposes of the definition of the mental impairments, "an arrested or incomplete development of mind" (MHA 1983 s.1(2)). In our Tenth Biennial Report we suggested that brain injuries might, however, *give rise* to mental illness or 'psychopathic disorder' that could warrant detention under the Act, although we suggested that the example of brain injury provided an argument for the abolition of the Act's categories of mental disorder provided that suitably robust thresholds for detention could be maintained[274]. The Mental Health Act 2007 will, as of October 2008 remove these technical barriers to the detention of patients with brain injuries under the 1983 Act.

Legal status	on admission	on census day
Informal	8	n/a
Section 2	1	1
Section 3	35	42
Section 37	3	4
Section 37/41	1	1
Section 38	1	1
CPIA	1	1
Total	**50**	**50**

Fig 26: Legal status of mental health and learning disability patients detained in Acquired Brain Injury Units on census date and on admission, 2006 Census.

Source: *Count Me In* census 2006

3.25   Given the widespread acceptance of the current law's apparent limitations with regard to the detention of patients with acquired brain injury, it is perhaps surprising to note that about a quarter of the 203 patients found to be resident in brain injury units at the time of the 2006

---

[274] See MHAC (2003) *Tenth Biennial Report 2001-2003: Placed Amongst Strangers* p.77

census were detained under the Act. Figure 26 above sets out the legal status of these 50 detained patients at the time of the census, and also indicates their legal status at the time of admission. The primary 'reason to be in hospital' was recorded as 'mental illness' for all but one of these patients. Forty-two patients (including the single 'learning disability' patient) were detained under s.3 at the time of the census. Eight patients who were detained at the time of the census had been admitted informally. Seven of these had been subsequently detained under s.3, and the eighth appears to have received a court order under s.37 whilst already a hospital inpatient[275]. It is likely that in most, if not all, of the 'mental illness' cases, the patients are being treated for concomitant mental illness (such as depression) that may or may not have a diagnostic connection to the brain injury.

3.26   An example of the difficulties experienced in providing the lawful authority for the care and treatment of a brain injury patient has been published by a neuropsychiatrist and a Mental Health Act administrator working in the Elm Park Brain Injury Service, Essex[276]. They describe the referral of a patient to their unit after he had been detained under s.3 on an NHS acute ward. Although the patient's clinical signs were confusion and agitation, he had been classified as suffering from severe mental impairment, and neither the examining doctors nor their legal advisers heeded a request from the receiving hospital that this classification was inappropriate. The RMO at the receiving hospital used his powers under s.16 of the Act to reclassify the patient as suffering from 'mental illness'. At this point a MHA Commissioner visited the ward and, in the words of the authors, "challenged not the problem but the remedy", but after some discussion the hospital's legal advisers agreed that the original detention was open to legal challenge and not rectifiable by reclassification. As such, the patient reverted to informal status whilst a further assessment was carried out. This found that the patient was suffering from mental disorder of the requisite nature or degree and he was again detained under s.3. The authors report receiving "several other" referrals of patients similarly misclassified with mental impairment or severe mental impairment since that time[277].

Consent status of patients with mental illness

3.27   The consent status of detained 'mental illness' patients from the 2006 census is shown at figures 27 and 28 below. This group is arguably the most heterogeneous of the three diagnostic categories of patients recognised by the census, and is certainly the largest. Figure 27 shows consent status split between civil patients (ss.2 and 3) and patients from the criminal justice system (part III of the Act). Figure 28 unpacks the various sections authorising detention of part III patients.

---

[275] Perhaps because s/he had been convicted of an offence committed whilst already an inpatient detained under civil powers.

[276] Bashir A & Tinto S (2006) 'Misapplication of mental impairment under the Mental Health Act 1983' *Psychiatric Bulletin* 30, 69-70.

[277] *ibid.*

(n = 12,551)		legal status on census date							
		s.2		s.3		Part III		Total (all detained patients)	
		number	% of legal category	number	% of legal category	number	% of legal category	number	% of legal category
consent status	consenting	528	47.3	4,175	52.4	2,404	69.3	7,107	56.6
	capable but refusing	154	13.8	1,312	16.5	442	12.7	1,908	15.2
	incapable of consent	226	20.3	1,767	22.2	495	14.3	2,488	19.8
	not known	208[278]	18.6	714[279]	9.0	126	3.6	1,048	8.3
	all consent status in legal category	1,116	100	7,968	100	3,467	100	12,551	100

Fig 27: Consent status of all patients admitted for treatment of mental illness detained under sections 2 or 3 on the 31 March 2006, all hospitals, England and Wales

Source: *Count Me In* census 2006

3.28 A comparison of the mental illness group against the other diagnostic groups highlights the following:

- Of those patients who are recognised as being in hospital primarily by reason of mental illness, approximately half of all civil patients, and over two-thirds those detained under part III criminal justice powers, are deemed to be capable and to be consenting to their treatment. These proportions are mirrored in learning disabled patients, but personality disordered patients are much more likely to be deemed consenting (fig 38, paragraph 3.53).

- 15% of all the patients in the mental illness group were recognised to have mental capacity and be refusing consent to treatment. This mirrors proportions found in personality disordered patients. There does not appear to be significant differences between civil and part III patients overall in this respect, although part III mental illness patients with restricted status are less likely to be refusing.

- One fifth of mental illness patients overall were deemed to be incapable of giving or withholding consent to treatment. This is half the proportion of learning disability patients recognised as incapable, but more than twice the proportion of incapable personality disordered patients. The proportion was less for some part III patients (particularly transferred convicted prisoners).

(n = 3,467)		legal status on census date														
		s.37		s.37/41		s.47		s.47/49		s.48		s.48/49		CPIA[280]		Other pt III	
		number	% of legal category	number	% of legal category	number	% of legal category	number	% of legal category	number	% of legal category	number	% of legal category	number	% of legal category	number	% of legal category
consent status	consenting	449	62.8	1380	71.7	27	69.3	328	79.6	11	61.1	90	61.2	61	52.7	58	61.7
	capable but refusing	105	14.7	228	11.8	7	17.5	43	10.4	2	11.1	24	16.3	20	17.2	13	13.8
	incapable of consent	119	16.6	265	13.8	4	10.0	29	7.1	4	22.2	25	17.0	33	28.4	16	17.0
	not known	42	5.9	52	2.7	2	5.0	12	2.9	1	5.5	8	5.4	2	1.7	7	7.4
all consent status in legal category		715	100	1925	100	40	100	412	100	18	100	147	100	116	100	94	100

Fig 28: Consent status of patients admitted for treatment of mental illness detained under part III powers on the 31 March 2006, all hospitals, England and Wales

Source: *Count Me In* census 2006

---

[278] Includes 99 's.2' patients categorised as 'informal: capable' and 55 as 'informal: incapable', probably due to clerical error or misunderstanding of the consent categories.

[279] Includes 376 patients marked as 'informal: capable' and 118 as 'informal: incapable' (see n. 278 above)

Patients with learning disability

Service provision for learning disabled patients – old wards and new challenges

3.29   Between the census collections of 2006 and 2007, the NHS closed approximately 12% of its learning disability inpatient beds. The 2007 census counted 3,217 occupied beds of this type in the NHS, compared to 3,669 in 2006. During this period the number of learning disability beds in the independent sector appeared to remain roughly constant at about 940 beds, two-thirds of which were occupied by detained patients in 2007[281].

3.30   The absolute number of specialist learning disability beds may have fallen in the period between the two most recent census counts, but this does not mean that hospital-based care for learning disabled patients is in any sense being phased out. The independent sector provides an increasing share of the market, especially in the provision of secure beds, as we show below.

3.31   In 2004, Professor Gregory O'Brien (who was then chair of the Royal College of Psychiatrists' Faculty of Learning Disability), noted that "we are beginning to see a growth in hospital care, particularly for those with learning disabilities who have committed offences"[282]. Professor O'Brien thought it unlikely that this signalled a return to "some kind of pattern of separate long-stay hospital care", not least because of a strong international political will against this. It is important that, in order to avoid such a return, services heed Professor O'Brien's plea that hospital placements must never be regarded as permanent, but always as "opportunities for people with learning disability who suffer from a mental health problem to receive help, over time, towards a pattern of inclusion and acceptance"[283].

3.32   There is a danger that long-stay ward environments may be institutionalising and unnecessarily confining for many patients with a learning disability, and indeed some such wards have been exposed as "institutionally abusive" towards such patients in this reporting period. In July 2006, the Healthcare Commission and CSCI published their 2005 findings of abusive behaviour and misuse of patients' money amongst learning disability services in Cornwall Partnership NHS Trust, including over-reliance on medication to control behaviour, as well as illegal and prolonged use of restraint. One person spent 16 hours a day tied to their bed or wheelchair for what staff wrongly believed was for that person's own protection[284]. The Healthcare Commission further reported in January 2007 on its inquiry into the care at Sutton and Merton Primary Care Trust's Orchard Hill Unit. There it found

---

[280]   Excludes patients detained subsequent to a finding under the Criminal Procedure (Insanity) Acts after to March 2005, who would be detained under s.37. (For the changes to the CPIA in 2005, see MHAC (2006) *Eleventh Biennial Report 2003-5: In Place of Fear?* para 5.25 et seq).

[281]   MHAC, CSIP, Healthcare Commission (2007) *Information from the 2007 Census*. Additional data from Jo Simpson.

[282]   O'Brien, G (2004) "A road map for care" in St Luke's Hospital Group (2004) *21st Century Asylums? Essays about low secure hospital care for people with learning disabilities.* London: Premium Publishing, page 58.

[283]   *ibid.*, p.60.

[284]   Healthcare Commission and CSCI (2006) *Joint investigation into services for people with learning disabilities at Cornwall Partnership NHS Trust*, July 2006

impoverished environments, poorly supported and trained staff, patients left with little to occupy their time, and unacceptable practices including the use of mechanical restraint. In one case, a woman had routinely been restrained for many years through the use of an arm splint, which was applied to prevent her putting her hand in her mouth[285].

3.33   In November 2006, as Parliamentary Under-Secretary of State for Care Services, Ivan Lewis MP, committed in the House of Commons to ensure that the abuse that occurred in Cornwall does not happen again[286]. The MHAC is a part of the Joint Policy Network with the Healthcare Commission and CSCI considering issues about learning disability services, and we acknowledge the Healthcare Commission's work in auditing learning disability services (which involved visits to 154 services), which is now published[287]. However, it should be a serious matter of concern that any learning disability unit that does not detain patients under the Act may still be relatively free of regular external visitation with the focus and methodology that the MHAC applies to its visits to detained patients. We believe that it is imperative that the government addresses this lack, both to comply with its obligations as a signatory to the Optional Protocol to the UN Convention against Torture (OPCAT) and to make good its commitment to preventing further neglect and abuse of this vulnerable population.

3.34   Much of the growth in long-stay facilities is taking place in modern, purpose-built facilities. Whilst such facilities may be free of the run-down, 'back-ward' atmosphere of the older services that are being closed, MHA Commissioners visiting some of the new services have been concerned at both the scale of some developments and, especially in some of the more secure services, at their design:

> The continuous build-up on this site ... when completed will resemble a rather remote medium-sized institution (which is what we have just escaped from). This unit is one of three high-quality buildings on site. Inside resembles a prison ... bleakness and lack of sensory stimulus. In 50 years I have never seen anything like it. These buildings include the reintroduction of fully-padded seclusion rooms (floors, walls and doors)[288].

3.35   Despite the potential problems of institutionalisation (or worse) noted above for long-stay wards, it is undoubtedly the case that some patients that we see have challenging and complex needs that surely justify an expectation of fairly long-term care. Furthermore, for many learning disabled patients long-stay wards may, notwithstanding their faults, be the most likely *hospital-based* environment to be equipped and staffed to meet their day-to-day needs, and preferable on that basis to admission to mainstream mental health facilities where the majority of patients have no learning disability needs. That is not to say that more learning disability patients should be treated in specialist facilities, but it rather implies that a balance must be struck between providing adequate care to learning disabled patients and achieving the aspiration of the 2001 White Paper Valuing People to "open up mainstream

---

285 Healthcare Commission (2007) *Investigation into the service for people with learning disabilities provided by Sutton and Merton Primary Care Trust,* January 2007.

286 Hansard, HC 6 Nov 2006 : Column 29WS. This interpretation of the statement is from Department of Health (2007) *Promoting Equality,* p.26.

287 In 2007 the Healthcare Commission audited learning disability services through self-assessment questionnaires. A sample of 154 sites were peer-reviewed, "including the best performing organisations, those that need most improvement and a random sample". See Healthcare Commision (2007) *A life like no other.* December 2007.

288 MHA Commissioner, communication with MHAC policy unit, 21 August 2007.

services, not create further specialist services"[289]. We welcome the Department of Health's best practice guidance *Commissioning Specialist Adult Learning Disability Health Services*[290] and will use this, as the document suggests that we should, to assist our role in visiting hospitals where learning disability patients are detained.

Admissions of learning disabled patients under the Act

3.36 Published statistics on the use of the Act to admit patients provide data by legal category of mental disorder only for NHS facilities, although the NHS Information Centre were able to provide us with such data for independent hospitals for the years 2002/03 to 2005/06. We have set out such data as is available at figures 29 and 30 below. It is striking that this is the one sector of inpatient care for detained patients where the independent sector now has more admissions than NHS hospitals. The overall numbers are too small to read apparent trends with any degree of confidence, although there does seem to have been a decline in admissions to the NHS sector over the nine years shown at figure 29, and figure 30 may show continuing growth in the independent sector. We know, in any case, that the independent sector has generally increased severalfold since the 1990s and, in particular, now provides a considerable number of 'long-stay' beds for learning disability patients. In the 2007 census, the independent sector provided 272 'long stay' beds for learning disability patients overall (about 6.5% of all beds for this patient group), of which 153 were occupied by detained patients. As such, nearly 10% of all learning disability beds occupied by detained patients were classified as 'long stay'[291].

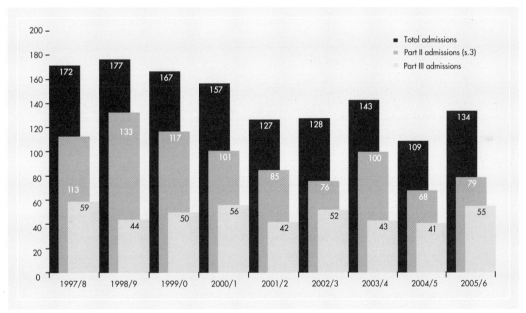

Fig 29: Admissions to NHS facilities of patients with the mental impairment or severe mental impairment category of mental disorder, 1997/8 – 2005/6, England.

Data source: Department of Health / Information Centre statistical bulletins
"Inpatients detained under the Mental Health Act 1983 and other legislation" 1986 – 2007

---

[289] Department of Health (2001) *Valuing People: A new strategy for learning disability for the 21st century.* Cm 5086l, March 2001. See para 1.14.

[290] Department of Health (2007) *Commissioning Specialist Adult Mental Learning Disability Health Services: Good Practice Guidance.* Office of the National Director: Learning Disabilities, 31 October 2007.

[291] Data from 2007 census. 153 detained patients were in long stay beds, out of a total detained population of 1,610 learning disabled patients in the NHS & independent sector. 272 detained and informal learning disability patients were in long-stay beds, out of a total learning disabled population (NHS & independent sector) of 4,153.

3.37 There are no discernable differences in the patterns of referral to NHS or independent hospitals. In either type of hospital, learning disability patients are more likely to be detained under the civil powers of section 3 than any other section. If they are detained as a result of a criminal justice disposal under part III of the Act, this is much more likely to be a court disposal than a transfer from prison. Roughly one-third of all admissions of learning disability patients under part III powers have restricted status[292].

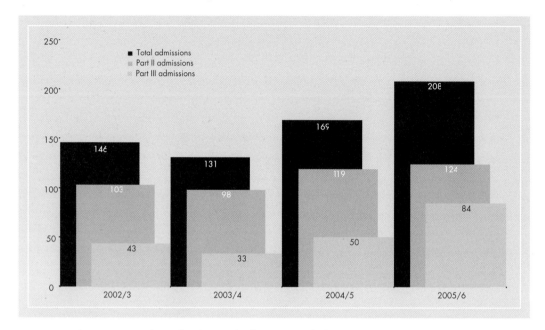

Fig 30: Admissions to independent hospitals of patients with the mental impairment or severe mental impairment category of mental disorder, 2002/03 – 2005/6, England.

Data source: Information Centre

The resident learning disability population subject to detention under the 1983 Act

Department of Health statistics

3.38 Department of Health statistics record 1,098 detained patients with the legal category of "mental impairment" or "severe mental impairment" resident on the 31st March 2006 (figure 31)[293]. By contrast, 1986 statistics reported a resident population of detained patients with mental impairment or severe mental impairment in NHS facilities (excluding High Secure Hospitals) of just 304[294]. Although this is less than half the number of patients with learning disability detained in NHS hospitals twenty years later (and less than a third of such patients detained in all hospitals in 2006), these official statistics suggest that the proportion of learning disabled patients in the resident population of *all* patients detained under the Act (i.e. whether for mental health or learning disability reasons) has not changed

---

[292] Restricted patients counted for 155 of the total (442) NHS part III admissions between 1997/8 and 2005/6, and 57 of the total (166) independent hospital part III admissions between 2002/3 and 2005/6.

[293] Department of Health / Information Centre statistical bulletins "*Inpatients detained under the Mental Health Act 1983 and other legislation*" 1986 – 2007.

[294] Department of Health and Social Security Statistical Note 1/88 *Mental Illness and Mental Handicap Hospitals and Units in England: Legal Status Statistics 1982 – 1986*, table 5.

significantly. In 1986, the 304 patients accounted for 6.6% of the detained population in NHS units. In 2006, learning disabled patients counted for 5.6% of the resident population detained in NHS units, but for 7.5% of the resident detained population in both NHS and independent units[295].

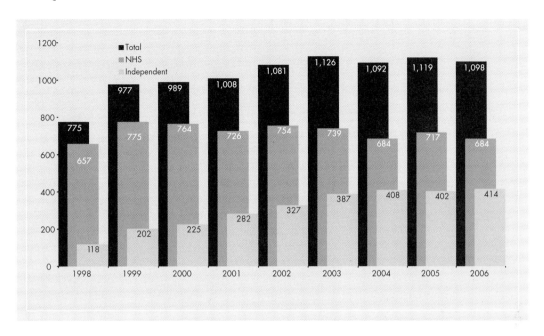

Fig 31: Resident population of patients with the mental impairment or severe mental impairment category of mental disorder, 1998 – 2006, all hospitals, England.

Data source: as for fig 29

3.39 It is notable that there has been more than a threefold increase in the detained learning disabled population resident in independent hospitals since 1998.

Count Me In census data

3.40 The *Count Me In* Census 2006 recorded 4,602 inpatients overall for whom the primary 'reason to be in hospital' was given as 'learning disability', as opposed to 'mental illness' or 'personality disorder'. Thirty-six percent of this group (1,636 patients) were detained under the Mental Health Act. The discrepancy between this total and the number of detained patients with mental impairments recorded by official statistics (1,098) is unsurprising, as the two data sets are not directly comparable, having both differences in coverage and definition[296]. In 2007, the census recorded 4,153 learning disabled patients (defined as above), of whom 1,610 (39%) were detained.

---

[295] Information Centre (2007) *Inpatients formally detained in hospitals under the Mental Health Act and other legislation, England, 1995-96 to 2005-06*, table 2. The categories 'mental impairment' and 'severe mental impairment' account for patients in 684 of 12,132 NHS beds (5.6%), or 1,098 of 14,625 NHS and independent sector beds (7.5%).

[296] The 'Count Me In' census had a wider coverage than the National Statistics Bulletin, in that it included Wales (where it found 34 learning disabled detained patients), and used a broad definition of 'learning disability' as the 'reason the patient is in hospital', whereas the national statistics collection counted only those patients who are detained in England and have a MHA category of 'mental impairment' or 'severe mental impairment'. As a result, the census returns may assign 'learning disabled' status to patients detained under MHA ss. 2, 5, 135 or 136, (and did so for a total of 46 learning disability patients in England and 7 in Wales), but may also count some patients who are detained under the classifications of psychopathic disorder or mental illness. Other potential causes of discrepancy between the two totals may be over or under-reporting in one or both data sets.

The 2006 census found that patients who were in hospital because of their learning disability counted for 11.3% of a total detained population of 14,488[297]; in 2007 such patients amounted to 10.6% of the total detained population.

3.41   The census data suggests that patients who were in hospital for the treatment of learning disability were therefore less likely to be detained than patients who were classified as being in hospital for treatment of mental illness or personality disorder. Whereas the 2006 census data suggested that 36% of all learning disability patients (defined as above) were detained, the comparable figure was 40% for inpatients with mental illness, and 74% for inpatients with personality disorder. Of course, the reality of many patients' diagnoses evades these neat categorisations, in that many hospitalised learning disabled patients may also have concomitant mental illness or personality disorder.

Characteristics of the detained population: age and gender

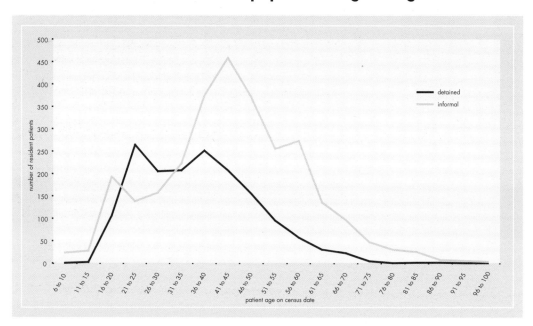

Fig 32: Distribution of detained and informal patients in hospital for reason of learning disability, by age at census date, all hospitals, England and Wales, 31 March 2006

Data Source: *Count Me In* census 2006

3.42   The detained group of learning disabled patients identified by the 2006 census showed some similar characteristics to those seen in relation to detained patients with mental illness. Male inpatients with learning disability were more likely to be detained under the Act: detained patients counted for 43% of all male patients and 27% of all female inpatients with learning disability. Detained patients with learning disability were also significantly younger than their informal counterparts: detained patients had an average age of between 36 and 37, whereas informal patients were, on average, between 45 and 46 years old. The quite different age profiles of detained and informal patients in this group is shown by figure 32 above.

---

[296]   http://www.healthcarecommission.org.uk/nationalfindings/nationalthemedreports/mentalhealth/countmein/2006.cfm., table x36n.

Ward type and security level for detained learning disability patients

			Detained patients			Informal patients			Total
			count	% of all detained patients	% within ward type	count	% of all detained patients	% within ward type	
Ward type	Assessment & treatment	2006	674	41.2%	53.8%	579	20.8%	46.2%	1,253
		2007	952	59.1%	61.3%	601	37.4%	38.7%	1,553
	High dependency, extra or intensive care, PICU	2006	100	6.1%	67.6%	48	1.7%	32.4%	148
		2007	57	3.5%	45.2%	69	2.7%	54.8%	126
	NHS campus bed / old long stay	2006	32	2.0%	5.5%	552	19.8%	94.5%	584
		2007	16	1.0%	2.3%	666	26.2%	97.7%	682
	Long stay (>1 yr)	2006	485	29.6%	34.9%	903	32.4%	65.1%	1,388
		2007	366	22.7%	31.9%	781	30.7%	68.1%	1,147
	Short stay (<1 yr)	2006	178	10.9%	54.9%	146	5.7%	45.1%	324
		2007	56	3.5%	31.8%	120	4.7%	68.2%	176
	Rehabilitation	2006	108	6.6%	42.5%	146	5.7%	57.5%	254
		2007	120	7.5%	64.2%	67	2.6%	35.8%	187
	Other[298]	2006	59	3.6%	12.5%	413	16.2%	87.5%	472
		2007	43	2.7%	15.2%	239	9.4%	84.8%	282
	Total	2006	1,636	100%	37.0%	2,787	100%	63.0%	4,423
		2007	1,610	100%	38.8%	2,543	100%	61.2%	4,153

Fig 33: ward type for detained and informal 'learning disability' patients from 2006 and 2007 census collections[299]

Data source: *Count Me In* census 2006, 2007

3.43 Census data for 2006 and 2007 shows detained learning disabled patients in most types of psychiatric ward, as is shown in detail at figure 33. We are not confident of the accuracy of returns relating to NHS 'campus beds' and 'old' long-stay units, given that the overall number of patients (both detained and informal) in these categories appears to rise between 2006 and 2007, despite the general trend towards closure of these types of ward, although the total number counted in each year appears to be significantly less than other sources suggest as a true value[300]. We suspect that services did not define these terms consistently

---

[298] Category of 'other' includes brain injury units (49 detained and 146 informal patients in 2006; 41 detained and 61 informal patients in 2007); and respite beds (16 detained and 122 informal patients in 2006, 1 detained and 64 informal patients in 2007).

[299] Total detained patients = 1,636 (2006); 1,610 (2007); total informal patients = 2,787 (2006); 2,543 (2007). Data source: 2006 and 2007 census collections.

[300] SHA-level statistics reported in the media suggest that "there are 1,683 people who definitely fall within the definition of campus resident but there could be hundreds more": 'Data black hole undermines NHS campus closure target' *Community Care, 14 June 2007*. On the government's undertaking to close all campus beds by 2010, see that article and MHAC (2006) *Eleventh Biennial Report 2003-2005: In Place of Fear?* footnote 25, p.118. For the NHS definition of 'campus bed', see n.267 above.

when completing census returns, and that there may be some confusion between 'old long stay' and 'long stay' wards. It is, of course, a matter of great regret that the census appears not to have provided reliable data on the numbers of patients in these specific parts of the service, given the general uncertainty over the numbers of patients involved and the high political profile of these wards[301].

3.44   Mental Health Act Commissioners are often told by staff and patients that wards designated as 'intensive care' or 'high dependency', including psychiatric intensive care units (PICUs), can be very unsuitable environments for the care of learning disabled patients. In 2006 the census counted 100 detained learning disability patients (approximately 6% of all such detained patients) and 48 informal learning disabled patients resident in such units. In 2007, we counted 57 detained patients (3.5% of all detained patients) and 69 informal patients in such units.

3.45   The level of security for learning disability patients is shown at figure 34. As may be expected, detained patients are more prevalent in secure facilities. Approximately three-quarters of the detained learning disability inpatients resided in conditions of low, medium or high security, whereas a similar proportion of informal learning disability inpatients reside on general wards with no specific security designation. We find nothing surprising in the fact that a quarter of detained patients in this sample should reside in general units of no particular security designation: more than half of all detained patients with mental illness reside in such units[302], and it is not a criterion for detention under the Act that a patient must reside in a designated 'secure' environment. By contrast, the informal admission of learning disabled patients to secure units engages issues of lawful deprivation of liberty[303]. There were 675 learning disabled patients admitted informally to secure units in 2006, and 514 such patients in 2007. It may be that a growing awareness of this issue is behind the shifting proportions of these patients between the two census collections, such as the greater number of patients who were detained rather than informal in low secure units in 2007 compared with 2006. In 2006, every other learning disability patient in a low secure unit had informal legal status; in 2007 the proportion was approaching one in every three patients. But the shift from formal status to informal was not uniform: although the number of informal learning disabled patients in medium secure units fell between the two census collections, so did the number of detained learning disabled patients in such units, and so the likelihood of informal admission (which is in any case very small) remained about the same.

3.46   Patients with learning disability who are admitted informally to secure services may well be particularly vulnerable in terms of unlawful deprivation of liberty, perhaps even more so than the larger number (1,798 in 2006; 1,260 in 2007) of informal patients residing in low or medium secure units for the treatment of mental illness (see paragraph 3.17). Whether or

---

[301]   The Sutton and Merton NHS Trust inquiry (see para 3.31 above) related to an 'old long stay' ward, and the main focus of the Cornwall inquiry was such a ward. The Government has described NHS campus facilities as "the service settings where there is the greatest misuse of psychiatric medication in [sic] people with learning disabilities" (Department of Health (2007) *Promoting Equality*, p.24).

[302]   See chapter 3.17 above.

[303]   On deprivation of liberty (and the *Bournewood case*), see MHAC (2006) *Eleventh Biennial Report 2003-2005: In Place of Fear?*, Chapters 1 and 3; also paras 3.17, 3.45 and chapter 8.8 of this report.

not such patients are in fact deprived of their liberty would have to be determined on the particulars of each case, but even if it may be true that most are not so deprived, the census results do at least point to a pool of between 1,775 and 2,500 patients in hospital[304] to whom the new 'Bournewood' safeguards could potentially apply.

		Ward type									
		General		Low security		Medium security		High security		Total	
		2006	2007	2006	2007	2006	2007	2006	2007	2006	2007
Detained Informal	count	431	422	496	755	658	387	51	46	1,636	1,610
	% of all detained patients	26.3%	26.2%	30.3%	46.9%	40.2%	24.0%	3.1%	2.9%	100%	100%
	% within security type	17.0%	17.3%	44.8%	61.0%	91.1%	92.6%	100%	100%	37.0%	38.8%
	count	2,105	2,021	611	483	64	31	–	–	2,787[305]	2,543[306]
	% of all informal patients	75.5%	79.5%	21.9%	19.0%	2.3%	1.2%	–	–	100%	100%
	% within security type	83.0%	82.7%	55.2%	39.0%	8.9%	7.8%	–	–	63.0%	61.2%

Fig 34: security type for learning disabled patients from 2006 census – detained and informal patients

Data source: *Count Me In* census 2006

3.47 The 2007 census did not record any instances of privately-funded learning disability placements (whether detained or not). Primary Care Trusts commission the largest number of learning disability beds in the independent sector, although significant numbers are also commissioned by local authorities or other NHS Trusts[307].

Out of area placements

"...since she's been in Essex, I've only been able to see her once a month... she cries and cries for her mummy and I can't get to her."

A Whitney mother's distress at out of area placements by Oxfordshire social services.
Her daughter had learning and behaviour difficulties, and a reported mental age of five[308].

3.48 *Valuing People* announced as a strategic aim that specialist learning disability services should have a role in enhancing the competence of local services, so enabling care to be provided without "the often high costs (both personal and financial) of specialist

---

[304] The total pool of potential 'Bournewood' patients would of course be much wider than this, as our data does not include any patient resident in a care home rather than in hospital.

[305] Seven patients out of the total 2,787 informal patients noted by the 2006 census (0.25%) could not be accurately ascribed a security status.

[306] Fifty-four patients out of the total 2,543 informal patients noted by the 2007 census (2.1%) could not be accurately ascribed a security status.

[307] MHAC, CSIP, Healthcare Commission (2007) *Information from the 2007* Census. From available data returns (75 independent providers returned invalid information), it appears that PCTs commissioned 42% of all independent sector learning disability beds; local authorities 24%; and other NHS Trusts 9%.

[308] 'Distress as daughter sent to Southampton for care', Oxford Mail, 20 November 2006. The daughter was in an out of area placement in Colchester, Essex, at the time of the article. Her mother's hopes for a placement within Oxfordshire were unlikely to be met as social services could not find a suitable place: another out of area placement in Southampton (60 miles from the mother) was under consideration.

placements out of area"[309]. In our last report we welcomed the government's issue of guidance on commissioning learning disability services, which sought to promote local and non-institutional support over such placements[310].

3.49   The *Count Me In* 2007 census returns provide the postcodes of hospitals in which learning disability patients reside, and, for 58% of such returns overall, also a postcode for each patient's normal residence. We were therefore able to calculate the distance between the two for this proportion of returns. The census returns that did not provide calculable postcodes are likely to relate to patients whose hospitalisation has lasted over a year, or where the hospital was deemed to be the place of normal residence by the completing administrator. The results are shown at figure 35 below.

	total number of patients	invalid returns	average distance (miles)	total detained	invalid returns	averae distance (miles)
NHS	3,217	1,102	17	988	318	27
Independent	936	664	82	622	389	82
total	4,153	1,766	–	1,610	707	–

Fig 35: Average distance from home for learning disability patients, by provider type

Source: *Count Me In* Census 2007

3.50   We must be cautious of over-interpreting these results, particularly give the high proportion of invalid returns from the independent sector. The most striking finding is that the average distance from home recorded for patients in the independent sector was 82 miles. Detained patients in independent hospitals were, on average, three times further away from home than patients who were detained in NHS hospitals[311]. This becomes a fourfold difference if all patients (i.e. both detained and informal) are considered. It is also notable that detained patients in NHS hospitals tend to be slightly further from home than all patients in such hospitals (although there was no difference apparent in the average distance from home for detained and informal patients in the independent sector). This may be a reflection of the greater specialisation (or at least level of security) found for detained patients' placements.

3.51   The MHAC will publish a report on out of area placements in low and medium secure units in 2008.

The consent status of detained learning disability patients

3.52   The consent status of detained learning disability patients from the 2006 census is shown at figure 36 below. Overall, the patterns of consent status are only slightly different across the three diagnostic categories (the others being mental illness and personality disorder) recognised by the census (see figure 27, paragraph 3.27 and figure 38, paragraph 3.53). A

---

[309] *ibid.*, para 6.30

[310] Department of Health *Commissioning service* close to home, note of clarification for commissioners and regulation and inspection authorities. www.dh.gov.uk/assetRoot/04/09/33/23/04093323.pdf

[311] It is important to note, however, that we were unable to calculate distances for over half of this group of patients.

comparison of the learning disability group against the other diagnostic groups highlights the following:

- In comparison with other categories of mental disorder, patients who are recognised as being in hospital primarily by reason of their learning disability are, as might be expected, much more likely to be deemed incapable of consent to their treatment (38% of all learning disability detainees compared with 20% of mentally ill detainees, and 7% of personality disordered detainees).

- It is more surprising, perhaps, that nearly half of the learning disability detainees (48%) are deemed to be capable and to be consenting, although the proportion of consenting patients in the other groups is higher still (57% and 74% respectively). However, the proportion of consenting *civil* learning disabled patients (shown in the column "s.2, 3") is significantly smaller than this at 37%. Learning disabled patients detained under part III of the Act after contact from the criminal justice system are much more likely to be deemed to have capacity and be consenting, with over two-thirds of such patients who are on restriction orders consenting to their treatment.

- Only 9% of all learning disability detainees were recognised to have mental capacity and be refusing consent to treatment. In other diagnostic groups, 15% of patients refused consent.

Fig 36: Consent status of patients admitted for reason of learning disability and detained on the 31

		legal status on census date												
		s.2,3		s.37		s.37/41		s.47		s.47/49		Other pt III		Total (all detained patients)	
(n = 1,637)		number	% of legal category	number	% of legal category	number	% of legal category	number	% of legal category	number	% of legal category	number	% of legal category	number	% of legal category
consent status	consenting	365	37.2	157	61.3	201	67.4	4	40.0	25	69.4	26	50.0	778	47.7
	capable but refusing	74	7.6	29	11.3	30	10.1	3	30.0	5	13.9	5	9.6	146	8.9
	incapable of consent	474	48.4	62	24.2	62	20.8	2	20.0	5	13.9	17	32.7	622	38.1
	not known	67[312]	6.3	8	3.1	5	1.7	1	10.0	1	2.8	4	7.7	86	5.3
all consent status in legal category		980	100	256	100	298	100	10	100	36	100	52	100	1,632	100

March 2006, all hospitals, England and Wales

Source: *Count Me In* Census 2006

Patients with personality disorder

3.53   The group identified in the *Count Me In* census 2006 as being in hospital for treatment of personality disorder differs from other diagnostic groups in that a majority (indeed roughly two-thirds) of the patients are detained rather than informal[313]. The referral routes for the detained population, and the consent status of patients categorised by such referral routes, is shown in figure 37 below.

---

[312] Includes 22 section 2 patients. The majority (48, or 72%) of all 'not known' returns in this category appear to result from incorrect coding.

[313] The 2006 census reported 1,296 personality disorder patients overall. Our analysis at figure 38 above suggests a detained population of 952 (73.5%), although there is a question over the consent status (and therefore possibly the legal categorisation) for 34 of this group (which, were they discounted from the detained population, would make that population 70.1% of all personality disorder inpatients).

| | consent status | | | | | | | |
| n = 918 | consenting | | capable but refusing | | capable of consent | | total | |
	number	%within referral route	number	%within referral route	number	%within referral route	number	%within referral route
prison	205	77.7	49	18.6	10	3.8	264	28.8
other inpatient service (NHS)	107	78.7	16	11.8	13	9.6	136	14.8
high security	103	88.0	10	8.5	4	3.4	117	12.7
courts	48	64.9	20	27.0	6	8.1	74	8.1
medium security (NHS)	58	77.3	12	16.0	5	6.7	75	8.2
medium security (private)	35	76.1	7	15.2	4	5.3	46	5.0
other clinical specialty	35	74.5	10	21.3	2	4.3	47	5.1
community team (MH)	30	69.8	6	14.0	7	16.3	43	4.7
other inpatient service (private)	22	73.3	4	13.3	4	13.3	30	3.3
GP / self / carer	14	63.6	6	27.3	2	9.1	22	2.4
community team (LD)	8	50.0	1	6.3	7	43.8	16	1.7
police	12	80.0	2	13.3	1	6.7	15	1.6
A & E	9	81.8	2	18.2	–	–	11	1.2
social services	8	61.5	0	–	5	38.5	13	1.4
probation	9	100	–	–	–	–	9	1.0
all referral routes	703	78.3	145	15.8	70	7.6	918	100

Fig 37: Referral route of all patients admitted for treatment of personality disorder detained on the 31 March 2006 by consent status, all hospitals, England and Wales

Source: *Count Me In* census 2006

3.54 At figure 38 below we show the consent status of personality disordered patients by the section of the Act under which they are detained, so that this can be compared with the other diagnostic groups recognised in the census collation (see fig. 27, para 3.27 and fig. 36, para 3.52).

| | | legal status on census date | | | | | | | | | | | | |
| (n = 952) | | s.2,3 | | s.37 | | s.37/41 | | s.47 | | s.47/49 | | other pt III[314] | | Total (all detained patients) | |
		number	% of legal category	number	% of legal category	number	% of legal category	number	% of legal category	number	% of legal category	number	% of legal category	number	% of legal category
consent status	consenting	197	68.6	111	74.0	253	77.6	17	85.0	112	77.8	15	60.0	705	74.1
	capable but refusing	41	14.3	20	13.3	49	15.0	3	15.0	25	17.4	5	20.0	143	15.0
	incapable of consent	34	11.8	13	8.7	17	5.2	–	–	4	2.8	2	8.0	70	7.4
	not known	15	5.2	6	4.0	7	2.1	–	–	13	2.1	3	12.0	34	3.6
all consent status in legal category		287	100	150	100	326	100	20	100	144	100	25	100	952	100

Fig 38: Consent status of all patients admitted for treatment of personality disorder detained on the 31 March 2006, all hospitals, England and Wales

Source: *Count Me In* census 2006

---

[314] Includes patients detained under powers of the Criminal Procedure (Insanity) Acts prior to March 2005. (For the changes to the CPIA in 2005, see MHAC (2006) *Eleventh Biennial Report 2003-2005: In Place of Fear?* para 5.25 *et seq*).

3.55 We note the following from the above data:

- A majority (nearly three-quarters overall) of patients who are recognised as being in hospital primarily by reason of personality disorder are deemed to be consenting to their treatment. This is particularly so for sentenced prisoners who are transferred to hospital (s.47, 47/49). Possible explanations for this may be that a personality disordered prisoner who is unwilling to engage with treatment is less likely to be transferred out of prison; that the treatments concerned are more likely to involve psychological therapy and, at least for some patients, less likely to involve neuroleptic medication; or that the detainees (especially those who have come from the criminal justice system, are habituated to its working, and may have been serving indeterminate or life sentences) recognise that they must 'earn' eventual release through co-operation and demonstrable 'progress'.

- By contrast with the other diagnostic groups of detained patients, personality disordered patients were least likely overall to be deemed to be mentally incapacitated. The small number of patients whose referral route to hospital involved community teams or social services noticeably bucked this trend (see figure 37).

- Fifteen percent of all the personality disordered patients were recognised to have mental capacity and be refusing consent to treatment. This mirrors proportions found in mentally ill patients. There does not appear to be significant differences between civil and part III patients overall in this respect, although part III mental illness patients with restricted status are less likely to be refusing.

3.56 The age profile of patients with personality disorder is shown at figure 39 below.

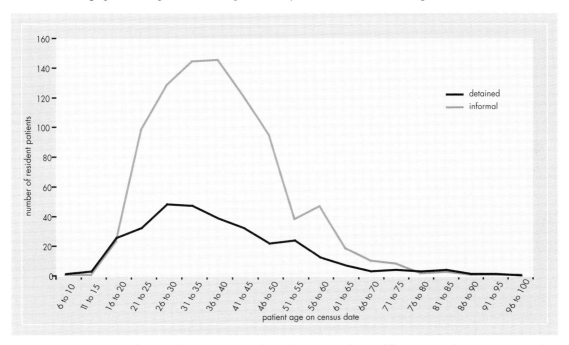

Figure 39: Distribution of detained and informal patients in hospital for reasons of personality disorder, by age at census date, all hospitals, England and Wales, 31 March 2006

Source: *Count Me In* census 2006

Children and adolescents

3.57 Figure 40 below shows the numbers of children and adolescent inpatients recorded in the 2007 *Count Me In* Census. Nearly 900 11-17 year olds were resident in hospitals on the 31 March 2007. Detained patients account for just over one third of this patient group overall, but 42% of the population in low-secure units, and 92% of the population in medium-secure units.

		service type						
		Mental health		learning disability		total (mental health & learning diability)		
		informal	detained	informal	detained	informal	detained	all patients
security level	general	425 (82.4%)	81 (33.9%)	48 (66.7%)	10 (14.1%)	473 (83.9%) (80.5%)	91 (16.1%) (29.3%)	564 (100%) (62.8%)
	low secure	78 (15.1%)	50 (20.9%)	24 (33.8%)	24 (33.8%)	102 (58.0%) (17.3%)	74 (41.0%) (23.9%)	176 (100%) (19.6%)
	medium secure	13 (2.5%)	108 (45.2%)	–	37 (52.1%)	13 (8.2%) (2.2%)	145 (91.8%) (46.8%)	158 (100%) (17.6%)
	total (all security levels)	516 (100%)	239 (100%)	72 (100%)	71 (100%)	588 (65.5%) (100%)	310 (34.5%) (100%)	898 (100%) (100%)
		755		143		898		

Fig 40: Psychiatric child and adolescent inpatients (aged 11 – 17) resident 31 March 2007, all hospitals, England and Wales.

Data source: *Count Me In* census 2007

3.58 In this data, 'informal' patients include those for whom the authority for their hospital admission is parental consent. From January 2008, amendments to s.131 of the 1983 Act[315] will provide that the capable consent or refusal of 16 and 17 year olds to be admitted to hospital cannot be overridden by those who have parental responsibility for them. Therefore, when a competent 16 or 17 year old refuses consent to hospital admission, parents may not override that refusal by giving their own consent, and the patient could only be admitted if the criteria for detention under the 1983 Act are met.

3.59 Figure 41 below shows the distribution of children and adolescents detained under the 1983 Act across the NHS and independent sector. The independent sector's focus on specialist areas of care is reflected in the fact that it cares for over half of this detained population.

		service provider					
		NHS		independent		total	
service type	mental health	116 (82.3%)	(48.5%)	123 (72.8%)	(51.5%)	239 (77.1%)	(100%)
	learning diability	25 (17.7%)	(35.2%)	46 (27.2%)	(64.8%)	71 (2.9%)	(100%)
	Total	141 (100%)	(45.5%)	169 (100%)	(54.5%)	310 (100%)	(100%)

Fig 41: Service providers for detained psychiatric child and adolescent inpatients (aged 11 – 17) resident 31 March 2007, all hospitals, England and Wales.

Data source: *Count Me In* census 2007

---

[315] MHA 2007 s.43, amending s.131 of the MHA 1983. See *MHA 2007 Explanatory Notes* paras 171-2, and the *MHA 2007 (Commencement No.3) Order 2007.*

The detention of children and adolescents on adult wards

3.60   The revisions of the Mental Health Act 2007 to the 1983 Act create a duty on PCTs and Local Health Boards to notify social services authorities of hospitals in their area that provide accommodation suitable for persons under the age of 18[316], and places hospital managers under a duty to ensure that children and adolescents (whether detained or not) are accommodated in an environment suitable to their age, subject to their needs[317]. In determining whether the environment is suitable, the managers must consult a "person who appears to them to have knowledge or experience of cases" involving child and adolescent patients[318]. The Minister has stated that "we should be seeking a situation where no child ends up in an adult ward environment … my view is that there are virtually no circumstances where that should be happening"[319]. We are delighted at the announced investment to increase bed capacity and improve children's facilities, and the commitment to end the treatment of under 16 year olds on adult wards by November 2008[320].

3.61   The definition of a person with knowledge of child and adolescent cases under the revised Act is capable of very broad interpretation. It could, indeed, include a representative of the MHAC (or our successor body), given the MHAC's past research into child and adolescent care and our close interest in certain individual cases. However, we would expect anyone seeking our help in this matter to also seek the involvement of a doctor with specific child and adolescent mental health training in a further advisory capacity. We hope that other persons who might fulfil the legal role under s.131A(3) would do likewise.

> **Recommendation 21:** Good practice in implementing the requirements of s.131A(3) in the revised Act should involve a doctor with specific child and adolescent mental health training.

3.62   The ending of admissions of children or adolescents to unsuitable adult facilities is an ambitious undertaking. In the usual course of its visits to hospitals between October 2004 and November 2006, the Mental Health Act Commission encountered 116 adult wards where one or two children under the age of 18 were detained[321]. In all, 132 children were accommodated in such situations. Eighteen of these wards were psychiatric intensive care units where the most disturbed and dangerous adults are treated.

---

[316] MHA 1983 s.140 as amended by MHA 2007 s.31(4).

[317] MHA 1983 s.131A(2) as inserted by MHA 2007 s.31(3). The 2007 Act also amends MHA 1983 s. 39 concerning the court's powers to request information about suitable accommodation for child and adolescent mentally disordered offenders.

[318] MHA 1983 s.131A(3) as inserted by MHA 2007 s.31(3).

[319] Ivan Lewis MP (as Parliamentary Under-Secretary of State for Care Services), BBC six o'clock news, 23 November 2006. See Press Association, 23/11/06: "'No child should be on an adult psychiatric ward' - minister".

[320] "Government invests £31m in children and young peoples' psychiatric wards". Department of Health Press Release, 14 November 2007.

[321] This data was first presented to Parliament in the Mental Health Bill debates by Lord Patel of Bradford, the MHAC chairman: see Hansard (HL) 15 January 2007: col 549 - 552

3.63   Between April 2003 and October 2006 we asked services to notify us of any occasion when a patient under the age of 18 was admitted to an adult ward under the detention powers of the 1983 Act. We received 1,308 such notifications: an average of about one admission every day over the three and a half year notification period. Given that authorities were not compelled to notify us, the real figure is likely to be higher still. We have no data on the numbers of children and adolescents admitted voluntarily or under the direction of their parents. Just over half of these admissions to adult facilities were 17 year-olds, with most of the remainder being 15 or 16. There were rare but extremely concerning examples of younger children being admitted to adult facilities under the powers of the 1983 Act. These involved twenty-two 14 year-olds, three 13 year-olds and two children under the age of 12.

3.64   The care packages provided to these children and minors was often inadequate, despite the best intentions of staff (figure 42 below). Very few staff working on adult wards had received any specialist training in working with children or adolescents with mental health needs, and a number of staff members expressed concerns over their lack of skills and knowledge for working with this client group. In some cases it was reported that they felt they could only offer containment until a more suitable placement became available. There were often no arrangements for the continuation of young people's education, even for those aged under 16 and of compulsory school age. Appropriate plans for the continuation of education during their hospital stay were in place for only about 10 per cent of the young patients visited, rising to just over 18 per cent for those under 16. Only one-third had access to a programme of activities appropriate to their age and abilities.

n=1,308	yes		no	
	number	%	number	%
Plans to transfer to age-appropriate surroundings within seven days	349	26.7%	959	73.3%
RMO specialist in child and adolescent psychiatry	887	67.8%	421	32.2%
Identified social worker	896	68.5%	412	31.5%
Identified key worker	874	66.8%	434	33.2%
Identified primary nurse	1,182	90.4%	126	9.6%
Of 409 female patients, detained on single sex ward	87	21.3%	322	78.7%

Fig 42: Care plans and situation of 1,308 children and adolescents detained on adult wards, April 2003 – October 2006.

Data source: MHAC data

Consent to treatment provisions for children and adolescents

3.65   Figure 43 below shows the number of SOAD visits to patients aged 17 years or under over the last four financial years, and the age at the time of the SOAD request. Over this period there has been a steady rise in the number of patients for whom such visits are requested.

Year	Patient age at SOAD request						Total patients under 18 (Total patients 16/17 yrs old)	Total SOAD visits (Total visits to 16/17 yrs old)
	12	13	14	15	16	17		
2003/4	–	1	4	15	38	42	100 (80)	130 (105)
2004/5	–	1	8	14	40	56	119 (96)	147 (121)
2005/06	1	8	6	23	53	52	143 (105)	190 (132)
2006/07	–	3	7	21	57	77	165 (134)	215 (176)

Fig 43: SOAD visits to patients aged 17 or under, England & Wales, 2003/4 to 2006/7

Data source: MHAC 'data warehouse'

3.66   Only 18 patients over the entire four-year period shown at figure 43 (and also at figure 44 below) were being considered for ECT. There were 20 SOAD visits to these patients overall. All but two of these patients received authorisation for ECT, although the authorisation for two of 18 patients who did receive ECT took place on a second SOAD visit, after an initial refusal. From our examination of these cases, we suggest that this indicates that SOADs were concerned to ensure the treatment was not used if alternative options had not yet been exhausted. Both of the patients for whom ECT was not authorised were male, as was one of the patients for whom ECT was only authorised after a repeat visit. The others were female. One patient was aged 15 (and had ECT authorised); the rest were 16 or 17 years old.

3.67   It seems unlikely that the introduction of a requirement for a SOAD authorisation for ECT in the case of any patient (whether detained or informal and consenting or not) in the 2007 Act[322] will increase the numbers of Second Opinion visits to consider ECT by a large number.

3.68   Figure 44 below shows the outcomes of the Second Opinion visits tabulated above. The rates of treatment approval and changes consequent upon visits are broadly comparable with those for the general detained population (see figure 66, chapter 6.20 below).

Year	Outcome of second opinion visit								Total second opinion visits in year	
	no change		slight change		significant change		not recorded			
	no	%	no	%	no	%	no	%	no	%
2003/4	88	68%	22	17%	4	3%	16	12%	130	100%
2004/5	108	73%	19	13%	8	5%	12	8%	147	100%
2005/6	156	82%	15	8%	7	4%	12	6%	190	100%
2006/7	171	80%	28	13%	3	1%	13	6%	215	100%

Fig 44: Outcomes of SOAD visits to patients aged 17 or under, England & Wales, 2003/4 to 2006/7

Data source: MHAC 'data warehouse'

---

322   MHA 1983 s.58A(4) as inserted by MHA 2007 s.27

3.69 We have noted some good practice in prescribing for detained children and adolescents, many of whom have complex needs and some of whom are treated on powerful psychotropic medication designed primarily for the treatment of mental illness in adults. We were pleased to learn, for example, of the care and attention that goes into the prescription practice at the Alpha Hospital, Woking, where the consultant attends a paediatric pharmacology group for peer support.

Black and Minority Ethnic Patients

3.70 Despite the high profile of the *Count Me In* census, we continue to find instances where the basic NHS Trust responses to Black and Minority Ethnic patients is unacceptable. For example, in one hospital in the Avon, Gloucester and Wiltshire Commission visiting area, a patient complained to the visiting Commissioner of racial abuse from another patient. We were told that staff were aware of the issue but felt unable to do anything about it unless the victim of the abuse involved the local police and pressed charges.

3.71 It is also clear that recording of self-reported ethnic status in Trust records continues to be significantly incomplete[323], although annual performance assessments of NHS organisations by the Healthcare Commission and its predecessor have included indicators on ethnicity coding levels since 2003 and there has been an improvement since that time[324]. Although ethnic monitoring of inpatients became mandatory in 1995, it is not so for patients treated in the community, and indeed overly cautious interpretation of the Data Protection Act by the NHS Information Standards Board may prove an obstacle to ethnic monitoring of such patients[325]. It is vital that government puts in place a clear requirement for ethnic monitoring of Community Treatment Orders before they come into force in the autumn of 2006, notwithstanding commissioned research on the use of CTOs generally[326]. This could be achieved by accepting the Healthcare Commission-sponsored proposal that ethnicity coding be made mandatory in all commissioning data-sets (CDS) and the Mental Health Minimum Data Set (MHMDS). In the meantime, the MHAC (and, we hope, our successor body) will consider ethnic monitoring of all patients subject to formal coercive powers to be an absolute minimum requirement in terms of compliance both with the Race Relations (Amendment) Act 2000 and with general good practice for hospital boards.

> **Recommendation 22:** Ethnic monitoring of patients subject to community treatment orders under the amended Mental Health Act should be an explicit mandatory requirement.

---

[323] Raleigh V S, Irons R, Hawe E, Scobie S, Cook A, Reeves R, Petruckevitch A & Harrison J (2007) 'Ethnic variations in the experience of mental health service users in England' *British Journal of Psychiatry* **191**, 304-312

[324] Raleigh V (2007) 'Race equality in mental health care: is routine data collection adequate?' (correspondence) *Advances in Psychiatric Treatment* **13**; 394.

[325] *ibid.*

[326] Oxford University and Oxfordshire and Buckinghamshire Mental Health Partnership NHS Trust have been granted at least £1/2m by the government to study CTOs over 21/2 years; a further £1/2m grant has been given to the University of Warwick and Birmingham and Solihull NHS Trust to research aimed at reducing inequalities and improving outcomes for BME patients. 'Tsar announces £1m in new research funding for mental health' Department of Health press release, 7 March 2007

3.72 Over the last year the Ministry of Justice Mental Health Unit (MHU) has written to hospitals requesting information on the ethnicity of restricted patients. The MHU currently holds ethnicity data on three quarters of the restricted patient population, which will limit its ability to comply with its duties under the Race Relations (Amendment) Act 2000 to monitor the impact of its policies on different ethnic groups. We understand that the MHU is to commission research into the race equality impact of its decisions that determine the granting of leave, patients' length of stay in hospital, their security level and recalls to hospital. We discuss the role of the MHU more generally at chapter 7.54 below.

3.73 Our own attempt to gather data on the ethnicity of all patients detained under the Act continues to elicit an incomplete response, although we are of course grateful to those hospitals that return our questionnaires. The resulting data collected over the last four years is set out at appendix B to this report.

3.74 A more complete data set, albeit one that takes a snapshot of services rather than monitoring use over the whole year, is provided by the *Count Me In* census that will run for its fourth year in 2008. The census, which is the subject of published reports available on the MHAC website[327], has consistently found overrepresentation of BME patients, with admission rates amongst Black and Black/White mixed groups three or more times higher than average, with other indicators of coercive treatment (such as seclusion rates) also disproportionately high.

3.75 Figures 45 and 46 show the age range of a selected group of the most populous ethnic categories of patients detained at the time of the 2006 *Count Me In* census. The census reports themselves standardise their data for age, but our presentation below shows how these categories have different age patterns. As might be expected, all the BME groups show less prevalence amongst the older hospital population, and a higher percentage of patients in the 25-45 age groups than the average overall. It is notable that the Black African group is the youngest on average overall, and the Black Other group has the highest proportion of patients aged 35-44, whereas the Black Caribbean population contains more older members. Amongst the BME groups shown, the Indian group is closest to the overall average age profile.

---

[327] See http://www.mhac.org.uk/census2006/ for census reports and other data.

Age band	gender	White British		Black Caribbean		Black African		Black Other		Indian		All ethnic categories	
		total gender	total - age band (% in ethnic cat.)	total - gender	total - age band (% in ethnic cat.)	total - gender	total - age band (% in ethnic cat.)	total - gender	total - age band (% in ethnic cat.)	total - gender	total - age band (% in ethnic cat.)	total - gender	total - age band (% in ethnic cat.)
<17	M	47	94 (0.90%)	3	4 (0.50%)	5	5 (1.20%)	2	2 (0.50%)	–	–	75	137 (0.10%)
	F	47		1		–		–		–		62	
18-24	M	772	1,106 (11.00%)	66	82 (9.30%)	58	69 (17.00%)	40	48 (13.00%)	15	17 (8.60%)	1,158	1,588 (11.50%)
	F	334		16		11		8		2		430	
25-34	M	1,574	2,179 (21.70%)	158	184 (21.00%)	103	127 (31.20%)	78	99 (26.80%)	36	54 (27.40%)	2,371	3,207 (23.20%)
	F	605		26		24		21		18		836	
35-44	M	1,804	2,546 (25.40%)	237	315 (35.90%)	109	145 (35.60%)	128	157 (42.40%)	39	62 (31.50%)	2,697	3,742 (27.00%)
	F	742		78		36		29		23		1,045	
45-54	M	1,074	1,673 (16.70%)	138	179 (20.40%)	32	41 (10.10%)	37	46 (12.40%)	26	39 (19.80%)	1,495	2,254 (16.30%)
	F	599		41		9		9		13		759	
55-64	M	714	1,177 (11.70%)	34	58 (6.60%)	5	15 (3.70%)	7	11 (3.00%)	6	10 (5.10%)	848	1,413 (10.20%)
	F	463		24		10		4		4		565	
65-74	M	309	772 (7.70%)	22	44 (4.60%)	3	4 (1.00%)	3	6 (1.60%)	4	8 (4.10%)	393	756 (5.50%)
	F	284		22		1		3		4		363	
>75	M	259	652 (6.50%)	3	12 (1.40%)	1	1 (0.20%)	1	1 (0.30%)	4	5 (2.50%)	293	740 (5.30%)
	F	393		9		–		–		1		447	
Total	M	6,553	10,020 (100%)	661	878 (100%)	316	407 (100%)	296	370 (100%)	130	197 (100%)	9,330	13,837 (100%)
	F	3,467		217		91		74		67		4,507	

Fig 45: Patients detained at the 31 March 2006 by age, gender, and selected ethnic categories, all hospitals, England.

Data source: *Count Me In* census 2006

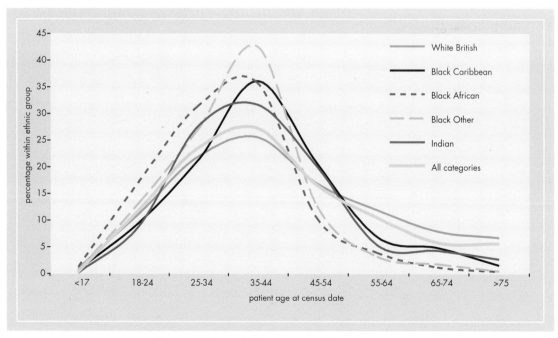

Fig 46: Age ranges of patients detained at the 31 March 2006 by selected ethnic categories, all hospitals, England.

Data source: *Count Me In* census 2006

Ethnicity and the prescribing of medication

3.76   The Royal College of Psychiatrists' consensus statement on high-dose antipsychotic medication states that there is evidence that African and African-Caribbean patients "may be prescribed higher doses of antipsychotics and more often receive depot preparations and conventional antipsychotics than second-generation antipsychotics"[328]. Much of the evidence for the disproportionate use of psychiatric medication amongst BME patients comes from American studies, where factors that are not relevant to UK services (in particular relating to issues about health insurance) may have a considerable role in any inequality of provision.

3.77   Although there is a generally disproportionate number of Black patients in the detained population in England (and as such there is a higher proportion of Black people prescribed antipsychotic drugs, and antipsychotic drugs above BNF recommended levels than would be expected from the proportion of Black people in the general community), there may be little evidence of disproportionate use of medication at supra-BNF levels within the Black detained population in comparison with the detained population as a whole. At figure 47 below we have tabulated requests for SOAD authorisation of medication above BNF limits by the ethnicity of the patient. For all but some White and Black ethnic groups, the numbers of patients concerned are too small to allow for confident interpretation, but it is notable that patients in the three Black groups (Black Caribbean; Black African and 'Black Other') for whom Second Opinions had been requested do not seem to be more likely (in terms of significant differences in this data) to be prescribed supra-BNF levels of medication than patients in the White British group. This finding would seem to echo in part a recently published study of 153 patients (of whom approximately 60% were detained) at the Maudsley, Bethlem and Lambeth hospitals, which found no statistical differences in the dose, type or number of antipsychotics prescribed between Black and White patients[329]. It remains the case, however, that Black patients account for a relatively high proportion of requests for Second Opinion authorisation for medication without consent: for example, Black Caribbean patients account for 7.9% of the Second Opinions in the table below, and males in that group account for 8.8% of all Second Opinions for male patients.

---

[328] Royal College of Psychiatrists (2006) *Revised consensus statement on high-dose antipsychotic medication.* Council Report 138, p.18.

[329] Connolly A, Rogers P, & Taylor D (2007) 'Antipsychotic prescribing quality and ethnicity – a study of hospitalised patients in south east London' Journal of Psychopharmacology 21(2) 191-197.

Ethnicity	<BNF limits	<BNF Limits as % within ethnic group by gender	>BNF limits	>BNF Limits as % within ethnic group	total	total as % within ethnic group by gender
British (White)	9,730	88.4%	1,282	11.6%	11,012	100%
Irish (White)	163	92.6%	13	7.4%	176	100%
Welsh (White)	78	79.6%	20	20.4%	98	100%
any other White background (White)	555	89.5%	65	10.5%	620	100%
subtotal (White groups)	**10,526**	**88.4%**	**1,380**	**11.6%**	**11,906**	**100%**
White and Black Caribbean (Mixed)	150	86.7%	23	13.3%	173	100%
White and Black African (Mixed)	52	91.2%	5	8.9%	57	100%
White and Asian (Mixed)	58	92.1%	5	7.9%	63	100%
any other Mixed background (Mixed)	133	92.4%	11	7.6%	144	100%
subtotal (Mixed groups)	**393**	**89.9%**	**44**	**10.1%**	**437437**	**100%**
Caribbean (Black or Black British)	1,138	88.9%	142	11.1%	1,280	100%
African (Black or Black British)	553	89.3%	66	10.7%	619	100%
any other Black background (Black or Black British)	167	90.3%	17	9.2%	184	100%
subtotal (Black groups)	**1,858**	**89.2%**	**225**	**10.8%**	**2,083**	**100%**
Bangladeshi (Asian or Asian British)	97	89.8%	11	10.2%	108	100%
Indian (Asian or Asian British)	288	91.1%	28	8.9%	316	100%
Pakistani (Asian or Asian British)	206	92.4%	17	7.6%	223	100%
Any other Asian Background (Asian or Asian British)	139	90.8%	14	9.2%	153	100%
subtotal (Asian groups)	**730**	**91.2%**	**70**	**8.8%**	**800**	**100%**
Chinese (other ethnic groups)	52	94.5%	3	5.5%	55	100%
any other ethnic group	207	93.2%	15	6.8%	222	100%
not stated	581	91.9%	51	8.1%	632	100%
Total	**14,347**	**88.9%**	**1,788**	**11.1%**	**16,135**	**100%**

Fig 47: SOAD visits to consider authorization of medication above BNF limits by ethnicity and gender of patient, 2005/6-2006/7

Data source: MHAC data

3.78   However, examination of the age-profiles of patients prescribed supra-BNF doses does suggest one possible difference between the White British and some Black Groups. Figure 47 above compares the age profiles of White British and Black Caribbean male patients against that of all patients in this study. This appears to show that the 40-49 year old group has the highest rate of supra-BNF doses in the Black Caribbean group, whereas for both the White

British group and all groups combined, patients aged 30-39 have the highest proportion of supra-BNF prescriptions. A similar pattern is apparent for women patients in the Black Caribbean group, and male patients in the Black African group (the next largest group amongst BME patients) prescribed supra-BNF doses show a similarly older profile, although numbers are rather small to interpret with confidence[330]. In the case of male Black Caribbean patients, the higher prevalence of 40-49 year olds prescribed supra-BNF doses is reflected in the higher than average proportion of requests for second opinion reviews of prescriptions for medication (whether supra-BNF or not) in this age band[331].

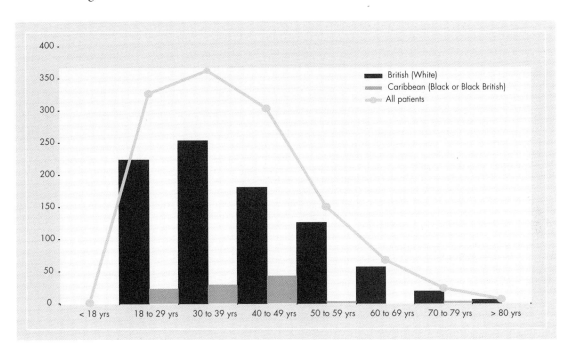

Fig 48: SOAD visits to consider authorization of medication above BNF limits by age and ethnicity of patient (male patients only), 2005/6-2006/7

Data source: MHAC data

---

[330] Second opinions for patients prescribed supra-BNF doses (MHAC data, showing percentage of age band within ethnic category):

	age band			
	18-29	30-39	40-49	50+
Black Caribbean Female	5 (13%)	10 (25%)	16 (40%)	3 (8%)
Black African Male	15 (31%)	12 (24%)	19 (39%)	3 (6%)

[331] Requests for SOAD authorisation of sub-BNF dosage medication (MHAC data, showing percentage of age band within ethnic category):

	age band			
	18-29	30-39	40-49	50+
Black Caribbean Female	179 (22%)	198 (25%)	270 (34%)	80 (30%)
Black Caribbean Female	92 (27%)	135 (39%)	97 (28%)	91 (27%)
Black African Male	133 (37%)	126 (35%)	68 (19%)	31 (9%)
White British Male	1,279 (22%)	1,379 (24%)	1,147 (20%)	2,022 (35%)

Overrepresentation of BME patients in the detained population: the policy context

3.79 In this reporting period the government has drawn back from its previous acknowledgement that mental health services are affected by institutional racism[332] (as defined by the McPherson Inquiry)[333], so that the Department of Health, for example, has stated that

> we just don't believe that 'institutional racism' would be a helpful label to apply – the solutions lie in the hands of individuals, not institutions[334]

3.80 The MHAC has been a party to the debate in psychiatric circles over institutional racism[335] which was instigated by the articles of Professors Singh and Burns[336]. We share the concerns of McKenzie[337] that the positions of that debate have been falsely polarised, in that each side appears to accuse the other making unscientific or false claims based upon generalisation or misuse of terminology. In this polarised view, those who support the Government's retraction of its previous position on institutional racism claim that pinpointing mental health services themselves as a cause of high rates of psychiatric diagnosis or coercion amongst BME groups ignores other causes in society for this phenomenon (many of which will be outside of health services' control); and that "political fashion" such as the concept of institutional racism is more likely to introduce bias in "sound clinical judgment" than to prevent such bias[338]. At root, this position seems to be concerned to protect the protection of psychiatry as a science (and sometimes psychiatrists as individuals[339]) from the suspicions of cultural bias or 'racism'. Whilst the MHAC has been depicted as occupying the other polarity of the debate (which is caricatured as laying all disparities of service provision traceable along ethnic lines as the sole product of mysterious forces of 'institutional racism'), our position is simply that the proportion of people from Black and minority ethnic groups admitted to and detained in mental health services is much higher than we would expect; and that the reason for this is should be looked for within the spectrum of possibilities between the extreme positions that there is either an epidemic of mental illness

---

[332] Murray R M & Feardon P (2007) ' Searching for racists under the psychiatric bed: commentary on … Institutional racism in psychiatry' *Psychiatric Bulletin* **31**, 365-6

[333] McPherson W (1999) *The Stephen Lawrence Inquiry*. London, Stationery Office: "the collective failure of an organisation to provide an appropriate and professional service to people because of their colour, culture or ethnic origin".

[334] Department of Health Media Centre, personal communication to Professor K McKenzie (2007), quoted in McKenzie K & Bhui K (2007) 'Better mental healthcare for minority ethnic groups – moving away from the blame game and putting patients first: commentary on … Institutional racism in psychiatry' *Psychiatric Bulletin* **31**, 368-9

[335] Heginbotham C & Patel K (2007) 'Institutional racism in mental health services does not imply racism in individual psychiatrists: commentary on … Institutional racism in psychiatry' Psychiatric Bulletin 31, 367-8; Heginbotham C & Patel K (2007) 'Institutional racism in psychiatry' (correspondence) *Psychiatric Bulletin* **31**, 397-8.

[336] Singh S P & Burns T (2006) 'Race and mental illness: there is more to race than racism' BMJ 333 648-651; Singh S P (2007) 'Institutional racism in psychiatry: lessons from inquiries' *Psychiatric Bulletin* **31**, 363-5

[337] McKenzie K (2007) 'Institutional racism in psychiatry' (correspondence) *Psychiatric Bulletin* **31**, 397

[338] Singh S P (2007) *ibid.*

[339] See, for example, Murray R M & Feardon P (2007) *ibid.*

amongst certain Black groups, or that such groups are corralled into detention without proper clinical cause. We doubt that either of these extreme positions holds the answer, and do not believe that setting them up as straw-man debating positions is helpful.

3.81   Nevertheless, we very much regret the reaction against the concept of institutional racism as an explanatory tool by some psychiatrists and the government, and find it particularly ironic that the government, in rejecting the concept as applicable to mental health services, has stated (as quoted above) that the problem is one of 'individuals and not institutions'. This implies that one reason for disproportionate detention of Black patients may be the individual racism of practitioners. Supporters of the concept of institutional racism are falsely accused of taking this position by those who applaud the government's line[340]. We are concerned that the Department of Health should appear so confused over the issue of institutional racism, particularly in the light of the Commission for Racial Equality's view that the Department of Health failed in its own legal obligations to undertake Race Equality Impact Assessments[341], and is guilty of "institutional complacency" with "probably the worst race equality record of any Whitehall department".[342]

3.82   Ministerial statements have, however, shown the way ahead. In February 2007 the Minister wrote to the chief executives of Strategic Health Authorities that

> we know that the reasons for the high numbers of people from some backgrounds in mental health services, and the high use of compulsion in care, are complicated. We know that many of the factors involved are outside the control of the NHS. That is not the same thing as saying that there is nothing we can do to address differentials in access to, or experience of, care for BME communities. And if more can be done, then it must be done. The moral – and legal – imperative is obvious. [343]

3.83   As such, practical measures to improve the experience of BME patients in mental health and address the overrepresentation of some BME groups in the detained population should not be dependent upon the outcome of the debate over 'institutional racism' and mental health care. But there is evidence that Black patients feel that they are racially discriminated against in mental health services. We recognise that work continues under the banner of the *Delivering Race Equality* five-year action plan, and that this has led to a number of examples of good practice as outlined in the Department of Health's *Positive Steps* report[344]. We will expect services that we visit to have taken note of that report in relation to their own practice.

---

[340] Murray R M & Feardon P (2007) *ibid*.

[341] Nick Johnson, Director of Public Policy & Public Sector, Commission for Racial Equality, letter to the Rt Hon Rosie Winterton MP, 13 June 2007: 'Mental Health Bill and accompanying Race Equality Impact Assessment'. Commission for Racial Equality.

[342] 'Department of Health's record on race 'probably Whitehall's worst'. *Community Care*, 31 Aug-6 Sept 2007, p.12.

[343] The Rt Hon Rosie Winterton MP, Minister of State for Health Services, letter to all Chief Executives of Strategic Health Authorities, 21 February 2007: 'Black and Minority Ethnic Mental Health'. Gateway reference 7888, Department of Health

[344] Department of Health (2007) *Positive Steps; supporting race equality in mental healthcare*. February 2007

4

The Mental Health Act in practice: admission and detention in hospital

Problems with admission

4.1   The MHAC continues to hear of problems in accessing the required professionals to complete applications for admission under the Act, as well as delays in admitting patients to hospital once an application has been completed. In both cases this can leave Approved Social Workers (ASWs) in the potentially dangerous position of being alone with a person who requires admission under the Act, or leaving that person without support. In our 2006 report on bed occupancy[345], we wrote that

> many parts of the country experience severe difficulties in locating available beds for acute psychiatric admissions… The MHAC was told about one case where an ASW made out two applications for the admission of a patient under the Act, and both applications (which are valid for fourteen days after the date of the last medical recommendation[346]) expired before a bed could be found. At one hospital we were told that some ASWs were refusing to undertake assessments where there was no potential bed identified. Nursing staff expressed general concern that extremely vulnerable patients could, for want of acute beds, be left in domestic situations when hospital admission was clearly indicated. Similar findings and concerns have been raised by the psychiatry subcommittee of the British Medical Association Central Consultants and Specialists Committee[347].

4.2   In May 2006, Manchester police were left unlawfully holding a mentally disordered male for three days in a police cell for want of a bed to admit him. The man had been arrested for carrying an offensive weapon, but it became clear that he was severely mentally disordered and a MHA assessment was completed for his admission to hospital. The Independent Police Complaints Commission found that the police had been placed in extremely difficult position by the failure of Manchester Health and Social Care Trust to find suitable facilities for this patient[348].

---

[345] MHAC (2006) *Who's been sleeping in my bed? The incidence and impact of bed over-occupancy in the mental health acute sector. Findings of the Mental Health Act Commission's Bed Occupancy Survey.* Suki Desai & Mat Kinton. December 2006 www.mhac.org.uk

[346] Mental Health Act 1983 s.6(1).

[347] *BMA News* 'Doctors warn of psychiatric bed shortages', 20 October 2006.

[348] "IPCC condemns Mental Health Care Trust treatment of vulnerable patient", press release, IPCC, 10/05/06

4.3   ASWs continue to have difficulties in obtaining support from other bodies. For at least some of this reporting period, police services in Wolverhampton refused to attend assessments unless a s.135 warrant had been obtained (a misunderstanding of the law dealt with in our Tenth Biennial Report[349]). There were also difficulties in obtaining the timely assistance of the ambulance service in Wolverhampton. The ambulance cannot be pre-booked, but has a target response time of two hours. It was not unusual that ASWs had to wait longer, as in the following examples:

- In July 2007, an ASW made an application for compulsory admission for an elderly woman with dementia who was threatening violence to family members. Police waited with the ASW for four hours. It was only when the police contacted the control room that the ambulance came within 30 minutes.

- An ASW made an application for an older man where police involvement was not necessary. An ambulance was promised within two hours, but after three hours waiting, the patient became more distressed. The ASW left the patient in the house on his own for the case to be picked up by another ASW the following day.

4.4   Following a meeting between social services and the MHAC in Dudley, where concerns had been raised about delays in admitting patients to hospital, the social services authority conducted an audit of problems experienced by its ASWs in order to identify and address problems. We commend this approach. Problems with the co-ordination of police and ambulance services were evident from the audit: on one occasion the police refused to give a time for their arrival until the ambulance was on scene, and on another occasion the ambulance would not attend until the police had arrived at the address.

4.5   Given such problems, it would seem imperative that social services and other authorities agree protocols over attendance for Mental Health Act assessments.

> **Recommendation 23:** Social services, police and ambulance authorities should agree protocols over attendance for Mental Health Act assessments

Section 5(2) – doctor's holding power

4.6   Under s.5(2), the doctor in charge of a patient's treatment may, if s/he feels that an application for admission under the Act should be made in respect of that patient, furnish the managers with a report to this effect, as a result of which the patient may be detained for up to 72 hours. In our last report we pointed to the decline in the use of s.5(2) from a peak at the turn of this century: this decline has continued (figure 49).

---

[349] MHAC (2003) *Tenth Biennial Report 2001-2003: Placed Amongst Strangers.* para 8.55.

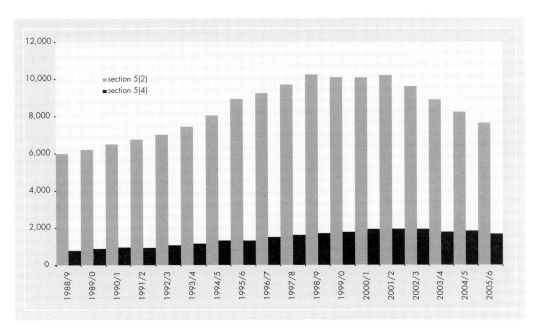

Fig 49: Changes from informal status to s.5(2) and s.5(4), 1988/9 to 2005/6, NHS facilities, England

Data source: Department of Health / Information Centre statistical bulletins *"Inpatients detained under the Mental Health Act 1983 and other legislation"* 1986 - 2007

4.7 The changing pattern of outcomes of s.5(2) detention over the last 18 years is shown at figure 50 below. The most noticeable trend is the increase in detentions under s.3 consequent to s.5(2) over the period. The outcome showing the steepest decline in the last four years is that in which patients revert to informal status. A patient detained under s.5(2) in 2006 would statistically have an even chance of reverting to informal status or being further detained under s.3: whereas in 1989, the odds on reverting to informal status rather than being detained under s.3 were roughly 3:1. This *may* signify improved practice over the period, in that it could indicate that the doctor's initial view that 'an application ought to be made' for further detention is well-founded and the holding power is not being used simply to keep informal patients in check. Alternatively, as we have suggested in previous reports[350], the rise may be a reflection of an increase in the numbers of informal inpatients who are otherwise settled (in the sense that they are known to and have been recently assessed by the clinical team) finding the hospital environment insupportable and seeking their discharge.

4.8 The statistics given above may not include the use of s.5(2) in general hospitals (i.e. hospitals that provide physical rather than mental health care), as such hospitals are less likely to complete the statistical returns. We suspect that s.5(2) is the most frequently used power of the Act used in general hospitals, but (as such hospitals are not included within our visiting schedules) out information is extremely incomplete.

---

[350] See MHAC (2006) *Eleventh Biennial Report 2003-2005: In Place of Fear?*, para 4.26 for a more detailed discussion of the possible causes of s.5 trends.

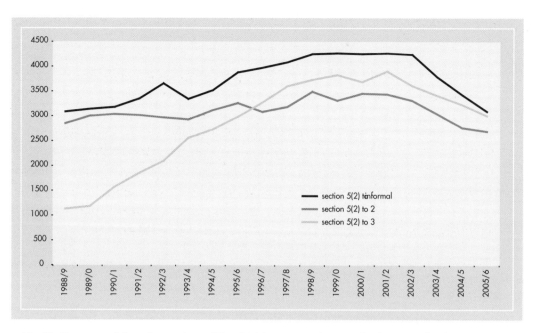

Fig 50: Outcome of detention under s.5(2), 1988/9 to 2005/6, NHS facilities, England.

Data source: as for fig 52A above

The following is an example of how the Act's powers are used questionably in a general hospital environment:

A patient on a general ward of a London hospital was held under s.5(2) on one early evening in June 2006. He remained on that ward for most of the 72-hour holding period, without being referred to the ASW service for an assessment. The doctor who initiated the holding power did not complete a medical recommendation. The patient was 'transferred' to a mental health unit managed by a different Trust towards the end of the holding power (despite there being no lawful authority to transfer a patient held under s.5(2)), where a MHA assessment took place leading to further detention.

4.9   It would seem that the purpose of s.5(2) holding powers is not always appreciated in general hospitals, where they may be used for inappropriate conditions, and treated as a free-standing detention power rather than as a means to facilitate a Mental Health Act assessment. In another general hospital we found the following note of a Senior House Officer's instruction in the medical record of a patient who had been detained under s.5(2) despite his presentation appearing to be related to alcohol withdrawal, with no indication of mental disorder within the meaning of the Act:

Patient can be kept under section 5(2) for 72 hours and treated under common law. If after 72 hours he needs further sectioning a consultant will have to come and do it

The s.5(2) form for this patient gave the following, quite inadequate, reason for his detention:

Problem of nausea, vomiting, epigastric pain and impression of alcoholic withdrawal and alcohol gastritis. Musculoskeletal pain.

4.10   In the same hospital, another patient's notes contained a statement:

Evidence of cognitive impairment secondary to brain metastases. Risk to health if returns home. Can be placed on section 5(2).

The patient was indeed detained, purportedly under the powers of s.5(2), with the reason recorded as

breast cancer with ?brain metastases? Treatment is required but unfortunately patient is refusing. Patient lives alone and is not safe to be d/c in current state.

4.11   It seems unlikely that secondary symptoms of cancer can be properly classified as mental disorder within the 1983 Act's definition. In these cases, the Act was being used to restrain a patient from leaving hospital so that treatment for physical disorder could be enforced against the wishes of the patients concerned. In the second example, this was even in the light of another entry in the medical notes which stated that the patient had refused oral antibiotics, where the professional making the record acknowledged that

I felt her logic to be reasonable and she appeared to have the capacity to make a logical decision.

In this case it appears that a Mental Health Act assessment (of some sort) did take place whilst the patient was held under s.5(2), although this quite understandably did not result in an application for admission under ss.2 or 3. However, it also appears that the holding power was not deemed to have lapsed at this point, but was allowed to run its full 72 hours, at which point it was 'renewed', with the new s.5(2) form marked clearly "renewal to previous 5(2)".

4.12   Thus we have noted examples of what almost certainly amounted to unlawful detention in general hospital environments. Additionally, the records display a worrying assumption that the patient's refusal of treatment and wish to be discharged wish to leave hospital was could be overridden was a patient who does not wish to receive treatment is, almost by definition, mentally disordered; that to make decisions seen as unwise by the health professionals amounts to mental disorder, and that to want to go home to die is not a valid choice.

4.13   The management of Mental Health Act matters is much easier in hospitals where there are large numbers of detained patients than where there are little more than a dozen detentions a year. Because they will only infrequently operate powers of the 1983 Act, staff in general hospitals should have access to advice and support from a competent Mental Health Act Administrator[351]. The hospital from which the above example was taken now has an exemplary service-level agreement of this sort.

> **Recommendation 24:** General hospitals should have service level agreements with neighbouring mental health services for the delivery of Mental Health Act Administration and training. Advice from the mental health service should be sought upon any use, or planned use, of the MHA within the general hospital. The service level agreement should also include:
>
> i) arrangements for regular scrutiny of all detention papers and the files of detained patients to ensure compliance with the requirements of the Mental Health Act and Code of Practice

---

[351] The MHAC also produces a Guidance Note *The use of the Mental Health Act in general hospitals without a psychiatric unit*, available from www.mhac.org.uk/Pages/guidancenotes.html

ii) The submission of six monthly reports on the extent of compliance to the chief executive of the general hospital

iii) An annual report to the general hospital's Board on its use of detention under the Act.

Section 5(4) – nurse's holding power

4.14 Section 5(4) of the 1983 Act requires allows a nurse "of the prescribed class" to instigate a six-hour holding power. The "prescribed class", as established by regulations, relates to the mental health and learning disability qualifications described in the register maintained under the Nurses, Midwives and Health Visitors Act 1997. In our last report[352] we highlighted the fact that the regulations in force since 1988[353] have, for some years, described these qualifications in out-of-date terms, and consequently so have the statutory forms established by those regulations and the Code of Practice outlining their effect.

4.15 We understand that the Nursing and Midwifery Council (NMC), in reviewing its pre-registration nursing programmes, has considered replacing the current four specialisms of adult, mental health, learning disability and children's nursing with a single generic nursing qualification that would enable its holder to practice in any setting. Many other countries have a generic nursing qualification of this type. Were such a change to take place, we suggest that further consideration should be given to circumscribing the sort of qualification that a nurse should have to exercise a power of detention. The evidence of misunderstanding and misuse of s.5(2) holding powers by general hospital doctors given above suggests that empowering general hospital nurses to detain patients under the Act, without any qualificatory requirement, is unlikely to result in a good application of the law.

> **Recommendation 25:** Exercise of nurses' holding powers under the 1983 Act should remain the preserve of suitably qualified and/or trained nursing staff, even under a system of generic nursing qualifications.

The role and displacement of the nearest relative

4.16 In past reports we have written of our longstanding concerns at the 1983 Act's framework for the appointment of 'nearest relatives', insofar as this is founded upon a hierarchical list without reference to patients' own wishes over whom amongst their family might be considered for this role[354]. This automatic identification of 'nearest relatives', coupled with the powers granted to persons who are so identified, has been found in certain circumstances to be in breach of Article 8 of the ECHR, as a disproportionate interference with the right to private and family life[355]. In response to the first challenge on such grounds

---

[352] MHAC (2006) *Eleventh Biennial Report 2003-2005: In Place of Fear?*, para 4.29.

[353] Mental Health (Nurses) Order 1998 (SO 1998/2625).

[354] MHAC (1999) *Eighth Biennial Report 1997-99*, para 4.46-51; (2003) *Tenth Biennial Report 2001-03; Placed Amongst Strangers*, para 2.56; *(2006) Eleventh Biennial Report 2003-05: In Place of Fear?* para 1.25-34.

[355] MHAC (2006) *Eleventh Biennial Report 2003-05; In Place of Fear?*, para 1.32.

to reach the European Court (in March 2000), the government promised to introduce changes now being implemented through the MHA 2007.

4.17 Under the 2007 Act amendments, patients are given the right to apply for the displacement of their nearest relative on the existing grounds[356], or on the new ground that that he or she is "not a suitable person to act as such"[357]. This is essentially the proposal made over seven years ago to the European Court in *JT v United Kingdom*, and was therefore implicitly accepted by the court at that time as a solution to the incompatibility of the law with human rights requirements. However, over the last seven years there has been a wide debate, including in Parliament during the passage of the new Act, over whether more radical measures might have been taken to protect the right to private and family life by introducing patient choice at the outset of the process whereby a nearest relative is identified. Government resisted calls for such a system, citing its fears that this could undermine the ability of the nearest relative to act in the patient's best interests, rather than according to the patient's wishes[358]. Government itself had proposed that patients would be able to nominate the equivalent of nearest relatives in the statutory framework presented in the Mental Health Bill 2004, but it argued against amending the 1983 Act in this way on the grounds that the nearest relative has essential powers under the 1983 Act of applying for admission and for the patient's discharge (which were not replicated in the 2004 Bill), which should be exercised independently both of mental health professionals and the patient concerned[359].

4.18 We remain concerned that in the wake of the 2007 Act revisions, patients will continue to have a nearest relative imposed on them, and any that object to such an imposition will be put in the invidious position of having to explain to a court why that person is not suitable to act as such. The draft 'illustrative' Code of Practice presented to Parliament stated that "a nearest relative cannot be rendered unsuitable on the basis that another person is deemed to be more suitable". This phrase has been omitted from the draft revised Code, published for consultation in October 2007, which simply allows that suitability is matter to be determined by the County Court[360], but there may be a real likelihood of further human rights-based legal challenge should any court adopt the approach that the government suggested to Parliament. In our view, the onus on the courts to act proportionately with ECHR Article 8 may well imply that they adopt quite the opposite approach in many cases

---

[356] "It is worth making clear that [patients] will be able to make … applications on all the existing grounds as well as on the new grounds that the nearest relative is not a suitable person to act as such" Lord Hunt of King's Heath, *Hansard* HL 17 Jan 2007 : Column 672. In practical terms it is difficult to envisage that the existing grounds for displacement will be of much use to a patient, with the possible exception of making a counter claim that a nearest relative applicant for admission is incapable of acting as such by reason of mental disorder (s.29(3)(b)). The other criteria are (in précis) that there is no nearest relative ((29)(3)(a)); that the nearest relative unreasonably objects to making a s.3 application (29(3)(c)); and that the nearest relative has exercised or is likely to exercise his or her power of discharge without due regard to the welfare of the patient (29(3)(d)). A patient arguing for displacement under (c) or (d) would effectively be arguing for their own detention, and as such undermining any argument that detention (rather than informal treatment) would be appropriate.

[357] MHA 1983 s.29(3)(e) as amended by MHA 2007 s.23(5)(b)

[358] *Hansard* HL 17 Jan 2007 : Column 670 -1 (Lord Hunt of King's Heath)

[359] *ibid.*

[360] Department of Health (2007) *Mental Health Act 2007 draft revised Code of Practice*. October 2007, para 8.19

presented to them, having no proportionate justification for disallowing the patient's exercise of choice.

4.19 We believe that the majority of applications for the displacement of nearest relatives under s. 29 are made by an ASW on the grounds that the nearest relative unreasonably objects to an application for the patient's detention under s.3. This is perhaps unlikely to change when the revisions of the 2007 Act take effect, although those changes will extend the range of possible applicants and reasons for applications. The new criterion for displacement ('not being suitable to act as such') is open to interpretation, and as such it will be important to ensure that any nearest relative who may be supplanted by an application to the court is aware of his or her legal position and rights. Our experience is that this is not always the case under current practices.

4.20 Whilst a displacement application has been made and is waiting to be heard, the original nearest relative will continue to enjoy the powers granted by the MHA 1983, until and unless the court appoints an acting nearest relative[361]. The nearest relative has also the right to appeal against the court decision. Furthermore, even after having been displaced, the supplanted nearest relative retains the right to apply to the MHRT for the patient's discharge once in every year after the court's order[362].

4.21 Although there is a clear procedure for making an application to the court, there is no statutory form or information provided to the nearest relative of the process of displacement. The only formal source of information for nearest relatives is contained within the Department of Health's leaflet[363]. This explains the powers of the nearest relative, including that a social worker considering applying for a patient's detention

> must take reasonable steps to consult you and obtain your agreement. If you object, then the patient cannot be detained. The social worker might then apply to the County Court and ask for you to be replaced as nearest relative; if this happens, and you object, you should consult a solicitor.

This leaflet (which tends to be kept by hospital administrators, rather than ASWs) is commonly only issued after the patient is detained, and is unlikely to be seen by any nearest relative who has been displaced in that process. Through our conversations with ASWs, we understand that the ASW seeking the nearest relative's displacement would very rarely be able or willing to provide information or support to any nearest relative who is to be subject to a displacement application, beyond advising that the nearest relative should seek legal representation and support. This is understandable, given the intrinsically adversarial nature of most displacement proceedings, but we are aware of occasions where the nearest relative first learns of displacement proceedings through the receipt of a notice from the court that the case is to be heard.

---

[361] Hewitt D (2007) *The Nearest Relative Handbook.* Jessica Kinsley Publishers, para 4.53
[362] MHA 1983 ss.29(6), 66(1)(h)(2)(g).
[363] Department of Health, Leaflet 21

4.22 It therefore seems likely that nearest relatives who are subject to displacement applications may be ill-served with information at the time of the application, and may not be provided with information on their rights after displacement. It is important that this is addressed with the coming into force of the broader powers of displacement contained within the 2007 Act. This may require a local agreement between social services and providers to ensure that an appropriate officer is designated to provide the nearest relative both with appropriate information.

Advance statements and crisis plans

4.23 From October 2007, the Mental Capacity Act 2005 gave statutory force in England and Wales to the common-law power to make an advance decision to refuse treatment. A valid advance decision to refuse treatment comes into effect when the patient who made it loses mental capacity to make contemporaneous treatment decisions, but acts as though that patient was contemporaneously refusing consent to the treatment specified.

4.24 At least until the Mental Health Act 2007 comes into force, this does not alter the fact that the refusal of consent to any treatment covered under part IV of the Mental Health Act 1983 (other than neurosurgery for mental disorder[364]) may be overridden if a patient is detained under the Act's powers. From the implementation of the Mental Health Act 2007 this will no longer be the case, as the law will not allow any 'valid and applicable'[365] refusal of consent to ECT to be overridden under the 1983 Act's powers, except in an emergency[366]. However, in relation to psychiatric medication, a detained patient's advance refusal of treatment will remain something to be 'taken into account' by mental health professionals, rather than something binding upon them. Indeed, where the advance refusal of consent relates specifically to hospital admission, a patient who is viewed as requiring such admission by mental health professionals would have to formally be detained under Mental Health Act powers, as this would be the only lawful means to facilitate admission. As a consequence, broadly-worded advance refusals of consent risk precipitating broad powers of coercion.

4.25 Although an advance refusal of treatment may be overridden by the use of Mental Health Act powers in many circumstances, and perhaps may even provoke the use of such powers, advance treatment planning that takes place in conjunction with mental health professionals has shown considerable promise as a means of reducing coercion at times of crisis. Initial findings from a study of Joint Crisis Plans (JCPs) in south London have shown that they can lead to a significant reduction in detentions under the Act[367]. The JCP is

---

[364] A patient's valid consent and certification by a SOAD is required for NMD or other treatments falling within section 57 of the MHA 1983: see chapter 6.87 below for further details.

[365] On the criterion that an advance directive must be 'valid and applicable', see (generally) Bartlett P (2005) *Blackstone's Guide to the Mental Capacity* Act 2005, Oxford University Press, paras 2.105 *et seq.* Bartlett claims there to be 'considerable elasticity' in the provisions of the MCA that allow for an advance decision to be held inapplicable or invalid.

[366] See Mental Health Act 1983 Section 58A, as amended by section 27 of the Mental Health Act 2007. This is further discussed at chapter 6.76 *et seq.* below.

[367] King's College London (2007) *Towards Mental Health; Health Service and Population Research at the Institute of Psychiatry* Number 2, 2007. p.11: *Can crisis plans reduce coercion?*

developed collaboratively between service users and mental health professionals, and involves reviewing past experiences of crises, and anticipating future crises whilst stating preferences and choices about future care when the service user may be incapacitated by his or her illness. The JCP also contains details of mental health workers to be contacted in a crisis, medical information (including diagnosis, current treatment and allergies) and information about early warning signs of relapse. The research, led by Professor Graham Thornicroft and Dr George Szmukler, has now been extended to a multi-centre trial of JCPs in London, Manchester, Birmingham and Leicester involving 300 patients, whose experience over 18 months will be compared against a control group of 300 patients without JCPs.

4.26   The Mental Health (Care and Treatment) (Scotland) Act 2003 enshrined advance statements in Scottish law and required that, from October 2005, advance statements about treatment and care should be taken into account by mental health professionals in their decision-making. It is a requirement that any overriding of advance decisions is notified to the Mental Welfare Commission in Scotland: between October 2005 and March 2007 the MWC reported 38 such notifications[368]. There will be no requirement for such notification under the law in England and Wales.

4.27   A study by the Mental Welfare Commission[369] on the prevalence of advance statements amongst 145 patients detained on community treatment orders in 2006 found that half of them had some knowledge of advance statements, although only six patients (4%) had made one. The MWC found that its raising of this issue with the patients studied uncovered 36 patients (26% of the 139 people visited who had not made an advance statement) "who were interested in making an advance statement or at least open to considering the idea"[370]. Of those who knew about advance statements, 29 (39%) expressed no interest in making one. A further 27 patients (19% of all patients in the study) were noted as being too unwell, or not capable, of making an advance statement.

4.28   The Scottish study suggests that advance directives can only have an impact on patient experience if services users are provided with information and support in making their preferences known. The Scottish Executive has produced a guide to advance statements, including a model form[371], and a MWC supported website[372] provides a range of resources for practitioners and service users to support good practice in the preparation of advance statements. We would welcome similar developments in England and Wales.

---

[368]   Mental Welfare Commission (2007) *The use of advance statements with compulsory treatment orders.* March 2007, p.3. At the time of writing a report on these cases was in preparation: see http://www.mwcscot.org.uk

[369]   *ibid.* The data was taken from 145 patients visited by the MWC between September and November 2006. http://www.mwcscot.org.uk/

[370]   *ibid.*, p.3.

[371]   Scottish Executive (2005) *A Guide to Advance Statements.* Edinburgh 2005.

[372]   www.principlesintopractice.net

4.29 Of course, making a crisis plan or advance statement may be difficult and emotionally painful. This is an area of patient care where the provision of a good advocacy service can make a very real difference.

Advocacy

4.30 The Mental Health Act 2007 introduces new sections 130A-D into the 1983 Act that, when implemented, will require government in England and Wales to make such arrangements as it considers reasonable to enable Independent Mental Health Advocates (IMHA) to be available for detained patients, patients subject to CTOs, and patients for whom treatment under ss.57 and 58A are under discussion[373]. Together with existing Independent Mental Capacity Advocates (IMCA), this goes much of the way towards meeting the recommendation of the *Kerr / Haslam Inquiry* Report that voluntary advocacy and advice services (independent of service providers) should be supported by central public funding to offer and advice and assistance to patients and former patients, particularly those who are mentally unwell[374]. The Durham University & Department of Health Good Advocacy Practice website provides guidance on advocacy, including research and guidance, and the beginnings of the development of an advocacy qualification[375].

4.31 In our Tenth Biennial report we reported findings that, in September 2002, 65% of adult acute inpatient wards were said to have advocacy input at least on a weekly basis[376]. In order to get a sense of developments in the subsequent five years, in June, July and August 2007 we asked whether advocacy services were available on every ward that we visited, and collated the responses.

4.32 When asked whether advocacy services were available to patients on 253 wards visited by the MHAC between the 1 June and 31 August 2007:

- 225 (89%) of wards reported that patient advocacy was available: and
- 24 (9.5%) that it was not[377].

4.33 When we asked whether advocacy was available only to individual patients upon referral to the service, 186 (74% of all wards) said that this was the case. This may indicate that many advocacy services are not resourced to proactively engage with patients, which may compromise their effectiveness. However, there was some contradictory evidence of advocates holding clinics and attending community meetings:

- Staff reported that advocates held clinics for groups of patients on 74 wards (29% of all wards). Of these, 33 (45% of clinics) were reported to be weekly events, with another 18

---

[373] MHA 2007, s.30

[374] Department of Health (2005) *The Kerr/ Haslam Inquiry.* Cm 6640-1, page 475.

[375] http://www.goodadvocacypractice.org.uk/home

[376] MHAC (2003) *Tenth Biennial Report 2001-2003: Placed Amongst Strangers*, para 9.9. Data from responses to the NIMHE LIT Stage IV Themed Review for Adult Mental Health Acute In-patient Care.

[377] Staff on four wards (1.5% of all wards) did not know whether patient advocacy was available. This would suggest that it was not, at least in any meaningful sense.

(24% of clinics) reported to take place at least monthly, although staff on 20 wards who reported such clinics taking place did not know how often they happened.

- Fifty-nine wards (23% of all wards) reported that advocates attended or facilitated community meetings on the ward, although 29 wards could not give a frequency for such meetings. Thirteen wards reported weekly community meetings with an advocate present, and 17 reported such meetings at least monthly.

4.34 To be fully effective, the new statutory advocates must similarly have a presence on inpatient wards, and make themselves available to patients. The government has indicated that patients who qualify for advocacy services by reason of their legal status (or because certain treatments are being considered in their case) under the revised Act should be informed of their eligibility as soon as is practicable, and can then elect to benefit from the advocacy service; and that advocates will meet with individual patients on the request of the patient, nearest relative, responsible clinician or any approved metal health professional[378]. This is a commendable basis for a referral-based advocacy service: we hope that advocates working within it will be enabled to go that one step further and advertise their availability to patients through their presence on wards and in group meetings, etc.

4.35 We also asked the patients that we met with on our visits in the summer of 2007 for their experience of advocacy services. Of 574 patients approached, 417 responded in some way[379]. Of those respondents, 184 (44%) had used advocacy while on the ward where we met them; 195 (47%) had not[380]. The majority of patients who commented upon the advocacy service they received were positive:

- Advocacy was useful because it supplied me with solicitors' names, made contact with my community team and represented me in discussion with staff.

- I really like the advocate, I see him every week. He has sorted out some problems for me; he talks to the staff for me.

- She can help you make a complaint. I made a complaint and she helped me. I think they take it more seriously if the advocate gets involved.

- The advocate came into ward round with me. She sorted out a problem with the RMO and he apologised.

- She helped me put my point across to the doctor

- The previous advocate was like a mum. I could talk to her about anything. She helped me with my care action plan and writing my life story.

- They are outsiders, not tied to the hospital. They are very pleasant. They come down when patients ask. Hospital complaints is rubbish and advocacy can help the patients to get things sorted. Patients' advocacy can liaise with staff/outside world.

---

[378] Department of Health (2007) *Mental Health Act 2007 Consultation on Secondary Legislation.* October 2007, para 3.1.3.

[379] Of patients who did not respond, incapacity was given as a reason for 99, and refusal for 58.

[380] Of the remainder, 31 patients (7% of the total group of respondents) could not remember whether they had used advocacy services or not, and 7 patients (2%) did not want to answer

4.36 It is apparent from some of these responses that advocacy services are being used to provide information, such as contact details of solicitors, that we would expect to be made available to patients by staff. However, it may be that advocates were representing information already offered by staff, or it may be felt that patients will more readily accept such information from advocacy services. The new provisions for statutory advocacy services under s.130A of 1983 Act will require advocates to help patients in obtaining and understanding information that hospital managers are already obliged, by s.132, to ensure that the patient understands insofar as is practicable. We hope that, when the revised Act is implemented, no managers will seek to discharge their duties under s.132 entirely through advocacy services, so that the introduction of statutory advocacy services does not lessen expectations upon nursing and medical staff to engage with patients in explaining and discussing patients' legal position and rights under the Act.

4.37 In 2007 we found detained patients being charged a fee of £20 for access to advocacy services at one independent provider. We have suggested forcibly that such charging is stopped, and that the hospital provides better access to advocacy services. The implementation of the 2007 Act's statutory right to advocacy should prevent such extraordinary practice.

4.38 The statutory requirement for advocacy will also fall upon some services where funding for advocacy services has been under threat. As this report was being finalised, one London PCT reversed its initial decision to completely decommission advocacy services provided by MIND to detained patients in a west London mental health unit, instead reducing the service to half-time with the instruction that it focus on representing individual patients at CPA meetings, ward rounds and Tribunals. This is part of the PCT's response to its need to make financial savings against spending deficits. We had protested at the original decision to stop advocacy services altogether, not only for the effect that it will have on the patients detained at the unit in question, but also because decommissioning the advocacy services may have provided a (very) short-term saving whilst there is no statutory duty to provide advocacy services, but would no doubt increase the overall expense (and possibly the effectiveness) of re-establishing a service when this becomes a statutory requirement later this year. The reduction of the service is clearly a better result than its closure, but as a result patients will not receive advice on benefits or housing from advocates. We hope that the unit management will monitor carefully any adverse effect on patients (especially in light of our concerns over delayed discharges, as discussed at chapter 1.51 above and that a full service will be restored in the next financial year through joint-commissioning strategies.

Section 2 and section 3

4.39 Our last report supported the contention of the *Mental Health Act Manual* that s.3 should only be used to admit a patient who is known to services and has been assessed in the recent past, and called for government to confirm or update its guidance in the light of the Manual's criticism of the wider use of s.3 powers[381]. We have suggested that this issue should be clarified with the publication of the revised Code of Practice necessitated by the passing of the 2007 Act.

---

[381] MHAC (2006) *Eleventh Biennial Report 2003-2005; In Place of Fear?* para 4.10 *et seq.*

4.40 Detention under the powers of the Act is a reaction to an event or chain of events, the significance of which should not be assumed. As such, the assessment provisions of s.2 will be the most appropriate initial detention power for many patients. Over the last five years of recorded data (figure 51 below), where either s.2 or s.3 was used as the initial detaining power, s.2 was used for 63% of admissions to hospital, and for 35% of detentions of existing inpatients. In 2005/06, these percentages were 64% and 39% respectively. It is possible that community-level support has provided the knowledge and recent assessment required in the one third of admissions that take place under s.3, although we believe that in many services the fact that a patient has had a previous admission or is otherwise generally 'known' to the service precipitates the use of s.3 without a recent substantial assessment.

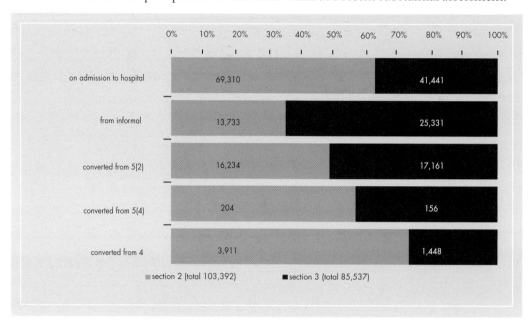

Fig 51: Uses of sections 2 and 3, NHS and independent hospitals, England, 2001/2 to 2005/6

Data source: Department of Health / Information Centre statistical bulletins
"Inpatients detained under the Mental Health Act 1983 and other legislation" 2002 - 2007

Section 17 leave

4.41 Although the Code of Practice allows that "short-term local leave" may be "managed by other staff" than the RMO, it is a legal requirement that the RMO authorises the parameters of such leave as the authorisation itself cannot be delegated. The Code states that "it is crucial that such decisions [as are taken by other staff] fall within the terms of the grant of periodic leave by the RMO"[382]. However, in one example, we found that an RMO had authorised leave in the broadest terms ("unescorted leave in the community at staff discretion") for a restricted patient, and that this authorisation, and others like it, were marked for review in four or five months from issue. In our view, this is inappropriate: the RMO's authorisation should be more specific, and should be reviewed more frequently.

4.42 The language used to describe the parameters of leave should be precise. It is unhelpful, for example, to specify that a patient may have leave to go to "local" shops if that term is capable

---

[382] *MHA 1983 Code of Practice*, para 20.4.

of different interpretations by nursing staff acting in a gatekeeping role. Inconsistency in such gatekeeping is unlikely to encourage patients to regard leave parameters seriously. We reiterate our concern at family members, friends or carers being designated as 'escorts' for patients at chapter 2.23.

4.43 Staff do not always record whether or not a patient's leave from hospital went well, or whether staff or the patient had any concerns in relation to the period of leave. In some hospitals, patients are encouraged to complete leave reports to put their view on record. Such reports, or verbal debriefing sessions leading to a nursing note in the records, are useful in terms of risk assessment and as a means to engage patients in discussion about their care planning.

> **Recommendation 26:** A record should be made of patient's views and concerns regarding every significant period of leave from hospital.

4.44 We have noted many examples where the Secretary of State's authorisation of s.17 leave is neither filed in restricted patients' notes nor kept alongside s.17 leave forms. It is sensible to have the letter of authorisation available to staff and administrators to ensure that leave granted falls within the permitted parameters set by the Mental Health Unit (see chapter 7.73).

Patients unable to take authorised escorted leave

4.45 In our comments on staffing levels in this report, we noted that some patients were unable to take escorted leave granted by their RMOs due to the unavailability of escorting staff (see chapter 1.35). In one hospital, nursing staff complained that the two RMOs with responsibilities for patients on a particular ward were granting a sum total of escorted leave that could never be provided under that ward's staffing ratios. We suggested that the ward manager should calculate the maximum capacity of his staff to escort patients on leave and seek the agreement of the doctors to be mindful of this limit. Whilst this is a pragmatic solution, the Code of Practice states that patients' leave can be an important part of their treatment plans[383], and it is important that the management of staffing levels is not allowed to compromise such plans.

4.46 For most patients, the parameters of discretionary or escorted leave authorised by the RMO are, of course, expressed as a maximum (e.g. "up to an hour's escorted leave a day"). Furthermore, in many cases the amount of leave allowed for in a care plan is used as an indicator of a patient's progress towards fitness for discharge, whether as a part of Care Programme Approach reviews or by hospital managers and the Tribunal considering appeals against detention. It is important that this is explained to patients, so that they understand the parameters of their leave as a maximum allowance rather than an entitlement. It is equally important to ensure that any review of the patient's care and treatment, or review of detention, is provided with information on the actual patterns of leave taken by a patient, as well as that which was authorised.

---

[383] *MHA 1983 Code of Practice*, para 20.1

4.47   In a number of cases patients were quite understandably frustrated by their inability to take authorised leave. One patient in a south London hospital in April 2006 reported having been able to take his authorised two-hour escorted daily leave on only three occasions over 35 days (and, speaking for all the patients on the ward, that "the boredom factor is doing us in"); and a patient in west London in August 2007 complained of having no leave since being transferred onto a particular ward twenty days earlier, despite having authorisation for half an hour's escorted leave twice daily. In these sorts of cases, there should be a record made of a 'service deficit' as a part of the Care Programme Approach review of care plans, which would allow the shortfalls to be noted (and addressed) in the individual patients' cases, but also for such shortfalls to be aggregated to provide a broader view useful for considering whether there is an adequate staff complement on the ward.

Photographing patients for leave documentation

4.48   In some parts of the secure sector, detained patients are photographed upon admission, primarily to provide a likeness of the patient to be used if that patient goes AWOL (staff also may take a note of patients' clothing when they go out on leave for the same purpose). In this period we have been asked for a view on the extension of such practices to open wards, and whether detained patients should be considered to have a right to decline to be photographed. In practical terms, we suggest that notwithstanding the arguments that may be made for or against deriving powers to photograph patients from the fact of their detention, no detained patient who declines to be photographed should ever be forced into posing for the camera in the manner of old asylum casebooks. However, where a risk assessment suggests that it would be prudent to possess an image of a patient, we can see no reason why the taking of such a photograph should not be stated to be a condition of that patient being granted leave of absence. If a patient continues to refuse to be photographed in such circumstances, the responsible medical officer should consider very carefully what meaning to attach to such refusal if he or she decides to reconsider the position.

Renewal of detention (section 23)

4.49   Within the final two months of a patient's current period of detention under s.3, the RMO may renew the authority for detention if, upon examining the patient, he or she determines that the conditions established in section 20(4) are met[384]. The renewal takes effect when the RMO's report, set out in statutory form, is "furnished" to the managers[385]. The point at

---

[384] See MHA 1983 s.20(3). The conditions at s.20(4) are

- that the patient is suffering from one of the forms of mental disorder specified in section 1 of the Act to a nature or degree that makes hospital treatment appropriate; and

- that such treatment is likely to alleviate or prevent a deterioration in the patient's condition (or, for patients with mental illness or severe mental impairment, that the patient would unlikely to be able to care for him or herself, obtain the care needed, or guard against serious exploitation); and

- that it is necessary for the health or safety of the patient, or for the protection of others, that the treatment is given and it cannot be given unless the patient is detained.

The second bullet-point above will no longer apply in the revised Act, where the test will be that 'appropriate treatment is available' to the patient.

[385] MHA 1983 s.23(3)(b).

which a report can be said to be "furnished" to the managers was considered in a Scottish case, which ruled that it was sufficient for the report to have been consigned to the hospital's internal post system[386].

4.50 Whilst it is a legal requirement that hospital managers record the renewal of authority for s.3 detention by the RMO in the form set out in regulations (Form 30), it is often mistakenly assumed that a failure to make such a record makes such a renewal invalid. We often receive queries from concerned administrators who find Forms 30 uncompleted by managers and seek reassurance over the legal status of the patient concerned. In 2007, we learned that an MHRT panel had declared a patient's s.3 detention invalid on the grounds that, at the time of its renewal, the managers had not had a hearing to consider whether to exercise their discharge powers, and had not completed Form 30. The MHRT panel was sitting six months after the renewal concerned, and one month after the hospital managers finally had met to consider the patient's case upon his request that they should do so. We consider the MHRT's assumption that the detention was invalid to have been incorrect in law. In the event, the question was not pursued as the hospital concerned was advised by its own solicitors against legal action, in part for reasons of cost, and the patient had in any case accepted inpatient treatment on an informal basis.

Renewal under the revised Act

4.51 The 2007 Act replaces the role of the 'responsible medical officer', who must be a doctor, with that of the 'responsible clinician', who may be any mental health professional who has been approved for that purpose (see chapter 1.45 *et seq*). We were among the many stakeholders in the debates leading up to the Act who expressed concern that the certification that the conditions of detention are met at the time of a renewal by someone who is not a doctor could fail to meet the 'objective medical evidence' standard required to justify psychiatric detention under Article 5 of the ECHR. Government informed us that its lawyers advised otherwise, and had stated that the responsible clinician's approval would provide sufficient qualification to meet this requirement, but this legal advice was never made available for our scrutiny. Many legal experts remain sceptical over this advice. In a late concession during the passage of the Bill, the government introduced an amendment that prevents the responsible clinician from renewing the detention of a patient without the agreement of another person who has been professionally concerned with the patient's treatment, but who is of a different profession to the responsible clinician[387].

4.52 In practice, it is quite possible that only a small proportion of responsible clinicians will not be doctors, at least in the early stages of implementing the revised Act. It is likely that prudent detaining authorities will establish policy-level requirements that, where a responsible clinician is not a doctor, he or she will involve a doctor as the second profession in the renewal process, if only to avoid becoming the test-case over whether a renewal of detention without the involvement of a doctor meets human rights requirements.

---

[386] Jones R (2006) *Mental Health Act Manual*, tenth edition, note under 'furnish' at p.128. The case is *Milborrow, Applicant*, 1996 S.C.L.R. 315, Sh.Ct.

[387] MHA 1983 s.20(5A) as inserted by MHA 2007, s.9(4)(b)

The provision of information to patients under section 132

Resolutions were taken as to the disposal of my person and my property, and communicated to me with about as much ceremony as if I were a piece of furniture, an image of wood, incapable of will and desire as well as of judgment

John Perceval (1840) *A Narrative of the Treatment Experienced by a Gentleman During the State of Mental Derangement* [388]

4.53 Throughout August, September and October 2006 the MHAC asked patients that it visited a series of structured questions concerning their experience of being given information under s.132 of the Act. The results of are set out at figure 52 below.

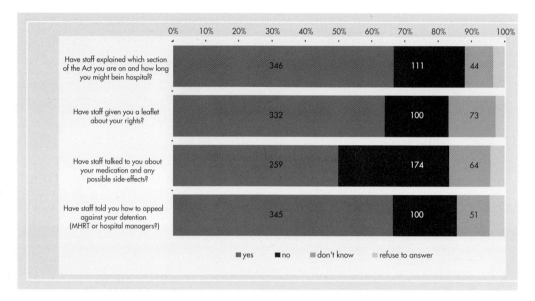

Fig 52: Responses of 519 patients met with on MHAC visits to a structured questionnaire on the provision of information under s.132 of the 1983 Act

Data source: MHAC data

4.54 We also asked if patients could recall when staff last spoke with them about their rights. 142 patients (27%) could remember, of whom slightly less than a third (44) had been spoken to within the last week and slightly over a third (52) had been spoken to over a month ago, with the rest in between.

4.55 It is of great concern to the MHAC that an average of nearly one quarter of the patients that we encountered told us that they had not received information from nursing staff to which they had a statutory entitlement. About one in five patients told us that staff had failed to explain to them the legal powers under which they were detained, how long they would be in hospital, or how to appeal. A similar proportion had not received the Department of Health leaflet (or any other leaflet) explaining these matters. One in three patients told us that staff had not talked to them about their medication. These findings suggest that a

---

[388] Bateson G (ed) (1961) *Perceval's narrative; a patient's account of his psychosis 1830-1832*. California, Stanford University Press, p.179

significant number of services are failing to meet their responsibilities under s.132 of the Act, and consequently may also be failing in their human rights responsibilities towards those that they detain: patients who are not well-informed are less able to exercise the rights that they are given in law.

4.56   Our survey reflects patients' subjective experience, and as such it is likely that some patients who claimed not to have been given information had forgotten or misunderstood it. However, the Act does not require only that managers give patients information (such that their duty might be discharged in a single act of 'giving patients their rights'), but rather that they take such steps as are practicable to enable patients to understand the information[389]. On some visits we have found that patients are 'given their rights' once, with no date set for a review of whether the patient understands or recalls the information, even when the rights had been explained soon after admission when many patients were at their most disturbed or distracted. On noting such practice, we have suggested that services audit which patients have had no recent discussion over rights to rectify the immediate problem, and instil systems whereby nursing staff are prompted to approach patients on a regular basis to prevent the situation reoccurring. It is important that such systems are not overly rigid, but encourage staff to approach patients at times that they think are best suited for the patient. One south Yorkshire based Trust had a system whereby nursing staff were instructed to make a second attempt to explain patients rights a fortnight after any unsuccessful first attempt: when this instruction was followed in explaining MHRT rights to s.2 patients, the opportunity for such patients to use the information and apply to the MHRT had passed[390]. The Trust changed its policy when we pointed this out.

4.57   These findings must not overshadow the good practice that is evident in some Trusts. In this reporting period, visiting Commissioners have commended the work of Janet Williams, the MHA Administrator at the Royal Glamorgan Hospital (Pontypridd and Rhondda NHS Trust), who has devised patient information leaflets concerning MHRTs and managers' hearings, alongside other local forms enabling RMOs to check that they have completed all the appropriate tasks before signing a Form 38 (see chapter 6.22) and to inform patients of SOAD decisions[391]; as well as forms to help statutory consultees record their part of the Second Opinion process (see chapter 6.71).

Section 136

Revision of the Act – ability to transfer between places of safety

4.58   We are pleased that the 1983 Act is to be amended by s.44 of the 2007 Act to enable a constable, approved mental health professional or anyone authorised by either of them to transfer a s.136 detainee between places of safety. We regret only that this revision has not been subject to early implementation, given the difficulties in operating safely and lawfully

---

[389] MHA 1983 s.132; see also *MHA 1983 Code of Practice*, Chapter 14.

[390] S.2 patients must apply to the MHRT within the first 14 days of detention: see MHA 1983 s.66(2)(a).

[391] See MHAC (2004) *Guidance for RMOs: R (on the application of Wooder) v Dr Feggeter and the Mental Health Act Commission*. Guidance Note available at www.mhac.org.uk

within the framework of the current Act. We have heard that some police services, faced with a person whom they suspect may be in need of urgent medical attention, have taken that person to an A&E department for assessment of the medical condition, and then continued on to a place of safety (whether in a psychiatric facility or police station), having considered the stop-over at A&E as a part of the conveyance process. We doubt that this is lawful, but understand the motivation. Other protocols for people in need of urgent medical attention have suggested that the police use powers of arrest for a breach of the peace in preference to s.136 powers[392]. This avoids the problem of having such a person 'stuck' in an A&E department whilst the s.136 assessment are arranged and carried out, but at the cost of criminalising mentally disordered behaviours that may otherwise have been dealt with in a medical context (albeit one that has its own consequences for a police record: see chapter 2.147 *et seq*).

Forensic Medical Examiners

4.59 Psychiatrists, social workers and staff in some NHS Trusts have expressed concern to the MHAC over the service provided in relation to s.136 detainees under contracts made between a number of police forces and a private provider of forensic medical services. One such concern relates to delays in attendance, but others were of a more fundamental nature.

4.60 In some cases, there was a suggestion that nurses employed by the private company might be expected to perform a triage function prior to the assessment required under s.136 of the Act. The implication of such a role is that the nurse could be responsible for deciding whether the detainee was suffering from a mental disorder within the meaning of the Act, and could terminate the s.136 process prior to attendance of a doctor and ASW if s/he thought that there was no mental disorder present. We do not believe that this is a proper role for a nurse. The Act states that the purpose of s.136 detention is for examination by a doctor. The Code of Practice suggests that the patient should be seen by a s.12 approved doctor, who may decide that the s.136 process must be terminated as the patient is not mentally disordered, and that any reason for not using such a doctor should be recorded[393].

4.61 Other concerns expressed to the MHAC have related to the professional background and decisions of some doctors provided to undertake the role of forensic medical examiners (FME). In one case, a consultant psychiatrist told us that he had been called by one such FME to see a young woman detainee, and was shocked to find that, although he could detect no sign of mental disturbance when he examined her, the FME had already completed a medical recommendation for admission to hospital under s.2 of the Act. We have also had (uncorroborated) reports of doctors supplied to undertake FME roles who have language difficulties, and whose medical speciality (in one case, plastic surgery) provided questionable qualification for the role.

---

[392] Heart of England NHS Foundation Trust (2007) *Managing the disturbed / agitated subject: a multi-agency partnership. July 2007.* The MHAC does not endorse this policy.

[393] *MHA 1983 Code of Practice*, para 10.12

4.62 Given the MHAC's remit and the need to target our resources, we do not think that it would be appropriate for us to investigate these claims, but we have sought to pass on concerns to appropriate bodies for action. In the meantime, police authorities should ensure that s.136 detainees held in police cells are seen by a doctor with s.12 approved status wherever practicable, perhaps in addition to the FME contracted to the authority.

> **Recommendation 27:** Police authorities should seek to ensure that arrangements for the medical assessment of s.136 detainees in police custody meet the expectations of the Code of Practice through being undertaken by a s.12 approved doctor wherever practicable, and that exceptions to this are recorded with reasons.

Defining a public place

4.63 Section 136 can be applied where a police officer "finds in a place to which the public has access" an apparently mentally disordered person appearing to need care or containment. The House of Lords' 2007 ruling in *Seal v Chief Constable of South Wales Police*[394] (see chapter 2.151) highlighted a situation where police were alleged to have made an arrest for breach of the peace in a person's home, and then detained that person under s.136 "as a result of what happened in the street"[395] outside the home. We do not know the details of this particular action (which in any case occurred in 1997), but we have heard of several other instances where s.136 has been used to detain a person who has been asked or made to step outside of their home (or another private property) by police. Indeed, at a meeting with one London-based social services authority in this period, we noted that its audit showed that 30% of s.136 arrests were recorded as having been made at or just outside the detainee's home. Police officers were 'inviting' people out of their homes, or arresting them for a breach of the peace and 'de-arresting' them once outside to then invoke s.136 powers. We suggested that this was at the very least a misuse of the powers given under the Act, and that the social services and police authorities should jointly explore alternative means of managing persons about whom the police have concerns that would not undermine the protections offered by the Act. We suggested, for example, that the police could be given a dedicated telephone number to contact ASWs and trigger an assessment under the Act.

4.64 Baroness Hale of Richmond noted, in her speech given as a part of the judgment in *Seal*, that "police officers lead difficult and dangerous lives [and] have to make snap decisions in complex situations", but that whilst "the police may have an answer to Mr Seal's claim… their case is not without difficulty"[396]. Lady Hale raised the difficulty of how Mr Seal could be said to have been "found in a place to which the public have access", as required under s.136, either whilst he was in his mother's house, or when under arrest in the street outside. The Court did not have to rule on this point, but Lady Hale's comment suggests that a future challenge to such an action would at least receive a hearing.

---

[394] *Seal v Chief Constable of South Wales Police* [2007] UKHL 31

[395] *ibid.*, para 3

[396] *ibid.*, paras 58, 60

Places of Safety

4.65   We welcome the emphasis given by government on ensuring that hospital-based places of safety are available, and the additional funding provided to establish them in some areas. As this report was in production, the Royal College of Psychiatrists was updating its Council Report on Standards of Places of Safety. We have had an input into this revision and will promote the final document amongst detaining authorities when it is published.

Appeals against detention

The Mental Health Review Tribunal

Problems in MHRT administration

4.66   The Mental Health Review Tribunal (MHRT) was transferred to become a part of the newly created Tribunals Service in April 2006, under the oversight of the Department of Constitutional Affairs. Later that year its secretariat for England was consolidated into a single, London-based office, although it is now planned to re-locate the secretariat to Leicester by the end of March 2008[397]. In our last report we highlighted the difficulties experienced in the administration of the MHRT in England, leading to late cancellations of hearings and adjournments; difficulties in listing cases; and unavailability of clerks for hearings[398]. We continue to hear widespread criticism of the logistical arrangements for Tribunals. Some of the problems experienced in MHRT administration were studied in a NIMHE/CSIP pilot study commissioned as a part of the Department of Health's preparations for the new Mental Health Act[399], and we note the significant efforts being made to improve the service. The MHRT has been dogged by administrative failings (and administrative upheaval) for a number of years now, and we hope that the relocation, and the already implemented move to a case-management system of working, will improve its service to hospital administrators, to its own members and, most of all, to the patients who appeal their detention.

4.67   Of particular concern to the MHAC are late cancellations of planned hearings (often due to the unavailability of key personnel, whether panel members or other professionals) and adjournments of Tribunal hearings that do take place. We have met with a number of patients who have been seriously distressed by cancellations of their appeal hearings, and some patients who had experienced more than one cancellation.

> On a visit in Norfolk, we met John, a restricted patient who had experienced three MHRT hearing cancellations in the last two years. Two of these hearings dates had been scheduled for early 2007, but both were cancelled the day before the hearing was due to take place. John told us that he felt "very upset, sick and disappointed" over these cancellations.

---

[397]   Mental Health Review Tribunal (2007) *MHRT Stakeholders e-mail bulletin, issue 1, July 2007.* http://www.mhrt.org.uk/news/documents/MHRT_stakeholder_emailBulletin_06Aug07.pdf

[398]   MHAC (2006) *Eleventh Biennial Report 2003-2005*; *In Place of Fear?:* para 4.108

[399]   Marsen-Luther Y (2007) 'Reforming the appeals process' *Mental Health Today February 2007, p18-20*; Marsen-Luther Y, O'Hare B, Symington J (2007) *Interim Report on Plan Do Study Act cycles on the recommendations arising from the MHRT improvement Pilot 2006.* NIMHE / CSIP

4.68 Whilst no national statistics are available on late cancellations of MHRT hearings, we hear anecdotally that they are a significant problem. It appears that the numbers of hearings adjourned on the day has grown significantly in recent years. The MHRT secretariat reported in 2005 that the rate of adjournments on the day of hearings grew from just over 1% in 2001 to just over 10% in 2004[400]. In its annual report for 2005/06, the MHRT reported that "nearly a quarter" of MHRT hearings were adjourned on the day[401]. The NIMHE/CSIP study findings on the reasons for 108 adjournments are reproduced at figure 53 below. This shows that causes of adjournments may be due to unavailability of reports or care plans, or to the unavailability of people. Technical problems in obtaining documentation may be eased by the MHRT's new secure e-mail system, although in many cases the delays in obtaining reports appears to be because they have not been produced, rather than because they are 'in the post': there is widespread failure by RMOs and social workers to provide their reports within the three-week time limit required by regulations[402].

Reasons for 'on the day adjournments'	number	%
Report related	**49**	**45%**
No report	17	15%
No CPA	11	20%
CPA / report problem	21	42
Attendance problems	**53**	**49%**
Patient non-attendance	17	15%
No RMO / doctor	14	13%
No solicitor	12	11%
No social worker	4	4%
No panel member	4	4%
No interpreter	2	2%
Miscellaneous	**6**	**5%**
Total	**108**	**100%**

Fig 53 : Reasons for adjournment of 108 MHRT hearings, England

Data source: NIMHE/CSIP pilot study, reported in *Mental Health Today*, February 2007[403]

4.69 We note that the problems with the availability of key people in the study on adjournments were more frequently related to RMOs or solicitors than panel members themselves. The CSIP/NIMHE study recommended that hospital MHA Administrators could co-ordinate bookings with clinicians and the patient's solicitor before offering dates to the MHRT secretariat[404], which might help to address such problems, albeit possibly at the expense of the goodwill of some hospital administrators who may feel that they are being asked to take

---

[400] Mental Health Review Tribunal (2005) Secretariat Activity Report 2001 -05. November 2005, http://www.mhrt.org.uk/resources/documents/pdf/mhrt_secretariat_activity_report_2001-05.pdf

[401] Mental Health Review Tribunal (2006) *Mental Health Review Tribunal Secretariat Annual Report 2006.* http://www.mhrt.org.uk/news/documents/mhrt_secretariat_annual_report_october_2006.pdf

[402] Marsen-Luther Y (2007) *op cit.*, n. 399

[403] *ibid*, p.19

[404] *ibid.*

up some of the burdens of the MHRT secretariat. The Mental Health Lawyers Association has stated that its members frequently chase up listing problems for MHRT appeals[405] (perhaps especially in relation to obtaining timely reports and care plans, as suggested in the Legal Services Commission guide for solicitors representing patients at the MHRT[406]), with the implication that mental health professionals are already engaged in administration that should be undertaken by the MHRT secretariat.

Number and outcomes of appeals

4.70 The Annual Report of the MHRT[407] records that, in 2005/6, it received almost 22,000 applications and referrals, of which 57% progressed to a substantive hearing. Hearings for unrestricted patients were arranged within an average of six days (for s.2 applications) and six weeks (for s.3 applications and referrals), although hearings for restricted patients' applications took an average of 18 weeks to arrange in 2005/06, compared with 16 weeks in 2004/05.

> I have found MHRTs to be a very beneficial way of getting professionals to review my situation
>
> *Dawn Cutler-Nichol, s.37/41, Derbyshire*

4.71 We are grateful to the MHRT secretariat for supplying us with data on the outcome of applications for hearings, which is set out at figure 54 below.

Outcomes of MHRT hearing application	Year	
	2005	2006
Total Hearings	9,522	8,778
Patient not discharged	7,935	17,417
Patient discharged	1,587	1,361
Absolute discharge	784	655
Delayed discharge	364	287
Conditional discharge	222	195
Deferred conditional discharge	217	224
% of discharges to hearings	14%	11%
Withdrawn applications	1,843	1,960
Discharges by RMO prior to hearing	4,760	4,629

Fig 54: Outcomes of MHRT hearing applications, 2005 & 2006

Data source: MHRT secretariat

---

[405] Mental Health Lawyers Association (2007) *Response of the Mental Health Lawyers Association to changes in the Unified Contract Mental Health Specification*. July 2007, para 30.

[406] Legal Services Commission (2007) *Mental Health - Improving Your Quality; A guide to common issues identified through Peer Review*. January 2007, p.15.
http://www.legalservices.gov.uk/docs/cls_main/MentalhealthBrochure-FinalJan07.pdf

[407] Mental Health Review Tribunal (2006) op *cit*. n.401.

4.72   The above data shows that more applications for MHRT hearings are withdrawn than are successful. It would seem likely that patients withdraw applications when they feel that they have little chance of a successful appeal: in some such cases the withdrawal may be tactical, so that the patient preserves the right to apply again within his or her current period of detention[408]. There are, of course, no similar limitations on the number of times a patient may request a managers' hearing (see paragraph 4.90 *et seq* below).

4.73   The data at figure 54 also shows that there are nearly one third as many MHRT applicants who are discharged by their RMO prior to their hearing as there are applicants who are discharged by the Tribunal itself. In many cases, the RMO's decision to discharge a patient from detention will be a foreseeable event (for instance, where the actual date of discharge is dependent only upon making suitable aftercare arrangements). The NIMHE/CSIP pilot study tested a system whereby RMOs classified their patients who made applications according to the likelihood of that patient remaining in hospital until the date of a hearing. In this way, the MHRT secretariat could prioritise the booking of hearings that would definitely take place before finding available panellists for those where patients may be discharged before their hearing date. Whilst we can see the logistic sense of such an arrangement, we hope that any wider application of it will be carefully monitored to ensure that it has no detrimental effect on the organisation of hearings for patients who were deemed more likely to be discharged by their RMOs: perhaps by definition, such patients may have the most to lose through delays and cancellations, as they are clearly perceived as being ready or almost ready to be discharged from formal powers.

4.74   We have previously suggested that the above data should be collated in such a way that it may be broken down by the section of the Act that is being appealed against, as there may be significant variation in discharge rates between, for example, civil detentions and restricted patients[409]. A key NIMHE/CSIP recommendation was that there should be ethnic monitoring of appeals and their outcomes[410]. In our view such monitoring must extend to all applications (including those that are withdrawn or where a patient is discharged before the hearing) and should include identification of the section under which patients are detained. Given the changes being made to legal aid funding of patients' representation at MHRTs (see paragraph 4.80 *et seq* below), it is particularly important that accurate and continued monitoring of the outcomes of MHRTs is undertaken.

> **Recommendation 28:** The MHRT secretariat should collate and publish data on MHRT applications and outcomes including patients' gender, ethnicity and the section of the Act to which they are subject.

---

[408] See MHA 1983, s.66 and 69: only one application to the MHRT may be made during detention under s.2; during the initial period of s.3 and in any renewed period of s.3; and in the second six months (and thereafter annually) of a s.37. Under the 2007 Act (schedule 3, regulation 18, amending MHA 1983 s.66) patients subject to a CTO will be able to apply to the MHRT once in the initial six months, and once in any renewed period (as with s.3). CTO patients will have an additional right to apply if they are recalled to hospital. If a Nearest Relative's application to discharge a patient from either s.3 or a CTO is blocked under s.25 there is a further right to apply to the MHRT.

[409] MHAC (2006) *Eleventh Biennial Report 2003-2005: In Place of Fear?*, para 4.119

[410] Marsen-Luther Y (2007) *op cit*, n.399; Marsen-Luther Y, O'Hare B, Symington J (2007) op *cit*., n.399.

Automatic referrals to the MHRT

4.75   The successful administration of the MHRT is, in practical terms, predicated on the fact that most patients will not exercise their legal rights of appeal. Only a minority of detained patients exercise their right to apply for an MHRT hearing of their case in any year. In 2004/05, for example, s.2 was used more than 21,000 times and there were just over 6,000 Tribunal applications[411]. Amongst the various likely reasons for the low rates of appeal, we would suggest that mental incapacity (whether in relation to understanding the legal position or the routes to challenge it) and lack of motivation are likely to be significant factors. Of course, the fact that a patient lacks the mental capacity to understand that they are deprived of liberty, or the motivation to challenge that deprivation, is absolutely no guarantee that the deprivation is justified or in their best interests.

4.76   It seems likely that older detained patients are significant less likely to appeal against their detention to either the MHRT or the hospital managers. Shah and Joels analysed data from all admissions under ss.2 or 3 to the Royal Free Hospital NHS Trust between 2002 and 2005, and found that patients under 65 years of age[412] were almost two and a half times more likely to appeal than those aged over 65. Rimmer et al previously found that younger patients were three times more likely to appeal than older patients[413]. It seems likely that there is a link between the reduced rates of appeal and incapacitating disorders such as dementia, in that patients who do not understand their legal position are unlikely to challenge it. The Royal Free Hospital data also shows that older patients with diagnoses of depression did not appeal, suggesting that lack of motivation may be another factor[414]. We would add that staff caring for older patients may also be less likely to encourage or help older patients to appeal against their detention in hospital, out of a sense that hospital care (and formal status) is the only viable option for clinical intervention.

4.77   Under the Act as it is now in force, patients who do not appeal their detention in the first six months of a s.3 should be referred to the MHRT automatically[415]. The 2007 Act changes this rule so that any time spent detained under s.2 will count towards that first six months[416]. This means that all civil patients who do not appeal their detention will now have an automatic referral at the same point, irrespective of whether they were initially detained under s.2 or s.3. For most patients this increases the protection offered by the Act. However, where a s.3 patient (or his or her nearest relative) had unsuccessfully appealed detention under s.2, but then made no further application to the MHRT, there will no longer be an automatic referral after six months of detention under s.3, and the next automatic referral will not take place until three years have elapsed from the last MHRT hearing[417]. In the event

---

[411] Lords Hansard 26 Feb 2007 : Column 1459 (Earl Howe)

[412] Shah S and Joels S (2006)'Appeals by the elderly against compulsory detention under the Mental Health Act 1983' *Int J Geriatr Psychiatry* **21**:1213-14

[413] Rimmer M A, O'Commor S, Anderson D (2002) 'Appeal against detention under the Mental Health Act 1983: relationship to age and incapacity'. *Int J Geriatr Psychiatry* **17**:1884-5

[414] Shah S and Joels S (2006) op *cit.*, n.412.

[415] See Mental Health Act 1983, s.68.

[416] Mental Health Act 1983, s.68 (as amended by s.37(3) of the MHA 2007).

[417] Mental Health Act 1983, s.68(6) (as amended by s.37(3) of the MHA 2007).

of such a case (and in any case where a relative's unsuccessful appeal to the MHRT has forfeited a patients' right to automatic referral), hospital managers should consider requesting that the Secretary of State exercise the power to make a special referral under s.67 of the Act[418].

4.78   Local systems should be in place to flag those patients who have not exercised their rights to appeal to the MHRT, to ensure that the hospital managers' duty to refer such patients under s.68 is met. In this reporting period we encountered one hospital where such a system appeared to be inadequate, leading to at least one case where the managers failed to make such a referral at the time of a patient's s.3 renewal.

4.79   The 2007 Act provides the Secretary of State with the power to amend by order the timescales for automatic referral to the MHRT. The Minister gave a commitment that it was the intention of government to reduce these timescales when resources in the NHS, local authorities and the MHRT allow[419]. In the absence of frequent automatic referrals, it is particularly important to provide detained patients with adequate information about and support in exercising rights to appeal. For patients who may be less likely to take advantage of legal rights and protections (whether because of the cohort effect of their diagnostic or social group, or because of the effects of their disorder) it may be necessary to engage assertive advocacy services which will be able to initiate discussions in an appropriate manner (see paragraph 4.30 above on advocacy).

Legal representation at Tribunals

4.80   The current arrangements for patients to engage legal representation for MHRTs and other matters operate through the Law Society's Mental Health Review Tribunal Panel. A list of members of that panel (the first such specialist panel set up by the Law Society in recognition of the specialist nature of the work involved) should be available to patients on wards: it is a requirement of the Code of Practice that patients be informed of how to contact a suitably qualified solicitor[420], and we recommended in our Ninth Biennial Report that all wards should have the relevant Law Society list available[421]. We often check on our visits that information on Law Society Panel members is available to patients.

4.81   The decisions taken by the MHRT, being questions of liberty, "are as intrinsically important as many of those of the Crown Court"[422], and access to the Tribunal engages rights under Articles 5 and 6 of the European Convention. Legal representation at Tribunals is one of the three core areas where legal aid is not means-tested[423]. Following Lord Carter of Cole's

---

[418] Indeed where hospital staff are concerned that limitations upon any patient's access to the MHRT may constitute a breach of Article 5 they should consider making such a request to the Secretary of State. See the comments of Baroness Hale in *R (on the application of MH) v Secretary of State (2004)*, and also Department of Health (2007) *MHA 1983 Draft revised Code of Practice*. October 2007, para 33.39.

[419] Lords Hansard 17 Jan 2007 : Column 746 -7 (Baroness Ashton of Upholland)

[420] *MHA 1983 Code of Practice*, para 14.5c.

[421] MHAC (2001) *Ninth Biennial Report 1999-2001*, para 2.13 (recommendation 6).

[422] Mr Stanley Burnton J in R *(on the application of KB) & Others v MHRT* [2002] EWHC 639 (admin), para 32.

[423] The other two are where a suspect is under arrest and for parents whose child is taken into care.

review of legal aid procurement, the Legal Services Commission (LSC) has developed a system of fixed fee remuneration to solicitors providing MHRT representation effective from the 1 January 2008. The LSC also proposes to introduce competitive tendering of contracts to provide such representation, and is considering means of reducing the costs involved in obtaining independent reports for Tribunal hearings.

4.82   The courts have recognised the specialist nature of legal work in mental health cases[424] and, indeed, have previously expressed disquiet over plans to rationalise legal aid funding for solicitors' MHRT work[425]. The Mental Health Lawyer's Association (MHLA), who represent about 80% of practitioners who represent patients before the MHRT, has been extremely critical of the LSC changes[426], arguing that the payment scheme provides inadequate financial reward for solicitors undertaking this work; will especially penalise specialist firms (such as those who work on forensic cases, due to the complexity and geographic spread of cases); and is incompatible with the expectation of working practices set out in the LSC's own guidance on mental health work[427]. It is, indeed, striking that the LSC guide states that "it is likely" that a solicitor representing a patient at a Tribunal (other than for s.2 appeals) "will need to visit the client several times prior to the hearing to take further instructions, and consider notes, section papers and Tribunal papers"[428]; and should consider "attendance at a s117 pre-discharge after care meeting"[429], although it is not clear how such activities could be funded under the new system[430]. The Legal Services Commission appear to have addressed some of the concerns expressed by the MHLA and other stakeholders, and has made some adjustments to its fixed fee scheme, although clearly not to the satisfaction of the practitioners of the MHLA. Lucy Scott-Moncrieff, a partner in the solicitors *Scott-Moncrieff, Harbour & Sinclair*, has stated that the firm

> will be dropping some of our more complicated and difficult mental health and Tribunal work … Of course, we hope that someone else will pick up those clients, but we don't see why anyone would. We are going to do a lot more straightforward work so that we can balance the books - that's what we are going to do because that is what we have been told to do. It doesn't seem like good value for money to me … [these] are stupid decisions in terms of using people's expertise[431].

---

[424]   see Brooke J (as was) in *R v Legal Aid Board and Lord Chancellor, ex parte Mackintosh Duncan* [2000] All ER(D) 189: "Reading the Report of a psychiatrist, identifying its areas of weakness, commissioning evidence and the appropriate expert challenge to it and representing a client at a Tribunal requires expert professional skills borne… of education and practical experience. It is not like going down to the Magistrates Court as a Duty Solicitor, arduous though those duties are."

[425]   *ibid.*: "We are worried, however, that the [Legal Aid] Board has not yet appreciated how difficult Mental Health Law is, and how generally solicitors cannot pick up the expertise needed to serve the clients effectively, unless they have strong and practical grounding in this field of Law. We hope that the Board will now take urgent steps to identify the really skilled solicitors who are willing to serve their clients in this field at Legal Aid rates of pay".

[426]   Mental Health Lawyers Association (2007) Response *of the Mental Health Lawyers Association to changes in the Unified Contract Mental Health Specification.* July 2007. www.mhla.co.uk

[427]   Legal Services Commission (2007) *Mental Health - Improving Your Quality; A guide to common issues identified through Peer Review.* January 2007.

[428]   *ibid.*, p.6

[429]   *ibid.*, p.11

[430]   See Mental Health Lawyers Association (2007) *MHLA Briefing for legal aid debate on the 12/07/07.* July 2007. www.mhla.co.uk

[431]   'Cashflow crisis', *Law Gazette*, 11 October 2007 (p.18).

4.83   We are concerned at these reports from practitioners over how they may adjust to the changed fee structures, and at the potential impact on patients of any retraction of the availability and quality of legal representation. We are concerned at the prospect of 'easy' MHRT cases being used to subsidise more complex ones. Whilst we will monitor the reported effects of the changes as we visit hospitals and talk with patients and mental health practitioners, we also recommend that government should fund an independent and appropriately detailed review of the effects of changes in due course, to identify (and if necessary counter) any detrimental effect on the protections offered to patients, and specifically on their access to appropriate legal representation.

> **Recommendation 29:** Government should commission an independent review of the effects of the fixed-fee scheme for mental health, with particular focus on patients' access to appropriate legal representation at MHRTs.

MHRT conflicts of interest

4.84   In our last report[432] we stated that we had made our views known to parties involved in a case[433] claiming a conflict of interest where a sentencing judge who had ordered a patient to hospital presided, fourteen months later, over his MHRT hearing. We had suggested that this should be deemed to present a potential "real danger of bias" and pointed to the Joint Committee on the Draft Mental Health Bill's recommendation that, under the revised Tribunal system proposed in the Mental Health Bill 2004, a member of a Tribunal system who has imposed an order should never hear the review or appeal of that order.

4.85   Mr Justice Bennett rejected the idea that the judge's participation in the Tribunal hearing posed a danger of bias. He especially relied on Lord Bingham's statement in *Brandenburg* that the MHRT role is to determine whether a patient is suffering from mental disorder at the point of the hearing, and that it therefore has no power to consider the validity of the admission which gave rise to the liability to be detained[434]. Bennett J concluded from this and other arguments that "a fair minded and informed observer would credit the legal member with the ability to listen… and revise or completely alter any previous view".

Community orders and outstanding MHRT appeals

4.86   Our last report[435] also discussed a patient's legal challenge to the MHRT's decision to consider his application for a hearing against his s.3 detention to be annulled after an application for supervised discharge had been accepted in his case[436]. We suggested that the principle established by a previous case that a Tribunal application is not annulled by a

---

[432]   MHAC (2006) *Eleventh Biennial Report 2003-2005: In Place of Fear?* para 4.120

[433]   *R (on the application of M) v MHRT* [2005] EWHC 2791 (7/12/05)

[434]   *R (on the application of Von Brandenburg) v East London & the City Mental Health NHS Trust & another* [2004] 2 A C 280, para 3.

[435]   MHAC (2006) *Eleventh Biennial Report 2003-2005: In Place of Fear?* para 4.116

[436]   *R v South Thames MHRT ex parte M* (1998) COD 83

patient's move from s.2 to s.3 should be extended to cover the movement from s.3 to aftercare under supervision, especially as the acceptance of a supervised discharge application does not automatically mean that a patient is released from s.3 detention.

4.87 The Court decided otherwise[437], reading the Act's restrictions over applications (s.66(2)) and criteria for discharge by a Tribunal (ss.72(1) and 72(4A)) as the expression of a clear intention by Parliament to treat appeals against detention and supervised discharge as separate issues. Therefore the patient would have had to make a new application to the MHRT to appeal his supervised discharge status.

4.88 Partly because the patient concerned in this appeal was on s.17 leave at the point when he was placed under supervised discharge, the question of whether a patient's supervised discharge status begins with the acceptance of the application or discharge from hospital was not ruled upon in the judgment. Mr Justice Burnton stated that "one would expect" that supervised discharge and detention under s.3 could not be concurrent, given the different criteria for each power and their different consequences for liberty. We might therefore assume that it is discharge from hospital rather than the acceptance of an application for supervised discharge that cancels a patient's detained status under s.3[438]. It is our understanding that the MHRT would require evidence that s.25A is *effective* (i.e. the patient has left hospital and is discharged from s.3), rather than simply that an application for s.25A has been accepted, before cancelling the application for a s.3 Tribunal in any future case.

4.89 Such cases are unlikely to be common, especially with the repeal of supervised discharge provisions with the implementation of the Mental Health Act 2007. However, the construction of the Tribunal's amended powers with regard to patients subject to the new community treatment orders introduced under the 2007 Act suggests that the ruling in this case (that discharge from s.3 onto a community power annuls any outstanding appeal against the s.3 status) will be applicable to the transition from detention under s.3 to being subject to a CTO. In some ways this creates a new anomaly, given that "the application for admission to treatment in respect of a patient shall not cease to have effect by virtue of his becoming a community patient"[439], although a patient's appeal against that application will be annulled at precisely that point, requiring a fresh application.

Managers' review of detention

4.90 Section 23 gives the managers of hospitals the power to discharge detained patients, without setting out any criteria or a specific procedure to follow when considering the exercise of this power. The Code of Practice devotes a chapter to addressing these questions, suggesting that the conduct of hearings "needs to balance informality against the rigour demanded by the importance of the task"[440], whilst establishing an expectation that in contested hearings

---

[437] R (on the application of SR) v MHRT [2005] EWHC 2923 (Admin)

[438] This question does not arise in the case of the CTO introduced as a replacement for supervised discharge under the 2007 Act, which is clearly stated to come into effect upon the discharge of a patient from hospital, even though such a discharge from hospital is not in fact a discharge from the effect of the s.3 application but might rather be seen as a variation of its condition (see para 4.89 above).

[439] MHA 1983 s.17D(1), as amended by s.32 of the Mental Health Act 2007

[440] *MHA Code of Practice* Chapter 23.16.

the hospital managers should obtain written reports in advance of the hearing from the RMO and other professionals directly involved in the patient's care (such as the key worker, named nurse, social worker and clinical psychologist), and implying that such professionals should appear at the oral hearing of the case and possibly be submitted to cross-examination[441].

The powers of managers' hearings

4.91 Just as the procedural aspects of managers' hearings resemble the MHRT, so do its outcomes. In our Tenth Biennial Report we stated our agreement with the contention of Richard Jones' *Mental Health Act Manual* (then in its eighth edition) that hospital managers exercise options similar to the MHRT, in that they may:

- discharge a patient directly;
- adjourn their hearing pending receipt of important information;
- make an unenforceable recommendation about the patient's care;
- order discharge at a specified future date to allow for preparations to be made; or
- order discharge subject to the achievement of a condition, such as obtaining hostel accommodation[442].

4.92 The tenth edition of the *Mental Health Act Manual*, published in this reporting period, omitted the final point above from its list of possible outcomes for managers' hearings, quoting from the 2005 case of *SR*[443] in which the judge appeared to state that managers had no power to order conditional discharge[444]. This interpretation of the case was challenged by Andrew Parsons in January 2007[445], and the 2007 *Mental Health Act Manual* supplement now states that the judge's remarks in *SR* do not have the general effect of prohibiting managers from ordering a discharge that is only to be effected upon the achievement of a specified condition, although it advises managers to be cautious in doing this[446]. Indeed, both Jones and Parsons suggest that managers might be better to adjourn to a specified date to consider whether any conditions that they view as prerequisite to discharge are then met. In our view this is sensible advice. It is true that there may be no great advantage in adjourning a decision where the aftercare requirement is clear and likely to be demonstrably satisfied in the near future (e.g. where suitable accommodation has been identified, and will shortly be available, but is not available at the time of the hearing), but many cases will present a more complicated scenario, in which the precise aftercare arrangements may be less clearly determined, or likely to be problematic to arrange. Managers should be wary of anticipating that a patient will no longer meet the criteria for detention under future circumstances which they cannot accurately predict, whether they do so by setting an as yet

---

[441] MHA Code of Practice Chapter 23.14 to 23.17.

[442] MHAC (2003) *Tenth Biennial Report 2000-2003: Placed Amongst Strangers.* para 9.58.

[443] *R (on the application of SR) v Huntercombe Maidenhead Hospital [2005]* EWHC 2361

[444] Jones R (2006) *Mental Health Act Manual*, tenth edition. Sweet & Maxwell, para 1-264 (penultimate sentence, p.146)

[445] Andrew Parsons (2007) *Hospital managers: can they order 'conditional discharge'?* RadcliffesLeBrasseur Mental Health Law Briefing Number 109, January 2007, www.rlb-law.com

[446] Jones R (2007) *Mental Health Act Manual, supplement to the tenth edition.* Sweet & Maxwell, para 1-264, p.13.

unrealized condition of discharge, or by setting a precise future date for a patient's discharge.

4.93 As we were writing this report we were approached for advice on an unusual hospital managers' decision of the latter type. The review hearing was convened in an independent hospital, following the renewal of a s.3 detention for a patient with severe mental impairment. The managers ordered a 'delayed discharge', but set the date for that discharge four months from the hearing. This is a surprisingly long period of time, especially given that, in setting an actual date for discharge, the managers appeared to have concluded that, at the time of their hearing, the patient no longer met the criteria for detention under the Act[447]. Whilst it can be lawful to determine that a patient no longer meets the criteria for detention but nevertheless delay discharge for a short period to enable aftercare to be arranged[448], we doubt that it is reasonable to anticipate that the patient's entitlement to discharge should be delayed for four months, as such a delay would be in danger of violating Article 5(1)(e) of the ECHR[449]. In our view, if the panel anticipated that making suitable aftercare arrangements would take up to four months, they would have been more prudent to adjourn their hearing to a future date near that time to reassess the situation of the patient at that time.

4.94 Having reached its decision that the patient no longer met the criteria for detention (even though they had deferred discharge for four months), the managers refused to complete the statement on Form 30 acknowledging receipt of the renewal report and stating that the managers 'have decided not to order that the patient be discharged'[450]. It is arguable that the wording of this statement on Form 30 inadequately provides for the various options exercised by managers when undertaking their review of detention following receipt of the renewal, although we felt that the managers could have completed the form (in that they had not in fact discharged the patient at the time of signing, but had established a date when he would be discharged). Despite our genuine concern over the appropriateness of the

---

[447] Although in this case the managers appeared to have determined that the conditions for detention were no longer met, a deferred discharge decision does not necessarily imply that this must be the case. For the MHRT, such a decision might be made in the context of the Tribunal's discretion to discharge a patient who continues to meet the conditions for detention (s.72(1)), and we submit that an analogous discretion may be read across to managers' powers. Jones ((2006) *op cit.*, para 1-815; (2007) *op cit.*, 1-815) contends that the MHRT's power of deferred discharge could be used if the Tribunal concluded that the patient would be fit for discharge at the expiration of a further short period of treatment (although a different opinion, albeit as an interpretation of an earlier authority, was set out by Eldergill A (1997) *Mental Health Tribunals Law and Practice*, Sweet & Maxwell, p.468). In practice, it is difficult to imagine common situations where it would be sensible for hospital managers to defer a discharge date in this way, and in doing so anticipate the effect of treatment and fetter the actions of the treating clinicians, rather than to refuse discharge but arrange to reconvene a hearing after the treatment had run its course to consider the matter afresh. Eldergill (1997) *ibid.*, p.471-2 submits that the *MHRT* is not empowered to adjourn hearings to a later date to see whether a patient's condition improves, for reasons in part to do with his reading of ss.66 and 72. There is, of course, no equivalent statutory framework for managers' hearings. We suggest that managers' hearings should normally come to a view about the patient's fitness for detention at the time of the initial hearing, to fulfil their role in protecting the patient's Article 5 rights, although there is no reason why a decision at that initial hearing should not be accompanied by a decision to reconvene the panel again in the near-future for any reason.

[448] For this in relation to MHRT powers, see Eldergill A (1997) *ibid.*, p.469, 471 (point 4); Jones R (2006) *ibid.*, para 1-814.

[449] See Jones R (2006) *ibid.*, para 1-814 (in relation to MHRT powers under s.72(3)).

[450] Mental Health Regulations 1983, Form 30, Part II.

managers' overall decision, we do not take the view that a failure to complete the managers' statement on Form 30 is, in general terms, material to the lawfulness of the patient's continued detention (see paragraph 4.50 above). However, upon examination of the documentation of the managers' hearing, the hospital's legal advisers suggested that the panel had not shown evidence of having considered whether the patient met the statutory criteria for detention, and recommended that a new panel be convened to reconsider the case.

4.95 The decision to 'overturn' the above managers' hearing raises some interesting legal questions. As a point of principle, as 'the managers' can utilise their power of discharge at any time, we suggest that there can be no legal difficulty in convening a fresh hearing where it is felt that at an earlier one had acted unlawfully in deciding *not to* discharge the patient. It is arguable that this is also the case where the original managers mis-conducted themselves in some other way, but we would suggest caution in rescinding decisions to discharge a patient on this basis. Managers' hearing decisions to discharge a patient (whether immediately or at a specified future date) are complete and in force once made, rather than provisional upon any future event or review by the panel[451], and as such there would normally be no legal authority for either the panel themselves, or the hospital managers on behalf of whom the panel acted, to rescind the decision and reconsider the matter. Although the lawfulness of such action might be argued on the basis that an original panel decision was itself defective in law, where the original decision gave the patient his or her liberty it would seem necessary to seek judicial review.

Outcomes of managers' hearings

4.96 Although we do not collect national statistics on applications for and outcomes of managers' hearings, the table at figure 55 below shows such data from five service providers (three NHS Trusts, one NHS Foundation Trust and one independent provider), for whose co-operation we are grateful. Out of 732 initial requests for managers' hearings that were dealt with in some way over the financial year 2006/07[452], 443 progressed to a hearing, from which 23 decisions to discharge were taken. Such a discharge rate (5%) is much lower than that of the MHRT (although of course our data below is just a sample and it is possible that practices vary from hospital to hospital). There appears to be no significant difference in the proportion of patients who are discharged by their RMO having made a request for a managers' hearing (27%) and the proportion discharged by their RMO having made an application to the MHRT (30%).

4.97 Of the five 'deferred' discharges shown at figure 55, in only one case was a specific date set for the patient's discharge (thus allowing professional staff a finite period of time to make necessary aftercare arrangement). In the others, the managers determined that the patients could be discharged at an unspecified date conditional upon the putting in place of specified aftercare arrangements.

---

451 See Eldergill A (1997) *Mental Health Tribunals Law and Practice*. Sweet & Maxwell, p.468 under 'discharge on a future date'. MHRT case law has, however, determined that decisions to discharge a patient subject to the achievement of a specified condition are by nature provisional.

452 The table excludes 30 requests for manager's hearings that were outstanding at the end of the financial year.

Outcomes of managers' hearing application in five service providers	2006/07
Total Hearings	443
Patient not discharged	**420**
Patient discharged	**23**
Absolute discharge	18
Deferred discharge	5
% of discharges to hearings	**5%**
Withdrawn applications	51
Discharges by RMO prior to hearing	195
Hearing not held for other reason	43

Fig 55: Outcomes of completed managers' hearing applications in five service providers, 2006/2007

Data source: information provided to MHAC [453]

Foundation Trusts and Managers' hearings

4.98   The legislation which was implemented in April 2004 to establish Foundation Trusts[454] established particular rules as to how such Trusts could undertake managers' hearings. As amended by the Foundation Trust legislation, sections 23(4) and (6) of the Mental Health Act stipulated, from that date, that the role of undertaking hearings was not delegable for Foundation Trust non-executive directors, even though the Act allowed such delegation for all other types of hospital. Until its repeal with the implementation of s.45 of the Mental Health Act 2007 on the 24 July 2007[455], this 'drafting error'[456], therefore placed Foundation Trust Managers in a situation unique at that time, although not unprecedented. A similar limitation was imposed on the power of delegation of the managers of NHS Trusts upon their creation in 1990, which was similarly repealed in 1994[457].

4.99   Before the 2007 Act resolved the problem, Foundation Trusts sought to manage the workload of managers' hearings in a number of ways. One 'solution' (also suggested at the time of the similar crisis in the 1990s) was to have the usual delegated panel conduct reviews and hearings, making full and reasoned recommendations to a specially comprised panel of three non-executive directors. Only if the latter managers had any qualms over following the

---

[453] Data source: Bedford & Luton NHS Trust, Dorset Healthcare NHS Foundation Trust, Hertfordshire Partnerships NHS Trust; Partnerships in Care (Kneesworth House), Pennine Care NHS Trust. The MHAC wishes to thank these organisations and their Mental Health Act Administrators for their co-operation.

[454] Schedule 4, paragraph 53 of the Health and Social Care Act 2003 amends section 23 of the MHA 1983 by adding a subsection (6) stating this requirement. See Jones' MHA Manual 10th ed. p.142 for the statute; there is no commentary on this change.

[455] Mental Health Act 2007 (Commencement No. 1) Order 2007

[456] Jones R (2007) *Mental Health Act Manual, supplement to the tenth edition*. Sweet & Maxwell, para 1-266, p.14.

[457] See MHAC (1995) *Sixth Biennial Report 1993-1995*, para 3.7: "an error in the NHS and Community Care Act 1990 resulted in a situation in which the power to discharge patients under section 23 could be exercised only by non-executive directors of a Trust…this caused major problems in many areas. The situation has now been corrected by the Mental Health (Amendment) Act 1994. Trusts can now appoint sub-committees…"

advice of their panel would they have held a hearing themselves (we are not aware that any such hearing was held in these circumstances). The *Mental Health Act Manual* also advised that the pressure on non-executive directors could be mitigated by advising patients to apply to the MHRT rather than for a managers' hearing[458]. Our initial scepticism over whether such strategies met the requirements of ECHR Article 5[459] were tempered by the fact that we had no alternative suggestions, and it was clear that, without some alternative arrangements, the system of managers' review in Foundation Trust hospitals would have become overwhelmed, leading to delays in hearings.

4.100   It is disappointing that the MHAC, as a body with some reserves of institutional memory over past difficulties in the administration of the Mental Health Act, and with a statutory remit that involves advising the Secretary of State on matters arising from its monitoring of the Act's use, was neither consulted on nor advised of the intended changes to the 1983 Act during the drafting of the schedules to the 2003 legislation regarding Foundation Trusts. We hope that government will take a lesson from this on the potential value of the resources available to it in maintaining such monitoring and institutional memory, particularly as the MHAC's functions pass to the Care Quality Commission.

---

[458] Jones R (2007) *ibid.*, note to s. 72(6), p.14

[459] An alternative view is that the MHRT itself is the body designed to guarantee to patients the right to have the lawfulness of their detention reviewed by an independent body (see Jones R (2007) ibid. p.14). If the system of managers' reviews is nothing more than a duplication of the role of the MHRT, then the collapse of the former would be immaterial in terms of Article 5 rights.

5

The Mental Health Act in Wales

The use of the Act in Wales

5.1   The use of the Mental Health Act 1983 in Wales over the last decade is shown at figure 56 below. This usage follows a similar trend to that in England (see figure 15, chapter 3.1 above), with a peak in admissions at the end of the 1990s followed by a levelling off at a lower rate. Overall admission rates have not changed significantly in this decade. In the last five years recorded at figure 56 below, there was an annual average of about 2,550 admissions; in the previous five years, the average was 2,600 admissions

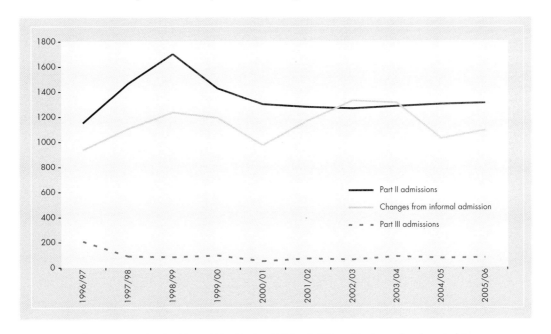

Fig 56: Admissions under the Mental Health Act, Wales (NHS and independent hospitals), 1996/7 – 2005/06

Data source: Welsh Assembly Government Statistics for Wales[460]

---

[460]   Data from National Assembly for Wales, Statistical Directorate website http://www.statswales.wales.gov.uk. Figure 56 above includes patients detained under 'other sections' (ss.38,44,46) in the part III totals. Neither this data nor 'changes from formal admission' was included in the graphic on admissions in Wales in our previous report (MHAC (2006) *Eleventh Biennial Report 2003-2005: In Place of Fear?* figure 45.

5.2 The pattern of detentions in Wales is distinctive from that in England, in that in Wales a higher proportion of civil patients are already in hospital at the time of detention under the Act. This is especially notable in the data for 2002/3 and 2003/4 at figure 56 above, where there were fewer admissions of patients under civil powers than there were uses of those powers on informal inpatients. The statistics for Wales are also notable in that, when informal patients are detained under the Act in Wales, they are almost as likely to be detained under s.2 as s.3, and are certainly more likely to be detained under s.2 than informal patients in English hospitals. Forty-nine percent of detentions of informal patients in Wales are under s.2 (figure 57 below), compared to no more than 39% of such detentions in English hospitals (see figure 51, chapter 4.40 above). It may be that the advice of the *Mental Health Act Manual* on the use of sections 2 and 3 is better followed in Wales than in England. A census count of patients in Wales from 2006 (figure 58) showed that 16% of patients detained under s.2 had been in hospital (presumably under informal status for part of the time) for longer than one month.

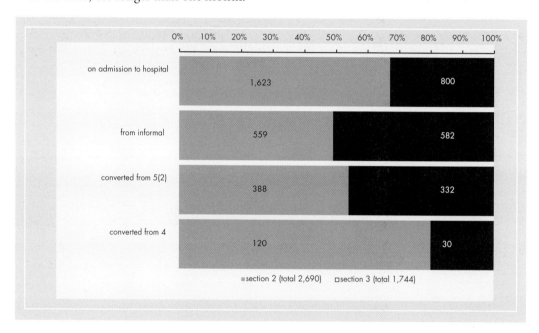

Fig 57: Uses of section 2 and 3, NHS and independent hospitals, Wales, 2004/5 to 2005/6

Data source: Welsh Assembly Government Statistics for Wales

5.3 Figure 58 below shows patients in hospital in Wales on the 31 March 2006 by gender, legal status and length of hospitalisation. That such data is collected and made available by the Assembly government is commendable. There is no comparable English data on, for example, lengths of stay, available from the Department of Health.

5.4 Over one-fifth (23%) of patients detained in hospital under s.3 in Wales had been there for more than one year, although only 6% of s.3 patients had been in hospital for more than five years. The longest stay patients detained under civil powers (i.e. the very few s.3 patients who had been in hospital for more than a decade) were learning disability patients: a far greater number of such patients were found in the long-stay informal population.

	Informal		s.2		s.3		ss.37, 37/41		ss. 47 & 48	
	M	F	M	F	M	F	M	F	M	F
0 – 1 month	(2) 200	(4) 258	32	25	37	42	3	–	–	–
1 – 3 months	(9) 130	(3) 165	3	3	(2) 53	(1) 42	(1) 5	1	2	–
3 – 6 months	(4) 175	(3) 107	2	–	(1) 35	18	4	–	2	1
6 – 12 months	(3) 90	(4) 75	1	–	(2) 47	(1) 22	18	2	3	2
1 – 2 years	(13) 78	(4) 94	1	–	(2) 21	12	16	2	1	–
2 – 5 years	(10) 74	(8) 81	–	–	12	(1) 16	18	3	2	–
5 – 10 years	(25) 50	(14) 46	–	–	9	(3) 7	4	1	–	–
10 – 15 years	(8) 18	(2) 7	–	–	1	(1) 3	–	–	–	–
15 -20 years	(5) 8	5	1	–	(1) 1	1	–	–	–	–
20 years +	(25) 38	(7) 16	–	–	(1) 1	–	–	–	–	–
	761 (104)	854 (49)	40	28	218 (9)	163 (7)	68 (1)	9	10	3
Totals	1,615 (153)		68		381 (16)		77 (1)		13	
	1,615		545[461]							

Fig 58: Mental illness and learning disability patients resident in hospital by gender, legal status and length of hospitalisation, Wales, 31 March 2006

Data source: Welsh Assembly Government Statistics for Wales[462];
figures in brackets indicate learning disability patients included in main total.

5.5   Women patients make up more than half (53%) of all informal inpatients, but only 37% of the detained population (figure 59 below). Women are similarly represented in the detained patient population in England (see figure 16, chapter 3.4 above), although admission rates over the last decade in both England and Wales show a roughly even split between male and female patients.

461   Includes six patients detained under 'other powers' (all mental illness, five male, only one resident for more than 12 months,) not otherwise shown in the table.

462   Data source: National Assembly for Wales Statistical Directorate (2006) *Statistical Bulletins* SB 61/2006 (table 15) & SB 62/2006 (table 9).

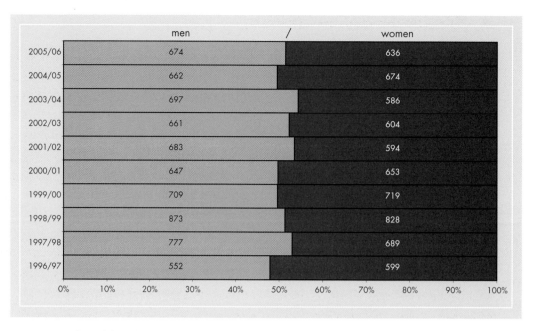

	men	/	women
2005/06	674		636
2004/05	662		674
2003/04	697		586
2002/03	661		604
2001/02	683		594
2000/01	647		653
1999/00	709		719
1998/99	873		828
1997/98	777		689
1996/97	552		599

Fig 59: Male and female admissions under part II of the MHA, all hospitals, Wales, 1996/7 to 2005/6

Data source: Welsh Assembly Government Statistics for Wales

5.6   Bed occupancy figures in Wales indicate some pressure on services. The bed occupancy noted by the MHAC on our 95 visits to acute wards in Wales over this reporting period is shown at figure 60 below. Forty per cent of all acute wards are operating over their capacity, with at least 10% operating at more than 120% capacity (see chapter 1.5 *et seq* above for further discussion of bed occupancy).

Occupancy Band	Number of Wards	Percentage band	
<= 90%	25	< 100%	34.7%
90%+ to <100	8		
Exactly 100%	24	= 100%	25.3%
100%+ to 105%	6	> 100%	40.0%
105%+ to 110%	14		
110%+ to 115%	4		
115%+ to 120%	3		
120%+ to 125%	3		
> 125%	8		
Total	95		100%

Fig 60: Bed-occupancy levels in 95 acute wards visited by the MHAC in Wales over 2005/6 & 2006/7

Data source: MHAC data

A distinctive policy climate

5.7   The policy agenda announced between the Labour and Plaid Cymru groups in the National Assembly have set the health service of Wales on a very different course to that likely to be taken by England. Whereas the government in England has announced that it intends to increase the involvement of the private sector in commissioning and delivering hospital services (see chapter 1.54 *et seq* above), in Wales the coalition parties forming the majority in the Assembly have committed to end the internal market in the NHS and eliminate the use of private sector hospitals by 2011[463]. The coalition is also committed to seeking legislative competence in relation to mental health, so that a Mental Health Act (Wales) could be a possibility for the future.

5.8   These policy commitments suggest potentially radical changes in service provision in Wales, and in the legislative context within which services work. Implementing such changes would appear to be a challenging policy agenda[464]. In terms of infrastructure, for example, despite a considerable infrastructure of independent hospitals in Wales, including a substantial forensic sector, we still find patients from Wales in out-of-area placements in the independent sector in England. The intention to stop using independent hospitals implies a considerable increase in NHS beds in Wales.

A Mental Health Act for Wales?

5.9   There is, of course, no reason in principle why Wales should not have a different legislative framework for mental health compulsion than England, just as Scotland now has very different mental health law to England and Wales. Wales (alongside many other legislatures around the world) may indeed look to Scotland for an exemplar of modern law in this area.

5.10   In response to the Assembly Government's consultation with stakeholders on the future direction of mental health legislation in Wales, the MHAC highlighted a number of its concerns with the 1983 and 2007 Acts that we felt had not been addressed in the review of legislation in England, and stated that we would welcome the Assembly Government taking steps to increase the rights and safeguards for patients. Such steps could include revisiting the criteria for (and exclusions from) detention under the 2007 Act; giving patients choice in the identification of their 'nearest relative'; or requiring automatic referral to the MHRT after a short initial period of detention. Primary legislation may not be needed to implement all of our suggestions (for example, regulating the use of seclusion and restraint, or extending the remit of the MHAC - or its successor body in Wales - to cover *de facto* detained patients).

5.11   However, we are aware of the considerable numbers of Welsh patients who are treated on out-of-area placements in English hospitals. Should Wales produce a law that differs on points of principle from the 1983 Act as amended, there must be a danger that such patients

---

[463] Welsh Assembly Government (2007) *'One Wales: A progressive agenda for the Government of Wales'* An agreement between the Labour and Plaid Cymru Groups in the National Assembly, 27 June 2007. http://new.wales.gov.uk/strategy/910682/onewales/e.pdf?lang=en

[464] For an overview of policy annoiuncements and implementation in Wales, see Drakeford M (2006) 'Health Policy In Wales: Making a difference in conditions of difficulty'. *Critical Social Policy* 26(3) 543-561.

(or their families or lawyers) would view as unfair the fact that the increased protections of Welsh law are being denied them for want of local (or at least Welsh) services. For some patients (for example, those requiring high security care), hospitalisation within Wales may be impossible.

5.12   Similarly, we are aware that mental health services in Wales suffer resource problems, particularly, for example, in maintaining sufficient psychiatrists in post for services' needs. As such, increased safeguards that might make an additional call on psychiatrists' time (for example in preparing for more Tribunals) might actually not help improve patient care. Whilst resources should not be an excuse to deny patients legitimate rights, it is perhaps important to be realistic about what can be achieved with the current Welsh service infrastructure and staffing.

Patient care in a time of change

5.13   We hope that any restructuring of services in Wales will be managed without detriment to patients' care. In part, our concern is the general one that planned restructuring of hospital services or the legal framework must not allow further 'planning blight' to effect services. In legislative terms, such 'blight' was apparent in that some incompatibilities between the 1983 Act and the European Convention on Human Rights went unresolved during the seven-year debate over the consecutive Mental Health Bills produced in Whitehall. In terms of the day-to-day management of hospitals, it is vitally important the services due for reconfiguration are not neglected during the development of their successors. Whilst there is already discussion over relocation from some sub-standard ward environments (for example, in some learning disability and older people's wards in north Wales and south-east Wales), it is important that such wards are maintained to a reasonable standard while they continue to house patients.

5.14   We have also heard of some examples where patients' needs seem not to have had priority in the reconfiguration of services. In a case that we were informed of as we were preparing this report, Health Commission Wales[465] had exercised its power[466] to transfer a patient from one medium secure independent hospital to another, despite opposition from the patient's original clinical team. We were told that HCW had informed the original hospital that they were under pressure to fill beds newly contracted with the second hospital. We understand that the patient's RMO at the time of the transfer had stated that the proposed MSU placement, which was in a larger unit further from the patient's family, would be detrimental to the patient's care. The patient had visited the proposed unit, under the impression that she could choose whether or not to move there, and had stated that she did not want to go. She was, nevertheless, subsequently moved there against her will without warning. In this case, the advised-against move proved to be a poor commissioning decision on grounds of practicality as well as ethics. It appears that the patient was quickly deemed to

---

[465] Health Commission Wales (HCW) is an executive agency of the Welsh Assembly Government commissioning tertiary and other highly specialised services throughout Wales.
http://new.wales.gov.uk/topics/health/hcw/?lang=en

[466] Under paragraph 7(4) of the Mental Health Regulations 1983.

be not suited to the new unit, having suffered deterioration in her mental and physical condition, and was likely to be moved again at the time of writing. We hope that this case will serve as a warning against lightly disregarding clinical advice over patient transfers.

Specialist service provision in Wales

5.15 The HCW's role in commissioning specialist service provision in Wales is an important one, given that NHS mental health and learning disability services are provided by integrated NHS Trusts (rather than specialist mental health Trusts) which can draw the focus of mainstream services away from mental health care.

5.16 In 2005, Health Inspectorate Wales (HIW) and HCW published its review of adult medium secure units in Wales[467], established at the request of the chief executive of NHS Wales in response to an independent review of a homicide in Prestatyn. The report focussed in particular on clinical governance and discharge arrangements, finding that:

- Links between medium secure services and local service commissioners were underdeveloped, leading to problems in planning discharge and discharge delays. There were particular problems with local health boards keeping track of patients, especially those detained outside of Wales.

- Discharge plans showed insufficient evidence of anticipating re-admission or recall to hospital, or regular review of patient needs and expectations. The Home Office reported delays in effecting the recall of some restricted patients.

- In only half of cases studied were risk factors and relapse indicators identified, with little evidence of non-clinical factors (such as housing) being addressed.

- Patients felt insufficiently involved in their care planning.

We are pleased that these matters have been addressed in the review and note that the recommendations should lead to service improvements, as should implementation of the best practice guidance on specifications for medium secure units[468]. The review did not consider the adequacy of service provision for medium secure care in Wales, although in the period since the review further independent medium secure facilities have opened in Wales.

5.17 The provision of specialist services other than medium secure units in Wales is a matter of concern to the MHAC. For example:

- There are no specialist eating disorder services in Mid and West Wales, leading to out of area placements in Shropshire and elsewhere in England. This can be a difficult journey, particularly in winter, and of course may lead to problems in co-ordinating aftercare services.

---

[467] Healthcare Inspectorate Wales, Health Commission Wales (Specialist Services) (2005) *Report of a review of Adult Mental Health Medium Secure Units in Wales.* October 2005

[468] Department of Health (2007) *Best Practice Guidance: Specification for Adult Medium Secure Services. Health Offender Partnerships 2007.* July 2007. This specification is common to all MSU services commissioned across Wales and England, irrespective of provider.

- There is also inadequate low secure provision for women patients in Mid and West Wales.

- We have heard of inadequacies in provision in Wales for patients with Aspergers' Syndrome, leading to patients with this condition being detained a long way from home, or waiting for acceptable placements for long periods, and/or being detained in wholly inappropriate placements.

- Delayed discharges are often reported, particularly for elderly patients, due to difficulties with aftercare planning or provision.

As such, we hope that the general lessons of the medium secure review will be extended across all specialist mental health service provision in Wales.

5.18   We note that the *One Wales* document promises "a new priority on providing for mental health, including child and adolescent mental health services"[469], and look forward to seeing developments in this area across Wales.

Smoke-free legislation in Wales

5.19   The Assembly Government's regulations for the purpose of the Health Act 2006 exempt designated rooms in mental health units that provide residential accommodation for patients from the ban on smoking in enclosed spaces[470]. As such, hospitals in Wales may retain their smoking rooms, whilst hospitals in England must close theirs by July 2008 (see chapter 2.61). We are pleased to note that, in hospitals where smoking rooms have been retained, this has not prevented smoking-cessation activity and support for patients.

5.20   Some hospitals, such as the Royal Glamorgan Hospital, have nevertheless declared themselves smoke-free and closed smoking rooms for detained patients. The transition of the Royal Glamorgan Hospital to a smoke-free environment has not denied those patients with access to the hospital's enclosed gardens the opportunity to smoke if they chose to do so, although patients in the supported recovery unit have no access to the enclosed garden and must therefore stand outside of the building in public spaces. It is not clear how such arrangements will work at night or in bad weather. Patients in a first-floor ward were using an uncovered balcony to smoke at the time of our visit.

5.21   Services that close indoor smoking facilities should undertake risk-assessments of the locations where patients will subsequently go to smoke, and ensure that they are as hazard-free as possible.

---

[469] Welsh Assembly Government (2007) *ibid.*, p.10.

[470] Smoke-free Premises etc. regulations (Wales) 2007, reg. 4(a)(iii)

Section 136 and places of safety

5.22 Pembrokeshire and Derwen NHS Trust provide ward-based mental health training events for police officers and police students, and also ward placements for police in training, with an ex-service user as a part of the training team. The training focuses on section 136 issues but also tackles stigma and broader issues about mental health. We welcome this ground-breaking initiative, which receives positive feedback from police and patients, and has facilitated the development of joint policies between the police and the Trust. One such policy commits the Trust to provide a first-level mental health nurse to stay with any person detained in the place of safety at Camarthen / Lanelli police station whilst awaiting transfer to a ward. The nurse is expected to provide nursing support and reassurance to the detainee; administer any medication prescribed as an emergency measure and monitor the patient afterwards[471]; to accompany the patient when transfer is finally arranged; and to keep a detailed nursing record of the time spent in police custody[472]. The nurse has direct telephone access to the ward manager and relevant psychiatrist for support during this time. The Trust aims to provide a nurse within four hours of being contacted by the police, or by 8 a.m. when contact is made during night duty. The policy does not presume that a police cell will be the place of safety: indeed it requires a review after every use of the police station for s.136 detention to evaluate the appropriateness of it as the first choice.

5.23 We commend this policy as a good example of arrangements suitable in particular for rural services, although we also hope that the ability to transfer patients from one place of safety to another provided in the Mental Health Act 2007 will enable patients brought initially to police stations to be transferred sooner to hospital accommodation (see chapter 4.58 *et seq*).

5.24 We have also noted good interagency working and compliance with the recommendations of Chapter 10 of the Code of Practice regarding s.136 in the North Glamorgan NHS Trust and Pontypridd and Rhondda NHS Trust in this period. However, whilst the facilities used as places of safety in one hospital (St Tydfil's, North Glamorgan NHS Trust) were very good, the facility at the Royal Glamorgan Hospital (Pontypridd and Rhondda NHS Trust) failed to meet the standards suggested in our last report on several counts. We understand that the PICU unit is often used in place of the designated place of safety. We are not aware that standards of places of safety are much of a priority in Wales, and suggest this should be considered as an area for focus and development across the country.

> **Recommendation 30:** Standards of places of safety should be considered as an area for focus and development at a national level in Wales.

---

[469] Welsh Assembly Government (2007) *ibid.*, p.10.

[470] Smoke-free Premises etc. regulations (Wales) 2007, reg. 4(a)(iii)

[471] Such administration would be under the authority of the Mental Capacity Act rather than the MHA 1983.

[472] Pembrokeshire & Derwen NHS Trust Mental Health and Learning Disabilities Division, Camarthenshire area, 'Protocal for nurses operating in a police environment' May 2006. Contact: Stuart Jones, Unit Manager, Cwm Seren, Pembrokeshire & Derwen NHS Trust.

6

Medical Treatment under the Mental Health Act 1983

6.1 At the end of our reporting period, an elderly man with dementia who was detained under section 2 of the Act died as a result of neuroleptic malignant syndrome following the administration of haloperidol in response to his difficult and aggressive behaviour. The coroner recorded a verdict of accidental death and made no observations regarding his care and treatment, describing the death as "an idiosyncratic reaction to an antipsychotic drug".

6.2 It is difficult to generalise any lesson from such a case, given its inherent rarity and unpredictability, save perhaps as a reminder that the psychiatric pharmacopeia is not without risks and that clinicians should always be aware of the possibility of adverse reactions or damaging side-effects. In this reporting period there has been useful discussion in the literature over cardiac safety and antipsychotic medication[473]. Psychiatric wards should have the equipment and trained staff to deal with medical emergencies, and patients should be provided with regular physical monitoring and health checks. In practical terms, this means that resuscitation equipment should be available and usable by staff, and that at least some clinical staff working on, or available to, mental health wards should be able to interpret electrocardiogram (ECG) readings, take blood for electrolytes and monitor potassium levels in patients receiving antipsychotic (and some antidepressant) medication. Patients should have a baseline ECG taken and there should be routine monitoring of weight, blood pressure, heart rate and glucose levels where any risks are perceived[474].

6.3 Although it is likely that the benefits of psychiatric treatment outweigh the risks and consequences for most patients who are detained under Mental Health Act powers, it is important to keep in mind that the imposition of psychiatric treatment without consent must be justified not only in terms of the violation of the human right to personal and bodily integrity, but also against the physical risks that such treatment poses to its recipient. The Second Opinion system is designed to provide an independent view of the possible justification for treatment without consent.

6.4 The MHAC's own role in administering the Second Opinion system demonstrates to us the need to strike a balance between organisational convenience and patient protection in systems for the approval and prescription of psychiatric treatment. Whilst it is important not to allow pragmatic considerations to chip away at the protections offered to patients by

---

[473] Abdelmawla N & Mitchell A J (2006) 'Sudden cardiac death and antipsychotics part 1: risk factors and mechanisms' *Advances in Psychiatric Treatment* 12; 35-44; 'Sudden cardiac death and antipsychotics part 2: monitoring and prevention' *Advances in Psychiatric Treatment* 12; 100-109

[474] For a fuller discussion, see Addelmawla & Mitchell (2006) *ibid.*, part 2.

the law, or to structure the medico-legal system for the convenience of practitioners at the expense of patients, excessively bureaucratic systems will be self-defeating and fall into being a 'rubber-stamp' rather than a real safeguard. It is also important, of course, that patients are not denied timely clinical interventions for procedural reasons, and the devolution of authority to nurses in the administration of medication (whether under existing 'PRN' prescribing practices or future nurse-based prescribing frameworks) can ensure that patients' clinical needs receive a prompt response.

6.5 The fragmentation of the inpatient unit estate into small, geographically scattered units, alongside the implementation of the European Working Time Directive, may lead to greater reliance on 'just-in-case' prescribing on a PRN basis, as it becomes increasingly difficult to secure the attendance of the doctor deemed to be patients' responsible medical officer under the Act. The devolution of legal responsibilities to clinicians who are not doctors under the 2007 Act is unlikely to alter this fact in the short-term, as doctors' involvement will still be required for a great deal of prescribing. The 1983 Act has historically limited the extent to which nurse prescribing for detained patients can be any more than an extension of the existing practice of giving nurses discretion in administering PRN medication. There is no doubt scope for more development in the future, particularly once the 2007 Act's amendments come into force later this year (see para 6.66 below).

> I remember once going up for my medication and was given the wrong stuff, which I spat back into the beaker. The nurse who gave it to me pleaded with me not to say anything.
>
> Joe, service user[475]

6.6 This opening up of prescribing practice is, however, taking place against a backdrop of increasing knowledge and awareness of complexity and unpredictability in drug interactions, such as that described by Davies et al[476]. We support their suggestion that information (and training) on drug interactions, particularly with regard to PRN and other episodic drug prescription such as the emergency treatment of acute psychosis, should be made available to all clinical staff responsible for prescribing and administering psychiatric drugs. Such staff should be aware of the potential for unpredictability in plasma concentrations, side effects and efficacy which PRN prescribing may cause through such interactions. There is a clear role for pharmacists in providing this information, and yet the Healthcare Commission has found that mental health Trusts, had "relatively weak investment in clinical pharmacy services compared with acute trusts"; mental health wards had less access to pharmacy staff than hospital wards dealing with physical disorders; and mental health patients were more likely than others to experience problems with their medication or to be taking it incorrectly[477]. Mental health Trusts should seek to address this imbalance in the interests of the safety of their patients, especially those whose liberty they remove in providing treatment.

---

[475] From chapter 9 of *Experiences of mental health in-patient care: narratives from service users, carers and professionals*, edited by Mark Hardcastle, David Kennard, Sheila Grandison and Leonard Fagin. London, Routledge, 2007

[476] Davies S J C, Lennard M S, Ghahramani P, Pratt P, Robertson A & Potokar J (2007) 'PRN prescribing in psychiatric inpatients – potential for pharmacokinetic drug interactions'. *Journal of Psychopharmacology* 21(2) 153-160.

[477] Healthcare Commission (2007) *Talking about medicines: the management of medicines in Trusts providing mental health services.* www.healthcarecommission.org.uk

Trends in Second Opinion usage

6.7 The number of Second Opinions arranged by the MHAC over the lifetime of the 1983 Act is set out at figure 61 below. This shows that, while there has been a slight decrease in the number of Second Opinions for ECT since the late 1980s, the volume of Second Opinions for medication has increased tenfold over the lifetime of the Act.

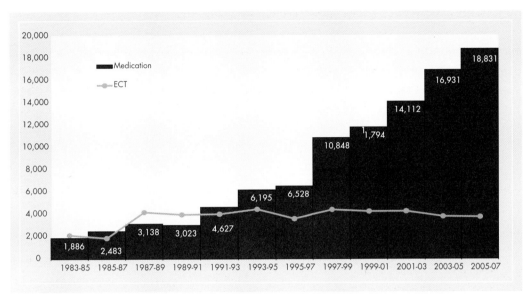

Fig 61: Second Opinions for ECT or medication over the lifetime of the Mental Health Act 1983[478]

Data Source : MHAC

6.8 The number of opinions has increased each year from between 1% to over 10%. Requests over the last eight years are shown at figure 62 below. Over the last five years shown, the number of Second Opinions has risen by 22%. The overall increase shown on the table is 28%. In our last report we suggested that the reason for these increases is not known, but that we suspect a combination of increasingly unwell patients and increasing awareness of consent issues by clinicians, the latter including a growing appreciation by clinicians of the Second Opinion service (whether as a protection for their patient or as a protection for themselves)[479]

---

[478] This chart excludes Second Opinion visits for both medication and ECT treatment, although such visits amount to less than 1% of SOAD activity – see fig 66 below.

[479] MHAC (2006) *Eleventh Biennial Report 2003-2005: In Place of Fear?* , para 4.65.

6.9 Under the 2007 Act, the role of SOADs will be extended into the community to provide Second Opinions for those patients who are on Community Treatment Orders. We expect that this will create an increase in the number of Second Opinions, particularly because of the requirement to perform a Second Opinion on consenting as well as non-consenting patients who are on CTOs. Although the actual numbers of CTOs likely as a result of the proposals is a matter of contention, the extension of Second Opinions to consenting patients is likely to have a significant effect. The census data showed that between 57 and 58 per cent of detained patients were consenting to medication, irrespective of how long they had been detained.

Review of the SOAD service

6.10 Late in 2005 the MHAC Board decided that a fundamental internal review of the SOAD service and its administration should be undertaken in the light of the rising volume of Second Opinions and the importance of the work. Consultation on the SOAD service took place with a range of interested groups and individuals, including patients, hospital staff and SOADs.

> SOAD visit – this elderly male psychiatrist did not give me time to answer his questions and spent the time discussing me with my husband. I sat silently.
>
> Kay Reed, detained under section 3

6.11 The main findings of our interviews with patients and consultation with SURP members can be summarised as follows:

- Few patients remembered having been given information about the SOAD service in advance of seeing a SOAD (although a number of patients suggested that they may have forgotten). Most patients did not think that they had been given a leaflet. Only one or two patients reported that they had been told in some detail about the SOAD service, were aware that the SOAD was independent, and that this was a chance for them to challenge the treatment plan. Where such an explanation had been given, it seemed to have been given by a nurse rather than the RMO.

- Some patients recalled clearly that they had received no advance notice of the visit. Even where patients had been told that a SOAD was coming, it seems that it is very rare for a date and time to be given. It seems to be common that the patient is simply told that there is somebody to see them. One or two patients felt that they would have liked some time to prepare for the meeting, although since most were unclear about the role it is not clear how they would have prepared. One patient felt very anxious in anticipation of the meeting, since she felt she needed to "put on a good performance" in order to prove that she was rational to the person who, she believed at the time, could get her discharged.

- Very few patients seem to have received a clear explanation of the SOAD role from the SOAD. One or two said that the SOAD explained his or her independence from the clinical team, but most said that the SOAD introduced themselves by saying something along the lines of "I'm here to make sure that they're looking after you well here", or "to check your medication". Some patients thought that the SOAD was another hospital doctor. Most misunderstood the Second Opinion to be a second diagnosis, and therefore a chance to be allowed out.

- The amount of time spent with the patient seemed to vary a great deal. Allowing for inaccuracy of memory (and several patients did say that they had some difficulty remembering) there seemed to be two groups. Some patients remembered that the

SOAD spent between half an hour and an hour with them, and others said that the SOAD only spent between two and five minutes. From our perspective, we could not say that the latter group of patients was likely to have been notably more ill or uncooperative than the first, and as such it would seem that some SOADs felt that it was enough to see the patient very briefly without engaging in a long conversation.

- We did not encounter any negative views of the SOADs' bedside manner. Patients felt that they were professional, "looked important", "obviously had experience", and were polite. Negative comments were more related to SOADs not asking enough questions; not being interested in listening or finding out enough about the patient; not spending enough time to make a proper diagnosis; and being 'in cahoots' with the doctors at the hospital.

6.12   The results of this survey were presented at a SOAD conference using many direct quotes. While the SOAD service has made a commitment to improve the information available about SOADs, we will inevitably be reliant upon detaining authorities to fulfill their legal duties under s.132 to give patients access to this information in advance of SOAD visits (see chapter 4.53 *et seq* above).

> **Recommendation 31:** Detaining authorities should ensure that patients due to receive Second Opinion visits are given advance notice of the visit and information about the SOAD role.

6.13   The report of the SOAD review was published in 2006 and is available on our website[480]: its nineteen recommendations were accepted by the MHAC Board in January 2007. Alongside improvements to data collection and administration (including enabling information from SOAD work to better inform MHAC visits), the review will also result in:

- Stricter recruitment procedure, training and monitoring of SOADs, including a focussed plan of recruitment in 2007 and a programme of re-assessment, leading to all SOADs being assessed against the new procedure by April 2008.

- A continuing programme of SOAD refresher training and opportunities for sharing practice, with an element of professional peer review and support and professional appraisal and validation agreed with the Royal College of Psychiatrists.

- Following piloting, the introduction of booked weekly, fortnightly or three-weekly SOAD attendances ("day-sessions") at hospitals with a high volume of Second Opinions. Such sessions would take place in addition to the existing call-out service for more urgent cases.

6.14   The MHAC's own performance indicators of Second Opinion attendance within five working days of request (or two days for ECT) will be reviewed, insofar as they may impede the administration of 'day-sessions' and also act as a perverse incentive against planning Second Opinion requests in hospitals. Many such requests are received for patients approaching the end of their three-month period, or in situations where there is no necessity for the request to be made when authorisation is required as a matter of urgency. In this reporting period we achieved these performance indicators for 88% of all Second Opinions for medication, and 78% of all Second Opinions for ECT[481].

---

[480] MHAC (2006) *Review of the Second Opinion Appointed Doctor Service*. www.mhac.org.uk

[481] MHAC (2007) *Mental Health Act Commission Annual Report and Operating Accounts 1 April 2006 – 31 March 2007*, table 6. www.mhac.org.uk

Second Opinions for medication

6.15 Figures 63 and 64 below show Second Opinion requests for medication broken down by gender and capacity status respectively. Male patients account for 63% of these Second Opinion requests, with just over half (53%) of all male and female patients for whom such a request is made being deemed incapable of consent by their RMO. This is a quite different pattern than that shown for requests to authorise ECT (figure 69, paragraph 6.74 below).

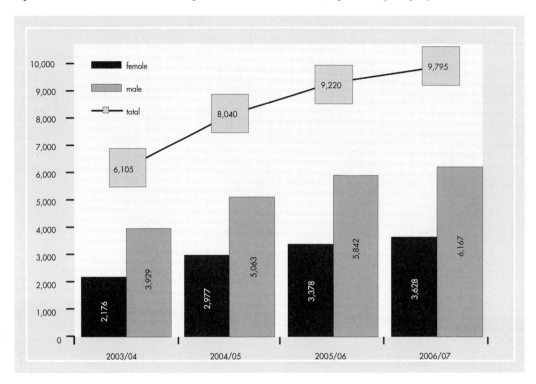

Fig 63: Second Opinion requests for medication by gender, 2003/04 to 2006/07.

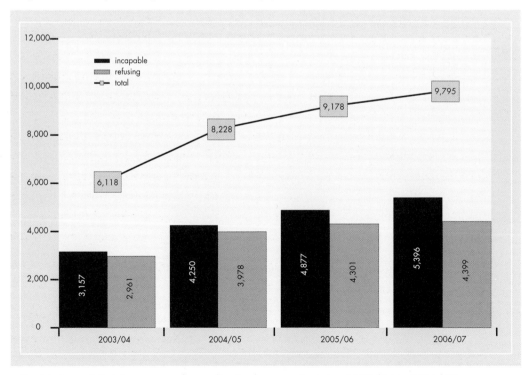

Fig 64: Second Opinion requests for medication by capacity status, 2003/04 to 2006/07.

Second Opinions by classification of mental disorder

6.16 Figure 65 shows Second Opinion requests over this reporting period broken down by the legal classification of the patient's mental disorder. As we would expect, the majority of Second Opinions are arranged to consider the treatment under s.58 of patients detained in hospital for treatment of mental illness. However, over the two years, Second Opinions were also arranged for a considerable number of patients with legal classifications of personality disorder or learning disability.

Classification of Mental Disorder	Second Opinions requested (number)	Second Opinions requested (%)
Mental Illness (MI)	21,520	88.2
Learning disability[482](LD)	933	3.8
With MI	1,020	4.2
With PD	118	0.5
Personality disorder[483](PD)	171	0.7
With MI	344	1.4
Not stated	302	0.1
Total	**24,408**	**100**

Fig 65: Second Opinion requests 2005/6 and 2006/7 by classification of mental disorder

Source: MHAC data

Second Opinions for patients with personality disorder

6.17 Over the two year period shown in figure 65 above, 633 Second Opinions were requested in total for patients with classifications of personality disorder (i.e. a legal classification of 'psychopathic disorder' under the Act). Of these Second Opinion requests, 344 were for patients with an additional classification of mental illness, and 118 for patients also classified with a learning disability (whether 'mental impairment' or 'severe mental impairment').

6.18 In the 2006 census, we found a total of 952 detained patients who were classified as being in hospital for the treatment of personality disorder (whether or not this was the only reason for hospitalisation), 705 (74%) of whom were deemed to be consenting to their treatment (see figure 38, chapter 3.54 above). If we assume the 2006 census data to be fairly representative of the general number of personality disordered patients detained at any one time, this implies a baseline population of something like 250 non-consenting personality disordered patients who may be eligible for Second Opinions on any particular day. It is likely that this population is fairly static, given that at least two-thirds of personality disordered patients are detained under part III powers and therefore likely to have relatively long hospital stays. Any interpretation of this data is necessarily speculative[484], but it does

---

[482] i.e. 'mental impairment' or 'severe mental impairment' under MHA 1983.

[483] i.e. 'psychopathic disorder' under MHA 1983

[484] Not least because the Mental Health Act and census categorisations of mental disorder are not exact equivalents, and because patients may be double-counted when the census data is divided into the three categories of mental disorder, as it is not possible to distinguish those patients who are listed in more than one category, although it is possible to distinguish such patients in the Second Opinion data collected by the MHAC, which excludes such double counting in that data-set.

appear to imply widespread prescription of medication for mental disorder (which would, after three-months' treatment under detention, trigger the Second Opinion) amongst detained patients with personality disorder who are not consenting to their treatment. It is not possible to say whether there is a connection between consent status and prescription of psychiatric medication (i.e. implying that consenting personality disordered patients may be subject to psychological rather than somatic treatment), or whether a significant proportion of personality disordered detained patients are consenting to the administration of psychiatric medication. Especially insofar as the 2007 Act was designed to ensure that no personality disordered patient is arbitrarily excluded from the provisions of the Act, it may be fruitful to research what treatment is actually provided to detained patients with diagnoses of personality disorder, although any such research would of course be complicated by the 2007 Act's abolition of legal classifications, which is expected to be implemented in October 2008.

Second Opinions for patients with learning disability

6.19 The 2006 census data recorded 1,632 patients in hospital for learning disability (whether or not they were also counted as being in hospital for another reason). Of these, 778 (47.7%) were deemed consenting to treatment (see figure 36, chapter 3.52 above). Thus we might assume a baseline population of about 850 detained learning disabled patients who are recognised not to be consenting to treatment on any given day, against an average of approximately four Second Opinions for learning disabled patients on every working day[485].

Outcomes of SOAD visits

6.20 Figure 66 below shows the recorded outcomes for Second Opinion visits over the five year period 2002 – 2007.

Treatment	No Change		Slight change		Significant change		No Outcome Recorded		Total	
MED	26,720	[80.91 %]	3,241	[9.81 %]	547	[1.66 %]	2,517	[7.62 %]	33,025	[100%]
ECT	5,640	[81.68 %]	456	[6.60 %]	242	[3.50 %]	567	[8.21 %]	6,905	[100%]
Both	246	[73.21 %]	36	[10.71 %]	29	[8.63 %]	25	[7.44 %]	336	[100%]
Total	32,606	[80.98%]	3,733	[9.27%]	818	[2.03%]	3,109	[7.72%]	40,266	[100%]

Fig 66: Outcomes of requests for Second Opinions between 1 April 2002 and 31 March 2007

Data Source: MHAC

6.21 The data shows that 11% of Second Opinions over this time resulted in some change to the patient's treatment plan. Although only 2% of all Second Opinion visits result in a 'significant' change, this still amounts to an average of three patients in every working week whose treatment plan is significantly changed as a result of the SOAD visit. An average of 14 treatment plans are slightly changed in each working week as a result of SOAD visits.

---

[485] See figure 36, chapter 3.52: there were 2,071 Second Opinions to patients whose mental disorder included a categorisation of learning disability in 2005/6 to 2006/7. We have assumed an average of 250 working days each year.

The boundaries of section 58 safeguards

Patients deemed to be consenting

6.22 Under the 1983 Act as it is currently applied, a Second Opinion is only made available to patients who cannot or do not consent to their treatment. This means that the majority of detained patients will not receive the safeguard of a Second Opinion, in part because they are deemed to be consenting by their RMO.[486]

6.23 The 2007 revisions extend the safeguard of a Second Opinion to all patients under 18 years of age who are considered for ECT, and for patients who are deemed to be consenting to the treatment that they are required to take as a condition of being on a community treatment order (CTO)[487].

6.24 The rationale is not clear for requiring Second Opinions for patients who are deemed to consent to their treatment whilst subject to a CTO, but not for those patients who are deemed to consent to treatment whilst detained in hospital. If the rationale for the former group of patients is a recognition of the need to interrogate the validity of any 'consent' given within a coercive framework, or at least to assume that a patient's consent in such circumstances is a guarantee that treatment is being appropriately administered, then such a rationale applies *(perhaps a fortiori)* to patients who are detained in hospital. The MHAC has great concern that 'consent' is equated with 'insight', which may itself be considered a precondition of some patients' discharge from compulsory powers or movement down the hospital security scale. In a number of cases it is

> "oh we didn't talk much about capacity – we used to talk about insight"
>
> Consultant Psychiatrists' comment noted by a
> MHA Commission observer at the inquest into a patient's death.

arguable that a patient's 'consent' fails the Code of Practice test of being permission given without unfair or undue pressure[488].

6.25 The MHAC often has cause for concern over the frequency and quality of contact between patients and their RMOs (see chapters 1.43 and 2.98 *et seq* above), although the Code of Practice requires that RMOs should personally seek the patient's consent[489]. The discussion with the patient, and the RMO's assessment of the patient's mental capacity, should be thoroughly documented in the patient's notes[490]. On our visits we often find inadequate recording of consent or capacity assessments and sometimes have reason to question whether a patient is in fact consenting as the doctor has certified, or indeed is capable of doing so:

---

[486] 57% of all detained patients were deemed to be consenting in the 2006 census. Many detained patients, consenting or otherwise, will be discharged within the 'three month period' before a Second Opinion is required.

[487] For ECT and under-18 years olds, see para 6.79 below. For consenting CTO patients, see MHA 1983 s.64B as amended by MHA 2007 s.35.

[488] *MHA 1983 Code of Practice*, para 15.13. For an example of such concerns relating to conditional discharge, see chapter 7.74 *et seq* below.

[489] *MHA 1983 Code of Practice*, para 16.13.

[490] *ibid.*

One of the patients who met with the Commissioner expressed his unwillingness to be on a mood stabiliser and the high dosage of the antipsychotic medication. The patient was under the impression that he had no choice as the SOAD had agreed to the treatment plan. On examination it was established that the RMO had completed a Form 38.

North west London, June 2006

The patient had a Form 38 completed. However the patient in an interview with the Commissioner stated that he was not happy taking the medication. The patient's notes recorded that on several occasions the patient refused the medication and in one episode it was recorded that the patient only accepted medication 'after much persuasion'.

Ashworth Hospital, March 2006

6.26 Where we have doubts over a patient's consenting status, we suggest that the RMO meets with the patient to reassess this and consider whether a SOAD review needs to be requested. Where there is doubt or disagreement about a patient's consent status, a SOAD visit should be arranged: a SOAD is empowered to complete either a Form 39 certifying treatment to be given in the absence of consent, or a Form 38 certifying that the patient gives valid consent.

> **Recommendation 32:** Detaining authorities should ensure that their responsible medical officers comply with the requirements of the Code of Practice in assessing the patient's mental capacity and consent status.

The three month period

6.27 Patients to whom part IV of the Act applies[491] may be given medication for mental disorder without the safeguard of a Second Opinion for an initial period of three months from the first administration of medication whilst they were detained.

6.28 In the debates over the Mental Health Bill 2007 there were calls for the duration of this 'three-month period' to be reduced. It remains in the gift of the Secretary of State to make such a reduction by order.

6.29 We are sympathetic to calls for the reduction of the three-month period. Many detained patients will never have their treatment subjected to the scrutiny of a statutory Second Opinion, because they are discharged within three months of treatment commencing. As we stated in our Sixth Biennial Report[492], some such patients may have repeated admissions to hospital which cumulatively amount to long periods of treatment under the Act without this safeguard applying to them. Others who remain in hospital and go on to see a Second Opinion doctor may quite justifiably wonder where that safeguard has been for the initial period of their detention.

6.30 The 2006 census data provides an idea of the numbers of patients who have no opportunity to receive a Second Opinion whilst detained under the Act. On the 31 March 2006 there were 14,574 patients detained under the Mental Health Act. Of these, we were able to

---

[491] i.e. patients detained under ss.2,3,36,37,37/41, 38, 45A, 46, 47, 47/49, 48 and 48/49.

[492] MHAC (1995) *Sixth Biennial Report 1993-1995*. London: Stationery Office, para 3.8.

ascertain the length of detention for 11,814 (81% of all patients detained on the day)[493]. The duration of detention for patients admitted to hospital under the Act and detained there on census day 2006 is set out at figure 67 below.

	Detained >3 for months	Detained for >2 months	Detained for >1 month	Detained on or before day of census
Consenting	4,650	5,088	5,659	6,848
Not consenting	3,261	3,598	4,022	4,966
Total	**7,911**	**8,686**	**9,681**	**11,814**

Fig 67: Patients admitted to hospital under MHA powers: length of detention on census day

Data Source: *Count Me In* 2006

6.31   The patients who would be eligible for a Second Opinion are those who are "not consenting". Under the current law, 3,261 patients (or 27.6% of the total patients admitted to hospital under MHA powers) were eligible for a Second Opinion. However:

- If the 'three-month period' was reduced to two months, 3,598 patients (or 30.5% of the total patients admitted to hospital under MHA powers) could have received a Second Opinion. This is an additional 337 Second Opinions, and an increase in Second Opinion activity of slightly over 10%.

- Had the 'three-month period' been reduced to a duration of one month, 4,022 patients (or 34.0% of the total patients admitted to hospital under MHA powers) could have received a Second Opinion. This is an additional 761 Second Opinions, and an increase in Second Opinion activity of perhaps 23%.

Recommendation 33: The Secretary of State should keep under active consideration the reduction of the three-month period under s.58(3) of the Act, and use his power to reduce this period as resources allow.

High-dose and combination prescribing of antipsychotic medication

6.32   In its most recent consensus statement on high-dose antipsychotic medication, the Royal College of Psychiatrists continues to state that current evidence does not justify the routine use of high-dose antipsychotic medication[494]. Despite this, a number of studies have shown that there is widespread prescription of antipsychotic medication in dosages in excess of those recommended in the British National Formulary (BNF)[495]. A 2002 audit found that 20% of inpatients receiving anti-psychotic medication were prescribed a total antipsychotic dose

---

[493] The census cannot reveal the length of detention for the remaining 19% of detained patients because it records legal status only on admission to hospital and on the census day for each patient. Where a patient was admitted informally and subsequently detained we cannot ascertain when that detention occurred. A further methodological limitation to this study is that it must assume that all detained patients are receiving medication and have done so from admission, whereas some patients may not receive medication immediately or (in the case of admissions where ECT is given) perhaps at all. It is likely that the overall effect of these limitations is an underestimation of the numbers. The latter limitation will tend towards an overestimation of the Second Opinions needed.

[494] Royal College of Psychiatrists (2006) *Revised consensus statement on high-dose antipsychotic medication*. Council Report 138.

[495] Joint Formulary Committee. (2007) *British National Formulary*. 54 ed. London: British Medical Association and Royal Pharmaceutical Society of Great Britain; Sept 2007

above BNF levels[496]. Other prevalence studies reveal that up to a quarter of psychiatric in-patients are prescribed a high dose of antipsychotic medication, with the highest prevalence figures being found in psychiatric intensive care units, rehabilitation wards and forensic units[497]. In its 2007 report[498], the Prescribing Observatory for Mental Health-UK (POMH-UK) found high-dose prescriptions in one third of the forensic patients studied[499]. It is important to recognise, however, that such studies count the prescription of drugs (including prescriptions for 'PRN' or 'as required' medication) and not drugs actually administered[500].

6.33 In the POMH-UK study, 88% of the prescriptions that exceeded BNF limits did so because two or more drugs were prescribed to be given simultaneously, of which nearly three-quarters (73%) involved 'PRN' medication[501]. Almost all PRN prescriptions were for 'first-generation' antipsychotic medication, even though the majority of patients were being regularly administered 'second-generation' antipsychotic medication[502]: as such, many of the advantages of prescribing the latter type of drug (i.e. fewer extrapyramidal side-effects) could be negated.

6.34 The POMH-UK study found that nearly half of all forensic prescriptions studied combined more than one antipsychotic drug[503]. There are some accepted reasons for combination prescribing:

- More than one drug may be prescribed during periods (ideally not exceeding six weeks) of titrated cross-over from one drug to another: this accounted for just 3% of combination prescriptions in the POHM-UK study[504].

- NICE guidance supports the strategy of 'clozapine augmentation', whereby patients who respond inadequately to clozapine alone may be prescribed a second antipsychotic[505]. Clozapine augmentation accounted for just 17% of the cases in the POHM-UK study[506]. Of the remainder, a further 15% were justified due to 'poor response to antipsychotic monotherapy', although there is little or no published evidence that combinations not involving clozapine are more efficacious than monotherapy.

---

[496] Harrington M, Lelliott P, Paton C, Okocha C, Duffet R, Sensky T (2002) 'The results of a multi-centre audit of the prescribing of anti-psychotic drugs for in-patients in the UK. *Psychiatric Bulletin* 26:414-418.

[497] Royal College of Psychiatrists (2006) *Revised consensus statement on high-dose antipsychotic medication.* Council Report 138, p.6.

[498] Prescribing Observatory for Mental Health-UK (POMH-UK) (2007) Topic 3 report 3a. *Prescribing of high-dose and combination anti-psychotics on forensic wards: baseline audit.* May 2007, Royal College of Psychiatrists.

[499] 642 patients in a baseline group of 1,891 were prescribed supra-BNF dosages of antipsychotic medication. See POMH-UK (2007) *supra.*

[500] See Royal College of Psychiatrists (2006) *op cit* n.797, p.14.

[501] POMH-UK (2007) *supra*, p.15.

[502] First generation' or older antipsychotics ('typical antipsychotics') such as chlorpromazine, haloperidol, sulpiride etc are more likely to cause extrapyramidal symptoms (tremor, abnormal face and body movements, restlessness) than the newer 'second generation' or 'atypical' antipsychotics (amisulpride, clozapine, olanzapine, quetiapine, risperidone, sertindole, & zotepine).

[503] 861 patients in a baseline group of 1,891 were prescribed more than one antipsychotic medication. See POMH-UK (2007) *supra.*

[504] Or 26 prescriptions: see POMH-UK (2007) *supra*, table 2.4 (p.32).

[505] National Institute for Clinical Excellence (2002) *Clinical Guideline 1. Schizophrenia: Core interventions in the treatment and management of schizophrenia in primary and secondary care.* NICE; December 2002. Page 18, para 1.4.5. http://www.nice.org.uk/pdf/CG1NICEguideline.pdf

[506] i.e. 146 patients; 128 for whom the reason for the combination was explicitly given as 'clozapine augmentation', and 18 others for whom clozapine was one of the drugs prescribed.

6.35 However, the most frequent reason given for combination prescribing in the POMH-UK study was control of behavioural disturbance or symptoms (388 patients, or 45% of all combination prescriptions). Combinations of antipsychotic drugs were also prescribed to 69 patients (8% of all combination prescriptions) to control persistent aggression towards self or others[507]. In such cases clinicians should be wary of relying on the sedating effect of medicines prescribed (and thus in effect prescribing medication for its side-effects) rather than addressing other possible causes of behavioural disturbance or aggression.

6.36 We discuss supra-BNF dosage and ethnicity of patients at chapter 3.76 *et seq*, using MHAC data collected on SOAD visits. MHAC data shows a relatively low level of supra-BNF prescription (approximately 11% of Second Opinions overall) in comparison to other studies. This may result from the fact that we ask SOADs themselves to identify whether they have authorised a supra-BNF prescription, and some SOADs may answer negatively when they have, in reality, authorised two or more drugs that cumulatively could be given over BNF recommended dosages. We are seeking to improve our data in this area.

> Selected recommendations of the RCPsych Consensus Statement on High-Dose Antipsychotic Medication
>
> • Each service should establish the audit of antipsychotic doses as a matter of routine practice. Careful watch should be kept on the dosage in terms of total percentage arising from drug combinations, and the use of PRN (as required) medication. Local systems should be developed to alert the responsible psychiatrist/clinical team to patients currently being administered or at risk of receiving high doses.
>
> • Before resorting to a high dose of antipsychotic medication, evidence-based strategies for treatment resistance should be exhausted, including use of clozapine.
>
> • The decision to prescribe high dose should be taken explicitly and should involve an individual risk–benefit assessment by a fully trained psychiatrist. This should be undertaken in consultation with the wider clinical team and the patient and a patient advocate, if available, and if the patient wishes their presence.
>
> • The decision to prescribe high dose should be documented in the case notes, including the risks and benefits of the strategy, the aims, and when and how the outcome will be assessed.
>
> • Before prescribing high-dose antipsychotics, carry out an ECG to establish a baseline, and exclude cardiac contraindications, including long QT syndromes. An ECG should be repeated after a few days and then every 1–3 months in the early stages of high-dose treatment. The ECG should be repeated as clinically indicated.
>
> • If high-dose antipsychotic treatment has been used in response to aggression with psychosis, it is particularly important that the routine monitoring of a sedated patient is carried out, with particular attention to regular checks of pulse, blood pressure, respiration, temperature and hydration. ECGs should be carried out frequently during dose escalation, if and when possible.

6.37 The MHAC has provided a guidance note to its Commissioners on the RCPsych consensus statement, including a list of the consensus statement recommendations of particular interest to the MHAC and an explanation of the 'percentage method' of calculating

---

[507] POMH-UK (2007) *op cit* n.498, table 2.4.

cumulative doses. That guidance is available on our website[508]. Where we see high-dose medication on visits, we seek to ensure that the clinical team are aware of the RCPsych statement and are implementing its recommendations. Over the last two years we have introduced the consensus statements onto a number of wards where it appeared not to have been previously noted.

> **Recommendation 34:** Detaining authorities should ensure that their clinical teams are familiar and comply with the RCPsych consensus statement through having local policies, with both the policy implementation and the use of high-dose medication audited and considered at Board level.

Covert medication

6.38 In our Tenth Biennial Report of 2003 we suggested dialogue between professional bodies and the Department of Health over the covert administration of medication, noting that this practice is likely to be more widespread in the treatment of informal patients than those detained under the Act[509]. We also suggested that it could be difficult to lawfully administer covert medication within the parameters of part IV of the Act, given the implicit assumptions of its framework (in part generated through the Code of Practice) that patients are given information about their treatment and therefore the opportunity, if they are capable of doing so, to give their consent[510]. In this reporting period, the new edition of the *Mental Health Act Manual* reiterated its previous charge that the MHAC has equivocated over this issue, and attempted itself to state a clear legal position[511]. We have suggested (in our response to the Department of Health's consultation on the draft revised Code of Practice) that the issue of covert medication should be explicitly addressed in the new Code. We hope that the Department will take up this suggestion and that this will lead to a wider debate and consensus regarding what is possible and permissible in this controversial area of mental healthcare.

6.39 In this reporting period, the Mental Welfare Commission for Scotland (MWC) published legal and practical guidance on covert medication that sets out useful principles and case scenarios, but focuses on mental incapacity legislation rather than the Scottish Mental Health Act[512]. The principles echo those of the 2004 Royal College of Psychiatrists' (RCPsych) consensus statement[513], especially in that both agree that covert administration of medication is unacceptable in the case of someone who is capable of deciding about medical treatment[514], and assume that the most common situation where covert medication might be justified was in severe dementia or profound learning disability cases, where the patient is unable to learn, even with support, that they are required to take medication and

---

[508] MHAC (2006) *Guidance for Commissioners: The RCPsych consensus statement on high-dose antipsychotic medication. 2006.* www.mhac.org.uk/

[509] MHAC (2003) *Tenth Biennial Report 2001-2003: Placed Amongst Strangers*, para 10.48 – 50

[510] *ibid.*, para 10.48

[511] See Jones R (2006) *Mental Health Act Manual* tenth edition, para 1-720 (a note to s.58(3)): "the legal position is that covert medication cannot be given to a mentally capable patient without his or her consent and may only be given to a mentally incapable detained patient the powers contained in either s.63 or under s.63 or under para. (b) of this subsection" (sic).

[512] Mental Welfare Commission for Scotland (2006) *Covert Medication.* MWC, November 2006 www.mwcscot.org.uk

[513] Royal College of Psychiatrists (2004) 'College Statement on Covert Administration of Medicines', *Psychiatric Bulletin*, 28, 385-386

[514] Mental Welfare Commission for Scotland (2006) *ibid.*, p.1

that this is in their best interests[515]. The RCPsych statement holds that covert medication of patients with mental illnesses such as schizophrenia is unacceptable on these grounds[516]. Both documents stress the multi-disciplinary nature of a decision to administer medication covertly; the advisability of discussion with relatives or carers; and the need to consider the best interests of the patient concerned in deciding upon any form of covert medication. Both documents should be read carefully by any clinical team considering the use of covert medication.

6.40   We have encountered a number of examples of the covert administration of medication to detained patients, and have been asked on several occasions whether such administration of medication is precluded by the terms of the Act, and if not, whether a SOAD's explicit authorisation is required. In one unusual example in December 2006, two nurses were suspended and subject to disciplinary measures for injecting a patient with water as a placebo in an independent hospital. The nurse who gave the instruction stated that this was viewed as acceptable practice in his home country of Trinidad, and he had not known it would be unacceptable in a UK hospital. We consider that practices based upon deception in this way can never be justified.

6.41   In general terms, we take the view that the Act itself cannot be said with confidence to preclude the use of covert medication to any detained patient, regardless of that patient's consent status or capacity to consent, although the fact that something is not precluded by the Act does not make it lawful in a wider sense, and in many cases it would be extremely hard to justify covert medication against the test established in Bolam ("in accordance with practice accepted at the time by a responsible body of medical opinion skilled in the particular form of treatment in question"[517]) or against the competing human rights claims of the patient concerned[518].

6.42   Our analysis of the basic legal and ethical framework within which any covert use of medication on detained patients must be applied is as follows.

Covert medication in the first three months of treatment

6.43   The authority to give medication in the first three months of a detained patient's treatment is provided by s.63 of the Act, which states simply that "consent… shall not be required". Whilst treatment is being given under this authority, there is nothing in the wording of the Act itself that would prevent covert administration. There is no authority under the Act for a SOAD to authorise the administration of medication in this period, and as such the MHAC cannot arrange a statutory Second Opinion.

6.44   The Code of Practice states that "even though the Act allows treatment to be given without consent during the first three months the RMO should ensure that the patient's valid consent is sought before any medication is administered" and proceed in the absence of

---

[515] Royal College of Psychiatrists (2004) *op cit* n.513, para 4.

[516] *ibid.*, para 14.

[517] *Bolam v Friern Hospital Management Committee* [1957] 1 W.L.R. 582.

[518] Any use of covert medication would have to be a justifiable interference with the right to private life protected by Article 8 of the ECHR, and in extremis could contravene the ECHR's absolute prohibition of inhuman or degrading treatment (Article 3).

consent only having considered the alternatives[519]. As the House of Lords accepted in *Munjaz*[520], a psychiatrist (or the detaining authority) can lawfully depart from the Code's guidance if there are "cogent reasons" for doing so. We advise that any such decision to depart from the Code's guidance, and the reasons justifying that departure, should be thoroughly recorded. The record should include an assessment of the patient's capacity to consent.

Covert medication after the initial three months of treatment

6.45 Once a detained patient has been receiving medication for three months, a SOAD's authorisation will be required for it to continue in the absence of consent. The Act sets out that the absence of consent can result from the patient's incapacity or refusal. As such, the SOAD who authorises treatment without consent must certify that the patient is either incapable of understanding the nature, purpose and likely effects of the treatment, or that the patient has not consented to it[521]. As we have stated in past reports, we are uncertain that either statement can be easily made when a patient does not know that they are receiving the treatment[522], at least insofar as the Act is interpreted through its Code of Practice. However, if the RMO or detaining authority finds cogent reason for departing from the Code's expectations, this should be recorded in the patient's notes as a part of the justification for covert treatment.

- For **patients with mental capacity** to give consent to treatment, the circumstances that might justify covert medication are almost inconceivable[523], and indeed the *Mental Health Act Manual* suggests that there could be no legal basis upon which a capacitous patient could be given covert medication without his or her consent[524]. In practical terms this may be broadly correct (not least because the wide consensus that such a practice would be unethical could cause it to fail the *Bolam* test[525]), and because logic suggests that a patient cannot refuse to consent to that of which they are unaware. As such, it would seem that a patient can only be deemed to have refused medication if his or her consent has been sought for it[526]. However, our close reading of the Act and the current Code of Practice does not identify any explicit or binding prohibition of covertly administering medication after consent for that medication has been solicited but refused. Such action would, however, do some violence to the Code's notion of capacity and consent as matters under continuous appraisal, and raise serious questions about compatibility with the patient's human rights. For these reasons, even if the law is flexible enough to allow the covert medication without consent of capacitous patients, the MHAC supports the view of the RCPsych and MWC that it would be unacceptable practice.

---

[519] *MHA 1983 Code of Practice*, para 16.11.

[520] *R v Ashworth Hospital Authority (Now Mersey Care NHS Trust) ex parte Munjaz* [2005] UKHL 58. See MHAC (2006) *Eleventh Biennial Report 2003 – 2005: In Place of Fear?* page 35 -37, and MHAC Briefing Note *The status of the Code of Practice following the House of Lords' Munjaz ruling* (www.mhac.org.uk) for discussion of this case.

[521] MHA 1983, s.58(3)(b).

[522] MHAC (2003) *Tenth Biennial Report 2001-2003: Placed Amongst Strangers,* para 10.48.

[523] Although the RadcliffesLeBrasseur Mental Health Law Briefing on *The Covert administration of Medication* (Number 101, June 2006 www.rlb-law.com) suggests as possible justifications "where this might enable treatment to be given without the use of considerable restraint of the patient, or risk to staff". We would advise extreme caution in justifying covert medication of capable patients on such grounds.

[524] Jones R (2006) *op cit*, n.511.

[525] See Mental Welfare Commission for Scotland (2006) *op cit*. n.512, p.1, Royal College of Psychiatrists (2004) *op cit*. n.513, para 4.

[526] See, for example, *MHA 1983 Code of Practice*, para 16.13.

- For **patients who lack capacity**, there may be circumstances where, if covert medication can be justified on clinical grounds, choosing to administer medication overtly using force may itself be a disproportionate breach of the patient's Article 8 rights, or even amount to a breach of Article 3 rights. Although the Code of Practice warns against a 'status' test of incapacity, suggesting that capacity should be assessed "in relation to the particular patient, at the particular time, as regards the particular treatment proposed" and that treatment plans should be explained in terms appropriate to enable patients to understand them[527], it is conceivable that for some patients (such as those with profound learning disability or dementia) the outcome of such capacity assessments are a foregone conclusion. In such exceptional circumstances we accept that a SOAD could legitimately certify that the patient is incapable of understanding the nature, purpose and likely effect of a treatment to be given covertly. However, particular care needs to be taken that the incapacitating effects of a broad range of psychiatric conditions – especially perhaps the paranoia associated with many types of psychotic illness which makes patients quite determined not to take medication – are not used to justify covert administration. Such a justification would be extremely counter-therapeutic and would breach the RCPsych guidelines that "the covert medication of patients with schizophrenia and other severe mental illnesses where patients can learn and understand that they will be required to take medication is unacceptable"[528].

6.46 Whether a patient has capacity to consent or not, the covert administration of medication under s.58 could only be lawful upon the authority of a SOAD. In deciding whether to certify that treatment should be given to a detained patient, a SOAD will also have to decide whether the means by which it is to be given are capable of being approved. We take the view that, in making the latter decision, the SOAD will have to have regard, not only to section 58, but also to *Bolam* principles and the Code of Practice.

6.47 Where an RMO presents a treatment plan for consideration by the SOAD, we would expect that any intention to administer part or all of that plan covertly should be made explicit. We will expect SOADs to look for evidence that the clinical team are aware of the RCPsych and related guidance, that alternatives to covert routes have been thoroughly considered, and that the clinical team have discussed the matter thoroughly between themselves and with any appropriate relatives, carers and advocates. We shall expect SOADs to document such compliance in general terms alongside their reasons for their decision, whether or not they authorise the covert route requested. Where a clinical team decide to resort to covert administration of medication that is authorised on an extant Form 39 (i.e. where that extant Form relates to a treatment plan that did not specify covert routes of administration), we would consider it to be good practice to request a further Second Opinion to reconsider the authorisation in this new context. Where the MHAC encounters covert administration on the basis of a Form 39 that did not specifically consider this, we will use our power under s.62(2) to withdraw the extant form and arrange a further SOAD visit.

> **Recommendation 35:** Covert administration of any part of a treatment plan authorised on an extant Form 39 should have been explicitly considered by the SOAD. Where a decision is made to covertly administer medication, a new Second Opinion should be requested even if the medication otherwise remains within the parameters of the extant authorisation.

---

[527] MHA 1983 *Code of Practice*, para 15.12.

[528] Royal College of Psychiatrists (2004) *op cit.* n.513, para 14.

6.48 A number of Trusts have formulated policies on covert medication that draw from the extant guidance in this area. The policy formulated by Bolton, Salford and Trafford Mental Health NHS Trust[529] includes a useful checklist for recording decisions to use covert medication that prompts clinical teams into compliance with good practice guidance, such as ensuring that attempts have been made to give the medication in its normal form; that the medication has been reduced to only that which is essential; that it has been discussed and agreed with the hospital pharmacist to ensure safe administration; discussed within the team and with relevant other parties; and (amongst other matters) that a care plan has been completed outlining the prescription and a date for its review.

Herbal remedies and certification under the Act

6.49 The MHAC is occasionally asked whether herbal remedies, such as St John's Wort, need to be certified under s.58 of the Act if they are to be taken by detained patients to whom that section applies. In our Tenth Biennial Report (2003) we stated that, in general, we would not consider herbal remedies to be 'medicines for mental disorder' falling within s.58. This position is open to the criticism that it adopts a rather arbitrarily restrictive definition of 'medicine' compared to the dictionary definition of the term[530], and so we have now revised our view and accept that herbal preparations may be considered as 'medicines for mental disorder'.

6.50 In general, the use of alternative medicines is usually initiated by the patient or carer, rather than being suggested or even imposed by the clinical team. As such, the practical question is most likely to be whether such medication should be included in the certification of medication to which the patient consents (i.e. on Form 38), although it is conceivable that family members might wish for such medication to be administered to an incapacitated detained patient, or a SOAD might be asked to allow for the continuance of such medication using Form 39 after a patient who has been using it has lost capacity,. We take the view that, at least insofar as any herbal remedy is prescribed or supplied by the patient's doctor to a patient subject to part IV of the Act who is no longer subject to the three-month rule, it should be certified on either of Forms 38 or 39.

6.51 If a patient is using herbal preparations having bought them over the counter (or having them brought into hospital by relatives or friends), it would not appear to be necessary in law for his or her doctor to certify the treatments on a Form 38, as the clinical team is playing no part in the administration of such medication and therefore needs no authority to do so. However, some herbal preparations can produce side effects or interactions with prescription drugs. Of all herbal remedies, the strongest claims for efficacy are made for St John's Wort, albeit only for mild to moderate depression[531], although this herbal preparation appears to have important and potentially dangerous interactions with many

---

[529] Contact: Joan Miller, Bolton, Salford and Trafford Mental Health NHS Trust, joan.miller@bstmht.nhs.uk

[530] See, for example, Jones R (2006) *Mental Health Act Manual*, tenth edition, paragraph 1-721, where Jones argues against the MHAC's rejection of placebo (in our Eighth Biennial Report of 1999) as 'medicine' on the grounds that 'placebo' is defined in the Shorter OED as, *inter alia*, "a medicine … prescribed more for psychological effect than for any physiological effect". This is a valid criticism, albeit one that Jones states is without practical consequences in the case of placebo medication, given the requirement to explain the nature, purpose and effect of medications proposed to detained patients.

[531] Ernst E (2007) 'Herbal remedies for depression and anxiety' *Advances in Psychiatric Treatment* 13, 312-6

prescription drugs, reducing their efficacy through lowered plasma levels[532]. It is also reported that it is suspected of triggering psychoses in patients who concomitantly take SSRI antidepressants[533]. That a patient may be choosing to take such preparations is therefore clearly relevant to a prescribing doctor, not least on grounds of safety.

6.52   It is therefore important that clinical and nursing staff are in a position to advise patients (and if necessary intervene) where patients are supplementing, or plan to supplement, their medication regime with herbal remedies. We recognise, of course, the limitations of the evidence upon which any such advice would have to be based. If a patient wishes to self-medicate with certain herbal remedies known to have potential interactions or side-effects, his or her doctor may wish to agree a particular dose (or even agree to provide and dispense the preparation). Whether or not any brought-in and self-administered preparation is recorded on a patient's Form 38, it is important that a record of what the patient is taking is made in the clinical notes, in the event of any side effects or drug interactions requiring intervention. Because of such interactions, patient's responsible medical officers may feel that they have to prevent individual patients from taking herbal preparations: we believe that authority for this can be inferred from the Act, but that any such action and its rationale should be carefully documented by the RMO.

Fish oils and certification under the Act

6.53   Although commonly thought of as an 'alternative' medicinal approach to the treatment of psychosis (perhaps because of their over-the-counter availability as a nutritional supplement), omega-3 fish-oils have a licensed prescription form used for lipid regulation in treating hyperlipidaemia[534]. Omega-3 fish-oil has also been reported to enhance the efficacy of antipsychotic drugs (especially clozapine) in poorly responding patients, and we understand that it is currently undergoing clinical trials for this purpose. We have been asked whether fish-oils used in these circumstances fall within the definition of medication for mental disorder.

6.54   It is the MHAC view that fish-oil used as an adjunctive treatment of psychosis does fall within the definition of medication for mental disorder and should be certified on Forms 38 or 39 if it is to be administered to a patient to whom s.58 is applicable. We have advised SOADs that the treatment should be certified as "one omega 3 marine triglyceride orally BNF 2.12 for adjunctive treatment of psychosis".

Use of Benzodiazepines

6.55   Benzodiazepines such as lorazepam or diazepam are widely prescribed to detained patients, often as an alternative treatment to antipsychotic medication for agitation associated with psychoses or mania. Whilst benzodiazepines do not cause the sorts of extrapyramidal side effects possible with antipsychotic medication, they can lead to severe withdrawal

---

[532] *ibid.*, p.315: see Box 2.

[533] Izzo A A & Ernst E (2001) 'Interactions between herbal medicines and prescribed drugs: a systematic review'. *Drugs* 15; 2163-2175

[534] Joint Formulary Committee (2007) *British National Formulary*. 54th ed. London: British Medical Association and Royal Pharmaceutical Society of Great Britain; Sept 2007, section 2.1.2.

symptoms on cessation, and therefore dependence, and are therefore generally indicated only for short-term use. For a very small number of patients with severely disabling anxiety, however, the benefits from long-term treatment with a benzodiazepine may outweigh concerns over dependence such that these patients should not be denied treatment[535].

6.56   In a study published in this reporting period, Choke *et al*[536] analysed the incidence of lorazepam prescription in a sample of 102 patients admitted in April 2005 to acute wards managed by South West London & St George's NHS Trust. They found that 83 patients (81%) were prescribed lorazepam, although only 45 of these had the drug administered during their hospital stay. Lorazepam was administered to these patients on a total of 143 occasions, although the reason for such administration was only clearly stated on either the prescription card or in the medical notes in 54 cases (51 of which recorded agitation, and 3 insomnia). A further 12 administrations (14% of all administrations) were recorded as being given at the patients' request without giving a clinical indication. The study found that half of the review dates for the prescriptions were set more than four weeks from the original prescription, despite guidelines stating that benzodiazepine treatment should be limited to 2 to 4 weeks (although of course many patients were prescribed but never given the treatment, or would have been given it only intermittently on a prn basis, which is less likely to induce dependence). For 12 patients, the review date was one year from the prescription date. The study found that in most cases (85% of administrations) between 1 and 2 mg of lorazepam was given to patients in any single administration, although three patients received more than the BNF daily recommended limit in a single administration. These excessive doses seemed to be the result of error, rather than responses to extreme clinical presentations.

6.57   As an adjunct to the study discussed above, in September 2007 we looked at the results of 100 Second Opinion Appointed Doctor visits to patients detained at South West London & St George's NHS Trust. We looked at the most recent SOAD visits, discounting abortive visits or visits for which paperwork was unavailable. Because four patients in the group had been visited twice, we identified data for 92 patients, which is set out at figure 68 below.

authorisation	Male		Female		Total	
	< 65 yrs	>65 yrs	<65 yrs	>65 yrs	<65 yrs	>65 yrs
no benzodiazepine	14	0	10	4	24	4
lorazepam	30	3	16	1	46	4
lorazepam & diazepam	4	3	3	0	7	3
diazepam	1	0	1	0	2	0
unnamed benzodiazepine	2	0	0	0	2	0

Fig 68: Benzodiazepine authorisation in 92 patients seen by SOADs, South West London & St George's NHS Trust, 2006-2007

Data source: MHAC

---

[535] *Maudsley Prescribing Guidelines*, 9th edition, May 2007. Benzodiazepines may also be given for severe insomnia. We would usually expect benzodiazepine use for insomnia in detained patients to be judged to fall within part IV of the Act (i.e. where severe and disabling insomnia is rooted in anxiety as a symptom of mental disorder), but in some cases the cause of insomnia may be judged to be separate to a patient's mental and therefore outside of the provisions of the Mental Health Act.

[536] Choke A, Perumal M V, & Howlett M (2007) 'Lorazepam prescription and monitoring in acute psychiatric wards' *Psychiatric Bulletin* 31, 300-303

6.58 By necessity, our review of SOAD authorisations shifts the focus from *all* inpatients in acute wards in the original study, to just those patients who are detained (not necessarily in acute wards) and who have been receiving medication for more than three months. This shift is reflected in the gender of the patients studied: male patients accounted for 32% of the original study group, whereas 68% of the MHAC patient group were male. The median age of the two groups was similar (39 and 43 respectively).

6.59 Our findings also shift focus from the *prescription* of benzodiazepines to the giving of permission for such prescription. The original study found that just over half of patients who were prescribed benzodiazapines actually received them, and remark that this may reflect a practice of doctors giving 'just-in-case' authority to nursing staff to cover any eventuality, resulting in "overprescription". We might expect that the proportion of patients for whom authority to prescribe benzodiazepines was obtained would show an even greater effect of such 'overprescription', but this is not the case: in the MHAC group 28% of patients were *not* being written up for benzodiazepines, as opposed to 19% of the more general population of acute wards in the original study. These differences may be explained by the different profiles of the patients involved, although the need to justify any prescription of benzodiazepines to a SOAD in the MHAC study group may also have had a restraining effect.

6.60 The BNF advises a maximum daily dosage of oral lorazepam of 4mg for adults, and 2mg for 'elderly or infirm' patients[537]. In the MHAC sample of patients for whom lorazepam was authorised, it was authorised within BNF limits for all patients aged under 65 (54 patients in total), and for three of the seven patients aged over 65. Four authorisations given in relation to patients aged between 65 and 70 specified between 3 and 4mg lorazepam daily (i.e. 150 to 200% the BNF dosage for 'elderly or infirm' patients). We were surprised to find that in only one of these cases the authorisation recognised that the dose authorised was above BNF recommendations: in the other three (one of whom had been visited twice and had two authorisations completed) it appeared that the SOAD had not taken into account the reduced BNF limit for elderly patients. We subsequently raised this as a training issue in our bulletin to SOADs.

6.61 Most clinical guidelines suggest that benzodiazepines should be used only for short term treatment, implying a review of their prescription not less than at monthly intervals[538]. It would be expensive and probably unhelpful to insist that all SOAD authorisations of benzodiazepines must be limited to expire within four weeks (particularly as many involve prn medication that is administered intermittently, if at all), but we suggest that all active prescriptions should be reviewed at no less than monthly intervals by the clinical team. Careful recording of the dosages administered, and the reasons for administration, will allow meaningful review, and may help prevent the numerous occasions when lorazepam is administered to a patient unlawfully: the MHAC often finds on its visits that lorazepam has been administered without authority, either because it is given in excess of the BNF dosage authorised, or because it is given without any authorisation under the Act.

---

[537] Joint Formulary Committee. (2007) *British National Formulary*. 54th ed. London: British Medical Association and Royal Pharmaceutical Society of Great Britain; Sept 2007, section 4.1.2.

[538] Choke et al (2007) *op cit.* list the Maudsley Prescribing Guidelines; NICE guidelines on the treatment of anxiety (2004) and the Committee on Safety of Medicines anxiolytics guidelines (BMA & Royal Pharmaceutical Society, 2005)

Review of treatment

6.62   Section 61 requires a report to be submitted to the MHAC where a patient has been given treatment following a SOAD authorisation, on the next renewal of detention (or, for restricted patients, after the first six months of detention, and subsequently when submitting a report to the Mental Health Unit[539]). In some cases, RMOs may be under the misapprehension that the requirement for a report under s.61 falls away if the patient consents to treatment at any point in the period between the SOAD authorisation and the point at which such a report is due. We found one concrete example of this on a visit in the Merseyside area, where the patient records contained the Mental Health Act Administrator's flagging letter requesting that the RMO should complete a s.61 report, annotated by the RMO with "changed to a Form 38". A report under s.61 had been neither completed nor submitted. This opportunity to review the patient's treatment and consent status would have served a good purpose in this case, as it might have highlighted other rectifiable shortcomings to the care team. We could find documented evidence neither of any discussion over consent to treatment with the patient, nor of any assessment of mental capacity to give valid consent, despite a recent CPA review noting some cognitive impairment in the patient's presentation. The Form 38 referred to by the RMO could not be found in the patient's notes, nor was it attached to the patient's medicine card, which was clipped to the original (and apparently superceded) Form 39.

Urgent Treatment under section 62

6.63   The provisions at s.62 of the 1983 Act, which provide authorisation for urgent treatment, are widely misunderstood. The Code of Practice requires that a form is devised to be completed by the RMO or doctor for the time being in charge of the treatment "every time urgent treatment is given"[540]. The MHAC is often asked whether it is necessary to invoke s.62 for every administration of treatment, or whether it can be invoked for a course of treatment. This question can be approached by considering the nature of the section itself:

---

[539] i.e. under sections 41(6); 45B(3) or 49(3).

[540] *MHA Code of Practice*, para 16.41.

214

- No treatment may be authorised under s.62(1) unless it is "immediately necessary". This will not change under the revisions of the 2007 Act[541]. Thus the decision to give treatment under this power cannot be foreseen, and the section cannot be invoked to provide authority for projected treatments at a future time. Once commenced, the treatment can only continue for as long as is necessary to achieve the statutory objective. As such, in the majority of cases, it is difficult to see how the RMO could avoid giving explicit authorisation for each administration of medication or ECT under s.62(1). The exception to this would be where discontinuing a treatment would end the alleviation of serious suffering, or end the prevention of the patient behaving violently or being a danger to self or others. In such circumstances, where the RMO is of the view that there is no likelihood of the patient's condition improving to the extent that such treatment could be suspended, the RMO might choose to authorise a course of treatment rather than individual applications. Such an authorisation should, however, be kept under constant review and discontinued when the urgency has passed. In our view, it is never appropriate to authorise more than a single application of ECT at a time under this power.

- Section 62(2) allows that a treatment which is already underway need not be discontinued if to do so would cause serious suffering, where either a patient who has been consenting to it withdraws that consent, or the SOAD authorisation for its administration to a patient without consent is withdrawn by the MHAC. In these circumstances, an RMO may well feel that a single authorisation is sufficient for the treatment to continue to be administered whilst a Second Opinion doctor is awaited to consider longer-term authorisation of the treatment.

6.64   Consideration of the use of s.62 should always trigger a request for a Second Opinion doctor's visit. The MHAC asks whether s.62 has been applied when taking requests for Second Opinions, and can prioritise those where a patient is being treated without the protections of s.58 of the Act.

6.65   It has been the practice of some SOADs, when authorising ECT for a patient who has already received one or more treatments under s.62 powers, to express that authorisation in terms of a course of ECT treatments (i.e. 12 treatments) including (or excluding) those that have already been given. We have asked SOADs not to do this, not only because it may give the incorrect impression that the SOAD can retrospectively authorise treatments already given under s.62, but as it may cause wider confusion. One RMO, having administered a 'course' of ECT to a patient upon such an authority, was refused authority to give another course of treatment by a SOAD, but upon reviewing the patient's file found that it could be argued that the patient could still have one further treatment before the limit of the previous authority was reached. The RMO contacted the MHAC to ask our view on whether that treatment could be given. We thought that the second SOAD's view that more ECT treatments should not be given must prevail and, using our power under s.61(3), we withdrew the extant Form 39, advising the RMO that he would have to justify the further treatment under s.62 if it was to be given. We have asked that SOADs now specify the number of ECT authorised in as simple a way possible.

---

[541]   The 2007 Act (at s.28(6)) does, however, restrict the application of s.62 to ECT treatment (allowing that it may be authorised only under the powers of 62(1)(a) or (b)). This means that ECT may only be given under emergency powers when it is necessary to save the patient's life or prevent a serious deterioration of his condition.

New roles, supplementary prescribing and part IV of the Act: new ways of working?

6.66 The concept of 'supplementary prescribing' – where nursing staff take limited prescribing responsibility in the place of doctors – pre-dates the Department of Health's 'new ways of working' initiative (see chapter 1.45 above) but could play an important part in meeting its aims of sharing the workload of consultants amongst the clinical team. As with 'new ways of working', there is a potential for misapplication of supplementary prescribing as a cost-saving measure, or as a means to manage services with fewer registered medical practitioners, but there is also considerable potential for service improvement of benefit to patients. Supplementary prescribing could enable patients to have medication adjusted without having to wait for the ward round, or for other contact with the psychiatrist, and could foster better provision of information, and choice, about medication and the ways in which it might be taken[542].

6.67 The 2007 Act abolishes the role of 'responsible medical officer' (RMO) under the 1983 Act. In its place, patients have a 'responsible clinician', who need not be a doctor. If the responsible clinician is neither a doctor nor another professional with the ability to prescribe medication, the role of the RMO in relation to the consent to treatment parts of the Act (such as signing Forms 38 certifying a patient's consent to treatment) must be undertaken by a doctor (who must also be an 'approved' clinician) who is 'in charge of the treatment in question.'[543] The draft revised Code of Practice suggests that in such cases, the responsible clinician "will maintain their overall responsibility for the patient's case, but that part of the treatment that they are not qualified to be in charge of will be the responsibility of another appropriately qualified member of the multi-disciplinary team"[544]. It is possible that the 2007 Act's rearrangement of responsibilities for detained patients' care will thus allow for the extension of non-medical prescribing beyond supplementary prescribing, so that an approved clinician becomes the independent prescriber of medication without becoming the 'responsible clinician' for the patient concerned[545]. It will be important that detaining authorities establish clear internal lines of accountability to avoid confusion of accountability, and to ensure that the requirements of the Act regarding patient's consent to treatment are met.

6.68 As we stated in chapter 1.48 above, a balance needs to be struck between maintaining adequate patient safeguards for patients subject to psychiatric compulsion, and not excluding them from any service developments fostered through new ways of working.

6.69 Authorities may be nervous of extending the new ways of working to some or all of the patients that they detain. For example, we have corresponded with services who, in adapting generic guidance on non-medical prescribing, had assumed that any patient who lacked

---

[542] Jones A (2006) 'Supplementary Prescribing: potential ways to reform hospital psychiatric care'. *Journal of Psychiatry and Mental Health Nursing* **13**, 132-138

[543] MHA 2007, Explanatory Notes, para 57.

[544] Department of Health (2007) *Mental Health Act 2007 draft revised Code of Practice*. Oct '07, para 13.9.

[545] For discussion of 'supplementary' and 'independent' prescribing, see National Prescribing Centre, National Institute for Mental Health in England and Department of Health (2005) *Improving mental health services by extending the role of nurses in prescribing and supplying medication: good practice guide*. NPC

mental capacity to consent to supplementary prescribing arrangements must be excluded from them. We questioned this assumption, suggesting that we could see no reason in law why this should be the case. Under current legal arrangements, the limits of an incapacitated patient's treatment with medication are established by the RMO or SOAD (depending on whether the three-month period has expired), but the administration of some medicines may occur on an 'as required' (i.e. prn) basis, within those parameters, at the discretion of nursing staff. We suggest that supplementary prescribing is an analogous arrangement, and as such is potentially applicable to any detained patient's care, provided that the supplementary prescriber works under the direction of the RMO and prescribes within the parameters established by the RMO (in the first three months) and within the parameters established by Forms 38 or 39.

6.70　There is also scope for 'patient group directions' for inpatient settings, where nursing staff are empowered by doctors to prescribe a range of medications within that setting, rather than being empowered to act as supplementary prescribers on an individual patient basis. In some Trusts, this arrangement is used simply to empower nursing staff to prescribe for common minor physical ailments without having to wait for the attendance of a doctor[546]. From the amendment of the Misuse of Drugs regulations in October 2003, patient group directions covering the administration of some medication used in the treatment of anxiety or used for night sedation, such as benzodiazepines, have also been permissible[547]. For detained inpatients, the broader scope that such group directions might provide would be limited, but, given our concern over the use of benzodiazepines, and the possibility that overmedication is usually the result of error at the point of administration, or repeated administrations, this underlines the importance of careful recording and audit of the use of these drugs (see paragraph 6.56 above).

The role of the 'second professional'

6.71　Section 58 requires that a SOAD must consult with a nurse, and with another person "professionally concerned with the patient's medical treatment" who is neither a nurse nor a doctor. The Code of Practice suggests that social workers, occupational therapists, psychologists, psychotherapists or pharmacists would all be appropriate second consultees, and lists the issues that a consultee should consider commenting upon, including:

- the proposed treatment and the patient's ability to consent to it;
- other treatments options;
- the way in which the decision to treat was arrived at;
- the facts of the case, progress, attitude of relatives etc; and
- the implications of imposing treatment upon a non-consenting patient and the reasons for the patient's refusal.

The Code also states that statutory consultees should ensure that they make a record of their consultation in the patient's notes[548].

---

[546]　*ibid.*, para 6.4

[547]　*ibid.*, para 6.5

[548]　*Mental Health Act 1983 Code of Practice*, para 16.34

6.72   We are pleased to note that this guidance remains unchanged in the draft revised Code of Practice[549]. MHA Commissioners frequently note that statutory consultees (whether nurses of others) fail to record their discussions with SOADs as the Code suggests: in this reporting period we have raised this issue on over 200 visits. We consider that this is an important part of the statutory consultee role, as an outline of the matters set out above from a member of the multi-disciplinary team should be a valuable part of records available for care-planning and review.

6.73   The MHAC is sometimes asked over the appropriateness of consulting with certain members of the clinical team. The final decision as to whether a consultee is appropriately qualified to take on the role is for the SOAD (and of course the consultee, who cannot be made to undertake the role), although we have generally advised that persons in 'assistant' roles who do not hold recognised qualifications and have little professional autonomy should not be expected to stand as second consultees. Whilst we continue to take the view that it would be unnecessarily restrictive to insist that the second consultee should *invariably* be professionally qualified and included in a professional register (as we stated in our Fifth Biennial Report[550]), since we first made that statement there has been a significant extension of professional regulatory provision in health and social care, as a response to the public perception that such regulation protects patients. As such, we suggest that the basic criterion for performing the role of a second consultee should be a recognised professional qualification relevant to the patient's medical treatment[551], and that wherever possible SOADs should consult with qualified persons who are also subject to professional regulation.

Electro-convulsive therapy (ECT)

6.74   The number of Second Opinions for ECT has not shown the same steep rise in recent years as we have observed in Second Opinions for medication (see figure 69 below). This graph

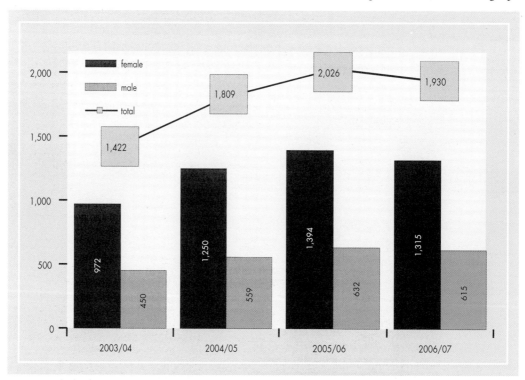

Fig 69: Second Opinion requests for ECT by gender, 2003/04 to 2006/07.

Source: MHAC data

---

[549] Department of Health (2007) *Draft revised Mental Health Act 1983 Code of Practice*, para 26.17 – 26.18.

[550] MHAC (1993) *Fifth Biennial Report 1991-1993*. para 7.16

[551] See Jones R (2006) *Mental Health Act Manual*, tenth edition, paragraph 1-709.

also shows that the gender profile for ECT is roughly a mirror image of that for medication, in that ECT is requested for more than twice the number of female patients than male patients (for data on medication, see figure 63 above).

6.75 ECT is most commonly used for elderly patients (figure 70 below), particularly females. It is likely that this preponderance of older patients is a significant cause of the higher proportion of incapable patients being considered for ECT (figure 71) in comparison to those being considered for medication (figure 64, paragraph 6.15). There is undoubtedly a preponderance of incapacitating illness amongst elderly detained patients, although it may also be the case that older women are more likely to be deemed to lack capacity to refuse consent by an assessing clinician.

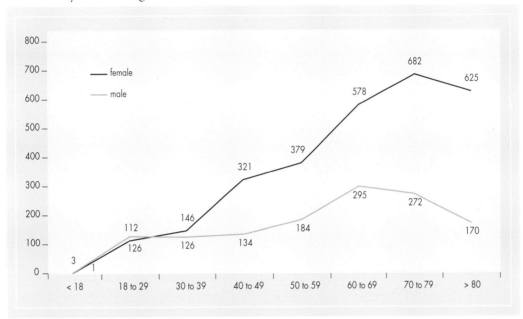

Fig 70: age range of patients receiving Second Opinions to consider ECT treatment, 2005/6 – 2006/7

Source: MHAC data

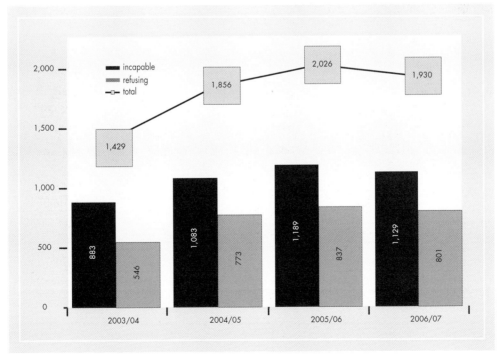

Fig 71: Second Opinion requests for ECT by capacity status, 2003/04 to 2006/07.

Source: MHAC data

219

ECT as a special case under the Mental Health Act

6.76   For many patients, the prospect of ECT treatment is frightening in the extreme[552], and indeed media images of the treatment reinforce this fear. The treatment is also particularly physical and arguably more invasive than other most other forms of psychiatric treatment (in that, for example, it requires general anaesthesia). It can be experienced as degrading, for example when patients feel that they are treated in a 'production line' on ECT clinic days[553], or if treatment and immediate recovery is not undertaken with sufficient privacy or care. However, ECT has also been described as a treatment 'opposed for political not clinical reasons'[554]. It is not reported to involve serious physical risks, although some patients report serious memory loss[555] and short-term disorientation[556]. A study of ECT in Denmark suggested that mortality rates from natural causes were lower for patients receiving ECT than for other psychiatric in-patients[557]. In Denmark (and the USA) ECT guidelines state that the only medical conditions contraindicating ECT are cerebral and other aneurysms, in comparison to UK guidelines that stress the identification and careful management of risk factors including cardiovascular disease or pulmonary disorders, and the Danish researchers therefore claim that their sample included patients who might be excluded from ECT treatment in this country on the grounds of cardiac contraindications[558].

6.77   Although government resisted calls for capacity-based thresholds for psychiatric compulsion in the debates over the Mental Health Act 2007, it conceded calls for such a threshold for the imposition of ECT (having suggested this itself in the draft Mental Health Bill of 2004). From the implementation of the 2007 Act, detained patients who give capacitous refusal of consent to ECT, or have done so in an advance directive or through a deputy or donee under the Mental Capacity Act's provisions, will not be liable to have the treatment imposed upon them. As is shown at figure 71, above, and as we have discussed in previous reports[559], such a legal threshold would, at least in theory, have prevented almost one third of SOAD authorisations of ECT over the last eight years. It is possible that actual ECT authorisations will not reduce by this number, but that patient presentations that would have been deemed capacitous under the current law will not be so deemed under the revised law.

6.78   As such, the actual effect of this revision to the criteria for compulsion should be studied as an important indicator for the future of mental health legislation in England and Wales. This change will, however, coincide with the demise of the MHAC as a discrete body able to

---

[552] Kershaw K, Rayner L, & Chaplin R (2007) 'Patients' views on the quality of care when receiving electroconvulsive therapy' *Psychiatric Bulletin* 31 414-417

[553] *ibid.*

[554] Bharadwaj R, Grover S (2007) 'Mortality and electroconvulsive therapy' (correspondence) *British Journal of Psychiatry* 191, 362-3. See also Shorter E & Healy D (2007) *Shock Therapy*. Rutgers University Press.

[555] See, for a recent example, Watkinson A (2007) 'ECT: a personal experience', *Mental Health Practice* Vol 10 No 7, p.32-35

[556] Kershaw K, et al (2007) *ibid.*

[557] Munk-Olsen T, Laursen T M, Videbech P et al (2007) All-cause mortality among recipients of elctroconvulsive therapy. Register-based cohort study. *British Journal of Psychiatry* 190, 435-9.

[558] See Le Strat Y, Gorwood P (2007) 'Mortality and electroconvulsive therapy' (correspondence) and the authors' reply, *British Journal of Psychiatry* 191, 362-3.

[559] See MHAC (2006) *Eleventh Biennial Report 2003-2005: In Place of Fear?* , para 4.71 – 4.75

determine its own research agenda in monitoring the revised Mental Health Act. It appears to us that the body responsible for monitoring the Act and managing the SOAD system will remain best-placed to do this, and as such we recommend this as a research agenda to our successor body.

> **Recommendation 38:** The Care Quality Commission should keep under close review the effect of the change in criteria for imposing ECT without consent to adult patients under the revised Mental Health Act 1983.

6.79   From the implementation of the 2007 Act, any administration of ECT to patients under 18 years of age must be certified as appropriate by a SOAD, whether or not the patient is consenting or incapable of consenting, and whether or not that patient is otherwise subject to the powers of the 1983 Act. This is further discussed at chapter 3.65 *et seq.*

Retraction of ECT services

6.80   In this reporting period we have heard of some closures of ECT suites, particularly where large Trusts who manage several hospitals centralise their ECT service within one hospital site. This "current trend of clinic closure and amalgamation"[560] is likely to be cost-driven, particularly given the higher costs of maintaining (or updating) ECT suites to a standard required by Royal College of Psychiatrists' voluntary ECT accreditation scheme, ECTAS, or even the administrative costs of ECTAS accreditation itself.

6.81   In our previous reports we have welcomed ECTAS, and called upon the Department of Health to give active encouragement to NHS services to sign up for approval[561]. We continue to support the ECTAS accreditation scheme as a necessary intervention to drive up standards in ECT practice (our own research suggested that in 2000/01, one in five ECT suites were operating with substantial departures from best practice, policy or training[562]). There does now seem to be some pressure on services to seek accreditation, particularly from the Healthcare Commission, but it may be that the 'active encouragement' required for the scheme to have a maximum benefit in terms of patient care should include funding, to counter any perverse incentives created by the scheme to reduce ECT services to a point where patients are having to undertake long journeys to receive the treatment. In an article on patient experience of ECTAS-approved clinics, Kershaw *et al* remark that patient anxiety is increased by travelling long distances to receive ECT, and that this may necessitate extra support to patients concerned[563].

> **Recommendation 39:** Government should consider specific funding for ECTAS compliance in ECT facilities, to preserve local amenities and avoid patients having to travel long distances for treatment.

---

[560]   Kershaw K *et al* (2007) *op cit* n.552.

[561]   MHAC (2006) *Eleventh Biennial Report 2003-2005: In Place of Fear?*, para 4.76 – 4.77

[562]   MHAC (2001) *Ninth Biennial Report 1999-2001*, para 3.31 *et seq.*

[563]   Kershaw K *et al* (2007) *op cit* n.552.

ECT and deprivation of liberty

6.82 Both the MHAC and the *Mental Health Act Manual* have in past years argued that unnecessary and therefore unlawful detention under the Act may have resulted from a common misunderstanding that ECT may not be given to compliant but incapacitated patients under the common law[564]. Research undertaken in September 2004 amongst 56 consultant psychiatrists in Wessex, in which the psychiatrists were asked to respond to case scenarios, found that roughly half would have sought to detain an incapacitated compliant patient on the basis that ECT was required, rising to three-quarters where the incapacity was founded in delusional beliefs[565].

6.83 Some commentators have since questioned whether, in the light of the *Bournewood* judgment and subsequent rulings[566], the legal position may now have changed, so that detention under the Act *is* appropriate for incapacitated but compliant patients receiving ECT[567]. This would be the case if the admission of a patient to hospital, and the process of administering ECT and caring for the patient between administrations, amounted to a deprivation of liberty. It has been argued that the degree of control involved in administering ECT is such that it should be seen as a deprivation rather than a restriction of liberty[568]. It is not clear to us what, excepting the requirement for general anaesthesia of the patient, makes ECT treatment so very restrictive that it must *necessarily* be viewed as a deprivation of liberty, when, for example, the admission of a patient onto a psychiatric ward where he or she will be medicated without consent is not so judged.

6.84 We rather doubt that a determining factor in deciding whether a medical intervention is a deprivation rather than a restriction of liberty can be whether or not it involves general anaesthesia. If we are wrong, a great deal of surgical interventions unrelated to mental health would involve unlawful deprivation of liberty where the patient has no capacity to give consent. This would considerably limit the generally-assumed scope of the MCA, and also considerably extend the reach of the new deprivation of liberty safeguards from that anticipated by government.

6.85 The existing Mental Capacity Act Code of Practice provides an example of "using the MHA" to detain a seriously depressed patient with learning disability who is being considered for ECT[569]. This scenario is not entirely helpful, however, as it is made explicit that the patient's consultant, who "has given him medication and is considering electro-convulsive therapy … thinks this care plan will only work if [the patient] is detained in hospital. This will allow close

---

[564] MHAC (2003) *Tenth Biennial Report 2001-2003: Placed Amongst Strangers*, para 10.59; Jones R (2004) *Mental Health Act Manual*, ninth edition, para 1-720.

[565] Law-Min R & Stephens J P (2006) 'Capacity, compliance and electroconvulsive therapy' *Psychiatric Bulletin* **30** 13-15

[566] See MHAC (2006) *op cit*. n.561, paras 1.1 to 1.24 and 3.1 to 3.26 for discussion of the *Bournewood* case and its sequelae.

[567] e.g. RadcliffesLeBrasseur Mental Health Law Briefing Number 92: *What implications does the Bournewood ruling have on ECT treatment?* www.rlb-law.com

[568] *ibid*.: "ECT almost inevitably involves a high level of control being exercised over a patient".

[569] Department of Constitutional Affairs (2007) *Mental Capacity Act 2005, Code of Practice, chapter 13.13*. London: Stationery Office, p. 230. www.dca.gov.uk/legal-policy/mental-capacity/mca-cp.pdf

observation and [the patient] will be stopped if he tries to leave"[570]. As such, it is the care plan as a whole that amounts to a deprivation of liberty, and the Code is silent as to the relative weight that should be given to the planned use of ECT in determining that such a plan tips the scales from a restriction to a deprivation of liberty. The answer could be that it is not a determinative factor at all, in that there is nothing inherent in the administration process for ECT that is necessarily a deprivation of liberty, but that the determinative factor is the degree of control exercised over the patient between ECT administrations, as the example suggests.

6.86   The MHAC has no legal authority to give a formal view on these matters, and each case should be considered on its own merits, although we doubt that there is anything inherent in the procedure for ECT treatment that amounts to a deprivation of liberty. This is one example where the government's reluctance to formulate clear guidance on determining what amounts to deprivation of liberty has increased rather than lessened the uncertainties for practitioners as we approach the implementation of the new MCA safeguards. In 2003 we called for the eventual revision of the Code of Practice to address directly the question of the lawful authority to give ECT to incapacitated patients[571]. We have repeated this call in our response to the revised Code of Practice consultation.

Neurosurgery for mental disorder

6.87   Requests for s.57 authorisation to undertake neurosurgery for mental disorder (NMD) continue to be rare (figure 72). In this reporting period, we were asked to consider seven cases; four in 2005/06 and three in 2006/07. Male patients accounted for two of the referrals in each year, with females accounting for two referrals in the first year and one in the second.

	1997-1999	1999-2001	2001-2003	2003-2005	2005-2007
Total referrals	17	9	13	7	7
Treatment authorised	17	9	6[572]	6	5
Treatment refused	–	–	3	1	2
Decision deferred	–	–	4	–	–

Fig 72: Section 57 referrals to the MHAC, with outcomes, 1997 – 2007

Source: MHAC data

6.88   The two referrals where the MHAC-appointed team refused authorisation for the procedure were made in 2005/06. The team had concerns over one female patient's preparedness to engage with a rehabilitation programme subsequent to the operation, and that patient also appeared to change her mind over consenting to the procedure. For one male patient, the team felt that NMD was not yet clinically appropriate, and that cognitive behavioural therapy should be attempted first.

---

[570]   *ibid.*

[571]   MHAC (2003) *op cit* n.564, p.160, recommendation 41.

[572]   Two patients were referred twice in this period. We have counted the initial visit to each of these patients as a deferral, as the operations were authorised only after the second referral in each case.

Deep-Brain Stimulation

6.89   We have written in past reports[573] about the developing treatment of deep-brain stimulation (DBS), which has been suggested as the likely successor to the types of neurosurgery for mental disorder discussed above involving ablation (cutting) of brain tissue[574]. In our last report we stated that a patient who was being considered for such treatment was detained under s.3: this was an error, and the patient actually had informal status. Nevertheless, we repeat our calls in the past two reports that it is time to consider safeguards for this treatment.

6.90   In our past reports we suggested that DBS, because it does not rely upon the destruction of brain tissue for its therapeutic effect, might be considered a suitable treatment for the safeguards afforded to ECT under s.58. In the meantime, the Scottish Parliament has extended the safeguards applicable to NMD patients (equivalent to s.57 of the 1983 Act) to DBS[575], thus providing a safeguard that is applicable irrespective of the patient's legal status. On reflection, and after consultation, we accept that this is the appropriate level of safeguard for DBS. The technique, which involves placing electrodes into the brain, does involve the risks of brain surgery and some inevitable damage to brain tissue; adjustment of the apparatus may require many visits to a doctor; and the pacemaker battery that operates the electrodes will need to be replaced every two or three years, requiring more surgery[576].

6.91   We were disappointed that the Department of Health's consultation on secondary legislation to the 2007 Act does not mention DBS, given our past recommendations. We have suggested in our response to that consultation that government should echo the safeguards applicable in Scotland and bring DBS within the scope of s.57 of the 1983 Act.

> **Recommendation 40:** The Secretary of State should consider the regulation of deep-brain stimulation for mental disorder, bringing the technique within the scope of s.57 of the 1983 Act.

---

[573]   MHAC (2003) *Tenth Biennial Report 2001-2003: Placed Amongst Strangers*, para 10.65 – 10.69; MHAC (2006) *Eleventh Biennial Report 2003-2005: In Place of Fear?*, para 4.83 – 4.86.

[574]   'Deep Brain Stimulation' *Harvard Mental Health Letter*, April 2006, p.3/4. www.health.harvard.edu

[575]   See Mental Health (Medical treatments subject to safeguards) (Section 234) (Scotland) Regulations 2005 (SSI No.291); and Mental Health (Care and Treatment (Scotland) Act 2003: Code of Practice Volume 1, Chapter 10.3.

[576]   'Deep Brain Stimulation' *Harvard Mental Health Letter*, April 2006, p.3/4. See also Shoter E & Healy D (2007) *op cit* n.554, chapter 11.

The 1983 Act and forensic psychiatry

7.1 Statistics on the forensic population have been published in this period by the Sainsbury Centre for Mental Health[577]. As we noted in chapter one, this shows that the number of patients in forensic beds is at a record level (see chapter 1.14). This chapter looks at aspects of the implementation of the powers contained in part III of the Act, relating to patients concerned with criminal proceedings or under sentence, and with related legal structures.

Prison transfers

> Perhaps future generations will look back on our generation which has criminalised a large section of its mentally ill as being just as misguided as previous generations which exhibited the mentally ill as freaks.
>
> All-Party Parliamentary Group on Prison Health (2006)
> *The Mental Health Problem in UK HM Prisons.* House of Commons, London

7.2 The massive and continuing increase in the prison population noted in our last report will inevitably have resulted in many more mentally disordered persons being kept in prison. The experience of England and Wales may be an example of the suggested inverse relationship between imprisonment numbers and mental hospital accommodation[578] that has been noted in other countries[579].

7.3 In its thematic report on the mental health of prisoners, published in October 2007, HM Inspectorate of Prisons stated that two things stood out starkly from their study;

- there are too many gaps in healthcare screening and healthcare provision in prisons, leading to too much unmet and sometimes unrecognised need; and

- the need will always remain greater than the capacity, unless mental health and community services are improved outside of prison and people are appropriately directed to them, before, instead of and after being received into custody.

---

[577] Sainsbury Centre for Mental Health (2007) *Forensic Mental Health Services: facts and figures in current provision.* Mark Rutherford and Sean Duggan, 'Forensic Factfile 2007' September 2007. http://www.scmh.org.uk/80256FBD004F3555/vWeb/flKHAL76WBRP/$file/scmh_forensic_factfile_2007.pdf

[578] Gunn, J (2000) 'Future directions for treatment in forensic psychiatry' *Br J Psychiatry* 176: 332-338

[579] Lamb H R & Weinberger L E (2005) 'The Shift in Psychiatric Inpatient Care From Hospitals to Jails and Prisons' *J Am Acad Psychiatry Law* 33:529-34

The report found that four-fifths of in-reach teams felt that they were unable to meet levels of need in their prisons, and that court diversion schemes remain under-funded and patchily implemented[580].

7.4   We welcome the Department of Health's renewed focus during this reporting period on transferring mentally disordered prisoners to hospital under the powers of the Act, and have participated in the its Prison Mental Health Transfer Project Steering Group. This project, which is one of a number of policy-level initiatives to improve mental health services for offender patients[581], aims to reduce the time taken to effect such transfers. Statistics published by the Sainsbury Centre for Mental Health show that, in 2006, an average of 42 patients per quarter waited for longer than three months for a transfer: this is an improvement on the previous year (an average of 53 patients per quarter) but only a slight improvement on 2004 (44 patients per quarter)[582].

7.5   Published data on transfers from prison under the Mental Health Act 1983 show that in the most recent year for which data is available, more mentally disordered offenders were transferred from prison under the Act's powers than at any time during the previous two decades that it has been in force, with over 830 transfers in each of the last two years recorded (figure 73 below).

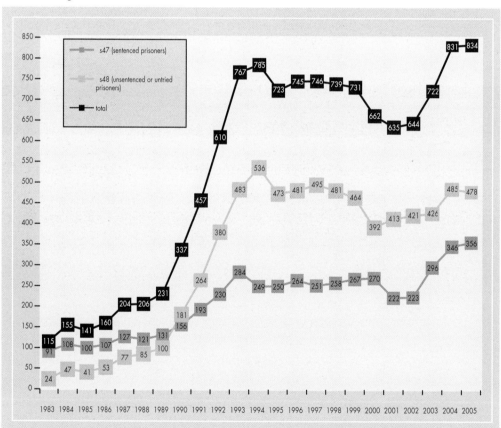

Fig. 73: Transfers from prison, restricted status, 1983 to 2005, England & Wales.

Source: Home Office Statistical Bulletins, *Statistics of Mentally Disordered Offenders, 1985-2006*

---

[580] HM Inspectorate of Prisons (2007) *The Mental Health of Prisoners: A thematic review of the care and support of prisoners with mental health needs.* October 2007.

[581] See www.hsccjp.csip.org.uk/our-workstreams/mental-health.html

[582] Sainsbury Centre for Mental Health (2007) *Forensic Mental Health Services: facts and figures in current provision.* Figure 7.

7.6   We welcome this progress, but whilst absolute numbers of transfers may be at a record level, the *proportion* of transfers from prison relative to the total prison population is actually lower than in many previous years, as we show at figure 74. If we assume a relatively constant rate amongst prisoners of psychotic illness or other conditions meriting transfer to psychiatric hospital, then the number of such prisoners who would have *remained* in prison in 2005 is also at a higher level than we can show for any previous year. If we assume that 10% of all prisoners have a serious mental disorder (and this is a modest assumption given current estimates[583]), over the sixteen years shown at figure 74, an average of only 12% of seriously mentally disordered prisoners were transferred to hospital. While the rate of transfer for the last two years shown on the table was close to the average rate (i.e. 11% of our estimated total of seriously mentally disordered prisoners), in the early 1990s there was a much higher rate, peaking at 17% in 1993.

year	prison population[584]	number of MHA transfers[585]	if 10% rate of psychosis in prison, number of psychotic prisoners not transferred	number of transfers per 1,000 prisoners
1990	45,466	337	4,210	07.4
1991	45,626	457	4,106	10.0
1992	46,832	610	4,073	13.0
1993	44,246	767	3,658	17.3
1994	48,879	785	4,103	16.1
1995	51,084	723	4,385	14.2
1996	55,256	745	4,781	13.5
1997	61,467	746	5,401	12.1
1998	65,727	739	5,834	11.2
1999	64,529	731	5,722	11.3
2000	65,194	662	5,857	10.2
2001	66,403	635	6,005	09.6
2002	71,218	644	6,400	09.0
2003	73,657	722	6,644	09.8
2004	74,448	831	6,614	11.2
2005	76,190	834	6,785	10.9

Fig 74: Prison population and transfers to hospital under the Mental Health Act 1983, England & Wales,1990-2005.

Data sources: see footnotes 584-5.

---

[583] The 10% estimate is taken for simplicity amongst the ranges of estimates of psychiatric morbidity in prison. The Home Office has that 11% of all male and 15% of all female prisoners suffer from psychosis (Home Office (2005) *Memorandum Submitted by the Home Office to the Select Committee on Home Affairs,* October 2005. Printed as HC-656-I, February 2006), although other estimates have suggested a range between 3% and 15% overall (Brooker C, Repper J, Beverley C, Ferriter M and Brewer N (2003) *Mental Health Services and Prisoners: a review.* Sheffield University School of Health and Related Research).

[584] Prison population data sources (population as at 31 June in each year): National Statistics (1999) *Prison Population 1971-1999: Social Trends 31;* National Statistics (2002) *Prison Population, 1990-2002: Social Trends 33;* Home Office (1998, 2003) *Statistics on Race & the Criminal Justice System* tables 7.3, 7.5 (1998), 9.3, 9.5 (2003); Home Office (2004, 2005) *Population in Custody Monthly Tables,* table 1

[585] Prison transfer data sources: Home Office Statistical Bulletins, *Statistics of Mentally Disordered Offenders,* 1985-2006

7.7   It would undoubtedly require a large investment in secure service beds to regain the proportionate levels of transfer achieved in the early 1990s at current prison population levels. Government figures point to marked increases of investment in secure and high-dependency services[586], but it would take a massive expansion in the number of forensic beds to enable transfers of all prisoners who are likely to be eligible. In its policy review *Building on progress: Security crime and justice,* government has stated that it is "considering the potential role of specialist 'hybrid' prisons for the most serious offenders with mental health needs who have not already been transferred to secure hospitals"[587]. Home Office officials told the press that such prisons were being considered as part of a 'third way' for the treatment of personality-disordered offenders, based upon the current Dangerous and Severe Personality Disorder (DSPD) units.[588]

7.8   The Prison Reform Trust is undertaking a UK-wide programme exploring and publicising the plight of people in prison who have learning disability and learning difficulties[589]. Learning disabled prisoners serving a sentence may be transferred out of prison to psychiatric care under the Act where their disability is of a nature and degree is associated with abnormally aggressive or seriously irresponsible conduct[590]; two doctors report that transfer to hospital is appropriate; and the Secretary of State agrees that it is expedient in the public interest and in all the circumstances of the case[591]. For unsentenced learning disabled prisoners, a further criterion is a need for urgent treatment in hospital[592]. It is likely that transfer powers are more often used for prisoners who are acutely mentally ill, or for those with personality disorder whose incarceration would otherwise be of limited duration (see paragraph 7.20 below) than for learning disabled prisoners, whose cases may be less visible and have less apparent urgency. As a result, there may be a large number of learning disabled people who are inappropriately in prison but for whom care in a mental health setting would be much more humane. As this report went to press, we learned of the death of Britain's longest serving prisoner[593], John Straffen, who had spent 55 years in the prison system despite having a clear diagnosis of serious learning disability (having, it was said, a mental age of ten years[594]); previous history of admissions to mental health care (including Broadmoor Hospital); and the commuting of his death sentence on grounds of insanity. At the time of Straffen's death, he was, aged 77, apparently "due for transfer"[595] to a secure mental health facility. We hope that government will give due attention to the Prison Reform Trust campaign and, as one consequence, actively seek to use the powers of the 1983 Act to transfer inappropriately incarcerated learning disabled prisoners to suitable placements.

---

[586] Mental Health Strategies (2007) *The 2006/07 National Survey of Investment in Mental Health Services,* pages 7 - 9.

[587] HM Government (2007) *Building on progress: Security crime and justice.* Cabinet Office, March 2007, p.33-4.

[588] 'Making sense of the hybrid hype', *The Guardian,* April 4th 2007.

[589] Prison Reform Trust, *No One Knows - Learning Disability And Learning Difficulties In Prisons.* See http://www.prisonreformtrust.org.uk/subsection.asp?id=525

[590] MHA 1983, s.1(2). Under s.1(2A) of the revised Act this remains a criterion for the detention of a person with learning disability (unless that person has concomitant mental disorder of another nature).

[591] MHA 1983, s.47.

[592] MHA 1983, s.48.

[593] Bob Woffinden 'John Straffen' (Obituary article), *The Guardian,* 22 November 2007.

[594] See MHAC (2006) *Eleventh Biennial Report 2003-2005: Placed Amongst Strangers?,* footnote 82, p.366, for an outline of Straffen's conviction.

[595] *op cit.,* n. 593.

Detention in prison of a mentally disordered offender found to be inhuman and degrading treatment

7.9 In July 2006, the European Court of Human Rights (ECtHR) found that containing mentally disordered offenders in prison can constitute a breach of ECHR Article 3. This may be a sign of developing case-law in this area. The court held unanimously in *Jean-Luc Riviere v France*[596] that the continued detention in prison of a seriously mentally disordered person, without medical supervision appropriate to his condition, amounted to inhuman and degrading treatment and as such was a violation of ECHR Article 3. The prisoner, who was serving a life sentence commuted from a capital sentence, had developed a psychotic illness in prison, and had twice been transferred for brief periods to hospital under equivalent provisions to the 1983 Act.

Prison as an appropriate treatment setting

7.10 By contrast to the above case, prison was affirmed as an appropriate treatment setting for a mentally disordered offender in the domestic courts. *R v Balderstone*[597] was an appeal against a prison sentence upon conviction for affray and arson. The prisoner, *B*, had attacked her husband and set a fire in their flat. She had a long history of psychiatric illness, but her psychiatric report at trial stated that there was no "evidence of mental illness as defined [*sic*] under the Mental Health Act 1983", in that her actions were attributable to "maladaptive behaviour" rather than psychosis. The report also stated that, in the absence of "any psychotic experiences which could impair her judgment at the time of the index offence", she should be considered responsible for her actions. The Court of Appeal noted that this report "effectively ruled out any possibility of a hospital order", but it did not consider in this context whether the patient might be classified with psychopathic disorder under the terms of the Act (it would seem self-evident that she *could* be so classified), and appears not to have considered that, at the time of this report, the psychiatrist was minded to recommend a community rather than custodial disposal on any finding of guilt (and so it was not material whether the patient was mentally disordered according to the Act's definition). In a second report, written after *B* had been in prison on remand for three months, the psychiatrist changed his mind about appropriate placements, noting that her behaviour was amenable to modification in a structured environment, and suggesting that she would best be served by "a secure setting such as prison or within medium security". This report recommended a custodial sentence "from where a hospital transfer could be pursued". A separate pre-sentence report warned of the potential of prison to "have a detrimental impact on her mental health".

7.11 The sentencing judge, in passing sentences totalling three and a half years, stated that he was giving less than usual credit for *B*'s guilty pleas, as to reduce the sentence would be counter-productive "because the mental health authorities need some considerable time to work with you in a closed, protective setting".

---

[596] *Jean-Luc Riviere v France* (11 July 2006, application no 33834/03)

[597] *R v Balderstone* [2005] EWCA Crim 3299 (6 December 2005)

7.12   The basis of this appeal was that the sentence was wrong in totality; gave insufficient credit for the guilty pleas; did not properly recognise the personality disorder which underlay the behaviour, and therefore (particularly in light of the fears of deterioration in mental state) "gave insufficient weight to the thought which everyone shared that what [B] needed was help of the most effective kind".

7.13   The Court rejected the appeal, finding that the sentence was not excessive, and that the sentencing judge, weighing the likelihood of B getting appropriate treatment in prison against the proven track record of the effectiveness for her of community-based therapies, was justified in making the decision that he did. Although the Court noted concerns raised by B's husband that B might self-harm in prison, and that whilst there she may not get appropriate therapies to address her alcohol abuse and depression, it concluded that she was receiving help in prison. It based this view upon psychiatric reports from her current prison placement which outlined that she had settled in prison and was engaging in therapeutic sessions appropriately, with further support from a visiting psychiatric nurse who would be able to plan an appropriate discharge package with her community mental health team.

7.14   In this case it appears that the judiciary have determined prison to be the best therapeutic setting for the treatment of a vulnerable woman with personality disorder, and that a custodial sentence could be tailored for such therapeutic effect. Whilst this in itself may set no particular precedent, we are concerned to note the grounds upon which diversion under the MHA was determined to be impossible in this case. We are equally concerned at the use of prison for essentially therapeutic aims and as an alternative to hospital.

Prison as an inappropriate setting for mentally disordered offender

7.15   A case heard by the appeal court in December 2005 (just too late for inclusion in our last report) showed the mechanism whereby mentally disorder offenders enter long-term punitive incarceration, and provided an unusual example of diversion to mental health services[598]. The offender, W, appealed against the life sentence she received for attacking a man with a brick. At the time of sentence she was recognised as suffering from a "low grade paranoid psychotic illness". The sentencing judge accepted a prognosis that W might develop further mental health problems, but suggested that she could be transferred under the Act in such circumstances.

7.16   After leave to appeal the sentence had been granted (the appeal was against the length of sentence and tariff for the nature of the offence) W was diagnosed with schizophrenia, probably of paranoid type, and transferred to hospital under s.47/49. It was held by at least one medical opinion that this illness had been developing for some years, and both psychiatrists recommended that W's interests would best be served by a hospital order with restrictions. An MHRT had upheld her detention in hospital prior to the Appeal Court hearing.

---

[598]   *R v Wang* [2005] EWCA Crim 3238 (1 December 2005)

7.17 In light of the medical recommendations, "because of the nature of the offence, together with the character and antecedents of the offender given her current mental ill health", the Appeal Court exercised its powers under s.11 of the Criminal Appeal Act 1968 and quashed the life sentence, replacing it with a hospital order under s.37/41.

7.18 In 2007 we were approached by a prison in-reach team concerning a different case. A patient, who was already detained under s.2 of the Act when she appeared before a magistrate's court, was remanded to Peterborough prison. We suggested that the magistrate could be asked to revisit this decision, and might be asked to consider remanding the patient to hospital under a s.35 order to run concurrently with the s.2 detention. Alternatively, we suggested considering the use of s.48 to transfer the patient from prison. Neither of these legal solutions proved necessary. Through the involvement of the court diversion team, the patient's solicitor reappeared before the magistrates to explain the situation, and the magistrate changed the disposal to one of unconditional bail. The in-reach team escorted the patient out of prison and handed her over to nursing staff waiting to return her to hospital.

Late transfers from prison

7.19 We continue to find cases of patients who are transferred at the end of their prison sentences, especially in the case of patients deemed to be suffering from personality disorder. Some complain that they were given neither notice nor explanation of the reasons for their transfer, and all understandably are shocked and disturbed to find themselves facing indeterminate detention in a psychiatric hospital when they had been expecting release from prison. At Broadmoor hospital in June 2007, we noted a number of such patients who were refusing to engage in therapy and otherwise proving to be a severe management problem due to their resentment at such late transfers. On patient told us that he had been assessed several times in prison and told that he did not have a mental disorder, before his sudden transfer towards the end of his sentence. He complained of being far from home, that his family had abandoned him and that he was nervous of the other patients. If transfers from prison are to serve a therapeutic purpose as well as that of containment, we feel that they should be managed much better than this and that transfer at the end of a sentence should be very much an exception.

Prison consent status

7.20 Figure 75 below shows the consent status of patients resident in hospital on the 31 March 2006, having been transferred from prison. We have shown the consent status of prisoners transferred after conviction and sentencing under s.47, and those transferred prior to conviction and/or sentencing under s.48, with or without restricted status under s.49.

		legal status on census date									
		s.47		s.47/49		s.48		s.48/49		Total	
(n = 786)		number	% of legal category	number	% of legal category	number	% of legal category	number	% of legal category	number	% of legal category
consent status	consenting	43	69.4	439	78.5	11	61.1	90	61.2	583	74.2
	capable but refusing	11	17.7	70	12.5	2	11.1	24	16.3	107	13.6
	incapable of consent	5	8.1	35	6.3	4	22.2	25	17.0	69	8.8
	not known	3	4.8	15	2.7	1	5.6	8	5.5	27	3.4
all consent status in legal category		62	100	559	100	18	100	147	100	786	100

Fig 75: Consent status on the 31 March 2006 of patients resident in hospital following transfer from prison under s.47 and s.48, all hospitals, England and Wales

Source: Count Me In 2006

7.21 Overall, three-quarters of patients who have been transferred from prison are deemed to be giving valid consent to their treatment. Patients transferred after sentence under a restriction order (i.e. under s.47/49) are the most likely to be consenting, and, as we have shown elsewhere in this report, of such patients, 85% of those with personality disorder are consenting[599], as are 80% of those with mental illness[600]. Patients detained under s.47 with or without restrictions have the lowest rate of mental incapacity of all other census categories of detained patients.

7.22 It is not immediately clear why transferred prisoners contain the highest proportion of patients who are deemed to be giving valid consent to their treatment, especially as (at least prior to the coming into force of the Mental Capacity Act 2005 in October 2007) we have often heard that an important factor in the instigation (or perceived urgency) of transfers is prison staff concern over their perceived inability to give compulsory treatment, almost always in the form of antipsychotic medication, in the face of the prisoner's resistance[601]. However, there are a number of possible explanations for the high proportion of capable and consenting patients in this group, including:

- Prison transferees may have a longer than average period of hospitalisation, and long-term detainees are likely to form a group of comparatively 'well' and insightful patients in the forensic system who may be more likely to be compliant with their continued treatment.

- Some patients will have experienced extremely distressing psychotic symptoms whilst untreated in prison, which were ameliorated when medication was administered following transfer. These experiences may increase the likelihood of future treatment compliance.

[599] See figure 38, chapter 3.54 above.

[600] See figure 28, chapter 3.28 above.

[601] From October 2007 the Mental Capacity Act 2005 provides a statutory framework within which prison staff may find the authority to impose treatment, using force where necessary, on a patient who does not have the mental capacity to give consent. See MCA 2005 ss. 5, 6.

- Transferees subject to restriction orders (who are even more likely to be consenting than the group as a whole) may be returned to prison if hospital treatment is deemed to be no longer necessary, or effective, in their case. Such patients may comply with their treatment regimes to avoid such an outcome.

- Patients with experience of serving prison sentences, especially if they have experience or knowledge of the parole system, may equate treatment compliance with the 'good behaviour' that leads to quicker release from custodial sentences or step-down from the higher security levels of the prison system, and (in most cases quite correctly) therefore view treatment compliance as likely to hasten their transfer to lower security hospitals and/or release into the community.

Immigration detainees and the Mental Health Act

7.23 In the twelve months to February 2007 we understand that eight immigration detainees were transferred from immigration removal centres (IRCs) in England to hospitals where they were detained under section 48 of the Mental Health Act[602]. The IRC population in England at December 2006 was 1,670[603]. If this was extrapolated into a rate of transfer comparable to known rates of MHA detention in other groups (and the small number involved makes this extremely speculative), it would suggest a proportionate rate of detentions under the Act per population second only to that within prisons[604]. A high rate of serious psychiatric morbidity is perhaps to be expected in this group, which consists of a high proportion of people arriving with underlying mental health problems (often linked to traumatic experiences) who are subject to indefinite and sometimes prolonged detention.

7.24 Six of the eight MHA transfers were from Yarl's Wood detention centre, a private facility which has a small inpatient unit and 24-hour healthcare[605]. Immigration detainees whose mental disorder cannot be managed elsewhere within the IRC system may be initially sent for treatment at Yarl's Wood, although not of course under MHA powers. The quality of mental healthcare at the unit was the subject of critical comment by an inquiry by HM Inspector of Prisons in February 2006, as was the management of mentally disordered detainees by Immigration and Nationality Department (IND) officers responsible for their cases[606]. From April 2007 the Immigration and Nationality Directorate (IND) became the Border and Immigration Agency (BIA).

---

[602] Data supplied to the MHAC by the Home Office Immigration and Nationality Directorate, UK Immigration Service Headquarters, April 2007. One further detainee in Dungavel IRC was transferred under section 136 of the Mental Health (Care and Treatment) (Scotland) Act to Hartwoodhill hospital, Lanarkshire.

[603] National Statistics (2006) *Asylum Statistics: 4th Quarter 2006 United Kingdom,* table 11. Home Office.

[604] In 2005, there were 834 MHA transfers from a prison population of 76,190 (1,095 per 100,000 population). Rates of MHA detention in the general population are 132 per 100,000 in the London Strategic Health Authority (SHA) Area and an average of 78 per 100,000 in all other SHA areas. Eight transfers from 1,670 immigration removal detainees in England is here taken to denote a rate of 480 such transfers per 100,000 population.

[605] Seven of the ten IRCs are privately run, and were not subject to the 2005 transfer of prison healthcare funding from the Home Office to the Department of Health. On the recommendation of the Prison Inspector (see discussion of report above) the IRC healthcare facilities have now been registered with the Healthcare Commission and are subject to its oversight.

[606] HM Inspector of Prisons (2006) *Inquiry into the quality of healthcare at Yarl's Wood immigration removal centre, 20-24 February 2006.*

7.25   In particular, the HM Inspector of Prisons inquiry suggested that emerging and often deteriorating medical conditions did not appear to be properly taken into consideration in decisions about continuing detention. Under the Detention Centre Rules, the IRC medical practitioner must report upon any detainee whose health is likely to be injuriously affected by continued detention or the conditions of detention, or who is suicidal, or who may have been the victim of torture, and such reports must be passed by the manager of the centre to the BIA (or IND prior to April 2007)[607]. The report gave examples of where there appeared to be no assessment of such medical reports in the case notes of the IND (as it was then), even after detainees had been transferred to hospital under MHA powers. In one example, a detainee who described a history of torture, whose solicitors had requested temporary release from IRC detention due to her deteriorating mental condition, was transferred for the third time to hospital under s.48 of the 1983 Act, and her case note stated "under no circumstances should this woman be TA'd [granted temporary release]. If she is sectioned, then she can remain there until she is fit enough to be released back to immigration detention". Subsequently, IND (as it was then) wrote to the detainee in hospital stating that "arrangements will be made to remove you from the United Kingdom once a flight and medical escorts can be secured, and you will be notified when this will be. Your case has been reviewed. It has been decided that you will remain in detention"[608].

7.26   The potential effects on severely mentally disordered patients of such restrictions and interventions by immigration officials are of particular concern, particularly as refugees as a whole are considered to be an especially vulnerable group for post-traumatic stress disorder (PTSD)[609]. The prison inspectorate report also found that screening for PTSD in Yarl's Wood did not meet NICE guidelines.

7.27   Patients who are transferred to hospital from the IRC system can also be severely disadvantaged in terms of their aftercare arrangements because they have no legal entitlements to welfare arrangements and it can be difficult or impossible to locate funding for ongoing social care arrangements were the patient to be discharged. This may lead to patients being returned to immigration detention after hospital treatment for want of any better arrangement that might support them in the community, even where BIA might otherwise allow a community placement after hospitalisation.

7.28   It has been suggested to the MHAC that failures to divert seriously mentally disordered persons from immigration detention, especially where the disorder involves a diagnosis of PTSD, can and has had extremely deleterious effects on the prognosis for such detainees' long-term care and treatment, in effect creating patients with an extremely high level of dependency[610].

7.29   The BIA has shared with us its action plan in response to the prison inspectorate report. The healthcare provision within the IRC system is to be registered with the Healthcare Commission, and discussions were ongoing with the Department of Health to consider establishing a medical advice facility. We will continue to take an interest in the mechanisms

---

[607] Statutory Instrument 2001 No 238, Rule 35. Such letters are referred to as "rule 35 letters".

[608] *op cit*, n.606 above, para 3.67- 9.

[609] Ahmed A S (2007) 'Post-traumatic stress disorder, resilience and vulnerability' *Advances in Psychiatric Treatment* 13: 396-7. See also Adshead G & Ferris S (2007) 'Treatment of victims of trauma' *Advances in Psychiatric Treatment* 13: 358-368.

[610] This view was outlined by the organisation *Medical Justice* at a meeting with IND/BIA officials in April 2007, attended by the MHAC.

of transfer under the Act of mentally disordered immigration detainees, and expect (notwithstanding the government's intention to legislate for a new immigration services inspectorate) that our successor body will do the same.

Section 35 remand to hospital

7.30　A patient who has been remanded to hospital under s.35 of the 1983 Act cannot be granted leave under s.17 of the Act. This causes difficulties in ascertaining how a patient may lawfully be absent from that hospital, even in situations such as when requiring physical treatment in another hospital. Many courts address this by specifying, when making the remand order, whether and where the patient may be taken whilst resident in hospital. We are sometimes approached by hospital staff where such specification has not been made, but a patient needs to attend an appointment outside of hospital (to doctors or dentists, for example) or the clinical team believe that there is a case to be made for compassionate leave under escort. In such cases, we advise hospital staff to approach the clerk to the court to request the court's permission for such visits, although we acknowledge that the legal basis upon which a court might give such permission is unclear. In one case at the end of our reporting period, a hospital administrator rang us with her concern that the court had stated that the patient should be allowed out under escort at the hospital's discretion, without specifying the actual places where such visits might take place. We suggested that the court must have intended this to be left to the discretion of the hospital. It is interesting that this hospital was so familiar with receiving 'permission' from courts to allow a patient escorted leave that it thought this example to be an irregularity.

Section 37 hospital orders

7.31　According to Department of Health statistics, over the last five years for which data is available there has been an annual average of 268 restricted hospital orders under s.37/41, and 333 unrestricted s.37 orders[611]. The numbers of s.37 court orders, restricted or unrestricted, reported by the Department of Health since 1987/88[612] are shown at figure 76 below.

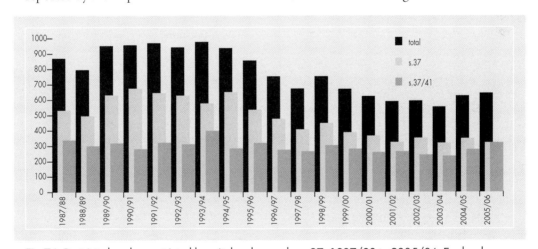

Fig 76: Restricted and unrestricted hospital orders under s.37, 1987/88 to 2005/06, England.

Data source: Department of Health / Information Centre statistical bulletins
"Inpatients detained under the Mental Health Act 1983 and other legislation" 1995 - 2007

---

[611]　Data from 2001/02 to 2005/6: see Information Centre (2007) *Inpatients detained under the Mental Health Act 1983 and other legislation*, Table 1

[612]　From this date the Department of Health collected data by financial year

7.32   The *Count Me In* census data from 2006 recorded 2,397 patients detained in hospital under s.37/41, and 1,019 detained under s.37 with no restriction.

7.33   In our previous report, we noted the discrepancies between Department of Health and Home Office data on the use of this section[613]. The 2007 Home Office bulletin noted "data quality issues" in areas of its information, which were therefore left unreported. This included the numbers of unrestricted hospital orders given by the courts. However, we have confidence in Home Office data on the numbers of restricted patients, which will have been taken from the case files of the Home office (now Ministry of Justice) Mental Health Unit. The number of restricted hospital orders made under s.37 over the 20 years from 1985 according to this data is set out at figure 77 below.

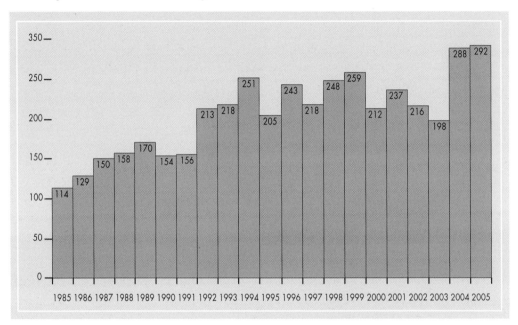

Fig 77: Hospital orders made under s.37/41, 1985 – 2005, England and Wales

Data source: Home Office *Statistics of Mentally Disordered Offenders* 1986-2007

7.34   We have no way of knowing the exact reason or reasons for the steep rise in restricted court orders over 2004 and 2005 shown in the Home Office data, although we might guess that the increasing availability of medium secure beds may provide more sentencers with the option of a hospital disposal. Without data on unrestricted orders, however, we are unable to say whether this shows an overall increase in the number of court orders made, or simply an increase in the numbers of patients going into hospital with restrictions. The Department of Health data at figure 76 also indicates an increase in restricted orders, which suggests a reverse in the declining trend of the total number in court orders that we noted in our last report[614]. Any overall rise in the numbers of court orders made under s.37 and s.37/41 should probably be welcomed as an indicator of increased diversion from custodial sentencing, although (as with the numbers of transfers from prison, discussed at paragraph 7.6 above), such increases must be seen in the context of a much greater proportional increase in the prison population. The number of court orders made under s.37 subsequent

[613] MHAC (2006) *Eleventh Biennial Report 2003-2005: In Place of Fear?*, para 5.84 *et seq.*

[614] *ibid.*, para 5.86

to a mentally disordered offender's conviction in the ten years to 2005/06 is substantially smaller than the number of such orders passed in the previous ten years, although the prison population (figure 74, paragraph 7.6 above) has grown by over 50% between 1995/96 and 2005/06.

Nearest relatives and patients detained under s.37

7.35 Some hospitals fail to distinguish that s.37 patients only have a nearest relative under the Act if they have unrestricted status. It is important to correctly identify whether a patient detained under s.37 could have a nearest relative, both to ensure that the provisions of the Act (such as those relating to the giving of information under s.132) are complied with, and to ensure that neither patients nor their families are given false information as to their legal position, or that hospitals do not unintentionally act incompatibly with a patient's Article 8 rights under the ECHR. Hospitals should, of course, attempt to ascertain who is the next of kin of any restricted patient and facilitate the passing of appropriate information to that person at the patient's request.

Section 45A hybrid orders

7.36 In January 2006 the Court of Appeal reconsidered the sentencing of an offender in December 2000 that resulted in a hospital direction under s45A of the 1983 Act[615]. At time of sentencing (December 2000) the patient, S, had disputed diagnoses all falling within the legal classification of psychopathic disorder, and had been found guilty but with diminished responsibility for the crime of manslaughter. There were differences of opinion over the presence of psychosis or developing mental illness, although no medical evidence suggested a classification of mental illness at the trial. S, who was 19 years old, had already been urgently transferred to Broadmoor from Holloway prison under s.48. The Broadmoor team had argued for s.37/41 disposal because they considered that the option of a return to prison could be used by S as a reason not to engage in therapy, and any such return would have a detrimental effect on her mental state. The Crown's medical evidence had expressed fears that S might refuse to engage with treatment and thus become entitled to release from a s.37/41 order if such were made.

7.37 The argument before the Court of Appeal was that S had, at the time of the appeal, been reclassified by the MHRT as suffering from mental illness in addition to psychopathic disorder, and that such mental illness was likely to have played a part in the index offence to a degree unappreciated by the sentencing court. Therefore the s.45A disposal (which was designed to apply to psychopathic disordered patients with treatability issues) should now be quashed and replaced with a s.37/41 disposal. Indeed, it was argued that had such a diagnosis been known to the sentencing court it would have taken a different view about culpability and treatability and disposed of the case with a s.37/41 order.

7.38 The Court dismissed the application. It did not accept that the new classification necessarily implied that the diagnoses at the time of sentencing were incorrect: the mental illness may have developed since that time. In any case, no professional had at any point of S's

---

[615] *R v Staines* [2006] EWCA Crim 15 (26 January 2006)

assessments and treatment argued that she had grounds for an insanity plea; therefore the Court had to accept that S was to some extent culpable for her offence. As to whether the reclassification prior to the appeal made S's present diagnoses relevant to the argument for s.45A to be quashed, the Court stated that there was nothing wrong with imposing s.45A on a patient whose classified mental disorders did not fall exclusively within the psychopathic range, provided of course that there was a diagnosis of psychopathic disorder. In part it relied for this conclusion upon the fact that the powers of s.45A were originally mooted for all classifications at White Paper stage; that a power to extend its provisions to all classifications was provided by its 1997 enactment; and that similar powers in Scotland apply to all classified disorders.

7.39 The Court rejected practical considerations against the continuance of the s.45A in this case, arguing that S's progress undermined arguments that the potential of return to prison impeded her treatment, and that there was no realistic possibility that S would in fact be returned to prison at the conclusion of successful treatment under the current powers. It was recognised that there was as yet no experience on which to draw over what would happen were S to complete her treatment whilst a s.45A patient, but the Court suggested a parallel with the arrangements made for s.47 patients with unexpired sentences for whom the MHRT is prepared to recommend release to the Parole Board. In such cases, patients remain in hospital whilst the Parole Board makes its decision[616]. Furthermore, the Court identified no particular or necessary disadvantage to arrangements for S's continued engagement with services were she eventually to be discharged under life licence rather than conditionally discharged under the MHA: the Parole Board could impose similar conditions to the MHRT.

7.40 Having taken a view that the s.45A was and continued to be an appropriate disposal in this case, the Court added its voice to calls for the power to be extended to be applicable to other classifications than psychopathic disorder. The Mental Health Act 2007 does have this effect, by abolishing the categories of mental disorder in favour of a broad, generic definition of the term. As such, it will be an available disposal for mentally ill offenders, as well as offenders whose learning disability is associated with abnormally aggressive or seriously irresponsible conduct[617].

Diversion from the criminal justice system

7.41 Of the four cases which were decided during this reporting period and are discussed below, the first two provide precedents regarding the processes of determining criminal responsibility for offences, and are as such may impact on the management of mentally disordered offenders. The third case provides further indication of the need for legal reform in the construction of the 'insanity defence' in England and Wales. The fourth case suggests some limitations in the use of coercive psychiatric treatment rather than criminal sanction, which may not be resolved by the changes to the 1983 Act brought about by the passing of the 2007 Act.

---

[616] An annual average of 111 restricted patients have been returned to custody over the last decade: see Home Office *Statistics of Mentally Disordered Offenders 2005* table 16.

[617] See MHA 2007, s.2 and schedule 1, section 1, 9, amending MHA 1983 s.1 and 45A(2).

CPIA defendant regains fitness to plead during the trial process

7.42   In December 2005, the Court of Appeal found that a patient sent to hospital under a restriction order following a CPIA finding of unfitness to plead may be returned to court for trial if s/he subsequently regains fitness[618]. In this case, the accused, having been found unfit, regained fitness before the disposal was decided, and the Court was asked to determine what should be done.

7.43   *H* was charged with assault, GBH and possession of an offensive weapon, but the judge found him unfit to plead under s.4 of the recently revised Criminal Procedure (Insanity) Act 1964[619]. That finding had not been contested. The next stage, at which a jury determined that the accused had done the relevant acts (a question that was again uncontested), took place within one month. The judge agreed to adjourn making a disposal to allow the defence to obtain up to date medical evidence from *H*'s treating doctor. At the adjourned disposal hearing, such evidence was that *H* was now fit to be tried. His defence team argued that the wording of the CPIA gave no discretion, once a finding of unfitness to plead had been made, to do other than proceed to the disposals offered by that act (i.e. a hospital order, a supervision order or an absolute discharge). Given *H*'s recovery only the latter – absolute discharge – was appropriate. The judge, however, preferred the Crown's submission that the right way forward was to arraign *H* for trial. The defence appealed this decision.

7.44   The High Court rejected the construction of the law suggested by *H*'s defence team. It held that there was nothing in s.4 of the CPIA that precluded holding a second hearing under its powers to determine again whether the accused is fit to plead. It was procedurally necessary to do this even if the outcome is obvious, to establish by the evidence of at least two doctors that the patient is so fit. It therefore quashed the first order for arraignment and remitted the case back to court for a second s.4 hearing to determine fitness to plead ("which may only be a formality").

Lords reject provocation as an insanity defence in homicide trials

7.45   Our last report predicted the demise of provocation as an insanity defence in homicide trials[620]. A House of Lords' judgment within two weeks of publication brought about that demise[621].

7.46   The *Morgan Smith* case in 2000 had extended the use of the provocation defence by determining that it was acceptable to take into account the individual characteristics of the defendant when deciding whether he or she had been provoked into killing: conditions affecting self-control such as mental disorder could therefore lower a threshold for successful use of the defence[622]. This interpretation had been rejected for the law of Jersey by a 2005 decision in the Holley case[623]. Here the court determined that "the sufficiency of the

---

[618] *Hasani v Blackfriars Crown Court* [2005] EWHC 3016 (Admin) (21 December 2005)

[619] For details of the relevant revision see MHAC (2006) *Eleventh Biennial Report 2003-2005: In Place of Fear?*, para 5.32.

[620] MHAC (2006) *Eleventh Biennial Report 2003-2005: In Place of Fear?*, para 5.47-8

[621] *R v James, R v Karimi* [2006] EWCA Crim 14. (25 January 2006).

[622] *R v Smith (Morgan)* [2000] UKHL 49. See MHAC (2006) *op cit* n.620 para 5.47.

[623] *Attorney-General for Jersey v Dennis Peter Holley (Jersey)* [2005] UKPC 23 (15 June 2005) 3 All ER 371

provocation ('whether the provocation was enough to make a reasonable man do as [the defendant] did') is to be judged by one standard, not a standard which varies from defendant to defendant".[624]

7.47 The *Holley* case was concerned with the law of Jersey, although it was heard by the Privy Council for that jurisdiction, which is essentially a panel of House of Lords judges. Thus, when the issue came up again for consideration under UK law, their Lordships were required to decide whether they had, with *Holley*, established a precedent, or at least a rival argument, to the approach adopted in *Morgan Smith*. Their decision that the *Holley* case should be construed as a precedent that they were bound to follow was reported as a very unusual constitutional event: a ruling of Britain's highest court was overturned by that of Jersey[625].

7.48 The practical result of the decision was that the two appeals against murder convictions failed. Both cases involved love triangles: James killed his wife in 1979 and Karimi his wife's lover in 1996. Both men claimed provocation and argued that their specific psychiatric profiles be taken into account in considering this defence. A defendant's psychiatric history is no longer likely to be considered relevant if the defence plea is provocation, although it is of course relevant to other manslaughter defences such as diminished responsibility.

The insanity defence and the M'Naghten test

7.49 In our last report we wrote of the limitations of the *Pritchard* test of fitness to plead and the *M'Naghten* insanity defence against legal responsibility, arguing that both are based in outdated psychology and, if interpreted literally, exclude the defendant's appreciation of the wrongfulness of his or her action even where this might be severely distorted by delusional thinking or other processes of mental disorder[626]. In January 2007, the insanity defence was considered in a legal appeal to the House of Lords, albeit (as with the *Holley* case discussed above) in the latter's capacity as the Judicial Committee of the Privy Council, this time hearing an appeal from the Court of Appeal of the Eastern Caribbean Court of Justice (St Lucia)[627].

7.50 The Privy Council gave a judicial interpretation of the insanity defence provided for in the St Lucia criminal code, which was first enacted in 1887, some 44 years after the *M'Naghten* rule was established. The insanity defence in s.21(a) of that Code echoes the *M'Naghten* rule[628], but adds a further test at s.21(b), which the Privy Council determined to be a

---

[624] *ibid.,* para 22

[625] See, for example, 'Privy council overrules Lords to put judgment back on track' *The Guardian,* 30 January 2006.

[626] MHAC (2006) *Eleventh Biennial report, 2003–2005: In Place of Fear?* paras 5.16 – 5.24.

[627] *Phillip & Another v The Queen (The Eastern Caribbean Court of Justice (St Lucia))* [2007] UKPC 31 (24 January 2007). The case concerned two self-acclaimed followers of Rastafarianism who, in a notorious incident in 2000, entered the cathedral in Castries during mass, armed with cans of petrol and flaming torches; attacked the congregation; set on fire the priest who remonstrated with them; and clubbed a nun who came to intervene. The priest and nun both died of their injuries. An insanity plea was lodged by the defendants on the grounds that both suffered from a delusional disorder, although the prosecution claimed that their beliefs were just normal if extreme emanations of Rastafarianism and that they were not mentally disordered. As a result of the Privy Council ruling, the appellants' murder convictions and death sentences were quashed and they were remitted for retrial.

[628] The first test of the insanity defence in the St Lucia Criminal Code is whether the accused "was prevented, by reason of idiocy, imbecility, or any mental derangement or disease affecting the mind, from knowing the nature or consequences of the act in respect of which he is accused, or if he did know it, if he did not know that what he was doing was contrary to law" (s.21(a)).

freestanding test "intended to encompass something more than the *M'Naghten* test contained in section 21(a)" and "getting away from the concept of the defendant's knowledge of the nature and quality of his act or that it was contrary to law"[629]. Their Lordships suggested that this aspect of the Criminal Code (which had been commissioned by the Colonial Office in 1877 from "the young barrister" R.S. Wright) was drafted in response to the contemporary criticisms of the *M'Naghten* rule[630]. The test that it establishes is whether the defendant acted "under the influence of a delusion of such a nature as to render him ... an unfit subject for punishment..."[631]. This was accepted as a test of appreciation by their Lordships.

7.51 Unlike the *Holley* case, this judgment has no direct consequence for the law in England and Wales that may be deemed a precedent of sorts for domestic cases. But it does contain an implicit criticism of the insanity test operative in England and Wales, in that the senior judiciary of England and Wales have recognised more than century-old criticism of that test, promoted as broad a definition of an alternative 'appreciation' test as "is necessary to meet the justice of the case"[632] and, of course, allowed that defendants in another jurisdiction might be diverted from punishment under criminal law on grounds of insanity that would not be applicable in domestic law. This surely underlines the need for a review of the insanity test in the law of England and Wales.

Community orders and personality disordered offenders

7.52 In August 2006 HHJ Alexander QC, sitting at Northampton County Court, wished to make a section 37 guardianship order in the case of Mr *B*, who had been convicted of affray. Mr *B* had a long history of mental disorder and many previous convictions involving violence and criminal damage, with much of his offending behaviour attributed to alcohol abuse. The judge's proposed disposal of the case was thwarted by Northamptonshire County Council, which was unwilling to receive the offender into guardianship[633]. In part, this reluctance was due to the Council's concern over how the limited powers of guardianship would be of use in managing Mr *B*'s aggressive behaviour and alcohol abuse without endangering the safety of its own staff and other residents in any residential placement. But the council also raised concerns that may be an indicator of wider obstacles to the use of any Mental Health Act powers of compulsion in cases such as this: it produced clinical opinion that the nature and degree of Mr *B*'s mental disorder (which one clinician described as alcoholism and emotionally unstable personality disorder) would mean that a guardianship order could be "psychologically and behaviourally detrimental" in that it might "reinforce his tendency to project responsibility on external factors and would undermine the likelihood of achieving any maturity and self-responsibility... it will serve no purpose"[634].

---

[629] *Phillip & Another* para 23

[630] *ibid.*, paras 21, 22

[631] St Lucia Criminal Code, s.21(b). The omitted words are, first, "in the opinion of the jury or the court" and, second, "of any kind in respect of such an act".

[632] *Phillip & Another* para 25

[633] A condition of guardianship under s.37(6) of the 1983 Act.

[634] *R (Paul Bukowicki) v Northamptonshire County Council* [2007] EWHC 310 (admin), para 23 (quoting Dr Al-Robb's report for the council as defendant to Mr *B*'s challenge to its decision).

7.53	In part, this case may be argued (as it was argued by medical opinion for Mr *B* in challenging the council's decision to reject him as a suitable case for guardianship) as an example of a person with treatable mental disorder being "needlessly rejected by mental health and social services due to his history of alcohol abuse"[635], or because of the challenges that treating his personality disorder would pose an authority with finite resources and a wariness of accepting potentially violent persons into community placements. As such (and irrespective of one's sympathies with one or the other opposing medical opinions in this case), it shows a form of 'treatability test' relating to personality disorder that is likely to survive the 2007 Act's rewording of both the definition of mental disorder and the conditions for detention and guardianship under the 1983 Act. Particularly in relation to community-based orders (including the new CTO under the 2007 Act), authorities faced with certain personality-disordered persons may weigh the exercisable coercive power granted by the Act against the way in which the person made subject to such compulsion is relieved of responsibility and self-determination, and decide that the coercive powers are either not worth the trouble or may be counter-productive. The medical opinion supporting a guardianship order for Mr *B* could only suggest that it would "provide [him] with a structure and statutory support within which he can work on his mental health problems"[636], about which the judge in the Court of Appeal stated "although I understand what the words say, I do not understand what the words actually mean in practical human terms relevant to guardianship".[637] In this case, the offender was given a supervision order for two years: we doubt that under the revised Mental Health Act, when that is implemented, a case presenting similar dilemmas (whether in relation to guardianship or any other MHA disposal) would necessarily be determined otherwise.

The management of restricted patients

The role of the Ministry of Justice in managing restricted patients

7.54	In our last report, we pointed out that the Home Office Mental Health Unit (as it then was[638]) is responsible for a minority of decisions to conditionally discharge restricted patients, and slightly less than half of decisions to absolutely discharge such patients[639]. The Mental Health Unit (MHU) has subsequently indicated to care teams that it is keen to work with them to increase the number of conditional discharges granted by the Secretary of State[640]. Our last report suggested that the review of the Mental Health Act should have provided an opportunity to reassess the relevance in a modern health care system of having a government minister's office make purely administrative decisions about individual's detention under mental health powers[641]. The narrowing of the terms of review of the Act subsequent to our report's publication rather precluded such a reassessment taking place. In 2006 a journal of the Royal College of Psychiatrists published an informative article on the

---

[635] *ibid.*, para 18

[636] *ibid.*

[637] *ibid.*, para 35

[638] The MHU passed from being a responsibility of the Home Office to being a responsibility of the newly created Ministry of Justice in April 2007.

[639] MHAC (2006) *Eleventh Biennial Report 2003-2005: In Place of Fear?* Paras 5.107- 5.113.

[640] Ministry of Justice (2007) *Mental Health Unit Bulletin,* Issue 1, August 2007, page 4. See also Srinivas J, Denvir S & Humphreys M (2006) 'The Home Office Mental Health Unit' *Advances in Psychiatric Treatment* 12, 450-458 at p.453 and the response by Eastman N (2006) 'Can there be true partnership between clinicians and the Home Office?' *Advances in Psychiatric Treatment 12, 459-461, p.461.*

[641] MHAC (2006) op cit., *recommendation 57*

MHU, written as a collaboration between clinicians and a casework manager from the unit, coupled with a commentary from Professor Nigel Eastman questioning the article's characterisation of the relationship between the MHU and RMOs as a "partnership", and calling for a closer ethical analysis of such collaboration where it might sit awkwardly with conventional medical ethics[642]. We would welcome the broadening of this debate. In practical terms, we are concerned that decisions about risk and mental disorder may be taken by the MHU at a purely administrative level, without benefit of independent clinical advice. We also believe that a more complete judicial check on the political administration of deprivation of liberty for reasons of mental disorder would be provided were the MHRT to have, at the very least, the same range of powers as the Secretary of State in whose name the MHU operates, so that it could direct transfer or community leave. A more complete separation of powers could be achieved were the MHU to act in a purely advisory capacity to the MHRT, with the latter body alone empowered to discharge restricted patients.

7.55   The report of the independent inquiry into the care and treatment of George Leigers[643], published in June 2006, questioned the role of the MHU in taking decisions about discharge in terms similar to those raised above. Mr Leigers' original index offence was the manslaughter of his wife, as a result of which he was detained under s.37/41 in 1986. In 1993 he was conditionally discharged into the community by the MHRT, with an original requirement that he live in a nursing home. He was allowed to move to independent accommodation in 1993 and, in January 1999, was given an absolute discharge by the Home Office. In 2003 he murdered a young woman at his home and was sentenced to life imprisonment, although he was subsequently transferred to Rampton Hospital. The inquiry made no specific criticism of the MHU decision to discharge Mr Leigers from all supervision (indeed it questioned the part played by mental disorder in the 2003 murder, and considered that nothing was known about Mr Leigers in the period leading up to it that would have indicated its imminence)[644] but it asked that consideration be given at government level to two issues:

i)   "Whether patients who have committed very serious offences and who have received restriction orders under s.41 of the MHA should remain under supervision for the rest of their lives".[645] The panel drew a comparison with those imprisoned for life for murder, who may be released after serving many years in prison but who remain under a lifelong licence[646].

ii)   Alternatively, if such patients are to be absolutely discharged, whether this would be undertaken only by the MHRT rather than by administrative action taken by the MHU on behalf of Secretary of State. The panel pointed out that the MHU decisions over absolute discharge "are usually wholly reliant on reports prepared by the team caring for the patient, and as such is dependent upon the quality of their assessments and conclusions. In contrast, the MHRT is able to carry out a much more extensive, and independent, review of a case, including information obtained from interviews carried out by its own medical member".[647]

---

[642] Srinivas J et al (2006) ; Eastman N (2006) *op cit.* n.640 above.

[643] County Durham and Tees Valley Strategic Health Authority (2006) *Report of the independent inquiry into the care and treatment of George Leigers.* June 2006. Paras 3.175-6 (p.80), recommendation 6 (p.87).

[644] *ibid.,* para 4.11

[645] *ibid.,* para 4.13 (recommendation 6)

[646] *ibid.,* para 3.175

[647] *ibid.,* para 3.175

7.56 These questions, at least in part, echo the concerns that we expressed in our last report. Even if government is minded to answer the inquiry's first question positively, we believe that the principle raised by the second question is also valid for decisions taken about conditional discharge of restricted patients generally. We recognise that the MHU has a valuable role in overseeing public safety in relation to mental disordered offenders, but we are uneasy at its role in determining whether a patient may be deprived of his or her liberty, and at the way in which having such powers leads the unit to automatically oppose any patient's appeal to the MHRT on the grounds that the Secretary of State has not exercised his or her own power to discharge the appellant patient. As we wrote in our last report[648], the MHU's consistently oppositional stance towards discharge at any MHRT hearing has led to accusations that it is selective in its presentation of information about patients to the MHRT, and to the danger that its representations are therefore seen as partial and given less weight than they deserve. In this sense, the effectiveness of the MHU might be enhanced, rather than diminished, were it to have a purely advisory role to the MHRT over discharge decisions.

Removal of patients' benefits

7.57 As a result of the general (if not universal) abolition of hospital downrating in April 2006 (see chapter 2.146 above), most long-stay detained patients receiving benefits had a substantial increase in their payments. As we discuss below, for some patients this will have provided a welcome opportunity to expand activities leading towards rehabilitation.

7.58 However, the benefits rules were also changed at this time to remove all eligibility for benefits from patients who are detained under sections 45A or 47 up to the expiry date of their sentence. Thus a minority even of part III patients - approximately 420 detained patients in England[649] and very few patients in Wales[650] - were deprived of all income as a result of this government decision. The Department of Work and Pensions wrote to these patients informing them of this change, but at the start of March 2006 not all patients had yet received letters, and Commissioners received many anxious enquiries from the patients concerned. In March 2006 the Department of Health circulated guidance to its chief executives on the change[651]. This stated that, where a patient was to be left unable to meet occasional personal expenses, it was expected that NHS commissioning bodies would meet these by making arrangements with hospitals to make appropriate payments. We understand that funding was made available to PCTs to enable them to pay the equivalent of the old hospital pocket-money rate (about £16 per week) to the patients concerned.

7.59 The removal of benefits from this minority of patients has led to considerable difficulties in this period. This has undoubtedly had a profoundly counter-therapeutic effect for the patients concerned, both in terms of general morale and also in relation to the work of rehabilitation that should be a central focus of their hospitalisation.

---

[648] MHAC (2006) *Eleventh Biennial Report 2003-2005: In Place of Fear?* para 5.110.

[649] Department of Health letter to all chief executives, 9 March 2006: 'Changes to benefit entitlements for patients transferred from prison to mental health units', para 3. Issued with DH *Chief Executive Bulletin* 308, 3 - 9 March 2006. Reproduced in MHAC Policy Briefing 13, March 2006.

[650] National Assembly statistics show an annual average of 28 admissions under section 47 (and no admissions under section 45A) over the five years 2001/02 to 2005/06. See National Assembly for Wales (2006) Statistical Bulletin *Admission of Patients to Mental Health Facilities in Wales 2005-06*, October 2006, table 4.1.

[651] See n.649 above.

Effect on Morale

7.60 It is particularly regrettable that the decision to remove benefits entitlement appeared to further undermine the concept of diversion of mentally disordered offenders from punitive sanction. According to the Department of Health's own statistics, nearly one in five sentenced prisoners who were transferred to hospital under the Act in the most recent two years' of reported data were not subject to restrictions under s.49, and as such the prison system lost all practical claim on them[652]), and yet such transferred prisoners will be deprived of any benefits until their sentence tariff has expired. A number of patients and staff reported disquiet at s.45A and s.47 patients being singled out as having the status of 'prisoners' (even at this technical level) amongst resident populations that contain many other patients who have been convicted of offences. Indeed, the removal of entitlement to benefits cannot be justified on the basis of culpability for a criminal offence: the government's own statistics show that, over the last five years of available data, roughly twice as many patients have been admitted under s.37 subsequent to conviction than have been admitted under ss.45A and 47[653], and patients detained under s.37 saw their benefits increase when the rules changed.

7.61 We are concerned to hear reports of "frictions" between patients with different incomes in some forensic services. Patients who have lost benefits entitlements have reported feeling that they had been unfairly treated over this issue, and at feeling infantilised by their 'pocket-money' income at the discretion of hospital authorities, when others around them were receiving newly upgraded state benefits.

> Patients' programmes include education, workshops and gardens. Some have paid work on the ward. This is particularly helpful for those transferred prisoners who have had their benefits stopped. According to a member of the nursing staff, the biggest problem is motivating patients to attend their programmes. In some cases the drop in motivation has been an unfortunate consequence of the increase in benefits for most patients.
>
> Broadmoor Hospital, January 2007

Effect on rehabilitation

7.62 Despite the specific allowances granted to such patients by some hospitals as a recompense for some of their lost income, many patients have been left in very unsatisfactory position and at a serious disadvantage to other patients who are detained alongside them. Patients who had lost benefits, or seen them replaced with pocket-money allowances from the hospital, particularly complained that they were being disadvantaged in terms of opportunities for rehabilitation.

---

[652] Information Centre (2007) *Inpatients formally detained in hospitals under the Mental Health Act 1983 and other legislation, NHS Trusts, Care Trusts, Primary Care Trusts & Independent Hospitals, England; 1995-96 to 2005-06.* See Table 1: of 700 s.47 transfers over 2004/05 and 2005/06, 128 are reported as being unrestricted.

[653] *ibid.* In the five years 2001/02 to 2005/06, 2,009 admissions under s.37 were recorded in England, against 1,511 admissions under ss.45A or 47. In Wales, there were 252 s.37 and 138 s.47 admissions (National Assembly for Wales (2006) *op cit* n.650).

The patient is on a s.47/49 transfer. Whilst she is grateful to the Trust for their support, including financial support, her position is unsatisfactory ... she finds the £13.40 to buy food not quite enough

South and East Wales Commission visiting area, October 2006

7.63 It is a matter of great concern that there should be such disparities of income amongst patients detained as mentally disordered offenders in secure facilities. The patients who have been deprived of benefits are put in a position of increased dependency upon the hospital that detains them, but are also at risk of forming dependent relationships with patients whose benefits have increased. There is considerable risk of exploitation in such patient relationships in this new, economically stratified, hospital environment, creating a new problem for hospital managers to try to deal with. We are very concerned to have heard reports of the beginnings of new barter economies in some secure facilities, where patients receiving state benefits were reportedly eliciting favours from others using cigarettes or confectionary as currency.

if rehabilitation is about trying to help people gain the skills to live in the community again, then treating them like children and giving them pocket money is scarcely helpful in achieving this.

MHA Commissioner, following a visit to a rehabilitation unit, August 2006

7.64 We are aware that one NHS Trust (Calderstones NHS Trust in Lancashire) adopted a principled position of paying its s.47/49 population the same benefit rate as its other patients receive in state benefits, on the grounds that doing otherwise could disadvantage their rehabilitative process, given that the majority will eventually be discharged into the community rather than returned to prison. The Trust has stuck to this position despite concerns expressed by other organisations that this may be setting a difficult precedent. Other NHS Trusts have found that they are being asked to fund through 'hardship grants' costs which might previously have been met through patient's benefits (such as money for patients to buy clothes).

Voting and patients detained under part III of the MHA 1983

7.65 In our last report[654] we highlighted the relevance to patients detained under part III of the MHA 1983 of the European Court of Human Rights' October 2005 ruling, in Hirst v UK[655], that the blanket deprivation of voting rights for convicted prisoners was incompatible with Convention rights. In the European Court, the UK government pleaded the punitive aspect of disenfranchisement as its justification. We recommended, in our last biennial report and in our response to the government's public consultation on this matter[656], that government should therefore redress its violation of ECHR rights to vote by extending the franchise to all

---

[654] MHAC (2006) *Eleventh Biennial Report 2003-2005: In Place of Fear?*, para 2.108

[655] *Hirst v United Kingdom (no.2)*, Application No. 74025/01, 6 October 2005.

[656] MHAC (2007) *Mental Health Act Commission response to Department of Constitutional Affairs consultation paper CP29/06: Voting rights of convicted prisoners detained within the United Kingdom - Government's response to the Grand Chamber of the European Court of Human Rights judgement in the case of Hirst v the United Kingdom.* 7 March 2007, available from mhac website.

detained patients, whether they have been convicted of an offence or not, as punitive or deterrent sanctions have no place in a hospital environment, whether or not it can be justified in a prison environment.

7.66 We believe that this is self evident in the case of hospital orders (i.e. MHA s.37), where there is no necessary connection between a judge's decision to dispose of a case through making a hospital order and that judge's view as to the need for punitive incarceration: indeed, a hospital order should be seen as a health measure designed to provide an offender with treatment.

7.67 We also believe that punitive measures have no place in hospital for transferred prisoners, as such transfers are, and should be recognised as, a diversion from the prison environment to a hospital environment.

7.68 Patients detained under sections 38, 44, and 51(5) of the Act should also be enfranchised because they are in hospital and not in prison, but also because, although these patients have been convicted of an offence, they have not been sentenced and their hospitalisation is an interim measure before a final disposal is made. Their final disposal may be community-based.

7.69 Patients who are detained under the Criminal Insanity Act or Criminal Appeal Act having been found not guilty by reason of insanity should not be disenfranchised as a result, because they are hospital patients and disenfranchisement could have no legitimate punitive or conceivable deterrent effect, and it is unjust that a person who is unconvicted under these circumstances should be subject to legal sanction with such stated aims.

7.70 We note that the Joint Committee on Human Rights has criticised the government for the long timetable of its consultation, and suggested that "the continued failure to remove the blanket ban, enfranchising at least part of the prison population, is clearly unlawful"[657]. It has also expressed regret that the government consultation invited views on whether it might retain the current blanket ban when in fact this is one option explicitly ruled out by the European Court[658]. We share the Joint Committee's hope that a draft remedial order will be published with the next consultation document, and that the question of enfranchisement be settled prior to the next general election[659].

'Shadow leave'

7.71 A practice variously known as 'shadow leave' or 'shadowed leave' involves granting apparently unescorted s.17 leave to a patient, but having that patient followed without his or her knowledge. We have only seen it proposed for forensic patients subject to restriction orders. In our last report we noted that the Home Office (now Ministry of Justice) Mental Health Unit claimed that shadow leave had been suggested in error and never implemented in a particular case that we raised with them, but reserved the position that such arrangements could be lawful and justifiable in exceptional circumstances[660]. We suggested

---

[657] Joint Committee of Human Rights (2007) *Sixteenth Report: Monitoring the Government's Response to Court Judgments Finding Breaches of Human Rights* HL 128/HC 728, 18 June 2007, para 78.

[658] *ibid.*, para 78.

[659] *ibid.*, para 79.

[660] MHAC (2006) *Eleventh Biennial Report 2003-2005: In Place of Fear?*, para 4.40

that the circumstances would have to be exceptional indeed to justify either the deception or the risk taken by authorities in having a patient unescorted but secretly observed.[661]

7.72 In a witness statement to the Court of Appeal in June 2006[662], the MHU explained why it had not agreed to an MHRT recommendation for 'shadow leave' made in February that year, in respect of a restricted patient whose paranoid schizophrenia appeared to be in remission. The MHU

> explained that shadow leave had in the past occasionally been agreed with care teams by the Secretary of State to meet the circumstances of patients for whom unescorted community leave was considered problematic. It enabled the patient to be followed by nursing staff from the hospital without him or her knowing this and enabled an informed decision to be taken on whether the patient could be trusted on unescorted leave in the future... The practice of shadow leave was discontinued over a year ago following disquiet about the practice for a number of reasons. First, the psychiatric community held it to be unethical to send patients into the community in the belief that they were unescorted but when in fact they were being followed... Second, there was also the possibility that shadow leave could lead to a patient developing paranoid delusions about being followed if they spotted the staff 'shadowing' them. There would not be delusions [sic] but these feelings could lead to deterioration in the patient's medical state thereby negating the intended effect of the leave.[663]

7.73 This slightly confused account of the MHU position at least makes clear that it recognises the clinical and ethical pitfalls of deceiving patients, and in this case acted accordingly. Historically, psychiatric practice has from time to time fallen into the ethical trap of believing that patients may be deliberately confused or deceived in the furtherance of their management or cure (see also chapter 6.38 on covert medication). There can be no room for such duplicity in modern practice, given the recognition today of human rights, and the importance of restoring personal autonomy and making patients – including forensic patients - partners in their recovery from mental illness.

Section 17 leave

7.74 In a number of hospitals we have noted that a copy of the Mental Health Unit authorisation of leave arrangements was not kept alongside local s.17 leave documentation completed by the RMO. We have advised that the documents should be kept together to allow easier checks that leave granted is within the parameters established. In one hospital, we found extremely general authorisations made by the RMO in respect of restricted patients, such as "unescorted leave in the community at staff discretion". We do not believe that such general authorisations are appropriate, especially in the case of restricted patients. While the Code of Practice allows that RMOs may authorise short-term leave at the discretion of staff, it also suggests that such discretion should operate within the terms of the periodic leave granted by the RMO, and that the RMO may not delegate the decision to grant leave[664].

---

661 *ibid.*

662 *R (on the application of OS) v Secretary of State for the Home Department* [2006] EWHC 1903 (Admin).

663 *ibid.*, paras 77-8

664 *Mental Health Act 1983 Code of Practice*, para 20.3, 20.4.

Recommendation 41: A copy of Mental Health Unit authorisation of leave should be kept alongside local leave documentation for restricted patients. RMOs should be careful to define the parameters of leave for such patients where elements of that leave are at staff discretion.

Compliance with medication as a requirement of conditional discharge

7.75 The High Court has ruled that it is acceptable for conditional discharge requirements to include a requirement that the patient complies with medication as prescribed by a specified doctor, but such requirements should only be made where the MHRT or Mental Health Unit had a proper basis to expect that the patient did and would consent to taking such medication[665]. The Court suggested that any expression of the condition should use some such words as "subject always to [the patient's] right to give or withhold consent to treatment or medication on any given occasion"[666].

7.76 In part, the Court's decision that the requirement of medication compliance is compatible with the conditionally discharged patient's right to consent or refuse consent to treatment with medication rests on the argument that there is no effective sanction for failure to comply with such a requirement. Although a conditionally discharged patient can be recalled to hospital by the Secretary of State, such recall must be justified (save in an emergency) by up to date medical evidence showing that the criteria for detention are met[667]. In this sense, the act of refusing consent to medication might break a requirement of the conditional discharge, but it would not in itself be sufficient for the sanction of recall to take place.

7.77 The reality of the patient's position was, however, a little different. In the skeleton argument to the court, counsel for the MHRT had argued that "it may be quite possible that if the claimant ceased to take his medication he would be recalled. But that would not be because he had broken the condition of his discharge. It would be because there was clear medical evidence that *if* he ceased to take his medication he would pose a serious risk to others"[668] (our emphasis). Thus, given the *nature* of the patient's illness, it was left open as to whether there need be any change in the *degree* of his illness to warrant recall should he refuse a depot injection: it appears to have been implicitly accepted that the very fact of refusal by person who has schizophrenia (even in remission) and an offending history similar to *SH*[669] could be medical evidence enough. This is, in effect, what the Administrative Court allowed in November 2006, ruling that a paranoid schizophrenic patient could be recalled on the basis of a breach of the condition that he abstain from the use of illicit drugs[670].

---

[665] *R (on the application of SH) v MHRT* [2007] EWHC 884 (Admin).

[666] *ibid.*, para 42

[667] *ibid.*, para 36 (*Kay v United Kingdom*, 1 March 1994, 40 BMLR 20; *B v MHRT and the Secretary of State for the Home Department* [2002] EWHC 1553 (Admin)).

[668] *R (SH) v MHRT* [2007], para 36

[669] *SH* had been convicted of manslaughter having strangled his wife in 2000.

[670] *R (on the application of MM) v Secretary of State for the Home Department & Five Boroughs NHS Trust* [2006] EWHC 3056 (Admin). We understand that the patient has sought to appeal this decision. See also RadcliffesLeBrasseur *Mental Health Law Briefing* Number 110: *Recall from Conditional Discharge*, February 2007. www.rlb-law.com

7.78 On these grounds, it seems to us to be far from clear that what the law now recognises as "a real or true choice"[671] over treatment compliance as a condition of staying out of hospital is in reality anything of the sort. The courts have recognised that they "must be alive to the risk that what may appear on the face of it to be true consent is not in fact so"[672], and have formulated as a test that "in order for an apparent consent ... to be less than a true consent ... there must be such a degree of external influence as to persuade the patient to depart from his or her own wishes"[673]. In part, the judgment in *SH*'s case appears to get around this test by taking the view that it is "the continuing conditional nature of his discharge, not the condition [of treatment compliance] itself" that puts "pressure" on *SH* to comply[674]. If this is taken as a general principle in future cases (for we suspect that there may be future cases), it seems to be dangerously close to sophism.

7.79 It is important to remember that *SH*'s appeal also failed on its facts: the patient was consenting to his medication. He challenged the conditional discharge requirement that he comply with medication not because he wished to cease such compliance, but because he wished to demonstrate that he would comply without any element of legal compulsion. As such, this judgment does not in any way change the fact that a conditionally discharged patient must be consenting to any treatment provided as a requirement of discharge. It does, however, highlight an aspect of risk-based practice that gives us pause in relation to the 2007 Act's introduction of community treatment orders (CTOs), and reinforces the concerns expressed in our last report that 'deinstitutionalisation', as the movement of treatment into the community, can have the perverse effect of creating more restrictive, and indeed institutional, practice in caring for patients outside of hospital[675].

7.80 In an earlier application to the MHRT (for an absolute discharge from compulsion), the patient had written that he recognised the ongoing need for his depot antipsychotic injections; did not suffer from side-effects; and had no wish to stop taking it[676]. Against this, his RMO stated that he was "convinced that *SH* does have full insight into his illness. He has mentioned on several occasions to his CPN that he wanted the medication to be reduced... if discharged off s.37/41 I am *not completely sure* that the patient will adhere to his care plan and will remain compliant with his medication"[677](our emphasis). We can see why the request for absolute discharge might be rejected on this basis, but we are concerned that, in the face of such mildly-worded doubts over the patient's future compliance, the patient was not subsequently given an opportunity to demonstrate that he would give consent to treatment freely by having the compliance requirement lifted whilst remaining under the general supervision of a conditional discharge. Denying the patient this opportunity placed him in a double-bind where the conditions of his discharge are considered necessary for reasons that must remain untested by their very nature. There are fears amongst service

---

[671] *R (SH) v MHRT* [2007], para 37

[672] *Freeman v Home Office (No.2)* [1984] 1 QB 524; see *R (SH) v MHRT* [2007], para 27

[673] *In re T (Adult:refusal of Treatment)* [1993] Fam 95, page 121E to F (Staughton LJ): see *R (SH) v MHRT* [2007], para 24

[674] *R (SH) v MHRT* [2007], para 38

[675] MHAC (2006) *Eleventh Biennial Report 2003-2005: In Place of Fear?* para 2.56.

[676] *ibid.*, para 6

[677] *ibid.*, para 5

users and some practitioners that such double-binds could be created by the treatment requirements of CTOs created by the 2007 Act, so that patients remain on orders for extended periods of time without being given the opportunity to demonstrate that they could be discharged. There should be robust monitoring of the implementation of CTOs to identify and challenge such practice at a policy level, whether by making recommendations for revisions to the Code of Practice, or through some other means.

Legal duties towards victims

7.81   In our last report[678] we noted new legal duties towards victims introduced under the provisions of the Domestic Violence, Crime and Victims Act 2004 ("the DVCV Act"). This change in the law extended to victims of some mentally disordered offenders with restricted status similar rights as are exercisable by victims of sentenced prisoners[679]. From July 2005, where the perpetrator of a sexual or violent offence has been sent to hospital upon conviction, prison transfer or a finding under the Criminal Procedure Insanity Acts, probation board victim liaison officers (VLOs) have been required to approach the victim of that offence (including victims' families where the direct victim is incapacitated or deceased) and offer to provide information and an opportunity of representation in respect of decision-making over discharge from hospital, including decisions over the precise terms of any conditional discharge.

7.82   The change to the law in 2005 placed the burden of statutory duties on the VLO (in liaising with the victim); the Home Office (now Ministry of Justice) Mental Health Unit and the Mental Health Review Tribunal (in providing the information to be passed on). However, the 2004 Act also provided a general power to provide "such other information as the [probation] board considers appropriate in all the circumstances of the case"[680]. The Home Office guidance required the patient's responsible medical officer (RMO) to be in contact with the VLO to facilitate this. The guidance states that the power to provide other information "is intended to allow the probation board the discretion to give information which will reassure victims. It is not intended to lead to the disclosure of any information which is covered by patient confidentiality"[681].

7.83   In our last report we expressed concern at the suggestion that victims should have an expectation of access and representation to the patient's care team through arrangements with their VLO. We believe that the new duties should not detract from the offender's status as a patient rather than a prisoner. Patients to whom the new rules apply may have been determined by a court to have reduced or negated legal culpability for the actions that made 'victims', and we would not want an assumption made that the status of victim provides a person with particular insight into clinical care of the mentally disordered offender. We have heard of one instance in this reporting period where a VLO appears to have passed on to a

---

[678] MHAC (2006) *Eleventh Biennial Report 2003-2005: In Place of Fear?*, paras 5.118 – 5.122

[679] The duties apply in the case of patients given restricted hospital orders under s.37/41 of the Act, or hybrid orders under s.45A, or to those who are transferred from prison with a restriction order under s.47/49, where such an order is made after July 2005 when the new powers came into force.

[680] See, for example, Domestic Crime, Violence and Victims Act 2004, s.38(3)(d)

[681] Home Office (2005) *Duties to Victims under the Domestic Crime, Violence and Victims Act 2004: Guidance for clinicians*. September 2005, para 8.

victim's family information about a patient's clinical presentation that should have remained part of the confidential medical record. It is important that VLOs respect boundaries of confidentiality in carrying out their role, and are open to guidance from clinical teams over what is and is not appropriate material to share.

7.84   However, our involvement with cases involving victims in this period has demonstrated how the new duties may provide useful certainty over the responsibilities of authorities towards victims. In November 2005 the MHAC was contacted by a Member of Parliament on behalf of his constituent, Ms W. She was both a close relative and victim of Mr Y, a patient detained under a restriction order in a High Security Hospital. Mr Y's detention predated the legal changes brought about by the DVCV Act. Although Ms W had been kept informed about MHRT hearings and proposals for trial leave in the initial years of Mr Y's detention, this information had ceased approximately four years before she finally contacted her MP with her "concern over not knowing [Mr Y's] situation or whereabouts". We contacted the Home Office and MHRT on Ms W's behalf. The MHRT, in accordance with its policy, immediately 'registered' her to receive notification of any Tribunal hearings of Mr Y's case[682]. The Home Office Mental Health Unit also re-established contact, and Ms W received an apology for the distress that she had been caused. It transpired that the Home Office's break in contact with Ms W resulted from a perception that such contact caused undue stress. Whilst this decision was clearly taken in good faith, Ms W felt it to be "somewhat arbitrary and unilateral", as well as based upon an incorrect judgment of her concerns. Although Ms W stated that she was generally very appreciative of the consideration and sensitivity of the Home Office team, and recognised the difficulties in their role, the case showed clearly the danger in taking decisions about victims without their involvement. Insofar as the new statutory framework should avoid this we welcome it wholeheartedly.

The expansion of duties towards victims in the Mental Health Act 2007

7.85   The Mental Health Act 2007 has amended the Domestic Violence, Crime and Victims Act 2004 to extend its coverage to any victim of a violent or sexual offence committed by any patient detained under s.37 or s.47, whether or not that patient has restricted status. The change has yet to take effect.

7.86   Because there is no Ministry of Justice Mental Health Unit involvement with unrestricted patients, specific statutory duties regarding such patients fall onto the hospital managers directly. Where a victim has indicated to their victim liaison officer (VLO) that they wish to receive it, hospital managers must provide the VLO with information about discharge proposals, including any proposal to place the patient on a Community Treatment Order and any conditions of that CTO relating to contact with the victim or victim's family. Alongside these quite specific statutory requirements, the new powers in the DVCV Act

---

[682] The MHRT has undertaken to use its existing powers under the MHRT Rules to provide, insofar as it can, equivalent access to information and representation for victims of sexual or violent offences who are not covered by the DVCV Act because the offenders were convicted or committed to hospital before its commencement date: see MHAC (2006) *Eleventh Biennial Report 2003-2005: In Place of Fear?*, para 4.124-5.

replicate that Act's general power and allows that hospital managers may provide "such other information as [they] consider appropriate in all the circumstances of the case"[683]. Whilst it would seem appropriate for the VLO to act as a conduit (and gatekeeper) for such information, there is nothing in the law that would prevent direct access to hospital managers by victims.

7.87 There is some risk of facilitating retributive acts if the information given to victims or their families about the discharge of an offender patient is mishandled. That such risks can be very real is perhaps indicated by Mr Justice Silber's acceptance that the Home Office Mental Health Unit was entitled to take them into account in refusing permission for a restricted patient's unescorted leave on two occasions in 2005 and 2006[684]. The Mental Health Unit's policies in relation to providing victims of restricted patients with information acknowledges the risks of retributive acts in that, for example, where victims are to be notified that a patient has been granted leave, they are not supposed to be told of the timing and purpose of that leave[685]. Similarly, the name or location of any hospital to which a patient is transferred is not supposed to be disclosed to victims[686]. We can envisage circumstances where placing such limitations on the information given to victims undermines the reassurance that such information might otherwise provide. Furthermore, limiting information about unrestricted patients in this way may not be possible under the requirements of the DVCV Act as it has been amended: for example, the revised Act requires that victims are told the name and address of the hospital in which an unrestricted patient is detained[687].

7.88 We therefore urge caution on hospital managers, and the clinical teams and responsible medical officers to whom they are likely to delegate liaison with VLOs or victims themselves.

---

[683] See, for example, DVCV Act 2004 (as amended by the Mental Health Act 2007), s.38A(7)(g).

[684] *R (on the application of OS) v Secretary of State for the Home Department* [2006] EWHC 1903 (Admin). In this case Mr Justice Silber accepted Home Office submissions that a relevant aspect of risk assessment in considering and rejecting the leave application was the patient's own fear of reprisals from the family of the man whom he had killed, as whilst on unescorted leave "he would …lack the protection afforded to him against those people while he remained in Chase Farm [Hospital]" (para 54).

[685] Home Office (2005) *Duties to Victims under the Domestic Crime, Violence and Victims Act 2004: Guidance for clinicians.* September 2005, para 16.

[686] *ibid.*, para 14.

[687] See, for example, DVCV Act 2004 (as amended by the Mental Health Act 2007), s.36A(3).

8

The future monitoring of psychiatric detention

The rationalisation of monitoring bodies

8.1   During this reporting period the Department of Health undertook a fundamental review of the regulation of health and adult social care in England, in addition to the decision already taken by Ministers to abolish the MHAC[688]. In large part the review (or indeed reviews, as there were two during this period), responded to wider central government drivers for change in regulation, led by the Better Regulation Executive of the Cabinet Office. The Chancellor's Budget Statement in March 2005 announced the merger of eleven public service inspectorates into four (covering health and adult social care; children; local services; and the criminal justice system). This formed a key element of the government's strategy to reduce spending on public service inspectorates by 30% - 35% by 2008/9 (which it considers a proxy for reducing the burden of inspection activity on frontline services). Other wider government initiatives in the preceding period included the Gershon Efficiency Review[689] and the Lyons review of public sector relocation[690]. As reported in our Eleventh Biennial Report[691], the Department of Health had already begun a programme of change in its arm's length bodies, which was itself part of a wider programme intended to improve efficiency and cut bureaucracy in the management of the NHS. During 2005, the Department of Health undertook what it described as a "wider regulatory review", which led eventually to publication in November 2006 of a consultation document entitled *the future regulation of health and adult social care in England*[692]. This outlined a number of new and revised regulatory functions which would be undertaken in health and adult social care from 2008 onwards and confirmed the commitment to establish an integrated health and adult social care regulator in England[693]. In Wales, there is no such initiative to integrate the

---

[688]   In 2004 that intention was confirmed through the 2004 Mental Health Bill. At that time, had the Bill gone forward, the functions of the MHAC would have been transferred to the Healthcare Commission.

[689]   *Independent Review of Public Sector Relocation. Sir Michael Lyons, March 2004.*
www.hm-treasury.gov.uk/lyonsreview

[690]   Releasing Resources to the Frontline: Independent Review of Public Sector Efficiency. Sir Peter Gershon, July 2004.
www.hm-treasury.gov.uk/spending_review/spend_sr04/associated_documents/spending_sr04_efficiency.cfm

[691]   MHAC (2006) *Eleventh Biennial Report 2003-2005: In Place of Fear?* para 3.79

[692]   Department of Health (2006) *The future regulation of health and adult social care in England*, November 2006.
www.dh.gov.uk/PolicyAndGuidance/OrganisationPolicy/HealthReform/fs/en

[693]   Inspection of children's social care services passed from the Commission for Social Care Inspection (CSCI) to the expanded children's inspectorate *Ofsted* in April 2007.

regulation and inspection of health and social care, but the functions of the abolished MHAC will find a home in the Health Inspectorate Wales.

8.2 The November 2006 consultation document announced that government intended to establish the new regulator (which at that time was to be called Ofcare) in 2008. This would replace the Commission for Social Care Inspection, the Healthcare Commission and the Mental Health Act Commission and would establish a new body rather than merging the current ones with functions unchanged. A final document setting out the response to the consultation, and announcing the Care Quality Commission, was published in October 2007[694]. We are pleased that the revised proposals take greater account than the original document of the importance of protection of human rights and of the centrality of service user involvement in the regulation of health and adult social care (not solely in the monitoring of the Mental Health Act). It also rectifies the omissions of the consultation document by making clearer the role of the new regulator in safeguarding the rights of patients subject to detention under the Mental Health Act 1983 (as amended), and new arrangements for monitoring the operation of the deprivation of liberty safeguards of the Mental Capacity Act 2005, as amended by the Mental Health Act 2007. The new regulator offers a welcome range of enforcement powers and sanctions which will provide the new regulator with much stronger "teeth" than any of its predecessor organisations. However, we remain concerned that the regulatory model which is proposed is essentially an economic one, and fear that an opportunity to promote the rights of service users in the regulation of services has not been fully exploited.

8.3 At the time of writing, it is expected that the new regulator will be established in October 2008 and become operational from 1 April 2009, with the three existing Commissions it is to replace (the Commission for Social Care Inspection, the Healthcare Commission and the Mental Health Act Commission) continuing until 31 March 2009. These proposals are subject to the passage of the Health and Social Care Bill through Parliament during the winter of 2007-08[695].

8.4 The planned retraction of monitoring bodies in the health and social care sector is no longer mirrored by a similar process in the criminal justice and immigration sector. Proposals to merge the role of HM Chief Inspectorate of Prisons (HMCIP) into a generic 'criminal justice' inspectorate were abandoned during this reporting period, and a new immigration services inspectorate was announced which will have an overlapping role with HMCIP in respect of immigration detention facilities, albeit one to be negotiated between the bodies themselves through "suitable protocols"[696].

---

[694] Department of Health (2007) *The future regulation of health and adult social care in England: response to consultation.* October 2007.

[695] The Health and Social Care Bill 2006 was introduced into the House of Commons on the 15 November 2007.

[696] Home Office (2007) *An Independent and transparent Assessment of Immigration – Policy Statement.* March 2007, para 11.

Optional Protocol to the Convention against Torture (OPCAT)

8.5 Under the Optional Protocol to the Convention against Torture (which was adopted by the UN General Assembly in 2002 and entered into force in June 2006), the UK is required to establish a National Preventive Mechanism (NPM). This is a system of regular visits to places of detention by independent expert bodies, in order to prevent torture and other forms of ill-treatment. The NPM complements a similar international function carried out by the UN Subcommittee on Prevention of Torture. Thus, by international agreement, the requirements on the UK government for independent monitoring of all those citizens who are deprived of their liberty, whether in prisons, psychiatric hospitals, care homes or other settings, is perhaps clearer today than it ever has been.

8.6 The Optional Protocol sets out fundamental requirements, but allows some flexibility for each country to structure its NPM according to its own circumstances. The UK government intends that the domestic requirements of the Protocol will be fulfilled by the collective action of all the existing statutory inspection bodies. It does not believe that in order to establish the UK NPM there is a need to create any new bodies, or that any additional activity by the existing bodies is necessary.

8.7 In most respects the MHAC can offer assurance of compliance with the NPM for psychiatric settings. The key requirements of the Optional Protocol are that the constituent bodies which make up the NPM meet criteria relating to their independence, capability, and professional knowledge or expertise[697]. The statutory basis on which the constituent bodies operate must either give the organisations unrestricted access to places of detention and to people deprived of their liberty – including the power to make unannounced visits – and unrestricted access to information about such persons and their conditions of detention; or, at least, contains nothing to prevent such access and such visits[698]. However, for psychiatric settings in England and Wales this assurance is subject to one important reservation, due to the MHAC's lack of authority to monitor *de facto* deprivation of liberty in psychiatric facilities.

8.8 In its *Guide on the Establishment and Designation of National Preventive Mechanisms*[699], the Association for the Prevention of Torture states that OPCAT extends to "instances where people were *de facto* deprived of their liberty, without any formal order but with the acquiescence of an authority"[700]. At present, the MHAC's legal remit extends only to patients who are formally detained under the powers of the Mental Health Act 1983, leaving a gap in the monitoring of de facto psychiatric detention that we have called attention to since the our first Biennial Report in 1985. The MHAC's current legal remit does not allow it access to de facto detained patients in the psychiatric facilities that it currently visits in pursuance of its statutory duties. We similarly are denied access to information about such

---

[697] These requirements are set out in some detail in Article 18 of the Protocol

[698] In accordance with Articles 19 and 20 of the Protocol

[699] Association for the Prevention of Torture (2006) *Establishment and Designation of National Preventive Mechanisms* APT; Geneva www.apt.ch

[700] *ibid.*, p.24

patients, including information relating to their treatment and conditions of detention. Psychiatric patients falling outwith the MHAC's legal remit do fall within the general powers of the Healthcare Commission, although the Healthcare Commission has a very different remit and methodology to the MHAC. This gap will remain at least until 2009 and the establishment of a new regulator with a duty to monitor deprivation of liberty under the Mental Capacity Act, and possibly beyond. At the time of writing, discussions are ongoing about the system to be introduced from 2009, and we would urge that the Department of Health and the new regulator put in place one that is compliant with the requirements of the Optional Protocol.

> **Recommendation 42:** The Department of Health should ensure that the new regulator for health and adult social care complies with the requirements of the Optional Protocol to the Convention against Torture, as part of the UK government's National Preventive Mechanism.

8.9   Putting aside this significant gap in the scope of the NPM in current arrangements, there is clear concordance between the requirements of the Protocol on the question of professional expertise and the arrangements for the appointment of members of the Mental Health Act Commission in England and Wales. Mental Health Act Commissioners are drawn from almost all of the categories of professional and other backgrounds recommended by the Association for the Prevention of Torture[701]. (In addition, members of the Commission include users of services, including service users who have been detained under the Act). Individual Commissioners are independent from the government, the judiciary, and the authorities responsible for places of detention (although whether this independence in their visits extends to true independence for the body as a whole is discussed below). The MHAC deploys its Commissioners in such a way as to ensure their independence from the services they visit: no Commissioner visits services provided by an organisation by which they are employed or which would in some other way present an actual or potential conflict of interest. Since October 2004, Commissioners have been organised into local teams, such that over several years usually the same area and local commissioners would visit services in a particular area and report on their findings. There is a risk with this approach that Commissioners might become overly familiar with the services with which they have contact, and could develop what is commonly termed an overly "cosy" relationship with service providers. There was a clear reminder of the lessons of failure to recognise how local practice may have fallen out of step with national practice in the report by the Healthcare Commission and Commission for Social Care Inspection into learning disability services in Cornwall (see chapter 3.31 above), although this related not to inspectorates but to the staff working within the Trust. However, given that most Commissioners have regular contact (often through other professional roles) with a variety of different services, and there is a clear system of management support and appraisal, this would not seem to present a very significant risk.

---

[701] Lawyers; doctors; psychologists and psychiatrists; persons with prior professional experience regarding policing, administration of prisons and psychiatric institutions; NGO representatives; persons with prior experience visiting places of detention; persons with prior experience working with particularly vulnerable groups; anthropologists; social workers.

8.10 At the time of writing, it is unclear whether the Commissioner role will be maintained in the same way in the future, under the government's proposals for abolition of the Mental Health Act Commission. The MHAC has watched developments in the Healthcare Commission since 2004 with some concern. In that body there have been changes from a specialist professional model of inspection for mental health services to a more generic model whereby not all inspectors assessing mental health services have a relevant background, and inspectors with specialist mental health expertise may also be deployed in inspections of other settings. Whilst the Healthcare Commission presumably has had sound pragmatic reasons for this methodology, the MHAC firmly believes that where issues of liberty are at stake, greatly increasing the risk of abuse of individuals' rights, those people tasked with providing an external check on behalf of the state must have a very high degree of understanding of the services in which patients are detained and treated under compulsion, and of the complexities of the law in this area. Indeed a model of generic inspection without a strong emphasis on training in these areas and sufficient experience would not meet the requirements of the Optional Protocol, and the Commission has drawn these matters to the attention of Ministers and officials in the Department of Health and the Welsh Assembly Government who are concerned with the establishment of new regulatory arrangements.

8.11 A further requirement for a satisfactory NPM under the Optional Protocol is that of independence of the monitoring body from government. Here the current arrangements in England and Wales through the MHAC are on slightly less certain ground than for the other areas described by the Protocol. That situation is unlikely to improve in any new arrangements in the future. We believe that the 'constitutional' position of the MHAC (i.e. its independence, including financial independence) is compliant with the requirements of OPCAT and the Paris Principles to which it refers at Article 18. It does not, however, meet all of the recommendations of the APT[702]. The MHAC is an arm's length body of the Department of Health, but remains accountable to the Secretary of State rather than to Parliament directly. It has annual accountability meetings with the Minister and, in point of law, its activities are almost entirely conducted on behalf of the Minister[703]. Its budget is determined by the Minister and not by Parliament. The law does not expressly prevent the Minister from issuing instructions to the MHAC (and in fact s.121(4) of the MHA 1983 expressly gifts the Minister with a power to direct the MHAC, albeit on the specific topic of the scope of its remit in relation to 'informal' patients). The law does not provide Mental Health Act Commissioners with legal immunity for actions undertaken in the course of MHAC duties, nor does it provide for an enforceable privilege against disclosure of information held by the MHAC.

8.12 From our understanding of the OPCAT and the Paris Principles, we do not take the view that these 'constitutional' issues compromise the functional independence of the MHAC to the extent that it is not compliant with their basic requirements. These are matters, however, which the government should consider when establishing a successor body that will undertake MHAC functions after its proposed merger into a wider health and social care regulator.

---

[702] Association for the Prevention of Torture (2006) *op. cit*, n.699, p.48

[703] See MHA 1983, ss.120 &121

8.13   The final key criterion for compliance with the Optional Protocol is the capability of the bodies designated to form the NPM. Article 1 sets out the purpose and key elements of the OPCAT. Several concepts appear in this article which are fundamental to the NPM:

- preventive visits
- undertaken on a regular basis
- that form part of an overall system of visits.

8.14   Visiting hospitals unannounced is a central part of the MHAC methodology, and one vital to its contribution towards providing the OPCAT monitoring mechanism for England and Wales[704]. We will visit unannounced not only those services who give us cause for concern, but also those whose care and treatment of patients appears to be of a high standard. In this way we are able to see what services are really like on a day to day basis, and also have a less mediated access to detained patients in all types of service. We believe that the less our visits are viewed as special events by patients and staff alike, the better we are able to fulfil our remit. In an ideal situation our visiting Commissioners would be seen as a potential presence on wards at any given moment.

> I was visited by an MHAC Area Commissioner; we had an excellent talk for some time. She really took the time to listen to me and relayed my thoughts back to the staff.
>
> *Richard, detained under s.3 in Hull*

8.15   By contrast, other health and Social Care monitoring bodies, which do not have a direct or central concern with issues of deprivation of liberty, use unannounced visits as a reactive tool where it has concerns about services. For example, the Healthcare Commission has indicated that it will make unannounced visits to wards where it sees "a cluster of concerns" and feels that it is "not getting the full picture" over possible compromised privacy, dignity or care of patients[705].

8.16   This is fundamentally different from the purpose of the NPM, and reflects the different remits of the Healthcare Commission and the MHAC – the former essentially tasked with assessing the quality of care provided by organisations, and the latter established as a protection for individuals. The UN Special Rapporteur on Torture has explained as follows:

> The very fact that national or international experts have the power to inspect every place of detention at any time without prior announcement, have access to prison registers and other documents, are entitled to speak with every detainee in private and carry out medical investigations of torture victims has a strong deterrent effect. At the same time, such visits create the opportunity for independent experts to examine, at first hand, the treatment of prisoners and detainees and the general conditions of detention. … Many problems stem from inadequate systems which can easily be improved through regular monitoring. By carrying out regular visits to places of detention, the visiting experts

---

[704] Association for the Prevention of Torture (2006) *op. cit*, n.699, para 6.1.3.

[705] Outrage over geriatric care' *The Observer*, 24 September 2007.

usually establish a constructive dialogue with the authorities concerned in order to help them resolve problems observed.[706]

8.17 We believe it to be vitally important that the transition to the new regulator must not diminish the present level of unannounced visits to mental health wards, or confine unannounced visiting to a reactive measure where services are under suspicion.

8.18 The MHAC has argued in strong terms to Government the need to ensure that future arrangements for monitoring deprivation of liberty contain all the attributes required by the Optional Protocol - independence, expertise and capability in the form of unrestricted access to places of detention and to people deprived of their liberty (including the power to make unannounced visits) and unrestricted access to information about such persons and their conditions of detention. This should apply to all deprivation of liberty, whether detention under the Mental Health Act, deprivation of liberty under the Mental Capacity Act 2005, as amended 2007, or indeed *de facto* detention outside any formal statutory powers.

8.19 The Health and Social Care Bill 2007 would seem to provide a sufficient statutory framework of safeguards in respect of Mental Health Act[707]. A test remains for the years to come: the extent to which the Board and senior management of the new regulator for health and adult social care in England, and Health Inspectorate Wales, will provide adequate organisational capability and resources to implement Parliament's intentions in this area, or whether the priority given to safeguards for those deprived of their liberty is contingent on the vagaries of other current priorities in the wider field of health and social care. Such issues of resource have ever been present: the Mental Health Act Commission has of course been limited in its activity by the amount of resource accorded to it by government. However, the concern now must be that squeezing of resources will be less noticeable in a combined regulator than in a single dedicated monitoring body.

---

[706] UN Special Rapporteur on Torture, 2006 Report to the General Assembly, UN Doc.A/61/259 (14/08/2006), para 72

[707] In relation to *de facto* detained patients, see paragraph 8.8 above and also MHAC (2007) *The Future Regulation Of Health And Adult Social Care In England, The Mental Health Act Commission's Response To The Department Of Health's Consultation.* February 2007, p.5. www.mhac.org.uk.

Appendix 1

Mental Health Act Commission

Maid Marian House   56 Hounds Gate   Nottingham   NG1 6BG   Tel: 0115 943 7100   Fax: 0115 943 7101
www.mhac.org.uk

30th July 2007

Rt Hon Alan Johnson MP
Secretary of State for Health
Department of Health
Richmond House
79 Whitehall
London
SW1A 2NS

Dear Secretary of State,

RE: Establishment of the Office of the Health and Adult Social Care Regulator (Ofcare)

First, may I offer my congratulations on your appointment as Secretary of State. I enjoyed good working relations with your predecessor and I look forward to meeting you and working with you.

I am writing to you on behalf of the Mental Health Act Commission Board to seek assurances about the continuation of Commission functions once the proposed new regulator is established. I worked closely with Lord Hunt, when he was the Minister responsible for Ofcare, the Office of the Health and Adult Social Care Regulator, and I look forward to close cooperation with you and your Ministerial colleagues during the passage of legislation that will give effect to Ofcare in 2008. Philip Hunt and I met on 14th June shortly before he was moved and he invited me to write to him with my concerns. Given the change of personnel I felt it would be both courteous and appropriate to write to you in the first instance, and to copy my letter to Ben Bradshaw MP, whom I understand, will be the Minister responsible for Ofcare establishment.

The Mental Health Act Commission recognises the importance the government places on developing a modern regulatory framework for health and social care, and in furtherance of that aim, the establishment of Ofcare. The government intends that this will be achieved by bringing together some or all of the present functions of the Healthcare Commission, the Commission for Social Care Inspection and the Mental Health Act Commission, subject to the outcome of consultation on the proposed regulatory framework and the passage of legislation. The Commission Board has considered a number of alternatives to merging functions, and retains an open mind about the best way forward.

By and large the Board wishes to be able to support the transition, but its enthusiasm is tempered, indeed severely diluted, by concerns about the government's commitment to protecting the rights of detained patients. The new organisation, Ofcare, should have the status, resources and organisational strength to ensure greater provider compliance with the law in meeting the rightful expectations of patents about safety and the quality of care. However, the Board remains deeply concerned that the proposals do not ground the Commission's current functions in ways that will ensure full protection for the rights of detained patients – perhaps one of the most vulnerable groups in society. In the Board's view it is essential that the current MHAC functions and the way in which those functions are performed are continued within Ofcare after 2009.

This letter describes the critical matters on which the Board would like to receive assurances from yourself and ministerial colleagues and officials within the Department of Health. In summary, the Board wishes to have assurances that the legislation and the regulatory framework, the resources available, and the operating arrangements for Ofcare will be written in a way that ensures explicitly a focus on the civil, legal and human rights of detained patients.

There are six functions or sets of functions, and the way in which those functions are performed, that the Commission considers to be vitally important for the new organisation. These are:

- Visiting detained patients and interviewing detained patients in private, and having the necessary breadth and depth of expertise of mental health care such that those undertaking visits and inspections are able to identify shortcomings or difficulties in mental health services;
- Engaging mental health service users actively as full partners in the enterprise of health and social care assessment, monitoring and inspection;
- Adequate organisational and personal accountability for monitoring and reporting on the needs and rights of detained patients;
- Statutory notifications of admissions, discharges and deaths of detained patients, and other relevant information;
- Ensuring adequate and appropriately trained staff, with the establishment of a specialist mental health team or department within Ofcare incorporating the present MHAC team;
- Having an overarching principle of equality and human rights, focussing at all times on the civil, legal and human rights of patients;

I will consider these in turn.

Visiting detained patients.

The Commission considers that regular and frequent visits to providers is the only way to ensure patients' rights are protected, the potential for abuse of patients is minimised, and appropriate care is provided at all times. Experience of visiting services demonstrates that the quality of care at a provider unit (notably at ward level) can deteriorate very quickly and is heavily dependant upon good middle and senior management staff. Recent scandals such as those at Cornwall, and Merton and Sutton, demonstrate what can happen if services are not visited on a regular basis. The Commission is Ministers' 'eyes and ears' and an important check on the possibility of patient abuse. Even with a Commissioner resource that equates to only 15 whole time equivalent staff the Commission finds abuses of patients and misuse of the law on a weekly basis.

Visits must be frequent and regular, with the opportunity for unannounced and short notice announcement visits. Visiting must be sufficiently frequent to ensure compliance of providers with the law and to give visiting inspectors the chance to see a sizeable proportion of detained patients in any year (approximately 45,000 people are detained on admission or following admission each year). The Commission seeks an assurance that the legislation establishing Ofcare will go as far as it is possible in legislative drafting to guarantee Ofcare will have a visiting programme, undertake regular unannounced visits, and have sufficient resources to visit regularly with an agreed minimum frequency. The draft legislation to establish Ofcare includes clauses to repeal sections 120 and 121 of the Mental Health Act 1983 and to give the visiting functions to Ofcare. The Commission wishes to receive an assurance that revised clauses will provide at least the same level of protection to patients as at present.

Engaging mental health service users actively as full partners in health and social care assessment, monitoring and inspection.

Involving service users is an essential step towards a full understanding of the impact of detention and the quality of care at individual providers. The Commission has made real progress on user involvement and seeks an assurance that this aspect of the Commission's approach will be maintained within Ofcare. Patients/service users must be able to contact the regulator at any time and to be treated with sympathy and understanding. At root, the role of the Commission is to get the heart of the patient experience, to understand the way the operation of the Act impacts on their lives, and to ensure as far as possible that the way the Act is operated encourages and facilitates improvements in care rather than the reverse. It is only by engaging users as the true voice of experience that the effect of detention can be assessed.

Adequate organisational and personal accountability for monitoring and reporting on the needs and rights of detained patients.

We believe that a specific duty should be placed on Ofcare, either on the Board, the Chief Executive or an identified member of the Board, to be responsible personally to Parliament for the monitoring of the Mental Health Act, for the protection of the rights of detained patients, and for reporting to Parliament regularly (annually) on the condition of services for detained patients and those subject to compulsion in the community.

I recognise how difficult it is in legislation to specify the level of resources that should be put into a specific function or, indeed, the precise way in which that function will be performed. Nonetheless the Board believes that legislation must provide a clear framework for these functions. We hope that the Minister, in speaking about these matters in the House, will provide a transparent indication of the government's intent, that the new regulator once established will give prominence to protecting patient's rights and will be required to devote sufficient resources to monitoring the Mental Health Act.

Ofcare will be expected to take on a wide range of regulatory functions as described in the Future Regulation of Health and Adult Social Care consultation paper. Yet two issues have seemed to dominate discussion in these early stages: registration of health and social care organisations, and risk management, both within an essentially economic rather than rights based regulatory framework. Whilst registration and risk are important, equally important are the rights of patients and the protection, and the enhancement of those rights. The Commission would like to receive an assurance that the regulatory framework will pay sufficient attention to patients' rights and will not be concerned solely with economic regulation.

Statutory notifications of admissions, discharges and deaths of detained patients, and other relevant information.

I shall welcome the opportunity to discuss with you and officials a list of items that will be mandatory for Ofcare to report on every year. Setting in place a minimum list of topics will have two effects: first, it will reassure patients/service users that Ofcare will be considering these matters regularly; and second, Ofcare will be able to make such reports only if it has visited and inspected the care and conditions of patients.

To undertake its functions adequately the new regulator will need high quality information on which to base decisions to intervene where it identifies a deterioration of care or the likelihood that patient's rights may be abrogated. Although, the Commission understands that the government intends to give the new organisation the power to obtain information on mental health services the Commission seeks an assurance that those powers will include:

- A notification of all deaths of detained patients and those notified to the coroner;
- A notification of all serious and untoward incidents and deaths of informal patients from unnatural causes;
- All homicides by detained or informal patients;
- All incidents of serious injury to patients receiving in-patient care; howsoever caused;
- A notification of all formal admissions and discharges including discharges to community treatment orders and compulsion in the community;
- All mental health review Tribunal decisions whether for continued detention or for discharge.

For all of these categories it will be essential to have information on age, gender and ethnicity.

Ensuring adequate and appropriately trained staff, with the establishment of a specialist mental health team or department within Ofcare, incorporating the present MHAC team.

Ofcare must have a mental health team of appropriately trained and expert staff, deployed specifically to monitor and inspect mental health care. The Mental Health Act Commission team offers one natural receptacle of expertise to complement the skills of those currently working within the Healthcare Commission and CSCI and others as appropriate. Whilst the Commission's concerns are with detained patients, each person's needs should be seen in the context of the overall patient pathway that includes other forms of community and institutional care.

Ensuring adequate communication between inspection staff and Second Opinion Appointed Doctors (SOADs) (and vice versa) will be an important function of this team, helping to identify shortcomings in services and potential abuses. The Board looks to the Minister for assurances that, either in legislation or through statements in the House, Ofcare will be encouraged to have such a team working to a nominated individual at Board level personal responsibility for Mental Health Act matters, and providing the necessary expertise to ensure that detained patients rights are properly protected.

Being detained compulsorily without court sanction is a disturbing and traumatic experience, made all the more so as it is done at a time when the person is in mental distress. Ofcare must be able to offer advice on the operation of the Act, give patients and their carers' information and advice on their rights, on services available and on remedies for wrongful detention or inappropriate care. The Commission maintains a small group of staff able to give patients advice and to support patients at times of extreme distress. This must continue to be available.

Ofcare must have available to it in future the expertise and breadth of knowledge that is available presently to the Mental Health Act Commission. Visiting staff will need to be comfortable meeting with mental health patients and service users who on occasions maybe highly disturbed. This is a specialist role and not one for people without adequate training experience or commitment. A very important feature of the Mental Health Act Commission is the passion and commitment that Commissioners, SOADs and Commission staff bring to the task. This is not simply a bureaucratic or organisational function, but is a matter of protecting people who have been detained compulsorily, usually against their will, ostensibly in their own best interests. Despite the Commission drawing attention repeatedly to substandard services, sadly many of the hospitals where people are treated compulsorily are not fit places to provide therapeutic care.

Having an overarching principle of equality and human rights, focussing at all times on the civil, legal and human rights of patients.

As you know I have been a strong advocate for a regime that promotes and enhances a culture of equality and human rights, recognising the multi-ethnic and multi-cultural nature of British society. Nowhere is this seen more clearly than in mental health care for Black and minority ethnic patients who are significantly more likely than average to be admitted to and detained in mental hospitals. Ofcare will be at the forefront of protecting their rights and freedoms and ensuring the Act is applied without adverse discrimination. The Commission believes strongly in applying principles of equality and human rights to all its work, and the Board will be seeking an assurance from the Minister that a similar principle or set of principles will apply in the new organisation.

I have written at length as the Board and I share a real and lasting concern for detained patients. We are worried that their protection will not be given sufficient attention in the new regulator, and look to you to assure us that our concerns will be addressed in legislation and in the performance framework you give to Ofcare once established. I look forward to meeting with you in the near future and discussing these points in greater depth once you have had time to consider the matters I have raised.

Yours sincerely,

Prof. Lord Patel of Bradford OBE

Appendix B

Ethnicity	gender	2003/04 n=14,146 (male) 11,266 (female)		2004/05 n=14,146 (male) 11,266 (female)		2005/06 n=20,974 (male) 17,630 (female)		2006/07 n=17,319(male) 14,665 (female)	
		%	%	%	%	%	%	%	%
British (White)	M	69.11	71.50	66.46	69.22	67.20	70.34	76.48	73.15
	F	74.49		72.61		74.07		69.82	
Irish (White)	M	0.86	0.84	1.06	1.00	1.08	1.03	1.32	1.25
	F	0.83		0.93		0.97		1.18	
any other White background (White)	M	4.40	4.54	4.48	4.68	0.19	4.75	5.46	4.76
	F	4.71		4.92		5.16		4.04	
White and Black Caribbean (Mixed)	M	0.80	0.66	0.80	0.57	0.82	0.63	1.40	1.03
	F	0.49		0.29		0.41		0.66	
White and Black African (Mixed)	M	0.28	0.26	0.45	0.38	0.41	0.86	0.56	0.42
	F	0.23		0.28		0.37		0.28	
White and Asian (Mixed)	M	0.17	0.18	0.24	0.24	0.29	0.29	0.36	0.35
	F	0.20		0.23		0.28		0.32	
any other Mixed background (Mixed)	M	0.47	0.42	0.57	0.45	0.83	0.73	0.66	0.49
	F	0.36		0.31		0.62		0.32	
Caribbean (Black or Black British)	M	5.40	4.47	5.72	4.57	5.10	4.20	4.74	3.84
	F	3.29		3.15		3.13		2.94	
African (Black or Black British)	M	2.80	2.35	3.33	2.98	3.48	3.05	3.14	2.64
	F	1.78		2.55		2.54		2.14	
any other Black background (Black or Black British)	M	2.45	2.00	2.28	1.88	3.02	2.32	2.22	1.72
	F	1.43		1.40		1.48		1.22	
Bangladeshi (Asian or Asian British)	M	0.38	0.30	0.81	0.65	0.06	0.48	0.50	0.42
	F	0.20		0.46		0.34		0.34	
Indian (Asian or Asian British)	M	1.85	1.75	1.77	1.75	1.66	1.48	1.90	1.70
	F	1.62		1.72		1.27		0.75	
Pakistani (Asian or Asian British)	M	1.51	1.36	1.74	1.46	1.80	1.38	2.46	1.89
	F	1.17		1.13		0.89		1.34	
any other Asian Background (Asian or Asian British)	M	0.82	0.70	0.91	0.81	1.30	1.20	1.56	1.33
	F	0.56		0.70		1.07		1.10	
Chinese (other ethnic groups)	M	0.32	0.35	0.19	0.29	0.30	0.35	0.40	0.39
	F	0.39		0.42		0.41		0.36	
any other ethnic group	M	1.98	1.64	1.97	1.74	3.02	2.32	1.80	1.45
	F	1.33		1.45		1.48		1.10	
not stated	M	6.50	6.69	7.23	7.33	6.17	5.93	3.32	3.17
	F	6.92		7.46		5.63		3.04	
total	M	100	100	100	100	100	100	100	100
	F	100		100		100		100	

Fig 78: Admissions of patients detained under the Mental Health Act 1983 by ethnicity and gender, 2002/03 to 2005/06, all hospitals[708], England and Wales

Data source: returns from MHAC questionnaires

---

[708] Questionnaires issued and returned: 288/167 (2002/03); 288/167 (2003/04); 235/171 (2004/05); 294/218 (2005/06). The data is thus substantially incomplete.

Appendix 3

Members of the Mental Health Act Commission, April 2005 to March 2007

Key to symbols:

~ appointment ended during period
® regional director

Region One[709]

Mr Richard Backhouse
Ms Hilary Bainbridge
Mr Alan Barrett
Mr Allan Bevan
Ms Linda Berry
Miss Anita Bowden~
Mrs Janet Buckley
Mr Brian Burke
Ms Patricia Chadderton
Ms Noelle Chesworth
Ms Jill Cox~
Ms Jennifer Creek
Ms Salle Dare
Mr Barry Delaney
Mrs Judith Foster
Ms Carolyn Fyall
Mr Philip Hindson
Ms Sue Jarvis
Ms Linda Jones
Mr Lionel Joyce~
Mrs Sue McMillan ®
Mr Leslie Marshall
Ms Sarah Matthews
Mrs Jean Meredith~
Mr Alan Milligan
Ms Glynis Morton

Ms Louise Relton
Ms Nigar Sadique
Mrs Christine Smithson
Ms Catherine Thompson
Mrs Lorraine Yearsley
Mr Barry Windle

Region 2[710]

Mr Salim Atchia
Ms Melanie Brooks
Ms Elisa Cioffi
Mr Felix Cofie~
Mrs Margaret Coombs
Ms Lyn Critchley
Miss Judith Croton
Ms Ann Davison
Mike Follows
Mrs Julie Gossage
Miss Sharon Hayles
Mr John Hewett ~
Mr Philip Howes
Ms Esther Jones
Mr Stephen Klein ®
Mr John Mclean
Mr Yens Marsen-Luther~
Mr George NazerMr Joe Nichols
Mr Nicholas North
Mr John Price
Mrs Kay Sheldon
Mr Gregory Steele
Ms June Tweedie~
Mrs Rhian Williams-Flew

---

[709] North of England

[710] Wessex & Trent

Region Three[711]

Mr Vincent Alexander
Mr Andrew Beaumont~
Ms Linda Bolter
Mr Robert Brown
Mrs Sue Campbell
Mr Christopher Chambers
Mr Jeff Cohen
Mr Brendan Commons~
Mrs Valarie Cranwell
Mr Cyril Davies
Ms Annette De La Cour
Mr Keith Dudleston
Mr William Evans
Ms Angela Flower~
Mr Navin Foolchand
Mr Robert Jones
Ms Joan Langan
Mrs Margaret Lloyd
Canon Frank Longbottom
Mr. Derek McCarthy
Ms Mary Nettle
Dr Ian Spencer
Mr Robert Southern
Mr Philip Wales ®

Region Three Commissioners visiting in Wales

Mr Kevin Barrett
Mrs Margot DosAnjos
Mr Michael Green
Mr Robert Holdsworth
Mrs Margaret Lloyd
Ms Jane MacKenzie
Ms Sarah Paxton
Mrs Carole Rees-Williams
Mr Philip Wales ®
Dr Anthony Williams
Mrs Nonn Williams~

Region Four[712]

Mr. Simon Armson
Ms Deborah Baldwin
Ms Jane Barnes

Ms Genevieve Bebiako-Bonsu
Ms Helen Bramley
Mr Michael Bryant
Dr Patrick Callaghan
Ms Louize Collins
Ms Sharon Cookson
Ms Suki Desai®~
Mr Richard Dosoo
Mrs Petrina Douglas-Hall
Mr Anthony Drew~
Mr Anthony Eaton
Mr Nihat Erol~
Mr Harry Field
Mr Norman Hamilton
Ms Katherine Herzberg
Mr Bakhtiar Hormoz~
Mrs Patricia Gregory
Ms Kathryn Johnson
Ms Maureen Napier
Ms Kate O'Regan
Mrs Parminder Parmar~
Mr Kuruvilla Punnamkuzhy
Ms Jennifer Scudamore
Ms Jennye Seres
Mr Paul Thompson
Ms Vimala Uttarkar
Mr Ivor Ward~
Ms Kate Whalley
Mr Alastair Williamson

Board members, 2007

Lord Patel of Bradford OBE (Chair)
Ms Deborah Jenkins MBE (Vice Chair)
Mr. Simon Armson
Dr Patrick Callaghan
Mrs Ann Curno
Mr Barry Delaney
Mr John Knox
Mrs Kay Sheldon
Professor Christopher Heginbotham
(Chief Executive)
Mr Martin Donohoe (Director of Finance)

Dr Mohammed Abdurahman

---

[711] London and the South East

[712] West and South West of England & Wales

Appendix 4

Second Opinion Appointed Doctors 2005 - 2007

Dr Syed W A Ahmad (dec'd)
Dr Peter Abraham
Dr Mahmood Al-Bachari
Dr Malikayil Alexander
Dr Delyth Alldrick
Dr Saravanamuttu Ananthakopan
Dr Tinnevely Ananthanarayanan
Dr Victor Atapattu
Dr Krishnapillai Balasubramaniam
Dr Colin Berry
Dr John Besson
Dr Eric Birchall
Dr Jeremy Bolton
Dr Michael Bristow
Dr Michael Browne
Dr Arnold Cade
Dr Nas Choudry
Dr John Colgan
Dr Colin Cowan
Dr Clive Cruickshank
Dr Rosemary Davenport
Dr Cyril Davies
Dr Martin Davies
Dr Shreema de Zoysa
Dr Peter Decalmer
Dr Alistair Drummond
Dr Gordon Dubourg
Dr Keith Dudleston
Dr Desmond Dunleavy
Dr Joyce Dunlop
Dr Robin Eastwood
Dr Christine Edwards
Dr Huw Edwards
Dr Stephen Edwards
Dr Anwar El Komy
Dr James Eva
Dr Leonard Fagin

Dr Graeme Feggetter
Dr Graham Gallimore
Dr Seng-Eng Goh
Dr Mestiyage Goonatilleke
Dr Gurmeet Grewal
Dr John Grimshaw
Dr Kailash Gupta
Dr Simon Halstead
Dr David Hargreaves
Dr Francesca Harrop
Dr Gwilym Hayes
Dr Pearl Hettiaratchy
Dr Sidney Hettiaratchy
Dr Robert Hill
Dr Michael Humphreys
Dr Mian Hussain
Dr Ghulam Ibrahimi
Dr Jagdish Jain
Dr Peter Jefferys
Dr Benjamin John
Dr Ben Johnson
Dr David Jones
Dr Patricia Jones
Dr Sikandar Kamlana
Dr Sunita Kanagaratnam
Dr Gunaseelan Kanakaratnam
Dr Alexander Kellam
Dr Lindsey Kemp
Dr Robert Londhe
Dr Michael Lowe
Dr Emanuel Lucas
Dr Godfrey Luyombya
Dr Hameen Markar
Dr Therese Markar
Dr Jose Mathews
Dr Gerard McDade
Dr Philip Meats

Dr Gyan Mehta

Dr George Milner

Dr Parimala Moodley

Dr Nagalingam Murugananthan

Dr David Myers

Dr Dewan Nabi

Dr Agnes Nalpas

Dr Gamini Nanayakkara

Dr Cheedella Narayana

Dr Hilary Nissenbaum

Dr Margaret O'Brien

Dr Satnam Palia

Dr David Pariente

Dr Ashokkumar Patel

Dr Abdul Patel

Dr Anthony Perini

Dr William Prothero

Dr Margot Quenstedt

Dr Ehsanullah Quraishy

Dr Dayananda Rajapakse

Dr David Ramster

Dr Bondada Kurma Rao

Dr Sudhir Rastogi

Dr Mohammed Razzaque

Dr John Rigby

Dr Maureen Royston

Dr Anthony Rugg

Dr Manga Sabaratnam

Dr Ruth Sagovsky

Dr Gurdarshan Sarna

Dr Abdul Sheikh

Dr Neil Silvester

Dr Marilyn Smith

Dr Ahmed Soliman

Dr Christopher Staley

Dr Richard Symonds

Dr Andrew Talbot

Dr Jennifer Tarry

Dr Shyamala Thalayasingam

Dr Rajaratnam Thavasothy

Dr Raja Thaya-Paran

Dr Rhinedd Toms

Dr Harinder Verma

Dr Sarla Verma

Dr Nicholas Wagner

Dr Gerald Wallen

Dr Dermot Ward

Dr Florence Watt

Dr Malcolm Weller

Dr Simon Wood

Dr John Yermilli-Rao

Dr Riadh T Abed

Dr Diwakar S Addala

Dr Roger N Bloor

Dr Andrew C Briggs

Dr Alexander Brown

Dr William J Charles

Dr Roger Chitty

Dr Miranda Conway

Dr Ian A Davidson

Dr Gerald H Dawson

Dr Navnitlal Desai

Dr Humayon B Dewan

Dr Andrew Easton

Dr Elizabeth Gallagher

Dr Prof George Mohan

Dr David M Hambidge

Dr Michael Hession

Dr Susan Joseph

Dr John M Kellett

Dr Lionel Kremer

Dr Marilyn Loizou

Dr Bryan Lowe

Dr Fiona McKenzie

Dr Terence Nelson

Dr Acha E J Okoko

Dr Julie Parker

Dr Gerard Roney

Dr Jacek Rucinski

Dr Catherine Ryan

Dr Girish Shetty

Dr Shashi Singhal

Dr Nawshad Suleman

Dr Narinder K Verma

Dr Christopher M Wallbridge

Dr Angela M Walsh

MHAC Death reviewers 2005 - 2007

Mr Simon Armson

Ms Elisa Cioffi

Mr Mike Follows

Canon Frank Longbottom

Mr Joe Nichols

Mr Alastair Williamson

Mr Allan Bevan

Mr Barry Delaney

Mr Robert Holdsworth

Ms Sue McMillan

Mr Nick North

Ms Linda Bolter

Mr Harry Fields

Mr Steve Klein

Mr Alan Milligan

Mr Egon Prtak

Mr Phil Wales

MHAC Section 57 (neurosurgery) panel members active from 2005 -2007

Dr C Bennett

Mr H Davis

Rev. B Lillington

Dr F Oyebode

Mr L Wilson

Mrs G Campbell

Dr D Dunleavy

Mrs M Morris

Mr R Ryall

Dr E Chitty

Dr P Jefferys

Ms M Nettle

Mr H Teaney

Index

The locators in the index refer to paragraph numbers. Figures are indicated by the paragraph number immediately preceding the figure, and are italicised with the letter 'f'; notes by the italicised number and 'n'; and recommendations by the italicised number and 'r'.